W9-BLG-626

DISCARD

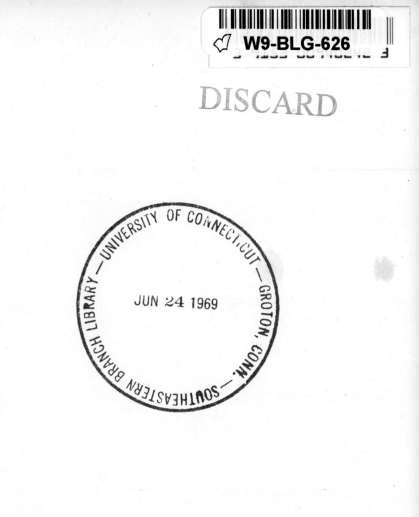

UNIVERSITY OF CONNECTICUT — GROTON, CONN. — SOUTHEASTERN BRANCH LIBRARY

JUN 24 1969

JUN 2 4 1966

Journey to America

PREVIOUSLY PUBLISHED

Alexis de Tocqueville

Journeys to England and Ireland

ALEXIS DE TOCQUEVILLE

Journey to America

Translated by George Lawrence

Edited by J. P. Mayer

New Haven and London: Yale University Press

COPYRIGHT © 1959 by J. P. Mayer
Issued as a Yale Paperbound January 1962
Printed in the United States of America by
The Murray Printing Company, Forge Village, Mass.
All rights reserved. This book may not be
reproduced, in whole or in part, in any form
(except by reviewers for the public press),
without written permission from the publishers.
Library of Congress catalog card number: 59–12699.

To Edward F. D'Arms

*with deep gratitude for his subtle
and tireless devotion which made my
work on Alexis de Tocqueville possible*
                                    The Editor

Contents

Contents

Preface

Tocqueville's notebooks which he kept during his journey through the United States of America appear here for the first time complete in English. They enable us to judge the mind of the author of the *Democracy in America in statu nascendi*. The text is based on vol. V, 1 of the *Œuvres Complètes* which I am directing. My foreword to the French edition expresses my gratitude to all those who helped me to establish a difficult text from the manuscript. The present edition has given me the opportunity of correcting a number of misprints and errors in the French edition. I have also added some further notes which may facilitate the understanding of Tocqueville's thought. They have been restricted to essentials. My short introduction uses material I have previously published in *Encounter* and I am indebted to the Editors of this admirable journal for allowing me to reprint it in the context of the present volume. Two friends have assisted me in seeing this book through the press: Miss Judith Steinhauer, an American lady, verified in particular things American; Miss Marjorie Nicholson who has also revised my previous volume: Tocqueville's *Journeys to England and Ireland*, has again scrutinized the proofs of this book. I am deeply grateful to both of them for their care and forbearance with the slave driver's reckless pace.

Finally, it gives me pleasure to thank my publishers, Messrs. Faber and Faber and the Yale University Press, whose public spirit made this book possible. It appears during the year when the world at large commemorates the centenary of Alexis de Tocqueville's death.

Stoke Poges, Buckinghamshire.   J. P. MAYER
February 26th, 1959.

Introduction

'To tell the truth I haven't written a word of the book itself. But I have worked at it a lot. I think about it every day and all day. I will explain the very odd way I work at it; in a notebook I put down day by day how the novel stands in my mind; yes, it is a sort of diary I keep, as one might keep one about a child. . . . Instead of concentrating on the solution of each difficulty as it turns up, I take each difficulty (the structure of every work of art is entirely built up out of the solutions of a heap of tiny difficulties as they come along), I take each of these difficulties and define and study it. You could call the notebook a continuous criticism of my novel; or better, of all novels. Think how interesting we should find such a notebook kept by Dickens or Balzac; if we had the diary of *L'Education sentimentale* or *The Brothers Karamazov*, the story of the work, of its gestation? But that would be thrilling . . . more absorbing than the book itself. . . . (André Gide, *Les Faux-Monnayeurs*.)

It is possible now to appreciate the influence of his travels on Alexis de Tocqueville's political and sociological thought. What he saw of peoples and their institutions gave birth to his books and his whole political activity. So his travel diaries deserve an important place among his works. As Aristotle wrote at the end of the classical period of Greece, as Bodin thought out his *Republic* at the beginning of the modern age, as Montesquieu published *De L'Esprit des Lois* in the last decades of absolute monarchy in France, so, too, did Tocqueville work out his political philosophy in a time of change. It was the time when the results of nineteenth-century industrialisation were beginning to show; social classes, states, and the whole of human existence were being remoulded in a huge crucible.

13

Introduction

A new world was coming to birth in America. Reform had begun in England. That is what makes the diaries so intensely interesting. We travel in the company of a subtle and profound thinker who is trying to understand the new social structures that are beginning to take shape. We know now what our own have turned into and that makes us feel at home in Tocqueville's world. We feel that Tocqueville lives in today's world, not because we have rediscovered him, but because his problems have become our problems.

He was twenty-two when he went to Sicily with his brother Edouard. But the travel notes of that journey already show the characteristic way of working which he developed in his later travels. His social theories are based on observed facts and always have a bearing on political action.

Three years later he started on his journey to America. This time Gustave de Beaumont was his companion. They arrived at New York on 10th May, 1831. They stayed in the United States until 20th February, 1832. At first their time was taken up by the official mission which had given the pretext for their journey, that is to say, the study of the penitentiary system in the United States.

Yet Tocqueville penetrated deeper and deeper into the study of American political and social institutions. The two friends visited the New England States of which, as Beaumont puts it, 'Boston is the head'. But they also went to the very limits of settlements in the West; *A Fortnight in the Wilderness*, and *A Journey to Lake Oneida*, breathe the air of those parts. They are within the tradition of Chateaubriand who was a relative of Tocqueville's. The travellers faced all the trials of a strenuous journey from Quebec to New Orleans.

Anyone who wants to follow their journey reconstructed day by day will find it all in George Wilson Pierson's authoritative *Tocqueville and Beaumont in America*, New York, 1938, which has made it possible to arrange the fourteen travel notebooks on America in the right order. But however important Professor Pierson's volume still is as a guide to the elucidation of Tocqueville's American contacts—I have constantly referred to it— Tocqueville's *texts* must from now on be studied in the form in which we present them here, for Pierson has used faulty and incomplete transcriptions without comparing them with the original manuscripts.

Introduction

That is how it has become possible to watch the birth-pangs of *Democracy in America*. There is no other book in the long history of political thought which gives us the same opportunity of following very closely a great thinker's process of work, except perhaps for the case of Montesquieu whose influence on Tocqueville was profound.

Perhaps some readers may feel that these pages give a fresher and more intriguing view of Tocqueville's social and political philosophy than does the finished work. Here are some instances. After a conversation with Mr. Quincy, President of Harvard, Tocqueville notes:

'One of the happiest results of lack of government (when a people is in the lucky, but rare, position of being able to do without it) is invariably a strong development of individual personality. Each man learns to think and act on his own, not counting on the support of an outside power which, however, watchful it may be, can never take thought for every need of society. . . . I admit that often a man actually achieves less than a central authority could have done for him, but the sum total of all individual enterprises taken together is a great deal more than any administration could undertake; besides, such a state of affairs has such a good influence on public morality that that alone would more than make up for any disadvantages there might be. But, I must say it again, very few peoples can do without government in that way. Such a state of affairs has only ever existed at the two extremes of civilisation. The savage, with only his physical needs to satisfy, relies on himself alone. A civilised man can only do the same if he has reached such an enlightened social state that he knows what is useful to do and his passions do not stop him from doing it. The chief care of a good government should be to teach people little by little to do without it.' (20th September, 1831.)

That is typical of the liberal outlook of the young Tocqueville. A few days later he summarises a conversation with Jared Sparks:

'The political dogma of this country is that the majority is always right. By and large we are very glad we have adopted it, but one cannot deny that experience often gives the lie to the principle. . . . Sometimes the majority has wished to oppress the minority. . . .' (20th September, 1831.)

Introduction

That is the germ of the great chapter of *Democracy in America* dealing with the tyranny of the majority. One finds other inspired sketches for chapters of the book.

But that is not all. Some of the young Tocqueville's observations—for example, the comparison between customary and written law, or the sketch for a history of English law—stand out against the background formed by the legal institutions of the Continent, and prove that Tocqueville's juridical sociology ranks in the same high class as his works on political sociology. These observations and many others are real sociological discoveries; I will just quote here some characteristic passages from the notebooks:

'Offspring of the Barbarians, customary law has all the imperfections of the civilisation that brought it into being, but it breathes the independence of the centuries in which it flourished. If one has to choose now between it and written law, one can only turn it down. But its abolition on the Continent of Europe has been a great misfortune. Whereas, I think, its maintenance in England has had a particularly marked effect in supporting conceptions and principles of liberty, and so, in that indirect way, in spite of its imperfections, has aided the progress of civilisation in that island; contrariwise, the introduction of written law on the Continent, albeit as law it is more complete, more supple, and more civilised, if one can put it so, has helped to establish despotism in Europe, and, as a result, has harmed the very cause of civilisation which it seemed to serve.'

Tocqueville continues: 'Quite apart from the political consequences to be traced from the preservation of customary law in England, I think its existence has notably helped to give a certain turn to English ways of thinking. It has given that nation what one might call its taste for precedents, that is to say, a certain turn of mind which leads men to try and find out not what is reasonable in itself, but what is done, not what is just, but ancient, not general theories, but particular facts. I have no doubt that habits bred from customary law, and the part that lawyers and judges have, in all ages, taken in political arguments, have proved strong allies of aristocratic institutions, and moreover have greatly helped to give the English that superstitious respect for the works of their fathers, and that hatred of innovation, which is peculiar to them.'

Introduction

Tocqueville was twenty-six years old when he wrote this and had never set foot in England. A deep natural affinity enabled him to understand the English turn of mind.

On 5th November, 1831, Tocqueville notes at the end of an interview with Charles Caroll:

'All the ways of his being and the turn of his mind make Charles Caroll the exact counterpart of a European gentleman. Probably the great Southern landowners at the time of the Revolution were all of such sort. That breed of men which provided the greatest names in America, is disappearing. With them the tradition of cultivated manners is going. The people become educated, knowledge spreads, and middling ability becomes common. Outstanding talents and great personalities are rare. Society is less brilliant and more prosperous. The various effects of the progress of civilisation and enlightenment, about which only Europe is in doubt, can be seen as clear as day in America. What is the basic reason for this? I cannot see it clearly yet.'

The notion of the mass era can already be seen in this passage: 'the facile age' as Goethe said, Goethe whose prophetic eyes were not yet closed when Tocqueville wrote these words.

Later in another fragment Tocqueville comes back to the same problem:

'Why, as civilisation spreads, do outstanding men become fewer? Why, when knowledge is accessible to all, are great talents rare? Why, when there are no lower classes, are there no upper classes either? Why, when understanding of government reaches the masses, is there a shortage of great minds to take the lead in society? America clearly raises those questions. But who can answer them?'

These two passages are plain proof of the penetrating restlessness of Tocqueville's thought. He is passionately seeking for the institutional means which could allow human liberty to be preserved. A few more extracts may help to show the importance of these new manuscripts for Tocqueville's sociological thought. The first two are dated 30th September, 1831:

'Two fundamental social principles seem to control American society, and one must always refer back to them to find the reason for any of the laws or customs which prevail among them. They are:

Introduction

'First. The majority may make mistakes about some little things, but by and large it is always right and there is no moral power higher than it.

'Second. Every individual, private person, society, community or nation, is the only lawful judge of its own interests, and so long as it does not harm anyone else's concerns, no one has a right to meddle. That is a point which one should always keep in mind.'

Indeed the first two volumes of *Democracy in America* are chiefly concerned with the elaboration of these two principles which could even serve as texts for them. But the following comment which bears the same date, is to the point:

'A completely democratic government is something so dangerous that, even in America, they have felt it necessary to take a great many precautions against the mistakes and passions of democracy. The two Houses, the Governor's veto, and above all the Judges. . . .'

The 'above all' is important; Chapter VIII of the second part of *Democracy in America* contains a masterly exposition of the spirit of law in the United States and how it serves as countervailing force against the power of democracy.

'Another principle,' Tocqueville continues, 'of American society, which one must always keep in mind is this: since every individual is the best judge of his own interest, society must not protect him too carefully, lest he should come to rely on it and so saddle society with a task it cannot perform.'

That is a far-sighted comment. A hundred and twenty years later, are not modern States still looking for the equilibrium between the rights of the individual and society?—As a political thinker Tocqueville was searching throughout his life for an ordered balance between rights and duties within the State. He may not have provided us with a ready-made concept, but he has certainly pointed into the direction of a possible solution.

It is not the least merit of his American notebooks that they reveal how, and to what extent, he formed from his observations and reflections in America his ultimate political philosophy.

J. P. MAYER

JOURNEY TO AMERICA[1]

I

Non-Alphabetic Notebook 1

VOLUME FOR GENERAL QUESTIONS[2]

Conversation with Mr. Livingston[3] at Greeburgh on the Hudson

I. It seems to me that American society suffers from taking too little account of intellectual questions.

He. I agree. Far from improving, we get daily worse in this respect.

I. Why do you think that happens?

He. Chiefly because of the law of inheritance. When I was young I remember the country peopled by rich landowners who lived on their estates as the English *gentry* do, and who used their minds, and had too a sense of tradition in their thoughts and manners. Then there was distinction in the behaviour and turn of mind of one class in the nation. The law making shares equal has worked continually to break up fortunes and form them anew; our former standards and conceptions have been lost and this process goes on from day to day. Land changes hands incredibly quickly, nobody has time to strike root in one place, and everybody must turn to some practical work to keep

---

[1] Tocqueville's *Journey to America* is based on fourteen notebooks, details of which can be found in my French edition (*Œuvres Complètes*, ed. J. P. Mayer, vol. V, 1, p. 1.

[2] This notebook begins with part of a draft of a letter, dated 10th June 1831, from Tocqueville to Ernest de Chabrol. Yale University Library has a complete copy of this letter dated 9th June 1831. It will be published in the Editor's edition of Tocqueville's *Correspondance Générale*.

[3] Cf. Pierson, op. cit., index, page 844. This Livingston may be either Edward Livingston (1764–1836) a well-known lawyer, at that time Secretary of State and afterwards (1833–5) American Minister in France, or his nephew John. The context makes the latter seem more probable.

up the position his father held. Almost all families disappear after the second or third generation.

I. Is there anything analogous to the influence, the patronage, of large landowners?

He. No. Only individual merit counts here.

I. How do the wealthy classes put up with such a state of affairs?

He. They put up with it as something inevitable since there is nothing whatsoever to be done about it.

I. But is there nonetheless some resentment between them and the common people?

He. None. All classes joined together in the Revolution. Afterwards the strength of Democracy was so paramount that no one attempted to struggle against it. Generally speaking the people show no distaste for electing the very rich or well-educated.

I. I am very struck by what seems an extreme equality in American social relations. The richest of men and the poorest artisan will shake hands in the street.

He. There is a great deal of equality. Less however than a foreigner supposes. The manners which strike you often count for no more than such a formula as 'your humble servant' at the end of a letter. Here we have to be polite to everybody as everyone has political rights. There is much pride of wealth among the new-rich of New York. Like the rest of the world we have our moneyed aristocracy, if one can use the word aristocracy of an ever-changing class which makes its pretensions but has no power.

I. In general what type of men hold positions in public service?

He. Generally they are held by men whose abilities and characters put them in the second rank. Such places do not carry sufficient pay, social consideration or power to attract men of distinction. But that was not so in the first years of Independence. Now we have no great men in politics. They use their energy and their resources in other careers.

(7th June 1831)

Mr. Livingston has been in Europe. He comes from a very old family and seems a man of culture.

* * *

Non-Alphabetic Notebook 1

Conversation with Mr. Gallatin[1] (who has spent several years as American Minister in France and in England)

He. We have no villages in America, that is to say none inhabited by people who cultivate the land. A landowner lives on his estate and the houses are scattered all over the country. What you take for villages had better be called towns as they are inhabited by shopkeepers, craftsmen and *lawyers*.

I. I take you up on the last word; so you have a great many lawyers?

He. Many more, I think, than anywhere in Europe.

I. What is their social standing and character?

He. The one explains the other: lawyers count among the top ranks of society and have much influence; so instead of having bustling, restless characters as in Europe, they tend to stability. Without the lawyers we should by now have revised our civil law, but they defend the abuses and ambiguities from which they profit.

I. Do they play a great part in elected bodies?

He. They form the majority of members of such bodies; but it has been noticed that the most distinguished speakers and, still more, the greatest statesmen have not been lawyers.

I. How are your judges chosen? What is their position and character?

He. The judges are all chosen from among the lawyers, and, bar the authority of the bench, remain on a footing of equality with them. Our judges are held in very high esteem. Being entirely dependent on public opinion, they need to make continual efforts to keep this esteem. Their integrity is unquestioned. I look on the judges, *supported as they always are by the lawyers* as a body, as the regulators of the irregular movements of our democracy, and as those who maintain the equilibrium of the system. Note that having the power to refuse to enforce an unconstitutional law, the judges are in some sort a political force.

I. Is it true, as I am told, that morals are chaste?

He. Conjugal fidelity is admirably secure; there is not always the same chastity before marriage. It very often happens in our country districts (not in the towns) that the extreme

[1] Cf. Pierson, op. cit., p. 136.

liberty enjoyed by young people of both sexes leads to trouble. The savage tribes that surround us go even farther in this disregard of chastity before marriage. They do not see it as a moral duty.

New York (10th June 1831)[1]

The same day while I was in a *club*, someone maintained that the Americans, as they stretched inland, would find their fleet diminishing. Mr. Gallatin has estimated at 60,000 (in round figures) the number of sailors at present sailing under the American flag. He has commented: 'As we neither have the English *pressgang* nor the French *inscription maritime* I forecast that at the first outbreak of war, it will be impossible for us to find enough sailors to man twelve of our ships.'

* * *

Conversation with Mr. Maxwell[2] on the (27th June 1831)

Mr. Maxwell has been a district attorney for ten years. He is one of the founders of the House of Correction, and is reputed to be a 'broad but very able man'.

I. What do you think of the penitentiary system?

He. One must make a distinction between penitentiaries properly so called and houses of correction. As to penitentiaries, I think the discipline is excellent as far as keeping order is concerned and getting useful work out of the prisoners; but I don't think it has an effective influence on their dispositions or bebehaviour. In general I do not think that *the criminal who is a full-grown man can be reformed*, however one treats the matter. My view is that he comes out of our penitentiaries 'hardened'. I take a different view about houses of correction: I believe in the reform of youthful offenders and I think that the only way to reduce the number of crimes in a country is to increase and to improve institutions of that sort. When I was district attorney, the number of young offenders had become decidedly alarming. It was daily increasing at a frightening rate. A few people had the idea of establishing a house of correction to remedy this evil. This conception had incredible difficulty in taking root in the

[1] *Œuvres* (ed. Beaumont), viii, 230 gives the date of this conversation as 7th June 1831.   [2] Hugh Maxwell, cf. Pierson, op. cit., p. 63.

public mind. Now success has made it popular. There is now a fifth or sixth as many young offenders compared to five years ago.

I. Have you documentary proof to establish that last fact?

He. No. But it is within my personal knowledge, and I can assure you of it. I think that houses of correction are multiplying not only in the different States, but also in the districts of the same State. In my view it is a great disadvantage if one has to send a child a very long way off to a house of correction. Such journeys necessarily involve considerable expense, and the young offender's moral sense is often lost during the move he has been forced to make.

Note: This belief in the uselessness of the penitentiary system as far as moral reform is concerned seemed to us to be shared by a great number more of able men, among others those with practical experience.

See under the heading Penitentiaries.[1]

* * *

Conversation with Mr. Elam Lynds[2] at Syracuse (on the 7th July 1831)

We felt great curiosity to meet Mr. Elam Lynds whose practical abilities are admitted by everyone, including his enemies, and who may be considered the father of the penitentiary system now in force, for it was his perseverance and energy which brought it about. So we were in good time for our visit to him. We found him in a hardware shop which belongs to him. He was dressed like a shop assistant and performed the duties of one. Mr. Elam Lynds looks like a very common man, and I believe his speech has the same vulgar quality. A note he sent us had shown that he could not spell correctly. Otherwise he seems very intelligent and singularly energetic. We could not talk to him at once as there was no one else to look after the shop, but half-an-hour later he came to visit us at our inn and we had the following conversation:[3]

[1] See below alphabetic notebook A, ff.

[2] See pocket notebook I, p. 129 and cf. Pierson, op. cit., p. 206 ff.

[3] This conversation is not found in volume viii of the *Œuvres* (ed. Beaumont), but it has been published because it figures, with cuts and modifications, in the notes of *The Penitentiary System in the United States* (2nd ed., 1836, ii, 189).

He. I have passed ten years of my life in the prison administration. I have long been a witness of the abuses that prevailed under the old system. They were terrible; the prisons cost the state a lot. The prisoners succeeded in losing their moral sense there; all sorts of disorder prevailed there. I think this state of affairs might have finished by bringing us back to the barbarous laws of the ancient codes. At least most people began to get disgusted with all philanthropic ideas, since the results as shown by experience were nil or bad. I undertook reform at Auburn; but at first I had great obstacles to overcome in the legislature and even from public opinion. There were outcries against tyranny. However I had my way in the end. When there was the question of building Sing-Sing and I offered to undertake it with prisoners working in the open fields, people would not believe that it was a practical possibility. Now that I have brought it off, many people are still ill-disposed or jealous towards me. A year ago I retired; I felt that I had done enough for the public good and it was time to pay attention to my own fortunes.

Q. Do you think that the system of discipline that you established could be applied elsewhere than in America?

A. I am sure it would succeed anywhere where it was undertaken as I undertook it myself. I even think that in France it has a better chance of success than with us. French prisons are under the immediate control of the government which can give solid and consistent support to its officers. Here we are the slaves of a perpetually changing public opinion. Now my theory is that the director of a prison, especially if he is an innovator, must be armed with absolute and assured authority. It is impossible for him to count on that in a democratic republic like ours. He must set himself at the same time both to win public favour and to carry his undertaking through to the end. Often the two objectives cannot be reconciled. In France the position is less difficult.

Q. We have heard Americans say, and we would not find this hard to believe, that the success of the penitentiary system is partly due to the scrupulous way in which the American people have become accustomed to obey the laws.

A. I am convinced of the opposite. A quarter of the prisoners at Sing-Sing are foreigners to America. I made them accept discipline just the same as the Americans. Those whom I found hardest to control were the Spaniards from South America, a race which is nearer to wild beasts or savages than to civilised man. The easiest to manage were the French. They were the quickest to accept their lot. Given the choice, I would rather govern a French than an American prison.

Q. What then is the secret of that powerful discipline of which you speak and of which we ourselves have seen the results at Sing-Sing?

A. I should find it difficult to tell you. It results from a series of daily efforts which you would need to see for yourself. One can't state general rules. It is a question of keeping work going and silence the whole time, and to achieve that one must never slacken in attention to one's job, supervising the wardens as much as the prisoners, being merciless and just. Once the organisation has got going, it will go on working very easily. If I were in charge of a government and wanted to alter the organisation of prisons, I should seek to choose an able, intelligent man; it would be desirable that he should himself have seen a prison like one of ours, or at least that he should have the most precise conception of such a prison. The man found, I would give him full powers to make changes. I have always held that for such work as this one must first concentrate all power and all responsibility in one man's hands. In that way the State stands a decidedly better chance of success and has real guarantees. When the inspectors wanted to harass me in my work, I told them: 'You are perfectly free to dismiss me; I depend on you; but while you keep me in office, I shall do nothing but carry out the plan I have conceived; it is for you to choose.'

Q. Do you think one can manage without corporal punishment?

A. I am completely convinced of the opposite. I regard punishment by the whip as the most effective and at the same time as the most humane, for it never makes a man ill and compels the prisoners to lead an essentially healthy life. Solitary confinement on the other hand is often ineffective and almost always dangerous. I have seen many prisoners who could not be brought to reason in this way, and who only left their cells to go to the hospital. I do not think you can control a large prison without the use of the whip whatever those may think who only know human nature from books.

Q. Do you not think it rash to allow the Sing-Sing prisoners to work in the open fields?

A. I should rather govern a prison where that system prevailed than one where it did not. In a closed prison one cannot get the same supervision or the same care from the wardens. Once the prisoners have been thoroughly broken to the yoke of discipline, one can set them to what work one thinks most useful and in the places one chooses. In that way the State can use criminals for various purposes, once it has improved the discipline of prisons.

Q. Do you think it completely impossible to maintain good discipline in a prison in which the cell system does not exist?

A. I think one could maintain strict order in such a prison, and one could make the prisoners' work profitable, but one could not prevent a heap of abuses which have very serious consequences.

Q. Do you think one could make cells in an old prison?

A. That depends on the structure of the place. No doubt the change could be made in most old prisons. It is very easy and inexpensive to put up wooden cells. But they have the disadvantage of holding bad smells and so sometimes become unhealthy.

Q. Do you decidedly believe in the *reform* of a great number of the prisoners?

A. We must understand each other. I do not believe in complete reform (except in the case of young offenders), that is to say I do not think one often sees a criminal of mature age turn into a religious and virtuous man. I put no faith in the saintliness of those who leave prison, and I do not think that either the chaplain's exhortations or the prisoners' own reflections ever make a good Christian. But my view is that a great number of former prisoners do not become recidivists and do even become useful citizens, having learnt a job in prison and formed a constant habit of work. That is the only reform that I have ever hoped to achieve, and I think that is all that society can ask.

Q. What do you think of hiring?

A. I think it very useful to hire out prisoners' labour, *provided* that the director remains in complete control of the prisoners themselves and of their time.

Q. In France the price for prison labour is put very low.

A. It would go up in proportion as discipline was improved. That is what we found here. Prisons were a great expense; now they bring in money. The well-disciplined prisoner works more and better and does not ruin the raw materials entrusted to him, as happens in ill-controlled prisons.

Q. What do you think the most important quality to look for in a prison director?

A. A practical capacity for handling men. He must above all be profoundly convinced, as I always have been, that a dishonest man is always cowardly. That conviction which he will be sure to communicate to those under his orders, will give him an irresistible ascendency and make a whole lot of things easy for him which at first sight might appear very dangerous.

During the whole of this conversation which, with intervals, lasted several hours, Mr. Elam Lynds came continually back to the idea that it was most important of all to break the prisoner in to a state of *passive obedience*. That point gained, the rest became easy no matter how the prison was built, and whatever the type or place of work.

*　　*　　*

Second conversation with Elam Lynds[1]

Q. What do you think his behaviour in prison proves for the future reform of a prisoner?

A. Nothing. If one had to make a guess, I would say that a prisoner who behaved perfectly in prison would probably return to his old habits on leaving it. I have always found that the worst types made excellent prisoners: they are generally more adroit and clever than the others. They see more quickly and clearly that the only way to make their lot less intolerable is to avoid the painful, repeated punishments which would be the inevitable consequence of bad behaviour. So they behave well without becoming better. The conclusion from that observation is that one should never give a prisoner remission because of his good conduct in prison. The opposite course has no certain success and only makes hypocrites.

Q. But do not almost all the theorists advise it?

A. In that as in many other matters they are wrong

[1] The second conversation is not reproduced in the *Penitentiary System*.

because they know nothing about those of whom they are
speaking. If Mr. Livingston, for example, had to apply his
prison system to men born like himself in a social position
where intelligence is developed and moral sensibility very
acute, I think his system would produce excellent results;
but on the contrary prisons are full of boorish men who have
no education and who have great difficulty in grasping any idea
or even any intellectual sensations. In wishing to apply to men
like that a system which would only be helpful to the former
type, Mr. Livingston, for all his talent, had fallen into the
almost inevitable mistake of which I spoke before.

* * *

*Conversation with Mr. Spencer; Canandaigua (17–18th July
1831)*[1]

Mr. Spencer is a distinguished man of law. He has been successively a lawyer, district attorney, and a member of Congress
and is at the moment a member of the New York legislature. He
has been one of the editors of the *Revised Statutes*.[2] Clearness
and perspicacity seem to be the guiding lights of his spirit.

Q. Are the members of the two chambers of the various
legislatures chosen in the same way and according to the same
rules of eligibility?

A. Yes. In the State of New York in particular there is just
the same type of man filling both chambers.

Q. But what then is the point of having two chambers?

A. It is immensely useful and so well appreciated that now
everyone in America accepts it as an axiom that a single legislative body is a detestable institution. Pennsylvania, which
began by making the mistake of having only one assembly,
has had to give it up. Here are the chief advantages of a legislative body with two houses: the first and most important is to
make a resolution pass two tests; between the two discussions
time passes to the advantage of good sense and moderation.
It is continually happening that the Senate, although composed
of similar elements and moved by the same spirit as the legis-

[1] Cf. Pierson, op. cit., p. 221 et seq.

[2] The 'Revised Statutes' is a periodic official publication of all the laws of the
United States.

lature, sees the matter in a different light and corrects mistakes which the former, prejudiced as it is by a first vote, would not be able to correct. The second advantage which I see in the institution of our Senate is that the senators hold office for longer than the Representatives and since they are replaced in batches, always form a body of men within the legislature who are knowledgable about precedents and have already been through their political education. They give our legislative assemblies a practical skill and a sense of continuity which without them would often be lacking.

Q. What generally speaking is the corporate attitude of the lawyers?

A. People complain that it is conservative. I know that the opposite complaint is made in France. I see these reasons for the difference: first, the body of lawyers in America have no interest in change. Our social organisation, as it now is, is the best possible one for them. Besides I think our civil laws have a different general principle from yours and that should give our lawyers an opposite turn of mind. Our civil law is entirely founded on precedents. A judge is completely bound by what another has decided before. As a result one can almost say that there are no arguments about law with us; everything reduces itself in some sort to a question of fact. One has to know what was decided in a similar case and argue for or against the application of that example. You can see that work of that sort is not apt to develop a taste for theories. Often it even narrows the mind. Your lawyers on the other hand, if I can judge by the reports of proceedings, feel they must delve down to the basis of society even in respect of a hole in a dunghill.

Q. Have the judges any disciplinary powers over them?

A. Yes. They can reprimand them, fine them, strike them off the roll, and even in extreme cases send them to prison. Otherwise the judges have no superior standing. Out of court they are on a footing of complete equality.

Q. What criticism is made of your judges?

A. The only criticism which I should feel able to make is that they are a little too fond of flattering the people, and that they will not fight courageously against a view that they believe is shared by the masses. We have seen some examples of that in cases with a political side to them. Usually and in ordinary cases they are inclined to leniency for this reason and not from their own convictions.

Q. What influence has the press on public opinion?

A. It has great influence, but it is not exercised in the same way as in France. For instance we attach very little importance to the opinions of journalists. They only gain influence by the facts they make known and the turn they give to them. Thus they sometimes manage to mislead public opinion about a man or a measure. To sum up, in all countries and under all governments the press will always be a formidable weapon.

Q. What limits do you impose on its freedom?

A. We have a very simple principle in this matter. Everything which is a question of opinion is perfectly free. One could go to print daily in America saying that monarchy is the best of all forms of government. But when a paper publishes libellous facts, when it gratuitously suggests culpable motives, then it is prosecuted and generally punished with a heavy fine. I recently had experience of an example. At the time of the case in connection with the disappearance of Morgan (a Masonic affair[1]) a newspaper printed that the jurors had pronounced their verdict of guilty from motives of 'party spirit'. I prosecuted the writer of the article and had him punished.

Q. What in your view is the way to diminish the power of journalism?

A. I am completely convinced that the most effective way is to increase the number of newspapers as much as possible and not to prosecute them except in extreme cases. Their power gets less as their number gets greater, a fact which experience has incontrovertibly proved to us. I have heard it said that in France there were only two or three newspapers that carried weight. I should suppose that in such a situation the press is an agent of destruction. Besides I think your social situation will always make the action of the press more to be feared with you than with us. Paris will always exercise immense influence over the rest of the kingdom. With us there are an immense number of factors dividing our interests. There is no great centre of

[1] Morgan, an American freemason, disappeared mysteriously in August 1826. His fellow masons were accused of drowning him in Lake Ontario to prevent him from revealing Masonic secrets. The formation of an anti-masonic party in the United States takes its origin from this affair.

activity; it is almost impossible to get public opinion excited over a large area. New York papers have no more influence over us than those of the nearest village. Another reason why the personal opinions of journalists carry very little weight is the bad use they made of them in the first years of Independence. It was then proved that most of them were sold to England. Since then they have lost public confidence.

Q. Are there influential men who write in your newpapers?

A. Party leaders often do, but they do not sign their articles.

Q. What causes the religious tolerance prevailing in the United States?

A. Principally the extreme diversity of sects (there is almost no end to it). If two religions faced each other, we should be cutting each others' throats. But as none has as much as a majority, all need toleration. Besides there is a general belief among us, a belief which I share, that some religion or other is needed by man as a social being. And all the more the freer he is. I have heard it said that in France there has been an attempt to dispense with all definite religion. If that is so, in spite of all your feeling for liberty, you will not quickly see free institutions firmly established, and you must rest your hopes on the next generation.

Q. What do you think can be done so that religion should regain its natural sway?

A. I think the Catholic religion less suited than the Protestant to come to terms with ideas of liberty: but if the clergy were completely cut off from all worldly concern, I think that in time they would win back the power over the mind which naturally belongs to them. I think that to seem to forget about the church without being hostile to it, is the best and perhaps the only way of serving it. If you act so, little by little you will see public education falling into its hands, and in time young people will have a different turn of mind.

Q. Do the clergy control public education with you?

A. Completely. I know of only two exceptions in the State of New York. That seems to me nature's way.

Q. What about your poor law?

A. In that as in many other matters we long followed the English example. We have ended by giving up their system which we thought too costly. This is the new system introduced in the last few years in the State of New York: every county has an *almshouse* to which vagabonds are forced by court orders to go, and which are also bound to receive those whom an official called the *overseer of the poor* sends as having no means of subsistence. A piece of land is attached to the almshouse, which the vagabonds and the local people shut up there have to cultivate. The object of the law is that this farmland should in time cover the expenses of the institution. We have great hopes of succeeding in this. It is not the place of birth but the place of residence which is taken to decide where the pauper should be sent.

Q. How do you manage about public education?

A. The State has special funds of   [1] set aside for this purpose. It makes grants from this fund to the local authorities who need them, in proportion to the efforts they promise to make on their own behalf. For it is generally accepted among us that the State should always *help* and never *do everything*. It is felt that people who give their money and who are on the spot, can and will give more careful attention to the way money is spent than is possible for a central administration. Moreover one wants to create as many local interests as possible. This combination of money from the State with money from the locality serves both these aims admirably. Here education rouses universal concern. The populace being really king, everyone feels the need to enlighten it.

Q. Have you noticed ill effects from the recent law abolishing all property qualification for electors?

A. No, just the opposite. The people being completely satisfied disregards the schemes of agitators.

*   *   *

Conversation with Mr. Mullon[2]

Mr. Mullon is a Catholic priest who seemed very ardent in his devotion. When I met him he was going to Michilimackinac to give religious instruction to a colony of Catholic Indians newly established at *Arbre croche.*

[1] Gap in manuscript.
[2] Beaumont, viii, p. 245 dates this conversation 7th August 1831; cf. Pierson, op. cit., p. 291 f. See pocket notebook 2, p. 145 f.

Q. Do you think that the support of the civil power helps religion?

A. I am profoundly convinced that it is harmful. I know that most Catholic priests in Europe hold the opposite view; I see why they think so. They mistrust the spirit of freedom whose first energy was directed against them. Moreover having always lived under monarchic institutions which protected them, they naturally miss this protection. So they fall into an inevitable error. If they could live in this country, they would not be slow to change their minds. All religious beliefs are on the same footing here. The government neither supports nor persecutes any of them; and without question there is no place on earth where the Catholic faith counts more ardent adherents or more numerous proselytes. I repeat the less religion and the clergy are mixed up with civil government, the less will they come in to political arguments, and the more will religious ideas gain in power.

Q. Which sects in the United States are most hostile to Catholicism?

A. All sects are united in their hatred of Catholicism; but only the Presbyterians are violent. It is they too who are the most zealous.

Q. Do you sometimes find traces of the labours of the Jesuits among the Indians?

A.[1] Yes. There are tribes which preserve confused ideas of the religion which the Jesuits taught them, and who come back to Christianity very quickly (at *Arbre croche* there are families who accepted the first principles of Christianity one hundred and fifty years ago, and they still preserve some traces of them), when one manages to reach as far as them. In general the Indian tribes venerate the memory of the *Black Robes*. From time to time one finds crosses in the wilderness which were put up by the Jesuits long ago.

Q. Is it true that the Indians have natural eloquence?

[1] Note by Tocqueville: M. (Mullon), like all the Catholic priests I have met so far, was in basic disagreement with the Protestant ministers; first in that he seemed a man of deep conviction devoted body and soul to his ministry; secondly, that he showed a strong inclination to intolerance and had little trust in the good faith of his opponents; thirdly, that he seemed not hostile to ideals of civil liberty, but far from fond of the democratic rule of the common masses. But that is a nuance that I must define more precisely from further information.

A. Very true. I have often admired the profound meaning and the conciseness of their speeches. Their style has something Spartan in it.

Q. Do they still make war as ferociously as ever?

A. Just the same. They burn and torture their prisoners in a thousand ways. They scalp the dead and the wounded. However they are gentle, honest people when their passions are not roused by war. I have seen their war dance. Never have I witnessed a more terrible sight. The warriors who are to dance first make themselves as terrifying as possible by smearing themselves with dyes. In the dance they mimic all the savage scenes which always take place in a war between Indians. Their pantomime sometimes shows them smashing an enemy's head, sometimes torturing him, sometimes scalping him. Some years ago the Bishop of Cincinnati suggested to an Indian tribe (I forget the name which Mr. Mullon mentioned) that they should send him some of their children to educate. I was present at the pow-wow to discuss the matter. Though they were all savages, the meeting, I assure you, was nonetheless impressive for that. They sat round in a circle, each spoke in turn with great seriousness and natural eloquence. An Indian never interrupts a speaker.

Q. What public authority exists among the savages?

A. They have their chiefs. Many of them are hereditary, and the family only loses its rights in case of some shameful crime. There is an Indian chief on the banks of the Saint Joseph River[1] who claims direct descent from an ancestor who met the first Frenchman in the country.

Q. Are the Indians of the *L'Arbre croche* zealous?

A. (Here Mr. Mullon's expression became extraordinarily animated.) I know no Christian to equal them. Their faith is complete; their obedience to the laws of religion is complete. A converted Indian would let himself be killed rather than break the rules for abstinence. Their life becomes very moral. You saw how eagerly the Indian population of Sault-Sainte-Marie came to look for me when they knew there was a priest on board.

Q. How is the American clergy recruited?

A. Up to now most of the priests have come from Europe. We

[1] Site of Indian settlement in Emmet County, Michigan.

are only beginning to have some native Americans. (Which is much better.) Now we have twelve or thirteen seminaries in the States. In the last forty years Catholicism has made incredible progress among us.

Q. How are Church expenses paid?

A. By voluntary gifts. The church pews of each family are the main source of revenue.

Q. How are Bishops appointed?

A. The Pope appoints them directly. But it is the custom for him to consult the existing bench of Bishops. He has sometimes been known not to do so, and in those cases his choice has seldom been a happy one.

* * *

Conversation with some French Canadians (trading with the Indians)

In the evening of 7th August walking by the banks of the Mackinac I came up to a bivouac of French Canadians. I sat down by their fire and had the talk that follows with their leader. (I have only noted in this conversation things which fitted in with all impressions I had formed before):

Q. What has become of the Hurons and the Iroquois who played such an important part in the history of the colonies?

A. The Hurons have almost disappeared. Almost all who remain of the Iroquois, for half of them too have perished, have amalgamated with the Chippewa. Many of them are based on Green Bay and the country round. The Iroquois were an astute tribe, always ready to come over to our side or to support the English as fortune seemed to favour us or them.

Q. Have you anything to fear from the Indians when trading with them?

A. Hardly anything. The Indians are not thieves and besides we are useful to them.

Q. Do you think that the Indians improve or get worse according to whether they are nearer to or further from Europeans?

A. I think they are much better when they have no contact with us, and certainly they are happier. There is more order, more government among them the further one goes into the wilderness. But I would make one exception for the Christian Indians and especially the Catholics. Those are the best of all.

Q. Do the distant Indians of whom you speak have chiefs?

A. Yes, sir. They have chiefs whose power is greatly respected in peace time. (They are hereditary and their origin is lost in the mists of the past.) They appoint an individual chief (the bravest) to lead them in war. They have not exactly got law. But when a murder has been committed, the murderer is handed over to the family of the dead man. Often he succeeds in buying himself off. Even more often he is killed and buried with his victim.

Q. How do the Indians of whom you speak live?

A. In a comfort entirely unknown among those who are near European settlements. They never cultivate the land. They are less well clothed and only have bows. But game is extremely abundant in their wilderness. I imagine it was like that right up to the Atlantic until the Europeans came. But game flies towards the west incredibly quickly. It goes more than a hundred leagues in advance of the whites. The Indian peoples who surround us would die of hunger if they did not cultivate the land a little.

Q. Have the Indians not got the idea that sooner or later their race will be annihilated by ours?

A. They are incredibly careless of the future. Those who are already half destroyed and those on whose tracks we are pressing, see the Europeans advancing to the west with despair, but there is no time left for resistance. All the distant nations of the west (I have heard it said that there were a good three million [sic]) seem unaware of the danger that menaces them.

Q. Is it true that the Indians like the French?

A. Yes, sir. Very much. They will only speak French. In the furthest part of the wilderness to be a Frenchman is the best recommendation to them. They always remember how well we treated them when we were masters of Canada. Besides many of us are related to them and live almost like them.

Q. How do the French Canadians put up with English rule?[1]

A. As with an evil that cannot be avoided. But we are not

---

[1] Tocqueville's notes published above come from pages 17–45 of the manuscript; but those which follow come from pages 1–15.

getting merged. We remain two distinct peoples. The French population of Canada has become very numerous.

*   *   *

Conversation with Major Lamard (12th August 1831)

Major Lamard is a well-educated man of good sense. He has been stationed for a year and a half on the *Prairie du Chien*. That is a huge plain by the Mississippi. The Europeans have an advanced post there and the place is considered by the Indians neutral ground on which the different nations can meet in peace.

Q. Do you think the Indians will ever adapt themselves to civilisation?

A. I doubt it. They are work-shy; and, more important, they have prejudices which will always hold them back in barbarism. The Negroes try to imitate Europeans and cannot succeed. The Indians could do it, but do not want to. They only value war and hunting and look on work as a disgrace. Far from desiring the comforts of civilisation, they scorn and despise them. I have seen Indians on the coldest days of the year with nothing but a blanket to cover them. Far from envying our furs and our cloaks, they looked on them with pity. They could not understand why one should wish for anything more than a wigwam, since one can sleep under cover in that, nor why one should cultivate a field when one could kill the game needed to live on with a gun.

Q. Do you suppose they ever think of uniting to attack the whites?

A. No. There are men among them who have seen the final fate of their race clearly and attempted to struggle. But generally the Indians are too busy with their private wars to think of uniting for a common interest. I was telling you a moment ago that Indian nature is untameable. Now here is an example. I knew the son of an Indian chief who up to the age of twenty was brought up in one of our best schools. At that age he went back to the woods. There was the war then between England and the United States. The young man marched with his tribe as part of our army. The Americans had strictly forbidden their Indian allies to scalp their dead enemies. After the first clash, the young man of whom I speak was met by one of our officers.

In course of conversation he could not restrain himself from showing with an air of glee a scalp which he had concealed between his waistcoat and shirt to stop the chiefs seeing it.

Q. What form of government do they have?

A. They have hereditary chiefs who only exercise some power if they are men of merit. Apart from that, in time of war they choose a war chief for his ability and courage.

Q. What sort of justice do they have?

A. When a man has killed another sometimes he is handed over to the family of the dead man. Most often public authority does not intervene at all. It is up to the victim's relations to avenge him. Very often they make a settlement.

* * *

Conversation with Mr. Quiblier, Father Superior of the Seminary at Montreal

Mr. Quiblier struck us as a good-hearted and enlightened cleric (24th August 1831). He is a Frenchman who came from France a few years ago.

He. I do not think there is a happier people in the world than the French Canadians. They have very gentle manners, neither civil nor religious dissensions, and they pay no taxes.

Q. But are there not some remains of the feudal system here?

A. Yes, but more in name than anything else. The greater part of Canada is divided up into seigniories. Those who buy or sell land in one of the seigniories are bound to pay a rent to the lord and a fee on transfer, but the rent is a trifle. The lord has no titular right, no superiority of any sort over his copy-holder. I think there is less distance between lord and copy-holder than between landlord and tenant in Europe.

Q. How are church expenses covered?

A. By the tithe. In general the clergy have no landed property. What is called the tithe is one twenty-sixth of the harvest. It is paid ungrudgingly and easily.

Q. Have you any monasteries?

A. No. In Canada there are only convents for women. Moreover all the nuns lead an active life educating children or tending the sick.

Q. Have you freedom of the press?

A. Complete, unlimited freedom.

Q. Have people sometimes tried to use it against religion?

A. Never. Religion is held in too high respect for a journalist to allow himself to indulge in the slightest attack on it.

Q. Are the upper classes religious?

A. Yes, very.

Q. Is there much animosity between the two races?

A. Yes. But it is not active. It does not extend to the ordinary relations of life. The French Canadians say that the English government only gives places to the English; the English on the other hand complain that it favours the French. I think both sides exaggerate their complaints. By and large there is little religious hostility between the two peoples, legal tolerance being complete.

Q. Do you think this colony will soon escape from the English?

A. I do not think so at all. The French Canadians are happy under the present government. They enjoy a political freedom almost as complete as that in the United States. If they became independent, there are a great many public expenses for which they would have to pay. If they joined the United States, they are afraid that their people would soon be absorbed in a deluge of immigrants, and that their ports, closed for four months of the year, would count for nothing if deprived of the English market.

Q. Is it true that education is spreading?

A. In the last few years there has been a complete change in this respect. Now the impulse has been given, and the French Canadians who are growing up now will not be at all like the present generation.

Q. Are you not afraid that this enlightenment may harm the basis of religion?

A. One cannot yet know what effect will be produced. But I do not believe that religion has anything to fear from it.

Q. Is French Canadian stock spreading?

A. Yes, but slowly and little by little. They have not got the spirit of adventure or the scorn of ties of birth and family which are characteristic of the Americans. Only ultimate necessity forces a French Canadian to leave his village and his relations, and he makes his new establishment as near as possible. Nonetheless there is a great deal of movement, as I was saying, and it will multiply a hundredfold as education increases.

* * *

Conversation with Messrs Mondelet[1] (*24th August 1831*)

Messrs Mondelet are lawyers at Montreal. They are intelligent and sensible young men.

Q. In what proportion does the French population stand to the English in Canada?

A. Nine to ten. But almost all wealth and trade are in the hands of the English. They have their families and connections in England and so have opportunities not open to us.

Q. Have you many newspapers in French?

A. Two.

Q. How many subscribers do they have compared to the subscribers to English papers?

A. 800 to 1300.

Q. Are those papers influential?

A. Yes. They have very decided influence, but less than one hears is enjoyed by papers in France.

Q. What is the position of the clergy? Have you noticed among them the political tendencies which they are alleged to have in Europe?

A. Perhaps one might detect in them a secret tendency to rule or direct, but it amounts to very little. Generally speaking our clergy are conspicuously nationalist. That is partly a result of the situation in which they find themselves placed. From the time immediately after the conquest up to our own days, the English government has worked in underhand ways to change the religious convictions of the French Canadians, so as to make them as a body more homogeneous with the English. So the interests of religion came to be opposed to the government and in harmony with those of the people. Hence whenever we have had to struggle with the English, the clergy have been at our head or in our ranks. They have continued to be loved and respected by all. So far from being opposed to ideas of liberty they have preached them themselves. All the measures we have taken to promote public education, which have been pretty

[1] Cf. Pierson, ibid., p. 316 f.

well forced through against the will of the English government, have been supported by the clergy. In Canada it is the Protestants who support aristocratic notions. The Catholics have been accused of being demagogues. What makes me suppose that the political colour of our priests is peculiar to Canada, is that the priests who occasionally arrive here from France, show, on the contrary, a compliance and docility towards authority which we cannot understand.

Q. Are morals chaste in Canada?

A. Yes, very chaste.

*　　*　　*

Conversation with Mr.[1]　　　*from Quebec* (*trader*)

Q. Do you feel you have anything to fear from the French Canadians?

A. No. The lawyers and the wealthy men of French extraction hate the English. They create a violent opposition against us in their papers and in their House of Commons. But it is just twaddle and that is all. The basic population of French Canadians has no political passions, and anyhow almost all the wealth is in our hands.

Q. But are you not afraid that this numerous and compact population which has no passions today may have them to-morrow?

A. Our numbers are increasing daily. Soon we shall have nothing to fear on that side. The French Canadians hate the Americans even more than they hate us.

Note: In speaking of the French Canadians Mr.　　's[2] phlegmatic face showed very apparent feelings of hatred and mistrust. Seldom does a man speak with such passion of those of whom he is not afraid.

26th August 1831

*　　*　　*

(*27th August 1831*). *Conversation with Mr. Neilson*[3]

Mr. Neilson is a Scot. Born in Canada and related by marriage to French Canadians, he speaks French as easily as his own

[1] Name left blank in manuscript.

[2] Name blank in manuscript.　　　[3] Cf. Pierson, op. cit., p. 326 f.

language. Mr. Neilson, although a foreigner, may be regarded as one of the leaders of the French Canadians in all their struggles with the English government. Although he is a Protestant, for fifteen years continuously the French Canadians have elected him as a member of the House of Assembly. He has been an ardent supporter of all measures favouring the French Canadians. He with two others was sent in 1825 [?] to England to plead for redress of grievances. Mr. Neilson has a lively and original turn of mind. The antithesis between his birth and his social position leads sometimes to strange contrasts in his ideas and in his conversation.

Q. What does Canada cost the English government in the current year?

A. Between £200,000 and £250,000.

Q. Does Canada bring in anything for it?

A. Nothing. The customs dues are used for the colony. We would fight rather than give up a penny of our money to the English.

Q. But what interest has England got in keeping Canada?

A. The interest that great lords have in keeping great possessions that figure in their title deeds, but cause them great expenses and often involve them in unpleasant lawsuits. But one could not deny that England has an indirect interest in keeping us. In case of war with the United States, the St. Lawrence provides a passage for goods and armies right into the heart of America. In case of war with the peoples of Northern Europe, Canada would supply the timber for building which she needs. Besides the cost is not as heavy as one supposes. England is bound to rule the sea, not for the glory of it, but for existence. The expenses which she is obliged to incur to gain that supremacy make the occupation of her colonies much less costly for her than they would be for a country only interested in intercourse with its colonies.

Q. Do you think the French Canadians will soon throw off the English yoke?

A. No, at least unless England forces us to it. Otherwise it is completely against our interest to make ourselves independent We are still only 600 [000] souls in Lower Canada; if we became independent, we should quickly be enfolded by the United States. Our people would, so to say, be crushed under an irresistible mass of immigrants. We must wait till we are numerous enough to defend our nationality. Then we will become the Canadian people. Left to themselves the people here are increasing as fast as in the United States. At the time of the conquest in 1763 we were only 60,000.

Q. Do you think the French race will ever manage to get free from the English race? (This question was put cautiously in view of the birth of the man to whom I spoke.)

A. No. I think the two races will live and mix in the same land, and that English will remain the language of official business. North America will be English; fortune has decided that. But the French race in Canada will not disappear. The amalgam is not as difficult to make as you think. Here it is above all *the clergy* who sustain your language. The clergy is the only *enlightened* and *intellectual* class which *needs* to speak French and which speaks it unadulterated.

Q. What is the character of the French Canadian peasant?

A. In my view it is an admirable race. The peasant is simple in his tastes, very tender in his family affections, very chaste in morals, very *sociable*, and polite in his manners; with all that he is very well suited to resist oppression, independent and warlike, and brought up in the spirit of equality. Public opinion has incredible power here. There is no authority in the villages, but public order is better maintained there than in any other place on earth. If a man commits an offence, people shun him, and he must leave the village. If a theft is committed, the guilty man is not denounced, but he is dishonoured and obliged to flee. There has not been an execution in Canada for ten years. Natural children are something almost unknown in our country districts.

I remember a talk with XX (I have forgotten his name); for two hundred years there had not been a single one; ten years ago an Englishman who came to live there seduced a girl; the scandal was terrible.

The French Canadian is tenderly attached to the land which saw his birth, to his church tower and to his family. It is that which makes it so difficult to induce him to go and seek his fortune elsewhere. Besides, as I was saying, he is eminently *sociable*; friendly meetings, divine service together, gatherings at the church door, those are his only pleasures. The French

Canadian is deeply religious; he pays his tithe without re-
luctance. Any one could avoid that by declaring himself a
Protestant, but no such case has yet occurred. The clergy here
is just one compact body with the people. It shares their views,
takes part in their political interests, and fights with them
against the powers-that-be. Sprung from the people, it only
exists for the people. Here it is accused of *demagogy*. I have never
heard that that is a complaint made against Catholic priests in
Europe. The fact is that they are liberal, enlightened and nonetheless deeply believing, and their morals are exemplary. I
myself am a proof of their tolerance; a Protestant, I have been
elected ten times by Catholics to our House of Commons, and
I have never heard it suggested that anyone had ever tried to
create the slightest prejudice against me on account of my
religion. The French priests who come here from Europe, have
the same moral standards as ours, but their political approach is
absolutely different.

I told you that our French Canadian peasants have a strong
social sense. That sense leads them to help one another in all
moments of crisis. If one man's field suffers a disaster, it is
usual for the whole community to set to work to put it right.
Recently XX's barn was struck by lightning; five days later it
had been rebuilt by the voluntary work of neighbours.

Q. There are still some traces of feudalism here?

A. Yes, but so slight that they are almost unnoticed; firstly,
the lord receives an almost nominal rent for the land which he
originally granted. It may for instance be 6 to 8 francs for
90 acres [about 135 English acres]. Secondly, corn must be
ground at his mill, but he may not charge more than the maxi-
mum fixed by law, which is less than one pays in the United
States where there is freedom and competition. Then there are
dues for 'lods et ventes', that is to say that when feudally held
land is sold, the seller must give one twelfth of the purchase
price to the lord. That would be rather a heavy burden, were it
not that the strongest determination of the people is to remain
invincibly attached to the land. Those are all the traces of feudalism that remain in Canada. Beyond that the lord has no titular
rights and no privileges. There is not and cannot be any nobility.
Here, as in the United States, one must work to live. There are
no tenants. So the lord is normally a farmer himself. However,

no matter how equal the footing on which the lords now stand, there is still some fear and some jealousy in the people's attitude towards them. It is only by going over to the popular party that a few of them have succeeded in getting elected to the House of Commons. The peasants remember the state of subjection in which they were held under French rule. One word lingers in their memory as a political scarecrow, that is the *taille*.[1] They no longer know exactly what the word means, but for them it stands for something not to be tolerated. I am sure they would take up arms if there were an attempt to impose any tax whatever to which that name was given.

Q. What conditions of eligibility are there for entry into your House of Commons?

A. There are none.

Q. Who are qualified as voters in the country districts?

A. Anyone with 41 francs income from land is a voter.

Q. Have you no fear of such a great mass of voters?

A. No. All the people have some property and are religious and order-loving; they make good choices and although they take a great interest in the elections, there are hardly ever disturbances at them. The English tried to introduce their system of corruption, but it ran completely aground against the moral standards and honour of our peasants.

Q. What is the position with regard to primary education?

A. It is a long story. In the time of the French there was no education. The French Canadian always had a weapon in his hand. He could not spend his time at school. After the conquest the English were only concerned for their own people. Twenty years ago the government wanted to start education, but it took the matter up clumsily. It shocked religious prejudices. It gave the impression that it wanted to get control of education and to direct it in favour of Protestantism. That at least is what *we* said, and the scheme ran aground. The English said that the Catholic clergy wanted to keep the people in ignorance. Neither side was telling the truth, but that is the way parties do speak. Four years ago our House of Commons saw clearly that if the French Canadian population did not become educated,

[1] The *taille* was exclusively paid by the non-noble class. In France it was either levied on land or on income. Cf. F. C. Green, the *Ancien Régime, A Manual of French Institutions and Social Classes*, Edinburgh, 1958, p. 17 f.

it would end up by being entirely absorbed by a foreign population that was growing up by its side and in its midst. Speeches were made, encouragement was given, funds were raised and finally school inspectors were appointed. I am one and I have just completed a tour of duty. Nothing could be more satisfactory than the report which I have to make. The impulse has been given. The people are most active in taking advantage of the chance to get educated. The clergy are all out to help us. We have already got in our schools half the children, about 50,000.[1] In two or three years I am confident we will have them *all*. Then I hope the French Canadian people will begin to leave the river banks and advance towards the interior. At present we stretch about 120 leagues along both sides of the St. Lawrence, but our line is seldom as much as 10 leagues in depth. However beyond that there is excellent land which is almost always given away for nothing (that is literally so) and which could easily be cultivated. Labour cost 3 francs in the villages and less in the country. Food is very cheap. The French Canadian peasant makes all necessities for himself; he makes his own shoes, his own clothes and all the woollen stuffs in which he is dressed. (I have seen it.)

Q. Do you think French people could come and settle here?

A. Yes. A year ago our House of Commons passed a law to repeal the aliens legislation. After seven years' residence the foreigner becomes a Canadian and enjoys citizen's rights.

We went with Mr. Neilson to visit the village of Lorette which is three leagues from Quebec, and was founded by the Jesuits. Mr. Neilson showed us the ancient church which the Jesuits had founded, and told us, 'The memory of the Jesuits is worshipped here.' The houses of the Indians were very clean. They spoke French and looked almost European, although their clothes were different. Almost all are of mixed blood. I was surprised not to see them cultivating the soil. 'Bah!' Mr. Neilson said to me, 'those Hurons there are gentlemen. They would think it degrading to work. To scrape the soil like oxen', they say, 'is only suitable for the French or the English. They still live on hunting and the little things their women make.'

Q. Is it true that the Indians have a predilection for the French?

[1] Or, 60,000.

A. Yes, that cannot be disputed. The French, who perhaps maintain their original identity longer than any other, none-theless adapt themselves most easily for a time to the customs, ideas and prejudices of those among whom they are living. It is by becoming savages that you have won from the savages an affection which still endures.

Q. What then has become of these Hurons who have shown such a constant attachment to the French and who have played such a great part in the history of the colony?

A. They have gone under little by little. But they used to be the greatest Indian nation on the continent. They could put up to 60,000 men under arms. You see what is left. It is thought that almost all the savages of North America have the same origin. There are only the Eskimoes of the Hudson Bay who clearly belong to a different race. With them everything is dif-ferent; language, boats (?). . . . I was speaking just now of your capacity for turning into savages. We had in Canada a breed of men, now almost extinct, who excelled in that aptitude. They were the agents of the fur trade called by the name of *Voyageurs*. They were recruited out of the whole population. I doubt if courage and the spirit of adventure have ever been pressed so far. They astonished and overawed the Indians even in their forests.

*　　*　　*

Boston (16th September)

I said to Mr. Dwight,[1] a very zealous Protestant clergyman who was talking to me about the good effects of education: 'There are people in France who have a blind love of education. They imagine that simply by teaching someone to read, write and calculate, they have made a good citizen and, almost, a vir-tuous man. Does one find the same mistake made in America?'

He answered: 'No, certainly not. No one here could be found to support the thesis, so often maintained in Europe, that education can have troublesome results; but everyone tacitly assumes that education will be moral and religious. There would be a general outcry, something like a popular rising, against anyone who wanted to introduce a contrary system, and everyone would agree that it were better not to have education than to have it given in that way. It is from the Bible that all our children learn

[1] Cf. Pierson, op. cit., index, p. 839.

to read. But I have before now heard a man of culture maintain that, albeit religious instruction was preferable to all other types, in his view education in general, no matter how it be given, was more useful for people than ignorance.'

Mr. Dwight added that he thought that the cause of religion was making advances in the United States. He told me that published reports established that the number of those who made their communion (Protestant) had increased greatly every year. But he admitted that the Unitarians had thirteen churches (I think) in Boston. There are sixty churches in all in Boston for 60,000 people.

* * *

Boston (18th September 1831). General comments.

So far I have been astonished to see how well able enlightened men in America are to discuss French affairs reasonably. I have not yet met a single man who thought we would be able to maintain a republic or democratic institutions. Perhaps it is that seeing close up the effects of popular passions working themselves out in full liberty among them, they are in a better position than we to judge how difficult it is to form a good government and, more especially, a stable government, out of such elements. They all think that, to be republican, a people must be *balanced, religious* and *very enlightened.* Many add that, in addition to these conditions, it is also necessary to have such a state of material well-being that there would hardly ever be internal troubles, resulting from unsatisfied needs. Such men let it be understood, or boldly affirm, that America must come round to Monarchy within a certain time. But that time is surely very far off. Enlightened people judge M. de Lafayette without any sort of infatuation. Almost all think that the Restoration régime was the happiest combination for France, and the present Revolution is a dangerous crisis which could be fatal for European liberty. But the middle classes, the people and the newspapers, expressing popular passions, have, on the contrary, a blind instinct which leads them to adopt all the ideas of freedom professed in Europe and the men who profess them. So it comes about that the most religious nation in the world puts all its hopes on the success of that political party among us which professes the least concealed hatred against all religions.

II

Non-Alphabetic Notebooks 2 and 3

(18th September 1831)

Today Mr. Clay[1] (Mr. Clay is a planter from Georgia. I have seldom met a more likeable or better informed man) pointed out to me several of the beautiful houses in Boston and told me that most of those who had built these sumptuous dwellings had made their fortunes themselves and had risen from very low down. He added: Fortunes change hands here at an incredible rate. It has been noted that a poor son almost always succeeds a rich father and that a family only stays down for one generation.

'How does that happen?' I ask; 'I understand that your law of inheritance tends to break up fortunes. But a still more democratic law is in force in France. Fortunes no doubt get smaller little by little, but they do not collapse like yours.' 'The reason for the difference', Mr Clay answered, 'is that great fortunes in France are landed, and in New England they are all trading fortunes. You know that in general in America one cannot find tenants: the opposite is an exception; land costs too little and its products are too cheap for anyone to want to cultivate it unless he is the owner. Without tenants, no great territorial fortunes. Now great commercial fortunes are won and preserved by industry and skill, things which cannot be bequeathed like dollars and seldom pass from father to son. In the South, on the other hand, where our slaves take the place of your tenants, fortunes do not disappear faster than with you.'

That led us to talk about the slaves. Mr. Clay said to me; 'In our Southern states there are a great many districts where white people cannot get acclimatised and where the blacks live and prosper. I imagine that in time the black population of the South, as it becomes free, will concentrate in that

[1] Cf. Pierson, op. cit., p 368 f.

49

portion of the American territory, and the white population on the other hand will gradually move out. In that way a population will be formed entirely descended from the Africans, which will be able to have its own nationality and to enjoy its own laws. I can see no other solution to the great question of slavery. I do not think that the blacks will ever mingle sufficiently completely with the white to form a single people with them. The introduction of this foreign race is anyhow the one great plague of America.'

Note: Must not this impossibility of which Mr. Clay speaks, of forming great territorial fortunes in the North of the United States (one cannot doubt that it is an impossibility) be an important contributory factor in shaping the commercial, manufacturing, restless state of mind which is so extraordinarily prominent among the men of this part of the States? In New England the urge to grow rich can only find satisfaction through trade and industry.

* * *

(*19th September 1831*)

Mr. *Sparks*[1] (a distinguished Boston literary man) said to me today: 'Most enlightened men now recognise that General *Jackson* is not fitted to fill the office of President; his limited experience of anything to do with civil government and his great age make him incompetent. But he will be re-elected.'

'And why will that be?' I asked.

'Our people,' Mr. Sparks answered, 'is not like yours. With us public opinion forms slowly. It is never carried away by surprise, although it is very subject to mistakes. It took long and patient work to put it into the head of the public that General Jackson was a great man and that he brought honour to America. The people were persuaded to believe this. There has not been time yet to bring them round to other feelings and the majority is still at the General's disposal.'

* * *

(*20th September 1831*)

Mr. *Quincy*,[2] President of Cambridge University [*sic* i.e. Harvard] said to me today: 'The State of Massachusetts is a union

[1] Cf. Pierson, op. cit., index.   [2] Cf. Pierson, op. cit., index.

of little republics who appoint their magistrates and manage their own affairs.' — 'But', said I, 'what is the central tie?' — 'The Legislature,' Mr. Quincy answered: 'These little republics have a sphere of action fixed by the Law, and outside that they become completely dependent on the great political body which represents the people. When individual communities break the Law, they are prosecuted in the courts by the State Attorney-General. They can also be sued by anyone who has been harmed by them. Such-and-such a town is bound to repair a road, neglects it and I break my carriage there. I bring an action for damages at once against the town.'

Mr. Quincy also said to me: 'I think our present happy state is even more due to circumstances outside our control than to our constitution. Here all a man's material needs are satisfied and furthermore we are born in freedom, knowing no other state. Massachusetts was very, very nearly as free before the Revolution as it is now. We have put the people's name in place of that of the king. For the rest one finds nothing changed among us.

Note: One of the happiest consequences of the absence of government (when a people is happy enough to be able to do without it, a rare event) is the ripening of individual strength which never fails to follow therefrom. Each man learns to think and to act for himself without counting on the support of any outside power which, however watchful it be, can never answer all the needs of man in society. The man thus used to seeking his well-being by his own efforts alone stands the higher in his own esteem as well as in that of others: he grows both stronger and greater of soul. Mr. Quincy gave an example of that state of things when he spoke of the man who sued the town that had let the public road fall into disrepair; the same goes for all the rest. If a man gets the idea of any social improvement whatsoever, a school, a hospital, a road, he does not think of turning to the authorities. He announces his plan, offers to carry it out, calls for the strength of other individuals to aid his efforts, and fights hand to hand against each obstacle. I admit that in fact he often is less successful than the authorities would have been in his place, but, in the total, the general result of all these individual strivings amounts to much more than any administration could undertake; and moreover the influence of such a state of affairs on the moral and political character of a people, would more than make up for all the inadequacies if there were any. But one must say it again, there are but few peoples who can manage like that without government. Such a state of affairs can only exist at the two extremes of civilisation. The savage with nought but his physical needs to satisfy, he too relies only on himself. For the civilised man to be able to do the same, he must have reached that state of society in which knowledge allows a man to see clearly what is useful for him and in which his passions do not prevent him carrying it out. The most important care of a good government should be to get people used little by little to managing without it.'

*   *   *

(*21st September 1831*) *Conversation with Mr. Gray*[1]

Mr. Gray is a Senator of the State of Massachusetts. He is moreover a very talented man.

'Have you', I asked him, 'a collection of laws regulating municipal government?'

'No,' answered Mr. Gray, 'we have general principles. All the rest is a matter of custom.'

Q. What are those principles and how are they applied in practice?

A. The general principle is that the whole people by its representatives has the right to look after all local affairs, but it should refrain from exercising that right in everything that relates to the internal management of the localities, police laws, administration of the revenues, and undertakings which only concern the locality. The Legislature never does interfere in these matters: the local authorities themselves do all these things through their annually appointed officers. The rule agreed is that as long as the local authority is acting only on its own account and does not injure anybody's rights, it is all-powerful in its sphere. Hence, it has the unlimited right to tax itself to meet the cost of certain undertakings, and its budget is never subject to review.

Q. When a local authority disobeys the law, what happens then?

[1] This is the conversation mentioned by Tocqueville in the alphabetic notebook B, under the letter J. Cf. Pierson, op. cit., p. 363.

A. The Prosecutor General cites it as it would an individual before the grand jury of the county in which it is placed. None of its inhabitants can be a juror, and if there is just cause, it is fined.

Q. How can one force a local authority to pay the fine? In France the Prefects are officially entitled to debit that expense in their budgets.

A. We have a different procedure; the law allows the creditor for the fine or damages to pick on any of the inhabitants of the locality he chooses. The inhabitant so picked becomes in this way in his turn the creditor of the local authority and can act in the same way, and so on. But that anyhow is pure theory. To avoid the exercise of such a right, the local authorities always make haste to pay.

Q. Do the judges have great political power?

A. Our courts are the chief power of the State. Everyone agrees that they can refuse to apply a law which they consider unconstitutional, and it is a daily occurrence for them to do so. I regard this power given to the judges as one of the strongest guarantees of freedom that a people can have. Besides the judges do not misuse it at all. They rouse no complaints. The people know them; they take part in their deliberations through the jury. I feel that one of the great advantages of having juries in civil cases is that relationship of which I have just been speaking, and the association and mutual confidence so created between the people and the judges, which greatly increases the moral standing of the latter.

Q. As we are talking of the jury, please explain why in America, or at least in the State of New York, you never let a jury decide cases which turn on a lack of good faith and other matters of the same sort which touch questions of conscience. It is especially, I should suppose, in cases of that sort that the jury is useful. What then is the significance of your Court of Chancery?

A. First of all you must know that the Court of Chancery is not organised in at all the same way in Massachusetts. Here the cases of which you are speaking are, like all others, within the competence of the jury, at least unless the parties wish it otherwise. That the Court of Chancery has been thoroughly established in the State of New York and in many other States of the Union, is because the English laws have been blindly followed.

Now this is the reason why the strange feature which you noted, and I agree with you, exists in English law.[1] England is a country in which, in the beginning, Roman law had completely ceased to be used. All the law was based on custom and all cases judged by jury. But when the nation began to get civilised, the deficiencies of customary law started to be felt. These deficiencies are such that I do not think a people could ever become enlightened if it remained subservient to customs. Little by little ideas were borrowed from the *written law*. The ecclesiastics, the learned and enlightened class, were those who began to bring this change about: from enlightenment and from ambition priests attracted a great number of cases to their courts on one pretext or another. Generally they were cases based on bad faith which involved questions of conscience. But before ecclesiastical courts and with written law there was no jury. So such cases ceased to come before a jury. Later the Court of Chancery took the place of the ecclesiastical courts, and although the same reasons for doing without a jury no longer applied, from habit matters continued to be conducted along the same lines. Thus an institution born from the power of the Roman church has lasted down to our own Republican and Protestant days.

* * *

(*22nd September 1831*)

Mr. Lieber[2] (a young German exiled for his liberalism, who has become known in the United States by his work entitled *Encyclopaedia Americana*) said to me this evening: 'We Europeans think we can make republics by organising a great political assembly. But on the contrary of all forms of government a republic is the one that grows most from roots in the whole of society. Consider this country. The republic is

[1] The system of Equity as administered by the Court of Chancery, independent of Common Law, is complex. For its early and subsequent history in English Law see Radcliffe and Cross, *The English Legal System*, London, 1937, pp. 108 ff.

[2] Cf. Pierson, op. cit., see the index of that work. Lieber (1800–72) who came from Berlin, served as a volunteer in 1815 and also took part in the war of Greek Independence. He became established in the United States in 1827 and worked from then onwards on his *Encyclopaedia Americana*. He wrote several important books on political science and translated Beaumont and Tocqueville's *Système Pénitentiaire* into English. Cf. also: *The life and letters of Francis Lieber*, edited by T. S. Perry, London, undated.

everywhere, in the streets as much as in Congress. If there is something blocking the public way, the neighbours on the spot form a body to discuss it; they appoint a commission and put the trouble to rights by their collective effort sensibly directed. When there is a public ceremony, or a banquet, you will see it is just the same, a meeting, a discussion and an executive power will spring out of it. The idea of an authority pre-existent to those who need it, does not come into anybody's head: the people have something of the republic in the marrow of their bones.

At another time he said to us: 'How can a man who has seen America imagine that one could transplant her political laws to Europe and, especially, do so all at once. Since I have seen this country I cannot believe that M. de Lafayette held his theories in good faith; one could not deceive oneself so clumsily. For my part I get more and more inclined every day to think that constitutions and political laws are nothing in themselves. They are dead creations to which only the manners and political situation of a people can give life.'

We asked him: 'Is it true that morals are as chaste here as people pretend?' He answered: 'Morals are less chaste among the lower classes than among the enlightened classes; but I think that they are better than among the same classes in Europe. As to the enlightened classes, one could not imagine more perfect morals. I do not think there has been a single intrigue in Boston society. A woman suspected is lost. But the women are very coquettish; they even are bolder in their coquettishness than our women are, for they know that they cannot go beyond a certain point and that nobody will think that they will go beyond it. But I still prefer our European women with all their weaknesses to the icy, egoistic virtue of the women of America.

Q. To what do you attribute the incredible control which people get here over their passion?

A. To a thousand causes: to the physical constitution, to the remains of puritanism, to habits of work, to the absence of an idle or corrupted class, such as a garrison for instance, to early marriages, even to the construction of the houses, which makes the secret of an illicit liaison almost impossible to hide.

Q. People say that the young men are not chaste before marriage?

A. No, they are like the English too, coarse in their tastes, but, like them, they make a complete distinction between the society in which they habitually live and that which serves for their pleasures. They are as two worlds which have nothing in common one with the other. They do not try at all to seduce honest women.

While we were walking with Mr. Lieber, he pointed out a gentleman who was passing near us and said: 'That man is the sheriff; he was a colonel in the army. Yesterday we met him in society at the house of the Mayor of the town, Mr. Otis.[1] (That was true.) Well, two months ago I saw him hang two men.'

'How could that be?' said we.

'In America the sheriffs perform the functions of executioner.'

Q. And there is no shame attached to such functions?

A. By no means. The sheriff executing a criminal is only obeying the law in the same way as the magistrate who condemns him to death; neither hatred nor contempt clings to his profession. It is this respect for the agents of the law, deriving from the extreme respect in which the law itself is held (because one has made it) that makes the people feel no animosity against police officers, tax collectors and customs officials. All those employments are respected.

He also said to us speaking of Germany: 'Our misfortune is not forming a single people. There is the Germany of literature, but there is no political Germany. I regard political unity as much more important, and much harder for a people to acquire than freedom. I should consider it as a great good fortune if the Germans could be subjugated under one yoke, albeit a yoke of iron. Then they would become a single people and in time would be free.

* * *

Reflection

What gives us most trouble in Europe is men born in a lower station in life, who have received an education which makes them long to get out of it without giving them the means to do so. In America this disadvantage of education is hardly noticeable.

[1] Cf. Pierson, op. cit., index, p. 846.

Education *always* provides the means needed to grow rich and does not create any social malaise.

*   *   *

(*28th September 1831*)

Mr. Gray told me today: 'I think it is even harder to establish municipal institutions among a people than great political assemblies. When I say municipal institutions I speak not of the forms but of the very spirit that animates them. The habit of dealing with all matters by discussion, and deciding them all, even the smallest, by means of majorities, that is the hardest habit of all to acquire. But it is only that habit that shapes governments that are truly free. That is what distinguishes New England not only from all the countries of Europe, but even from all the other parts of America. Even our children never turn to their masters. They manage everything among themselves, and there is no one of fifteen years old who has not performed a juror's functions a hundred times. I make no doubt that the humblest man of the people at Boston has a more truly parliamentary spirit, and is more accustomed to public discussion than the greater number of your deputies. But then we have worked for two hundred years to create this spirit, and we had the English spirit and a completely republican religion as points of departure.'

Q. Do you not think that the political character of the inhabitants of New England springs largely from their natural disposition?

A. Natural disposition counts for something, but it is above all the creation of laws and even more of customs.

*   *   *

(*29th September 1831*)

Mr. *Everett*[1] (Alexander), former United States Minister in Spain and a distinguished writer, said to me this evening: 'The

[1] Cf. Pierson, op. cit., index. Everett (1792–1847) had been Minister at the Hague and at Madrid. He then edited the 'North-American Review', and was a Deputy in the legislature of Massachusetts. In 1822 he had written a book about Europe and its future, which was very well thought of, and in another work published in 1827 he had examined the same problem for America.

57

point of departure for a people is of immense importance. The consequences for good or evil have a bearing which constantly surprises one. Our English forefathers allowed imprisonment for a proved debt; they even allowed the much more question-able practice of imprisonment before proof. That legislation passed on to us. But it is under attack and several States have begun to modify it. In the State of New York a law which will come into force next year entirely abolishes imprisonment for debt. In Kentucky imprisonment for debt has been abolished in the case where the debt is proved, but the plaintiff is still allowed to have his adversary imprisoned before the trial. So difficult is it to overcome the habits which a nation inherits from its origin.'

* * *

Mr. Sparks[1] said to us today: 'There are general political questions concerning the whole Union, which occupy the atten-tion of all provincial papers. They all take sides for or against the central administration. In that their collective effect is, in its lesser degree, comparable to the effect produced by the two or three great Parisian newspapers. In fact it is fairly rare for them to take sides even about the administration of a particular State. The papers are little concerned with that, and are absorbed in the petty interests of the localities where they are published. At least that is how it is in Massachusetts.'

Q. Representatives and senators are elected every year. Is there sometimes as a result a complete change of the legislative body?

A. No. Generally three-quarters of the members are re-elected.

Q. Does the choice of Governor give rise to a lot of intrigue and are the elections stormy?

A. The Governor of Massachusetts has but little power and only holds office for a year. It follows that there is no great passion in men's longing to achieve that position and they can always hope to succeed in a year's time; this moderates the heat

---

[1] Cf. Pierson, *op. cit.*, index. See also Herbert B. Adams, *Jared Sparks and Alexis de Tocqueville*, Johns Hopkins University Studies in Historical and Political Science, Series XVI, No. 12, Baltimore, 1898.

of faction. In Pennsylvania where the Governor has a great deal of power, for instance that of *removing* as well as appointing public officials, and where he stays in office for three years, the elections are often strongly contested.

Q. Is it essential for the President of the United States, in order to carry on the government, to have a majority in Congress?

A. No. The opposite has often happened. General Jackson did not have a majority in the last Congress.

Mr. Sparks added: 'The political dogma of this country is that the majority is always right. By and large we are very well satisfied to have adopted it, but one cannot deny that experience often gives the lie to the principle. (He quoted several examples of this.) Sometimes the majority has wished to oppress the minority. Luckily we have in the Governor's *veto*, and especially in the judges' power to refuse to apply an unconstitutional law, guarantees against the passions and mistakes of democracy.'

He also said: 'I think our origin is the fact that best explains our government and our manners. When we arrived here we were enthusiastic republicans and men of religion. We found ourselves left to our own devices, forgotten in this corner of the world. Almost all societies, even in America, have begun with one place where the government was concentrated, and have then spread out around that central point. Our forefathers on the contrary founded *the locality before the State*. Plymouth, Salem, Charleston existed before one could speak of a government of Massachusetts; they only became united later and by an act of deliberate will. You can see what strength such a point of departure must have given to the *spirit of locality* which so eminently distinguishes us even among other Americans, and to republican principles. Those who would like to imitate us should remember that there are no precedents for our history.'

*　　*　　*

Boston (30th September 1831)

Mr. Coolidge[1] said to me today: We are not afraid of Catholicism in the United States because we are sure that with us it will

[1] See notebook F, p. 290. Cf. Pierson, op. cit., p. 366.

be so modified that it will have no influence on our political approach. Here we have noticed that the Catholics always vote for the most democratic party. It is true that they are the poorest. Baltimore, where they predominate, is the most democratic town in the Union.

Charles Carroll[1] is a Catholic.

Q. Do you sometimes feel the absence of government?

A. No, far from that, what worries us is the fear that it may interfere in matters where its intervention is not indispensable.

* * *

Boston (1st October 1831)

Interview with Mr. Adams[2] (the former President). We met him when we were dining with Mr. Everett. He was received with great politeness, as an honoured guest, but that was all. Most of those present called him 'Sir'. Some gave him the courtesy title of 'President'. Mr. Adams is a man sixty-two-years old who seems still to enjoy full strength of mind and body. He speaks French with ease and elegance. I was put next to him at table and we had a long conversation together.

I told him how surprised I was to see how far the American people were able to get along without government; I commented among other things on the way any group of opinion was allowed to send representatives to an agreed rendez-vous and so form a convention. Mr. Adams answered: 'The practice of having these conventions is only five or six years old. Now we have them for all sorts of things. But to tell you frankly what I think, I find these assemblies dangerous. They usurp the place of political bodies and could end by completely thwarting their action.'

We spoke of the character of Americans in general and he said: 'There are two facts which have had a great influence on our character. In the North the political and religious doctrines of the founders of New England; in the South, slavery.'

Q. Do you look on slavery as a great plague for the United States?

[1] Cf. Pierson, ibid, index and below p. 85.

[2] John Quincy Adams (1767–1848), son of John Adams, second President of the Union, and himself the sixth (1825–9). He had defeated Jackson who took his revenge at the next election.

A. Yes, certainly. That is the root of almost all the troubles of the present and fears for the future.

Q. Do the Southerners realise that state of affairs?

A. Yes, at the bottom of their hearts. But it is a truth that they will not admit, although they are clearly pre-occupied about it. Slavery has altered the whole state of society in the South. There the whites form a class to themselves which has all the ideas, all the passions, all the prejudices of an aristocracy, but do not be mistaken, nowhere is equality between the whites so complete as in the South. Here we have great equality before the law, but it simply does not affect our ways of life. There are upper classes and working classes. Every white man in the South is an equally privileged being whose destiny it is to make the Negroes work without working himself. You cannot conceive how far the idea that work is shameful, has entered into the spirit of the Americans of the South. Any undertaking in which the Negroes cannot serve in a subordinate role, is sure not to succeed in that part of the Union. All those who trade in a large way in Charleston and the towns, have come from New England. I remember a Southern congressman who was dining with me in Washington, and who could not conceal his surprise at seeing white servants serving us at table. He said to Mrs. Adams: 'I feel that it is degrading the human race to have white men for servants. When one of them comes to change my plate, I am always tempted to offer him my place at table.' From the idleness in which the whites in the South live, spring great differences in their character. They devote themselves to bodily exercises, to hunting and races. They are strongly built, brave and very honourable; they are more touchy about 'points of honour' than people anywhere else; duels are frequent.

Q. Do you think that actually it is impossible to do without Negroes in the South?

A. I am convinced to the contrary, Europeans cultivate the land in Greece and in Sicily; why should they not do so in Virginia or the Carolinas? It is not hotter there.

Q. Is the number of slaves increasing?

A. It is diminishing in all the provinces to the East of the Delaware, because there wheat and tobacco are grown, and for those crops Negroes are more hindrance than help. So they are sent from there to the provinces where cotton and sugar are grown; in those provinces their numbers increase. In the States of the West where they have been introduced, their numbers remain small. I know nothing more insolent than a black, when he is not speaking to his master and is not afraid of a beating. It is not rare even to see Negroes treating their master very badly when they have to do with a weak man. The Negro women especially very often take advantage of their mistresses' kindness. They know that it is not the custom to inflict corporal punishment on them.

We spoke of religion which Mr. Adams seemed to consider as one of the principal guarantees of American society. I asked him whether he thought that religious feeling was on the decline in the United States.

'If one compares the present with the state of affairs a century ago,' he answered, 'yes; but if one compares things as they are today with how they were forty years ago, I think religion has gained, not lost, ground with us. Forty years ago the philosophy of Voltaire in France, and the school of Hume in England, had shaken all the beliefs of Europe. The rebound was felt in America. Since then the crimes of the French Revolution have made a profound impression on us; there was a spiritual reaction, and one feels the effect of it still.'

'But consider,' I said to him, 'the road which men's minds have travelled since their point of departure in Catholicism. Do you not think that this progress is continuing, and do you not see the Unitarianism of this country as the last link in a chain leading from Christianity to natural religion?' Mr. Adams agreed that that was his view. He added; 'Nevertheless all the Boston Unitarians protest strongly against this consequence of their doctrine, and firmly stick to the extreme position they have taken up.'

Mr. Adams appeared to think that one of the greatest guarantees of order and internal security in the United States was found in the movement of the population towards the West. 'Many more generations yet will pass,' he added, 'before we feel that we are overcrowded.'

I then spoke to him about the more immediate dangers to the Union and the causes which might lead to its dissolution. Mr. Adams did not answer at all, but it was easy to see that in this matter he felt no more confidence than I did in the future.

Mr. Adams has just been elected to Congress. Many people are surprised that he accepted. He is the first President who has re-entered public affairs.

*   *   *

(*12th October 1831*)

Today I went to see Mr. *Channing*,[1] the very celebrated preacher and the most noteworthy writer in the America of today (in a serious vein). Mr. Channing is a small man who seems worn out with work. But his eyes are full of fire and his manners kindly. He has one of the best-carrying voices I have heard. He received us warmly and we had a long conversation of which the following are extracts:

We spoke of the paucity of religion in France and he answered: 'I take the most keen and constant interest in France, and I believe that the destiny of the whole of Europe is joined to hers. You wield an immense moral power around you, and all the nations of the continent will follow you on the road on which you set out. You have in your hands more power for good or evil than any people that has ever existed. I do not think one should despair of seeing France religious. Everything in your history bears witness to your being a religious people. And besides I think that religion is so pressing a need of the human heart that it is contrary to the nature of things that a great nation should remain irreligious. I hope on the contrary that you will make a new step towards human perfectibility, and that you will not stop like the English in midroad. They have stopped at the Protestantism of the seventeenth century. I am confident that France has been called to higher destinies and will discover a still purer form of religion.'

We talked to Mr. Channing about Unitarianism, and we told him that many people belonging to other Protestant sects had spoken to us about it with disfavour.

'The question between them and us,' Mr. Channing said, 'is to know whether the seventeenth century can come back, or whether it is past beyond return. They have opened the road and claim to stop exactly where the first innovator stopped himself. But we, we claim to go on; we maintain that if human

[1] Cf. Pierson, op. cit., p. 837.

reason is progressing to greater perfection, what it believed in an age still coarse and corrupt cannot be entirely fitting for the enlightened age in which we live.'

'But are you not afraid,' I said frankly to him, 'that by your efforts to purify Christianity, you may end by making its very substance disappear? I am afraid, I admit, of the road which the human spirit has taken since Catholicism; I am afraid that it may in the end come to natural religion.'

'I think that such a result,' replied Mr. Channing, 'is little to be feared; the human spirit needs a positive religion, and why should it ever abandon Christianity? Its proofs have nothing to fear from the most searching examination by reason.'

'Allow me to raise one objection,' said I. 'It applies not only to Unitarianism, but to all Protestant sects, and even has a great bearing on the political world: do you not think that human nature is so constituted that, however education and the state of society may be perfected, one will always find a great mass of men unable by the nature of their situation to make their reason work on theoretical or abstract questions, and who, if they have not a dogmatic faith, will believe in precisely nothing?'

Mr. Channing answered: 'The objection that you have just made is indeed the most serious that can be raised against the basis of Protestantism. But I do not think it is unanswerable: First, to begin with I think that for every right-hearted man religious questions are not as difficult as you seem to believe, and that God has put their solution within the reach of every man; secondly, I do not think that Catholicism removes the difficulty at all; I admit that once one has admitted the dogma of the infallibility of the Church, the rest becomes easy, but to establish that first point you must clearly make an appeal to reason.'

That argument seemed to me more specious than solid, but as we only had limited time, I took up the question from another angle, and went on: 'It seems to me that Catholicism had established the government of men of understanding or an aristocracy in religion, and that you have introduced democracy there; but I must confess that the possibility of governing religious society as political society is governed, by means of democracy, does not seem to me as yet at all established by experience.'

Mr. Channing answered: 'I do not think one should carry the comparison between the two societies too far. For my part I think that every man has the capacity to understand the truths of religion, and I do not think that every man has the capacity to understand political questions. When, for instance I see the *tariff* question, about which the greatest economists are divided, submitted to the judgment of the people, I think one might as well take my son over there as judge (pointing to a child of ten years). No, I cannot believe that civil society was made to be controlled directly by the masses who are always comparatively ignorant. I think that we are going too far.'

*   *   *

(*2nd October 1831*)[1]

I was with Mr. Clay today (Mr. Clay is a very zealous Presbyterian). He warmly argued the case for democracy and for religion. 'I admit,' said he to me, 'that we are in a special position which is very favourable. But nonetheless I am not at all without hope that all enlightened nations will follow our example.'

'What!' I said. 'You think that the time will come when all the great nations of Europe will be able to achieve an unlimited democracy like yours?'

'That is what I hope,' he said. 'Especially those nations which are already or will become Protestant. I think Protestantism is indispensable for a republican people. With us religion is the surest guarantee of freedom. Religion progresses hand in hand with freedom, and pours it blessings on its principles. If ever we cease to be religious, I shall feel that our condition is very dangerous. All enlightened men among us share this view. We know that the immigrants to the West are getting somewhat detached from the religious habits of their fathers. We are acutely disturbed about this and appreciate so clearly the political danger of allowing an irreligious society to get established near us, that we are spending enormous sums in helping the peoples of the West to found schools and churches. Many New England families have gone to settle in the Mississippi valleys simply in order to form a nucleus of religious people there.'

[1] It seems that Pierson has not noticed this note; cf. op. cit., index.

I said to Mr. Clay: 'One thing that particularly favours a republic with you is that your country is composed of little, almost entirely separate nations.' He answered: 'That is even truer than you realise. Not only does each State form a nation, but each town in the State is a little nation. Each ward of a town is a little nation and has its own particular interests, government, representatives, in a word its own political life. As long as Paris remains France, you will have the rule of the populace, not of the people.'

* * *

(*2nd October 1831*)

Mr Sparks said to me today: 'Landed estates in Massachusetts are no longer being divided up. The eldest almost always inherits the whole of the land.'

'And what happens to the other children?' I asked.

'They emigrate to the West.'

Note: the bearings of this fact are immense.

* * *

(*5th October 1831*)

Mr. *Dens*, a judge at Hartford [?] said to me today :'Last year I was at Congress. There I found thirty-six members who originally came from Connecticut, on such a scale is our emigration. Connecticut itself has only six representatives.

* * *

(*5th October 1831*)

Mr. *Winthrope*,[1] the son of the lieutenant-governor of Massachusetts and a member of the Legislature, said to me today: 'It is a sad thing to assert but true, that with us the most enlightened provinces produce the most criminals.' This assertion astonished me. It was the first time I had heard anything of the sort in America.

'How did you get the proof of this fact?' I asked him.

[1] Pierson, op. cit., p. 441.

'It is enough to compare the population figures with the criminal statistics.'

Note: This observation needs confirmation.

* * *

(*13th October 1831*)

Mr. Vaughan,[1] Franklin's disciple, and an old man very much respected in Philadelphia, said this evening in speaking about the penitentiary system: 'Our prison at Walnut Street is in a terrible state. Things were different when the Quakers looked after it, but the political party opposed to the Quakers having won the elections some time ago, the Quakers have been turned out of all their employments.'

'But', said I, 'what has politics got to do with prisons?'

'Nothing, certainly,' answered Mr. Vaughan. 'But official positions of all sorts rouse envy, and when a party triumphs, it takes care to give them to its supporters.'

'This effect of the democratic system is so well known,' added Mr. Coxe,[2] a judge from Philadelphia, who was present at the conversation, 'that to try and put a stop to the evil, the Legislature has entrusted the appointment of the *Warden of the Penitentiary* to a commission, a majority of whose members are *judges*. It was thought that, holding office for life, they would be less likely to let politics influence their choice,'

* * *

(*16th October 1831*)

Mr. *Richards*[3] (Mayor of Philadelphia and a man who seems to be much respected in this country) told me today that in general the people showed much good sense in their choices.

'It has not always been like that in France,' I answered. 'With us there is an old feud of the people against the upper classes, which means that when the people are masters, one often sees them elect men who have no education, and for whose behaviour there is no social guarantee.'

Mr. Richards answered: 'We have never seen anything like that here. It is true that in America what one might call the upper

[1] Pierson, op. cit., p. 461.   [2] Ibid.   [3] Cf. Pierson, op. cit., p. 477.

classes have never had privileges, and have never ostensibly been separated from the people in politics. But you must understand how we are placed. One might call our republic the victory and the rule of the middle classes. In the Central States and in New England, for instance, there is no real link between the people and the real upper classes. The latter do not restrain their lack of faith in popular wisdom, a certain scorn for the passions of the multitude and a certain distaste for their manners; in fact they isolate themselves from them. The people on their side, without animosity exactly, but from a sort of instinctive repugnance, but seldom elect them to offices: generally they choose their candidates from the middle classes. Those it is who really rule.'

Q. Do you think that a good thing?

A. The middle classes are the most useful to society, and we find them as apt for business as the others. But what I have just been saying does not apply at all to the South. And as to the West, the progress of society is so fast, and there is such confusion of all the social elements mixed up there, that one can not make a similar comment.'

* * *

(*27th October 1831*)

Mr. Roberts Vaux[1] said to me today: 'I regard manufacture as a social necessity, but as a fatal necessity. It depraves the population and often exposes it to terrible deprivations. There are special dangers in introducing the industrial system into a country as completely democratic as ours. In France or in England, when the industrial population is frustrated by poverty and would disturb public order, there is a force outside it ready to maintain that order. But with us where is there a force outside the people?'

I answered: 'But take care. What you are saying has wide bearings. For if you admit that the majority can sometimes desire disorder and injustice, what becomes of the basis of your government?'

Mr. R. Vaux replied: 'I admit that I have never approved of the system of universal suffrage, which really does give the

[1] Cf. Pierson, op. cit., index.

government over to the most excitable and worst informed classes of society. Here we really have no guarantees against the people. The legislative powers have no independence. I should like the Senate to be chosen by the great landowners. But as it is chosen by the same electors as the Legislature, the one shows no more resistance than the other to popular frenzy.'

Mr.   ,[1] a distinguished lawyer from Philadelphia, said to me: 'We had a bankruptcy law, but although it had nothing to do with politics, it was repealed when the party which brought it in, lost its majority.'[2]

*   *   *

Conversation with Mr. Duponceau[3] *(27th October 18?1)*

Mr. Duponceau is an old man, the author of several well-considered books, and well known for his learning. He is French, but has lived in this country for nearly sixty years. He said to us, discussing France as if she were still the same as he remembered her: 'One thing that goes to the shaping of your morality in France is that with you each man is shut in in a certain sphere from which he does not hope to escape. Here on the contrary since the road to riches and fortune is open to everybody no matter from where they start, there is a restlessness of spirit and a greed for wealth which it would be hard for you to understand. You must appreciate that everybody here wants to grow rich and rise in the world, and there is no one but believes in his power to succeed in that. From that there springs a wearisome social activity, ever-changing intrigues, continual excitement, and an uncontrolled desire of each to outdo the others.'

'But in all this frenzy,' said I, 'what becomes of equality?'

'Equality only exists in the market place,' answered Mr. Duponceau. 'Money makes extreme inequalities in society. No doubt an able man, whatever his fortune, is received everywhere; but people are at pains to make him realise that he is not rich, and his wife and children are not received. "We cannot

---

[1] A blank in the manuscript.
[2] See alphabetic notebook I, bankruptcy, page 181.
[3] Cf. Pierson, op. cit., see the index.

go visiting those people there," say the women, "they have an income of only two thousand francs and we have ten." It is this uncontrolled wish to shine that drives many families into luxurious habits and spoils life's simplicity. One sees the same wish to shine between State and State. What a lot of money vanity has made us throw out of the window!'

'I have heard it asserted,' said I, 'that in general you have appointed incompetent people to run your undertakings.'

'That is true,' answered Mr. Duponceau. 'Seldom does the choice fall on an able man. All official positions are given for political reasons; the spirits of faction and intrigue grow here as they do under monarchies. Only the master is different.'

Another time Mr. Duponceau said: 'How strangely blind men can be to the effects of what they themselves have caused! I am sure that if England had not conquered Canada in 1763, the American Revolution would not have taken place. We should still be English. The need to resist French power in the North and the Indians, natural allies of the French in the West, would have kept the colonies in dependence on Great Britain. If they had attempted to throw off the yoke, France, for fear of insurrection in Canada, would not have dared to take their side. Nevertheless no nation has ever been more drunk with triumph than the English at the time of which I speak.'

He also said: 'The great plague of the United States is slavery. It does nothing but get worse. The spirit of the times works towards granting liberty to the slaves. I do not doubt that the blacks will all end by being free. But I think that one day their race will disappear from our land.'

'How will that be?' I asked.

'Never will white and black blood mix among us. The two races abhor each other and yet are obliged to live in the same land. That state is contrary to nature. It must end in the destruction of the weaker of the two enemy peoples. Now the white race, supported as it is in the West and North, cannot go to destruction in the South. The blacks will arm against them and will be exterminated. We will not get out of the position in which our fathers put us by introducing slavery, except by massacres.'

* * *

Conversation with Mr. Brown (28th October 1831)

Mr. Brown is a distinguished lawyer and a rich planter from Louisiana. He was ambassador in France for eight years.

We were speaking of the Quakers and he said to me: 'It is a great pity that the Quakers decided to wear a ridiculous dress, and to forbid in all circumstances resistance to oppression. Their doctrine otherwise is admirable. Of all the religious sects they are the only one that has always practised tolerance and Christian charity to the full extent. Amusements are forbidden to Quakers; their money has nothing to do; *doing good* is their only pleasure. Unfortunately their numbers are diminishing and they are also divided among themselves. For a long time they professed the doctrine that it is works and not beliefs that bring salvation: but later they abandoned that salutary principle; today they form two distinct churches one of which comes very close to the Unitarians' standpoint, and like them denies the divinity of Christ.'

'While we are on the subject of religion.' I said. 'Tell me what I am to think about the religious basis in this country. Is religion only superficial? Or is it deeply rooted in men's hearts? Is it a belief or a political doctrine?'

'I think,' said Mr. Brown, 'that for the majority religion is something respected and useful rather than a proved truth. I think that in the depths of their souls they have a pretty decided indifference about dogma. One never talks about that in the churches; it is morality with which they are concerned. But in America I have not met any *materialist*; I am convinced that a firm belief in the immortality of the soul and in the theory of rewards and punishments is, one can assert, universal; that is the common ground on which all the sects meet. I have been a lawyer for twenty years, and I have always found great respect for the sanctity of an oath.'

We spoke of New Orleans where he lived for twenty years. He said to me: 'At New Orleans there is a class of woman dedicated to concubinage: they are the coloured women. Immorality is for them in some sort a professional duty which they perform faithfully. A coloured girl is destined from her birth to be a white man's mistress. When she reaches nubile age, her mother is at pains to place her. It is a sort of temporary marriage. It usually lasts for several years, during which time it is seldom that there is a complaint of infidelity about a woman so attached. They pass like that from hand to hand until they have made a sufficient fortune, when they marry for good a man in their own station, and send their daughters out into the same way of life.'

'That', I said, 'is a state of affairs very contrary to nature; it must cause great disruption in society.'

'Not as much as you would suppose,' answered Mr. Brown. 'The rich young men are very dissolute, but the immorality is restricted to the sphere of coloured women. The white women of French and American extraction are very chaste in their ways. They are virtuous because, in the first place, I suppose, they like virtue, and then because the coloured women are not so; to have a lover would be to become like one of them.'

'Is it true', I asked, 'that there is a great difference in character between the Americans of the North and of the South?'

'An immense difference,' answered Mr. Brown. 'The Americans of the North are all full of intelligence and activity; the joys of the heart hardly play any part in their existence. They are cold, calculating, and reserved. The Americans of the South, on the other hand are open and eager; habits of command give them a certain hauteur and an altogether aristocratic susceptibility to points of honour. They are much disposed to idleness and look on work as degrading.'

'Does it not often happen in America,' I said some other time to Mr. Brown, 'that the people make mistakes in their choice?'

'Yes, that is frequent,' he replied.

Then yet another time Mr. Brown said to me: 'It is an odd thing, at New Orleans the coloured men always make common cause with the white against the blacks.

* * *

Conversation with Mr. Latrobe,[1] *a very distinguished lawyer from Baltimore* (*30th October 1831*)

He said to us: 'I think the constitution of Maryland is the most democratic in America. No property qualification is demanded for the electors. Any man who is a citizen of the United States

---

[1] Cf. Pierson, op. cit., p. 493.

and has been living for a year in the Republic is an elector.

'Do you not find', I said, 'that this universal suffrage has disadvantages?'

'There are some,' said Mr. Latrobe. 'The choices are not always good. It has been noticed that we have fewer able men in our Legislature than the Virginians have in theirs.'

'But,' I answered, 'since your Legislature is so democratic, is it not true then that Maryland is the place in the United States where the spirit of aristocracy is most in evidence?'

Mr. Latrobe answered: 'Our outward habits have indeed kept an aristocratic cast which is found neither in our laws nor in our political practice. So there is more luxury here than anywhere else: in the streets you see four-horse carriages, *jackets*, something like liveries; the members of different families are distinguished by names of estates.'

'Formerly your laws, like your manners, were aristocratic?'

'Yes, Maryland was founded by English nobles, and moreover the first emigrants professed the Catholic religion which itself is favourable to aristocracy. So they divided the territory into great estates; but America does not at all favour the existence of great landed fortunes, and the landowners were never able to get large incomes from their lands. Up to the Revolution however Maryland had the appearance of an English county; birth was as much valued there as on the other side of the Atlantic; all the power was in the hands of the great families.'

'What changed this state of affairs?'

'The law of inheritance. With equal shares, fortunes were quickly divided up. Some families, that of Charles Carroll for instance, having only one representative during several generations, kept their fortunes, but in general the great estates have been divided into a thousand fragments. With the small landowners and commercial industry, democracy was born. You see what progress it has made.'

'But how have the members of the great families put up with this change? What is their position over against the people, and what do the people think of them?'

'The people has not, as you seem to think, any hostility against the members of the old families. It shows no discrimination against them in appointments to all the offices. On their side the members of the old families do not *show* any hostility against the present order. This state of affairs is due to two circumstances; when war broke out with Great Britain, the great families of Maryland zealously supported the cause of independence. They shared the passion of the people and led them on the field of battle. After the war of Independence the political question dividing people was concerned with the Constitution. The nation was split between the Federalists who wanted to give the Union a very strong central power, and the Democrats or Republicans who wanted to keep almost complete independence for the States. The latter party, which won in the end, was the most popular. Now it happened that the Maryland aristocrats, from love of power and a wish to keep their local importance, almost all supported it. So these were two great occasions on which they went with the people and won rights for them. I was speaking just now of Federalists and Republicans and told you that in the end the Republicans carried off the victory. That is to say that they came to power in the end. For the rest, once in charge of the government, they managed things in almost all respects in the same way as their adversaries would have done. They allowed a central power, a standing army, a navy. . . .[1] Oppositions never can govern with the principles that have brought them to power. Now, to put the matter truthfully, there are no parties in the United States; everything turns on questions of personalities. There are those who have got power and those who want to have it; the "ins" and "outs".'

'What class is most usually elected by the people?'

'Lawyers. The United States are ruled by lawyers. It is they who hold almost all the offices. The President is a military man, but look at all his ministry; there is not one minister who is not a lawyer. The lawyers here have even more preponderance than in the rest of the Union, because here it is the custom before an election for the candidates to address the people. We often see the eloquence of one of them carry an election by surprise against an opponent whose real merit should have decided the matter.'

'Is there still slavery in Maryland?'

'Yes. But we are making great efforts to get rid of it. The law allows the export of slaves and does not allow their import.

[1] The dots are Tocqueville's.

74

Cultivating wheat we can very easily do without the blacks. It is perhaps even an economy.'

'Is enfranchisement allowed?'

'Yes, but we often find that enfranchisement brings great evil in its train, and that the freed Negro finds himself more unhappy and unable to help himself than the slave. One odd thing is that west of the Chesapeake, the Negro population is increasing faster than the white, whereas to the east of that bay the opposite is true. I think the reason is that the west is divided into great estates which have no attraction for the hard working, free population.

'Baltimore which now has a population of 80,000, did not have thirty houses at the time of the Revolution.'

'What then has made that city grow so fast?'

'First as a result of our Revolution; then the ruin of San Domingo which sent many French families as refugees to us and gave us the victualling of the colony, and finally the wars of the French Revolution in Europe. England was at war with the whole continent and ruled the seas; we became Europe's manufacturers.'

'Is it true that there are great differences between Americans of the North and those of the South?'

'Yes, at Baltimore we think we can recognise a Yankee in the street, and even an inhabitant of New York or of Philadelphia.'

'But what are the principal traits that distinguish the North from the South?'

'I would express the difference like this: what distinguishes the North is the *spirit of enterprise*; what distinguishes the South is the *spirit of chivalry*. The manners of a Southerner are frank and open; he is excitable, even irritable, and very ticklish on a point of honour. The New Englander is cold, calculating and patient. As long as you are staying with a Southerner, you are made welcome, and he shares all the pleasures of his house with you. The Northerner, when he has received you, begins to think whether he can do business with you.'

(Having painted this spirited portrait, Mr. Latrobe seemed to be afraid that he had been talking too frankly to us, and he added several details to diminish the effect.)

'But your present legislation, your law of inheritance among other things, should change the look of your society?'

'Yes, we used to have a race of landowners living on their estates. In general those were the most distinguished people in the country. They had received an excellent education, and had the manners and standards of the English upper classes. We still have a certain number of these "gentleman farmers"; but the law of inheritance and democracy are killing them. In two or three generations they will have disappeared.'

'Do you not regret that it should be so?'

'Yes, from some points of view. In general that class was a seedbed of distinguished people for the legislature and the army. They were our best statesmen and our finest characters. All the great men of the Revolution came, in the South, from that class. But nonetheless I am inclined to think that, all things considered, the new order is better. Our upper classes now are less remarkable, but the people is more enlightened; there are fewer distinguished men, but more general happiness. In a word we are daily getting more like New England. Now New England, in spite of all I was saying to you about it, is well ahead of us in everything to do with the economy of society. I think that the whole American continent must model itself one day on New England. What hastens this tendency is the perpetual flow of people from the North to the South. Their will to grow rich and their spirit of enterprise are continually driving them among us. Little by little all trade and control over society is falling into their hands.'

'Do you think you could do without slaves in Maryland?'

'Yes, I am convinced of it. Slavery is in general an expensive way of farming, and it is more so with certain crops. Thus wheat-farming requires many labourers, but only twice in the year, at sowing time and at harvest. Slaves are useful at those two seasons. For the rest of the year they must be fed and kept without, one may say, employing them. Besides, on a farm with slaves there are always a multitude of women and children who must be fed without being employed. So generally speaking slavery is worth nothing in wheat growing country. And that applies to the greater part of Maryland. In the South where the crop from the plantations is very large, one can employ slaves.'

'But if sugar and coffee are more profitable crops than corn, and if slave labour for agriculture is more expensive than free, it surely follows that the Southerners *can* keep their slaves, but it also follows that they would get a better return from their lands if they cultivated them themselves or employed free labour?'

'No doubt, but in the South the white man cannot, without getting ill or dying, do what the black does easily. Besides there are certain crops that are raised much more economically by slaves than by free workers. *Tobacco* for instance. Tobacco needs continual attention; one can employ women and children in cultivating it. In a country where labour is as expensive as it is in America, it would be difficult to grow tobacco without slaves: it is a crop admirably suited for slave labour. Tobacco is the only Southern crop grown in Maryland. People will end by giving up growing it in proportion as slavery disappears. It would be better to lose that source of income than to keep it. All that I have been telling you just now is not only my own opinion, it is an expression of public opinion. Over the last fifteen years there has been a complete revolution in people's attitude to this matter. Fifteen years ago one was not allowed to say that slavery could be abolished in Maryland; now no one disputes that.'

'Do you not think that the law of inheritance should have a great influence on the existence of slavery?'

'Yes immense. The division of properties multiplies small fortunes and quickly creates a class of white labourers who start competing with the slaves. Everywhere in Maryland where properties have been divided up, slavery has disappeared and the white population has developed extraordinarily.'

'In Maryland do you have a code for the blacks?'

'No. The penal code applies to both races. There are however some offences which can only be committed by a black. A black for instance, even if free, cannot carry arms. A black slave cannot buy or sell on his own account without the written permission of his master. Free blacks cannot come together for meetings.'

'Do enfranchised blacks have political rights?'

'None. The law gives them them in Pennsylvania, but in practice they do not use them any more than with us.'

'Is it true that public education in Maryland is infinitely less advanced than in New England?'

'Yes. We have only just set out on the road along which the Northerners have been going for two hundred years. We find the chief obstacle in the sentiments of the people themselves. A curious thing has long happened and still happens with us: the enlightened classes of the population feel the need for public education and work ceaselessly to spread it. But the people who still do not see the need to give their money to attain this object, does not re-elect to office those who thus work for their welfare in spite of themselves.'

'Do you realise that what you are saying is a very strong argument against the principle of the sovereignty of the people?'

'No, at least not in my view. The people is often blind and falls into incredible mistakes. But I have always found that it ends up by understanding its own interests. And then it does more than the strongest power could do. So in public education it has long been impossible for us to do anything; but now public opinion begins to turn to our side. The impulse has been given and nothing will now stop it.'

'How do the Catholics in America prosper?'

'They are increasing extraordinarily and are pursuing a very skilful policy. The Catholics are the only congregation that is never divided about doctrine. They march united like a single man. For the last twenty years they have very skilfully diverted all their efforts towards education. They have established seminaries and colleges. The best educational institutions in Maryland are Catholic. They have even colleges in other States. These colleges are full of Protestants. There is perhaps no young man in Maryland who has received a good education who has not been brought up by the Catholics. Although they are very careful not to speak of their beliefs to their pupils, you realise that they always exercise a certain influence. They have also very cleverly directed their chief attention to the education of women. They think that where the mother is Catholic, the children will almost always become such. Generally their bishops in America are able men.'

'What are the doctrines of the American Catholics about the question of Church government?'

'They recognise the Pope's right to appoint the bishops, and the bishops' right to appoint the parish priests. As to matters of faith they think that only an Ecumenical Council presided over by the Pope has a right to pronounce.'

* * *

Non-Alphabetic Notebooks 2 and 3

Conversation with Mr Stewart[1] (*1st November 1831*)

Mr. Stewart is a distinguished Baltimore doctor.

He said to me: 'Doctors have some political influence in America. In the small places they have the confidence of the people and are often sent to the legislatures and to Congress. Sometimes ecclesiastics too are sent there. But that is a very rare event. The general tendency is to keep the clergy in the Church and separate from the State.'

'What do you think about the state of religion in the United States? I admit that I am inclined to see a profound indifference beneath all religious beliefs. I imagine that the greater part of the enlightened classes have many doubts about dogma, but that they are careful not to show them; for they feel that positive religion is a moral and political institution which it is important to preserve.'

'There is some exaggeration in that picture. The vast majority in the United States, even among the enlightened classes, but especially among the people, is truly *believing*, and holds firmly to the view that there is no guarantee for the social behaviour of a man who is not a Christian. This view is so firmly rooted that it gives rise to an intolerance of which you can form no idea. It gives the clergy great indirect influence. So if a clergyman known for his piety gives it as his opinion that a man is *unbelieving*, that man's career will almost certainly be broken.

'Another example: a doctor is clever, but he has no faith in the Christian religion. However, thanks to his ability, he gets a good practice. No sooner is he introduced into a house than a zealous Christian, a clergyman or another, comes and seeks out the head of the family and says to him: "Be careful of that man. Perhaps he will cure your children, but he will seduce your daughters or your wife; he is an unbeliever. But here, on the other hand, is Mr. So-and-so who is as good a doctor as the other and who is also religious. Trust me and entrust the health of your family to him." Such advice is almost always followed. So one cannot exactly say that the clergy are a civil power with us; but it is at least certain that *religion* exercises immense power outside the church, and even has a prodigious influence on the affairs of the world.'

[1] Cf. Pierson, op. cit., p. 499 f.

'Does not such a state of affairs make for many hypocrites?'

'Yes, but especially it keeps them from speaking. Public opinion does with us what the Inquisition could never do. I have met, I have known a lot of young people who, having received a scientific education, thought they had discovered that the Christian religion was not true; carried away by the ardour of youth they have started loudly proclaiming this opinion; they have grown indignant against the intolerance of zealous Christians, and have been open in their hostility towards them. What then! Some have been forced to leave the country or to vegetate miserably there. Others, feeling the struggle unequal, have been constrained to an external religious conformity, or have at least kept quiet. The number who have thus been suppressed by public opinion is very considerable. Anti-Christian books are never published here, or at least that is very rare. However irreligion is beginning to penetrate into some newspapers. There is a newpaper of that sort at Boston, one in New York, one in Jersey, and another in Cincinnati. But the progress of that attitude is very slow. However several of our great men have shared it. One does not know what view Washington held about Christianity; he never expounded it. But Jefferson, Franklin and John Adams were decidedly deists. On the other hand one must recognise that a great many of our able men have been and are still firm believers. But I imagine that their number is diminishing.'

* * *

Conversation with Mr. Cranche[1] (2nd November 1831)

Mr. Cranche is a Catholic priest and vice-president of the college of St. Mary at Baltimore. Almost the whole of the present generation has passed through this college. It was founded forty years ago by Mr. Dubourg, a French priest. Since then it has had great additions.

Q. How are the Catholics in the United States governed?

A. In the United States there is a metropolitan archbishop who resides at Baltimore, and thirteen suffragan bishops. When a bishopric becomes vacant, each of the remaining bishops sends

[1] Cf. Pierson, op. cit., p. 499.

a list of three candidates to the archbishop. It is from among those candidates that the Pope chooses.

Q. Is that procedure a law or a custom?

A. A custom. In theory the Pope's choice is free, but he always does select one of the bishops' candidates.

Q. How are the lower members of the clergy appointed?

A. All the *governmental* power is concentrated on the episcopate. In Europe the parish priests can only lose their positions in case of bad conduct. America is regarded as a pagan country where there are no resident clergy, but only missionaries. The bishops choose these missionaries, appoint them and call them back at their pleasure.

Q. So you have nothing resembling the old French *officialités* here?

A. No, we have no sort of ecclesiastical tribunal.

Q. Is Catholicism spreading in the United States?

A. Yes, prodigiously.

Q. But is it spreading through conversions, and have you an idea of the number of converts?

A. We have not got an idea of the number of converts; but we know that there are a great many.

Q. I see there are many Protestant children with you. Do they sometimes become Catholic?

Mr. Cranche, with some animation answered, 'No.' 'At least it is a rare event,' he added. 'We are careful never to say anything to them against the religion of their parents. Two children who talked among themselves about points of controversy with the Protestants would be punished. It is true however that we make them attend our religious services. But their parents know that before they send them to us.'

'But it seems to me that, though you are careful not to talk to your pupils about the Catholic religion, they cannot live like this in a completely Catholic atmosphere without it producing a strong impression on them in favour of your doctrines?'

'The impression is strong enough to take away all their prejudices against Catholicism; not strong enough to convert them. What is more sure of effect is the marriage of a Protestant with a Catholic girl. Such marriages are forbidden in Europe; we favour them here. We have noticed that when the mother is Catholic, the children always and the husband often become

Catholics. At Baltimore there are a great number of women's organisations concerned with education. It is not rare to find young girls becoming Catholics.'

'Establishments like yours are multiplying from what I have heard in America?'

'This is the first one; it has 180 pupils. There is another in Maryland which is run on the same plan by the Jesuits, and there is a third in the district of Columbia.'

'What is the opinion of the Catholics in America about the power of the Pope and its independence of general councils?'

'It would be very difficult to say. In America as in Europe there are "Gallicans" and "ultramontanes". The latter have the Jesuits as leaders. But up till now these questions are only asked within the circle of those who study theology; the masses have never come into it, and it would be impossible to say what is the view of the majority.'

'Are American Catholics zealous?'

'Yes, I think America is called to become the hearth of Catholicism. It is spreading freely without the help of the civil[1] power, without rousing hatred, simply by the strength of its doctrine and in perfect independence of the State.'

'Do the people subscribe liberally to church expenses?'

'The clergy are not rich, but have what they need.'

'Do you think it is better to meet expenses in this way rather than by enforced contributions?'

'Yes, certainly, in America.'

* * *

(*3rd November 1831*)

I dined yesterday with Mr. James Carroll. Among several other guests were the Governor of Maryland, Mr. Howard, son of Colonel Howard, the chief judge of the criminal court, and Mr. Finley;[2] most of these gentlemen belonged to the old families of Maryland. There was talk about the political constitution of this State and all agreed that they had gone too far in widening the franchise. As a result, these gentlemen said, it is really the least enlightened part of the nation that rules the other. Then

---

[1] The word 'civil' ends non-alphabetic notebook 2. What follows is the beginning of non-alphabetic notebook 3.   [2] Cf. Pierson, op. cit., p. 501.

I took Mr. Finley aside and had the following conversation with him.

'I am sorry', he said to me, 'that you could not come to Baltimore at the beginning of last month. The members of our legislature were elected then, and the sight of our elections would have provided lively interest for you.'

'Could you not', I answered, 'describe them to me?'

'All the better,' replied Mr. Finley, 'since I played a part. The Republicans, or the anti-Jackson party, chose me as their candidate. My opponent happened to be one of my best friends. We went together two days before the election to Washington Square where a platform had been erected for speakers at the *town-meeting*. I got up first and began to explain to the audience —there were at least 10,000—the mistakes which General Jackson and the present administration had committed since they came to power, whereas my opponent made the case for the government. When I say we did that, we tried to do so; for the boos of the opposing party continually drowned the speaker's voice. Several men came to fisticuffs. There were several broken limbs and finally everyone went to bed. The next day my adversary and I went off to tour the different parts of the county. We travelled in the same carriage, ate at the same table, lodged at the same inns and then appeared as adversaries on the same *hustings*.'

'But do you see nothing to fear in such disorderly and tumultuous assemblies?'

'For my part I think the hustings system detestable. But it does not present the dangers you imagine. Our people is accustomed to that type of election. They know just how far they can go, and how much time they can devote to this sort of ancient saturnalia. The evening of an election at which people have fought with sticks is as peaceful at Baltimore as Ash Wednesday at Rome. Besides the very excess of democracy partly saves us from the dangers of democracy. All public appointments are annual. The party that loses this year, hopes to succeed the next. So why should it resort to illegal means?'

'You argue as a man who has never seen a people stirred by *real* and *profound* political passions. Everything with you up to now has been on the surface. There have been no large substantial interests at hazard.'

'That may be true; note that I only speak about us and about the present time.'

'No doubt with you as in New England it is the municipal authorities who summon the town-meeting.'

'It ought to be so; but our custom is different. In Maryland any individual, by announcing its date and object in a newspaper, can call a meeting together. At election time I have known innkeepers announce such meetings near their inn to attract customers; and the plan succeeded perfectly.'

'Is it true that you impose no property qualification for the vote?'

'Not the smallest; I have seen elections swayed by the paupers from the alms-house, whom one of the candidates had had fetched.'

'Do you approve of such a state of affairs?'

'No. In thus pressing democracy to the utmost limits, we have in actual fact handed over control of society to those who have no interest in stability since they possess nothing and have but little understanding. Also we have built our social order on ever moving ground. With us every year not only do public officials change, but principles, maxims of government and parties succeed to power at an incredible rate. Social standing and wealth are everlastingly caught up in this all-embracing change. There is no continuity in undertakings.'

'But it is yourselves, the members of the upper classes, who have made the existing laws. You were the masters of society fifty years ago.'

'Yes certainly, but each party, to gain power, chose to flatter the people, and bid for its support by granting new privileges. Thus by degrees the most aristocratic State in the Union has become the most democratic.'

*   *   *

(*3rd November 1831*)

Today I said to Mr.   ,[1] a criminal judge at Baltimore: 'In civil law you have two jurisdictions for cases that are almost the same, two codes of procedure, two laws. Do you not think that one could simplify that state of affairs?'

[1] A blank in the manuscript.

He answered: 'Yes, I am convinced of it. But how can one get our legislature to do such work? We cram politics into everything. All our laws are political. One party has them passed; another opposes them. It is the two-sided interests of parties, not the interest of the State, that leads to action. How can one make good civil laws in the midst of such fluctuations?'

* * *

(*3rd November 1831*)

Today I was saying to Mr. Latrobe.[1] 'I will allow, if I must, that democracy is able to control the internal affairs of society. But I cannot persuade myself that it is in a state to manage foreign affairs. All the peoples who have shaped the world, all who have achieved great deeds beyond their frontiers, have been ruled by strong aristocracies. Take the Romans in time past for example, or the English now.'

Mr. Latrobe answered: 'I agree with you on that point. That really is the stumbling-block for democracy. But we have not had occasion to suffer from it yet. We have no neighbour. *In general,*' he added, '*I feel that America proves absolutely nothing in favour of Republicanism.*' He also said: 'One does not take habit enough into account in the history of peoples as well as of individuals. One seeks far-fetched reasons why we uphold a Republic. The most important, to my mind, is that we are used to it. What needs explaining is how we came to get used to it. The reason why we suffered such a severe social malaise during the first ten years following the Revolution, is that we were not yet used to governing ourselves as an independent State, although we were already used to administering our own affairs within each State.'

* * *

(*5th November 1831*)

This evening we paid a visit to Charles Carroll.[2]

Charles Carroll is the last survivor of the signatories of the Declaration of Independence. He is descended from a very ancient English family. He owns the most huge domain in

---

[1] Cf. Pierson, op. cit., pp. 493.
[2] Cf. Pierson, op. cit., and above p. 60.

America now. The estate on which he lives comprises 13,000 acres and 300 Negro slaves. He has married his grand-daughter to the Duke of Wellesley[*sic*]. He is a Catholic. Charles Carroll is ninety-five years old. He holds himself very erect, has no infirmity, his memory is rather uncertain. Nonetheless he still talks very well as an informed and likeable man. He was educated in France. He welcomed us with great kindess and friendliness. Conversation turned on the great time of his life, that is the Revolution. He reminded us with very natural pride that he had signed the Declaration of Independence, and that by so doing he risked, together with his life, the most consider-able fortune that there was in America. I ventured to ask him whether from the beginning of the quarrel the colonies had had the idea of separating from Great Britain.

'No,' Charles Carroll answered me, 'we were strongly attached in our hearts to the Motherland. But she forced us by degrees to cut ourselves off from her.' He added with much warmth: 'No, doubtless we did not believe that things would go so far. Even after we signed the Declaration of Independence, we thought that Great Britain, frightened by that, would seek to get closer to us, and that we could be good friends. But the English pressed their point of view, and we ours.'

We talked of the government of the United States. Charles Carroll showed that he regretted the old aristocratic institutions of Maryland. The general tone and content of his conversation breathed the spirit of the English aristocracy, mingled sometimes in a peculiar way with the habits of the democratic government under which he lived and the glorious memories of the American Revolution. He ended by saying to us: 'A mere Democracy is but a mob. The English form of government,' he said to us, 'is the only one suitable for you; if we tolerate ours, that is because every year we can push our innovators out West.'

The whole way of life and turn of mind of Charles Carroll make him just like a European gentleman. Probably the great Southern landowners at the time of the Revolution were very much after this fashion. This race of men is disappearing now after having provided America with her greatest spirits. With them the tradition of cultivated manners is lost; the people is becoming enlightened, attainments spread, and a middling ability becomes common. The striking talents, the great characters, are rare. Society is less brilliant and more prosperous. These various effects of the progress of civilisation and enlightenment, which are only hinted at in Europe, appear in the clear light of day in America. From what first cause do they derive? I do not yet see clearly.

* * *

(5th November 1831)

Mr. James Carroll[1] said to us today: 'One must not exaggerate the disadvantages of democracy with us. No doubt in a lot of details, in a great number of particular cases, the people lack common sense, but by and large nevertheless the machine works and the State prospers. No doubt universal suffrage presents dangers, but it has this advantage that with it there is no hostility of one class against the others: there is general well-being spread through the nation. I think that whatsoever be the disadvantages of democracy, *when it can function*, it does even more good than harm. It encourages throughout the body social a lively activity which no other government would know how to create. However I am very far from thinking that it can function everywhere. I think that, as we are placed in unique circumstances, our experience proves nothing.'

'What do the wealthy classes of society think of the present state of affairs?'

'The upper classes see very clearly the blunders and passions of the people; they think that in a lot of matters they would guide society more successfully than the people. But they recognise all the same that, considering everything, the State prospers; they submit to the present order, recognising the good in its ultimate result, though quite conscious of the faults in the details.'

Note: Mr. James Carroll has a cool, just mind in which, I think, one can have confidence.

* * *

Philadelphia (18th November 1831)

Mr. Biddle,[2] President of the Bank of the United States, is one of the most distinguished men in this country. I said to him

[1] Pierson has not been able to identify this gentleman.
[2] Cf. Pierson, op. cit., p. 535.

today: 'What I least understand in America is the nature and ways of activity of the political parties. In France, and elsewhere in Europe, society is divided by two or three important conceptions round which definite interests and emotions group themselves. In America I see nothing like that: one might say that there are nothing but coteries here and no parties properly so called. Personalities are everything, and principles of little account.'

Mr. Biddle answered me: 'I can believe that you find it difficult to understand the nature and activity of parties in America, for we get lost ourselves in just the same way. There has been a mix-up of all the old parties and today it would be impossible to say what is the political belief of those who support the administration, or of those who attack it.'

'But it has not always been like that?' I asked.

'No, certainly not,' replied Mr. Biddle, 'this is something quite new with us. For a long time we were divided between *Federalists* and *Republicans*. Those two parties were very like what you have in Europe; they had political doctrines to which interests and emotions were attached. They fought bitterly until the Federalist party, always short in numbers, was completely crushed by its adversary: tired of their vanquished position, the Federalists ended by giving up their own cause; they either merged in the successful party, or rallied, under other names, about questions of detail. But the party standard has really been knocked down for good and all. This revolution finally worked itself out when General Jackson came on the scene; he claimed to make no distinction between the old parties in his choice. Since then there have been people who support the administration, and people who attack it; people who extol a measure, and people who abuse it. But there are no parties properly so called, opposed one to the other and adopting a contrary political faith. The fact is that there are not two practicable ways of governing this people now, and political emotions have scope only over the details of administration and not over its principles.'

Q. With you the Head of State can have the majority of Congress against him without public business suffering?

A. Yes, certainly. Our political machine is organised so that it can work by itself. The situation of which you speak has already come about several times; even now the President has lost the confidence of Congress and of informed opinion. His proposals are not adopted and his selections are turned down by the Senate; nonetheless public business is carried on just as well as before and no one has any fears for the future. I regard as one of the severest tests of the excellence of our institutions this ease with which we succeed in getting along without government or going upstream against it.

* * *

Philadelphia (20th November 1831)

Mr. Poinsett[1] who was for a long time the American Ambassador in Mexico, and has the reputation of being a very outstanding man, said to me this evening; 'It is in Kentucky and Tennessee that one should judge the character of the Americans of the South. The Kentucky people are descended from the Virginians and have never been mixed with outsiders. They have kept their spirit and manners better than the people of any other province. Ohio on the other hand, Illinois and all the West have been populated by emigrants from all parts of the Union but particularly from New England. The emigrants show a restlessness of temper which is very extraordinary: the land never stays in the hands of the one who clears it. When it begins to yield a crop, the pioneer sells it and plunges again into the forest. It would seem that the habit of changing place, of turning things upside down, of cutting, of destroying, has become a necessity of his existence. Very often the second owner too cannot persuade himself to stay still. When the land is in full cultivation, he sells it in his turn and goes further on to work up a newer piece of land. But the third emigrant stays; it is they who make up the population. The others are as it were the advance-guard of civilisation in the wilds of America.'

* * *

Cincinnati.[2] Conversation with Mr. Storer,[3] the leading lawyer in Cincinnati (2nd December 1831)

Q. Your judicial institutions are different from those of other States?

[1] Cf. Pierson, op. cit., p. 643.
[2] See the notes on Ohio and Cincinnati in notebook E, pp. 261 ff. and in pocket notebook number 3, pp. 162 ff.   [3] Cf. Pierson, op. cit., p. 554.

A. In one point especially: our judges are appointed by the legislature and for a term of seven years only. I think that in the whole Union there is only Vermont that has done the same as we.

Q. Do you think that innovation good?

A. I think it very pernicious. The judges ought to be independent of political passions. That is the greatest safeguard of our liberties. Here they are under the yoke of party spirit.

Q. Is the evil felt by the masses?

A. I think it is. We hope soon to change that part of our Constitution. But for that one must call a convention together, and we are afraid that with the existing political passions it might not be well composed. That which made our present Constitution in 1802 was composed very badly. Ohio then was populated by people not at all to be recommended, and the morality of the voters was reflected in their choice. We have granted too much to democracy here.

* * *

Mr. Walker,[1] *a very distinguished young lawyer from Ohio (2nd December 1831)*

Q. Do you think that your system of appointment for the judges is good?

A. I think it very dangerous, and experience has already shown up its vices. In general our Constitution tends towards too unlimited a democracy. It has other defects too; for our legislative body is too small in number, and that takes away some of its moral standing; one is never certain that it really represents the will of the people.

Q. I have heard talk of the extreme fertility of this part of your territory; is what is said about it true?

A. Yes; I was born and have spent part of my life in Massachusetts. There an acre yields 25 to 30 bushels a year. Here, from 70 to 80.

Q. Is it true that part of the population of Ohio is already getting under way to cross to the right bank of the Mississippi?

A. Yes. This is what is happening: those who possess land generally keep it and stay here. But their sons go to seek their

[1] See below pp. 94–98, and notebook F, p. 306. Cf. Pierson, ibid.

fortune further West in the States where the land is still un-inhabited. Moreover every year a crowd of workmen, prole-tarians from other States or from Europe, arrive in our towns. These men stop here for two or three years. The price of labour is so high (*one third more than in New England*) and the cost of living so low, that in two or three years they can put by some capital. Then they leave us and go West to buy lands and become landowners.

Q. Is it true that there is never a man of leisure in your towns?

A. I know no one who does not have a profession and work at it.

Q. How do you stand with regard to public education in Ohio?

A. The State of Ohio which contains about 25,000,000 acres, is methodically divided up into townships each comprising the same acreage. When Congress registered Ohio as a territory, it ordained that one 32nd[1] or 36th part of all the land in each township should not be sold but should provide funds for public education. It established the same rule in favour of religious worship. We already find that these funds supply our greatest provision for the establishment of schools. What holds up the progress of education with us is the lack of good teachers.

Q. Does the government concern itself with education?

A. One must make a distinction: everyone is free to establish a school or a college; in that respect the State has nothing to do with education. But you see that for its part the State is con-cerned to provide free education, and so it reserves control, in-directly it is true. So the schools are subjected to inspectors, not central ones but inspectors appointed by each locality, and they examine the masters, their methods and the progress of the pupils.

Q. With what State does your local government system have most analogy?

A. With the local government system of Pennsylvania which is the neighbouring State.

---

[1] This figure has been crossed out.

* * *

(2nd December 1831)

Mr. *Chase*,[1] a Cincinnati lawyer, said to me today: 'We have carried democracy here right to its ultimate limits. The suffrage is universal. The result is very bad choices, in the towns especially. Thus the four last members elected for the county of Cincinnati are absolutely unworthy to hold the position to which they have been elevated.'

Q. But how did they manage to get appointed?

A. By flattering everybody, a thing which men of character will never do; by mixing with the mob; by basely flattering its emotions; by drinking together. But it is not generally to the State assemblies that the people send men like that. One sees a lot of them in Congress. In spite of all however it is still the influence of men of talent that governs us.

Q. But do you not think that when the electoral franchise is so widespread, the people must necessarily often make a bad choice?

A. I think, and I am convinced that there is not a man of distinction in the Union but feels that a very extended suffrage is a fatal thing. But they cannot fight against the flood of public opinion which is flowing perpetually in this direction. We have seen an example in Virginia. Virginia was the State of the Union where the landowners had succeeded in maintaining an electoral property qualification up till now. A year ago at last they were overcome. They began to lower the property qualifications. Now they have no power to stop themselves. It is only in New England and particularly in Massachusetts, of which I can speak as my family comes from there, that the people are sufficiently enlightened and masters enough of their passions always to elect the most remarkable men. But I believe that that is an exception.

Q. What is the ordinary revenue of the State of Ohio?

A. About half a million francs. But it often makes extra-ordinary outlays. The canals have already cost 6,000,000. It has covered that expense by a loan. Just to indicate how poor America still is in capital, to find that sum it had to go to Europe.

Q. Do you in Ohio have the local government system of New England?

[1] Cf. Pierson, op. cit., p. 554.

A. No. Our system is more like that of Pennsylvania. We have townships, but they do not as in New England form a single, constant entity having but one will and one government. In Ohio one often finds in the township a town having its own separate government, independent of the township. I find the system in New England simpler and more consistent.

Q. Do you not think that in Ohio you have done something dangerous in having the judges appointed by the legislature and limiting their term of office to seven years?

A. Yes. I think that measure dangerous. The judges in America are there to hold the balance between all parties, and their function is particularly to oppose the impetuosity and mistakes of democracy. Springing from it, depending on it for the future, they cannot have that independence. Moreover Vermont goes even further than we as it has them elected every year.

* * *

Mr. MacLean,[1] *judge of the Supreme Court of the United States* (*2nd December 1831*)

He said to us: What I find most favourable with us to the establishment and maintenance of republican institutions is our division into States. I do not think that with our democracy we could govern the whole Union for long, if it formed but one single people. That is all the more true for the great nations of Europe. I hold too that the federal system is peculiarly favourable to the happiness of peoples. The legislature of a great nation can never enter into the details of local interests as the legislature of a small nation can. By our federal organisation we have the happiness of a small people and the strength of a great nation.

Q. Do you know how many voters there are in Ohio?

A. About 150,000. At General Jackson's election 130,000 voted. Election time is much less stormy than you would expect, because of the extreme care taken to avoid large assemblies of people. Each township has an electoral college. In six hours the election is finished for the whole State, without disturbance, without travelling and without expense.

[1] Cf. Pierson, op. cit., p. 554 f.

Q. Do you know why there are so few banks in Ohio?

A. Ten years ago there were some forty, but they all went bankrupt, and the people have certainly lost confidence in them. Besides the large quantity of paper that they issued gave a distorted value to the various consumer goods. Now scarcely any notes are accepted except those of the Bank of the United States.

Q. Is there not an urge to abolish the privilege of the Bank of the United States?

A. Yes. Party politicians exploit for their own benefit the instinctive hatred to which the thought of privilege or monopoly always gives rise. I do not trust the good faith of the enemies of the Bank. The effects of its operations are clearly beneficial especially in the West where it provides a trustworthy, portable currency. Apart from its other advantages, it scores by preventing the establishment of bad banks. It refuses to accept their notes, and so discredits them on the spot.

*   *   *

(*3rd December 1831*)
Second conversation with Mr. Walker: *important*.

Our Constitution was drafted at a time when the democratic party represented by Jefferson was triumphing throughout the Union. One cannot fail to recognise the political feelings under the power of which it was drafted. It is democratic. The government is a very great deal weaker beyond bounds than any other. The Governor counts for absolutely nothing and is only paid 1,200 dollars. The people appoint the Justices of the Peace and control [?][1] the ordinary judges. The Legislature and the Senate change every year. In general what distinguishes our legislation and that of all the new States of the West is boldness of innovation, mistrust of the past and of caution, the need to have a clean slate and to shake free from legal *technicalities* so as to get quickly to the bottom of things. There is this same freedom of mind everywhere. Nothing is fixed, nothing regulated with us, neither in lay society nor even in religious. Everything is driven by individual impulse which shows a complete absence of established opinions.

[1] Word doubtful in French manuscript.

Q. Does the people often make good choices?

A. No. It almost always makes indifferent or bad ones. Here one finds a permanent and active jealousy on democracy's part, not against the upper classes for they do not exist, but against all who rise from its ranks by their wealth, their talents and their services. We saw a striking example of this at the last election. General Harrison, a former member of Congress, a well-known general, governor of a territory and twice a minister abroad, put up as a candidate for our legislature. He failed. His chief opponent was a young man whom we had seen three years before selling cakes at street corners. Since then, it is true, he had studied to become a lawyer: he succeeded. In Massachusetts which I consider the most perfect model for a republican government, there is no ostensible canvassing for votes; the people by itself almost always chooses the most noteworthy men. In the West a candidate must go and harangue his partisans in the public places, and drink with them in the taverns.

Q. Are you not at all afraid of this excessive development of the principle of democracy?

A. Yes. I would never say it in public, but I admit it between ourselves, I am afraid of the movement that carries us along. The United States seems in a state of crisis. At the moment we are making the experiment of a democracy without limits; everything tends that way; but can we make it work? No one can yet assert that.

Q. I appreciate the distinctive features characteristic of the social and political condition of the Western States. Will they not, what is more, bring into the affairs of the Union interests which are peculiar to them and of a nature calculated to upset the present equilibrium?

A. That question needs a full answer: The West has no interests contrary to those of the rest, at least not at present, and there is no sign that it may develop them one day. The North of the United States is almost exclusively manufacturing, and the South exclusively agricultural. The West is both one and the other at the same time. Nothing indicates a future collision between its interests and those of other parts of the United States. However its growth must necessarily give a different look to the Union. There are already 5,000,000 inhabitants in the Mississippi valley. I do not doubt that in twenty years time the majority of the population of the United States will be to the West of the Ohio; the greatest wealth and the greatest power will be found in the basin of the Mississippi and Missouri. Then it will be necessary to change the position of the capital which will have come to be at the edge of the nation. The movement of power and wealth will of necessity bring new combinations which it is impossible to foresee.

Q. Have you no fear that it may be impossible to hold together this huge body?

A. Everything is going well up till now; there is even at the bottom of our hearts a strong interest attaching us to the Union. However I am not without my fears about its duration. There are several causes weakening the federal bond. First of all in all the States there is a fund of jealousy of the central government. It is easy to notice that. The excessive development of the principle of democracy in the West makes the new States even more impatient of the yoke of the Union and the restrictions it puts on their sovereignty. I cannot stop worrying about the tariff affair. South Carolina has really taken a menacing attitude; she is supported by almost all the Southern States.[1] The party leaders in that part of the Union seem determined to gain power, cost what it will, and inflame passions which, in my view, are unreasonable. The growth of the North and the weakening of the South have partly destroyed the equilibrium of the Union. A question which is full of menace still in the future is that of the uncultivated lands. You know that Congress owns all the uncultivated lands. It also possesses immense tracts of land enclosed within the new States. These States are beginning to make loud claims for the possession of these lands. Indiana and Illinois have already pressed their claims energetically. That is one point of collision between the States and the Union. There are several others as well.

Q. Is it true that the central government distributes all the places to its dependants without bothering about their ability?

A. Yes. When General Jackson came to power he dismissed 1,200 officials for no other reason than that he wanted to put

[1] It was a question of the very protective tariff of 1828, which, aggravating the provisions of that of 1824, had raised the cost of manufactured goods at the very moment when the price of cotton, the only export from the South, was falling. The Legislature of South Carolina maintained that this tariff was contrary to the pact of federation and claimed to exercise the right of 'nullification' against it.

his partisans in their place. Since then he has continued with the same folly. Places have served to pay for services to him personally. That is what I blame him for most; he has introduced corruption into the central government and his example will be followed. All the journalists who worked for him have been given places. For appointments even up to the Supreme Court he has picked among his friends.

Q. To return to Ohio; is it true that religious ideas have less power there than in the other parts of the Union?

A. There are many unbelievers in Ohio, and, especially, they flaunt themselves more openly than elsewhere. For, as I said before, there less than anywhere else are there accepted standards to which everyone must submit. Everyone is more himself. But the mass of the people is at least as much, and perhaps more, soaked in religious feeling there than in any of the other States of the Union, not excepting New England. It is, it is true, a less enlightened religion. Living in the forests, having to fight against all the ills of life, the inhabitants of the new States can not receive the same education as those in the old States. The sect of Methodists predominates in all the valley of the Mississippi and of the Ohio. But the lack of established rules and of method makes itself felt in that as in all other matters. Much of the population has neither church nor regular worship. Travelling clergy come to preach the Gospel to them. Often the first comer performs that function. One never sees in the country districts there, as in New England, pastors of recognised competence with fixed stipends.

Q. Is it true that there is a great difference between the spirit of Ohio and that of Kentucky?

A. Prodigious. However Kentucky was peopled twenty years before Ohio; the soil there is as fertile; the climate more temperate; the country lovely. But Ohio has three times as many inhabitants as Kentucky, and its enterprises are ten times as great. The population of Kentucky increases, but its prosperity is stationary. The only reason that one can give for this difference is that slavery reigns in Kentucky, but not in Ohio. There work is a disgrace, here it is honourable. There, there is idleness, here endless activity. Kentucky receives no emigrants. Ohio attracts industrious people from all parts of the Union; the South, which moreover receives none, sends its inhabitants there; the poor classes from the South come to Ohio because they can work there without disgrace. I can see no reason why slavery should cease in Kentucky. The existing population, though recognising the evils it causes, is unable to learn to do without it; there is no emigration.

Q. In Ohio you have made very severe laws against the blacks.

A. Yes. We try and discourage them in every possible way. Not only have we made laws allowing them to be expelled at will, but we hamper them in a thousand ways. A Negro has no political rights; he cannot be a juror; he cannot give evidence against a white. That last law sometimes leads to revolting injustices. The other day I was consulted by a Negro who had supplied a lot of victuals to the master of a steamboat. The white denied the debt. As the creditor was black, and as all his assistants were the same and so could not give evidence on his behalf as they could not appear in court, there was no way of even starting a case.

Q. Are the laws changed often?

A. Incessantly. That is one of the greatest disadvantages of our democracy. However, as a result, many parts of our legislation are good.

* * *

(*3rd December 1831*)

Mr. Drake,[1] the leading doctor in Cincinnati, said to us today: Our democracy is unlimited, and I admit that the people is not at all happy in its choices. I have noticed that in general outstanding men do not get its votes. However the State enjoys an immense prosperity. Its enterprises are great and favour general prosperity. I have never heard talk of the slightest resistance to the law. The people are happy and tranquil. If there was only one demagogue in the direction of our affairs no doubt they would go very badly; but they keep one another in control and harm each other. The ill effects produced by the peoples' choice are not so bad as one might have believed.

* * *

[1] Cf. Pierson, op. cit., p. 554.

Louisville.[1] Conversation with Mr. MacIlvaine,[2] one of the greatest merchants of Louisville (9th December 1831)

Q. They say that the prosperity of Louisville has made great strides in the last few years?

A. Immense. When I came to settle here seven years ago Louisville had only 3,000 inhabitants; it reckons 13,000 today. At the moment I by myself do more trade than the whole of Louisville was doing seven years ago.

Q. Why has there been such a rapid increase?

A. Principally the incredible flow of emigration which is directed towards the West. Louisville has become the entrepot for almost all the goods that go up the Mississippi to provide for the emigrants. I think that Louisville is destined to become a very large town.

Q. Is it true that there is a great difference between the prosperity of Kentucky and that of Ohio?

A. Yes, the difference is striking.

Q. What is the reason?

A. Slavery. I think that slavery is even more prejudicial to the masters than to the slaves. The slaves in Kentucky are treated very gently, well fed, well clothed. Nothing is more uncommon than to see them flee from their master's house. But slavery prevents emigrants from coming to us. It deprives us of the energy and spirit of enterprise that characterise the States that have no slaves.

Q. Is it true that slavery prevents a State from becoming industrialised?

A. Many people think that the Negroes cannot become good workers in factories. I hold the opposite view. When blacks are placed young in a factory, they are as apt as the whites to become good workmen. We have an example of that in Kentucky; several factories, worked by slaves, prosper there. If the South is not as industrialised as the North, that is not because slaves cannot work in factories, it is because slavery deprives the masters of the necessary industry to establish and manage them.

Q. Is it true that public opinion begins to be against slavery in Kentucky?

[1] See Tocqueville's notes on Kentucky and Tennessee in notebook E, p. 266.
[2] Cf. Pierson, op. cit. p. 382.

A. Yes. In the last few years there has been an incredible mental revolution. I am convinced that if one canvassed opinions man by man in Kentucky, the majority would come out for the abolition of slavery. But we do not know what to do with the slaves. Our fathers did us terrible harm by introducing them among us.

Q. But since opinion is so decidedly against slavery, why did Missouri obstinately refuse to abolish it, when it was so easy to do so?

A. At that time the mental revolution of which I was speaking just now, had by no means come about. Besides it is so convenient for new emigrants to have slaves to help them cut the trees and clear the ground in a country where it is hardly possible to find free labour, so it is understandable that the distant benefit of the abolition of slavery was not felt at its true value in Missouri. I think, too, that now they feel the mistake they made.

Q. Is the black population increasing fast in Kentucky?

A. Yes, but it can never become dangerous for the white population. The land in Kentucky is divided into small holdings; on each small holding there is a white family with a few slaves. The division of land and the type of cultivation which require few slaves, prevents us having hundreds of Negroes cultivating the land of one white man as one sees in the South. With us slavery is a great evil, but not a peril.

Q. What is cultivated in Kentucky?

A. Corn, wheat, flax, tobacco.

Q. Do you think that for those various crops, slaves would be more economical than free labour?

A. I think the opposite. Slaves work less well than free labourers, and also they are an expense the whole time. They must be brought up, and supported in their old age.

* * *

Conversation with our host at Sandy Bridge,[1] a farmer (15th December 1831)

He came a few years ago from South Carolina to settle in this place

[1] Cf. *Œuvres* (ed. Beaumont), viii, 293. Sandy Bridge is in Tennessee. Beaumont notes that it was at Sandy Bridge where Tocqueville fell ill.

Q. Then tell me why all the dwellings we come across in these woods offer such imperfect protection against bad weather. Daylight shows through the walls so much that rain and wind blow freely in. A dwelling like that must be uncomfortable and unhealthy for the owner as well as for his guest. Would it really be so difficult to keep it covered?

A. Nothing easier, but the dweller in this country is generally lazy. He regards work as an evil. Provided he has food enough and a house which gives half shelter, he is happy and thinks only of smoking and hunting.

Q. What do you think is the chief cause of this laziness?

A. Slavery. We are accustomed to doing nothing for ourselves. There is no small-holder in Tennessee so poor but he has one black or two. When he has no more than that, he often has to work with them in the fields. But suppose he has about ten, as often happens, then there is one white man to give orders and he does absolutely nothing but ride and hunt. There is not a farmer but passes some of his time hunting and owns a good gun.

Q. Do you think cultivation by slaves economical?

A. No. I think it costs more than using free labour.

* * *

New Orleans. Conversation with Mr. Mazureau,[1] one of the leading lawyers in Louisiana (1st January 1832)

Q. Before you came under American rule, did you have any of the forms of free government?

A. No.

Q. Was the change from complete subjection to complete freedom difficult?

A. No. Congress has been careful to give us independence by degrees. At first its rule was almost as absolute as that of our old Governors. Then it gave us the status of a territory. Finally it incorporated us in the Union as an independent State. We get on in that capacity as well as the other States of the Union, although the majority are still Creoles. In my view Congress could even have done without putting us through an apprenticeship. A small State, placed as we were, is always able to govern

[1] See pocket notebook number 3, p.164, pocket notebook number 4, pp. 171–173, and cf. Pierson, op. cit., p. 625. Also cf. Appendix, pp. 383–384.

itself. Hardly any of the troublesome consequences of the sovereignty of the people are to be feared in small societies.

Q. Do you think that in Louisiana the whites could cultivate the land without slaves?

A. I do not think so. But I was born in Europe and arrived here with the ideas you seem to have on that point. But experience has seemed to me to contradict the theory. I do not think that Europeans can work the land, exposed to this tropical sun. Our sun is always unhealthy, often deadly. It is not that I think it completely impossible to work. But the white, to escape death, is bound to work in such a limited way that he can only barely gain his living. We have an example in the district of Arkapas; Spain formerly sent peasants from the Azores to this part of Louisiana, and they settled there and have remained without slaves. These men work the soil, but so little that they are the poorest people in Louisana.

Q. But might not their poverty be attributed to their laziness rather than to the climate?

A. In my view the climate is the chief reason.

Q. People say that at New Orleans one finds a mixture of all the nations?

A. That is true. Here you see a mixture of all the races. There is not a country of America or of Europe that has not sent us some representatives. New Orleans is a sample of all the peoples.

Q. But amid this confusion which race dominates and sets the pace for the rest?

A. The French race up till now. It sets the tone and shapes manners.

Q. Are the ravages of yellow fever here as bad as is said?

A. I think people exaggerate the evil. My experience indicates that of ten foreigners who live sensibly and do not allow themselves excesses of any sort, only two die. I speak of people who do not have to work with their hands to live. For of the same number of working-class men who spend the day in the open air, perhaps seven or eight would succumb. Besides you know that yellow fever is confined to the town of New Orleans. Two miles above or below no one ever has it.

Q. What is the lot of the Negroes in Louisiana?

A. Fairly pleasant. Severity towards the Negroes is exceptional. The condition of the Negroes has singularly changed during the last twenty years. Time was when they lodged in wretched huts which gave them, one may say, no protection from bad weather; their clothing was a blanket, and for food they were given a barrel of corn (containing about two bushels) for the month. Now they are generally fed enough and given proper clothes and healthy quarters.

Q. Does the law protect their lives?

A. Yes. I remember while I was Attorney General having a master condemned to death for killing his slave.

* * *

Conversation with Mr. Guillemin,[1] French Consul at New Orleans (1st January 1832)

Mr. Guillemin is certainly an able man and, I think, of means. All that is exceptional. For incompetence among French agents abroad seems to be the rule. He has been living in New Orleans some fifteen to seventeen years.

This country, he said to us, is still essentially French in thoughts, manners, opinions, customs and fashions. We ostensibly model ourselves on France. I have often been struck by the echoes our political passions have had here, and the analogy still existing in that matter between the population of Louisiana and the population of France. I have often been able to predict, from the impression an event made here, what would be the reaction in France, and I have always guessed right. The inhabitants of Louisiana are more concerned with French affairs than with their own.

Q. That temper must be favourable to the trade relations between us and the United States.

A. Yes, very. I consider it a matter of great interest for France that French manners should be preserved in Louisiana. In that way one of the great American doors is open to us. It would have been very difficult for us to have kept Louisiana as a colony, but we ought at least to have been able to keep it long enough and take enough trouble about it to establish a French population there, which could afterwards look after itself. We are now in a very weak position to hold our own against

[1] Cf. Pierson, op. cit., index, p. 841.

the pressure of the American peoples. Almost all the land in Louisiana is still in French hands, but big business is in American hands. There is, one must admit, a great difference between the dispositions of the two peoples towards business. The French of Louisiana are not enterprising in business; they do not at all like to risk what they have got on a chance, and they fear the disgrace of bankruptcy. The Americans who descend on us every year from the North, are eaten up with longing for wealth; they have long given up everything else for that; they come with little to lose and very few of the honourable scruples the French feel about paying their debts. It is interesting here to study the striking differences between the two races, and see the good and bad in each.

Q. Does not the struggle which seems to exist between the Americans and the French in Louisiana result in bitterness between the two nations?

A. Each criticises the other; they do not see each other much; but at bottom there is no real hostility. The French here are not at all a conquered people as in Canada; on the contrary they live on a basis of real and complete equality; there are frequent marriages between them and the Americans; finally the country enjoys immense prosperity. A prosperity that increases daily. New Orleans has a very great future. If we succeed in conquering, or only in greatly diminishing, the scourge of yellow fever, New Orleans is certainly destined to become the largest city in the New World. In fifty years the Mississippi valley will hold the mass of the American population, and here we hold the gate to the river.

Q. Do you think that part of this prosperity is due to the free institutions given to Louisiana?

A. One must have seen close up as I have for fifteen years the way business is conducted in a little, completely democratic republic, to be convinced that prosperity is not due to political institutions, but is independent of them. You have no idea of such a Bedlam. The people appoint intriguers without talent to office, while outstanding men seldom achieve it. The legislature ceaselessly makes, alters and repeals the laws. It is Penelope's loom; the most important measures are sidetracked in some sort of underhand way. The government is a prey to factions. You see what a state of neglect and dirt the town is in; it has a revenue of a million francs. But much squandering of public money prevails. People say that by widening the franchise one increases the independence of the vote. I think the opposite. In all countries the working classes are at the disposition of those who employ them; and in those where they decide elections, it is the intrigues of a few industrialists that fix the supposed free choice of the people. However, as I was saying to you, the prosperity of Louisiana is very great and is perpetually increasing. This government here has the merit of being very weak, and of not hampering any freedom. But here and now there is nothing to fear from freedom. That does not apply only to Louisiana but to the whole of the United States. I have never been able to make out how one could draw general conclusions from American institutions; the situation of America is so special.

Q. They say that religion has little sway here over men's souls?

A. It does not have much, but I think that that is partly due to the bad priests they have sent us from Europe. We are flooded out with Italians who have nothing in common with the local people, and whose morals are detestable. However there is no political animosity of any sort against the ministers of the Catholic religion, who, for their part, never meddle in affairs. Recently they broke the windows of a parish priest who refused to bury a suicide in holy ground, but I am sure the people acted very largely in imitation of the scenes at Saint-Germain-l'Auxerrois.[1] From what I see here and in the other States of America, I am profoundly convinced that, in the interests of religion, one ought to make an absolute division between the clergy and the State, and leave religion to exercise the influence proper to it.

Q. How are the priests paid in Louisiana?

A. The State does not come into it at all. But the localities generally have landed property devoted to this pur ose, besides there are usual receipts, voluntary gifts, pews. . . .[2]

Q. It is said that morality, particularly among the coloured population, is very bad?

A. Great immorality does indeed prevail among the coloured population. But how could you expect it to be otherwise? The

---

[1] At Paris on the 14th February 1831 the legitimists wanted to celebrate a memorial service for the Duke of Berry in the church of Saint-Germain-l'Auxerrois. The mob broke into the church and sacked it as well as the presbytery and the Archbishop's palace. [2] The dots are Tocqueville's.

law in some sort destines women of colour to wantonness. You
have no doubt noticed at theatres and elsewhere in the places
reserved for half-castes, women as white as the most beautiful
European women. Well! Nonetheless they belong to the proscribed race, because tradition makes it known that there is
African blood in their veins. These women, and many others, too,
who are not as white as they, have nonetheless by now almost
the colour and graces of Europe, and have often received an
excellent education. And yet the law forbids them to marry into
the reigning and wealthy race of whites. If they want to contract
a legitimate union, they must marry men of their caste and share
their humiliations, for men of colour do not even enjoy the
shameful privileges that are accorded to their women. Even
though neither their colour nor their education comes to betray
them, and that is often the case, nevertheless they are condemned
to continual indignities. There is not a white beggar but has
the right to bully the wretch he finds in his way and throw him
in the dirt, crying out: 'Get off, mulatto!' At the head of any
document he executes, the law obliges him to write: 'man of
colour, free'. He cannot hope for anything. But I know some
of them who are excellent and prosperous men. It is by obstinately isolating itself from all the rest that the white aristocracy
(as is true in general of all aristocracies) exposes itself to dangers on the American continent and to almost certain destruction in the Antilles. If, without giving rights to the negroes, the
white race had at least admitted into its circle those coloured
people whose birth and education make them closest to it, it
would infallibly have attached them to its cause, for they really
are very much nearer to the whites than to the blacks; and that
would have left nothing but brute force on the side of the
Negroes. By rebuffing them, on the other hand, they have given
the slaves the one kind of power they lacked in order to become
free, that of intelligence and leaders.

* * *

*With a very well-known New Orleans lawyer whose name I have
forgotten (1st January 1832)*

He said: When the legislature is in session so-to-say all legislation is in question. Our Houses are largely made up of young,

ignorant and very scheming lawyers. (Everyone here thinks he can be a legislator.) They make, unmake, lop and cut at random. Here is an example: after the cession to Spain many points in our law were taken from Spanish laws. Late in 1828, at the end of a session, a bill was passed unnoticed repealing these laws in a body without putting anything else in their place. Waking up the next day the bar and the judges discovered with horror what had been done the day before. But the thing was done.

Q. But why do men of note not get into the legislature?

A. I doubt the people choosing them. Besides little importance is attached to public offices, and outstanding men do not canvass for them. (*This is what makes the State function so badly and at the same time saves it from revolutions.*)

Another example of the same sort given by the Consul: three years ago, on the last day of the session, the Legislature, in unnoticed fashion, passed, in an act having no reference to this matter, a law ordaining that from thenceforth the tenth part of the property of foreigners dying in Louisiana should go to the State. This was nothing less than the *droit d'aubaine*.[1] 'I made representations,' said the Consul, 'many members seemed to me surprised themselves at what they had done. This act was repealed in the next session.'

Points on the positive side: the present Governor of Louisiana is a man of talent and character. The two Senators for Louisiana, Mr. Johnson and Ed. Livingston, are two of the leading men in the Union. Yet they were elected.

* * *

Conversation with a lawyer from Montgomery (Alabama) (6th January 1832)

I travelled for two days with this young man. I have forgotten his name which anyhow is very obscure. But I think I ought to note the conversation down. It is stamped with much practical

---

[1] Ancient French law which made the stranger on a baron's land almost into a slave. (The word *aubin* is derived either from *alibi natus* or *Albion*, because the inhabitants of the British Isles were regarded as foreign travellers. The *droit d'aubaine* was abolished by the French Constituent Assembly on August 6th, 1790. Cf. A. Chéruel *Dictionnaire historique des Institutions, Moeurs et Coutumes de La France*, Paris, 1874, vol. I, p. 52 f.

good sense. Besides what he says is corroborated by several pieces of subsequent information:

The erroneous opinion is spreading daily more and more among us, he said, that the people can do everything and is capable of ruling almost directly. From that springs an unbelievable weakening of anything that could look like executive power; it is the outstanding characteristic and the capital defect of our Constitution, and of those of all the new States in the South-West of the Union. That has grave consequences. Thus, we did not wish to give the Governor the right of appointing the judges; that was entrusted to the Legislature. What results? That responsibility for the choice is divided; that little coteries and little, local intrigues are all-powerful, and that instead of calling competent men to our tribunals, we put there little party leaders who control the elections in the districts and whom the members of the Legislature wish to attract or reward. Our magistrates are completely incompetent; the mass of the people feels it as we do. So no one is disposed to appeal to regular justice. This state of affairs which is common to the States of Kentucky, Tennessee, Mississippi and even Georgia, is, to my way of thinking, the chief factor causing these fierce manners for which the inhabitants of those States are justly blamed.

Is it then true that the ways of the people of Alabama are as violent as is said?

Yes. There is no one here but carries arms under his clothes. At the slightest quarrel, knife or pistol comes to hand. These things happen continually; it is a semi-barbarous state of society.

Q. But when a man is killed like that, is his assassin not punished?

A. He is always brought to trial, and always acquitted by the jury, unless there are greatly aggravating circumstances. I can not remember seeing a single man who was a little known, pay with his life for such a crime. This violence has become accepted. Each juror feels that he might, on leaving the court, find himself in the same position as the accused, and he acquits. Note that the jury is chosen from all the free-holders, however small their property may be. So it is the people that judges itself, and its prejudices in this matter stand in the way of its good sense. Besides, my informant added, I have been no better myself than another in my time; look at the scars that cover my head (we did see the marks of four or five deep cuts). Those are knife blows I have been given.

Q. But you went to law?

A. My God! No. I tried to give as good in return.

Q. Do the people choose good representatives?

A. No, in general they choose people on their own level who flatter them. I have no doubt of the advantage that would come from restricting the franchise. The choices would certainly be better. But it is in the nature of things in a democratic State that the franchise should be extended by an irresistible movement until everyone is a voter, as happens with us. I predict that in France, too, you will not be able to stop yourselves indefinitely.

Q. But from these bad choices there must result bad laws and bad government?

A. Not nearly so much as one might expect at first glance. There are always some men of talent in our assemblies; from the first days these overwhelm the others and absolutely dominate business. It is really they who make and discuss the laws. The rest vote as they do. We have had representatives who could not read or write.

Q. Do you yourself see a great difference between the social state of the North and that of the South?

A. Immense. We Southerners have perhaps more natural advantages than those of the North, but we are much less energetic and, especially, less persevering. Our education is much neglected. We have no regular school system; a third of our population cannot read. One sees none of the same care given to the needs of society, or the same thought for the future.

Q. What power has religious feeling among you?

A. There is infinitely less morality with us than in the North. But religious feeling properly so called is perhaps more enthusiastic with us. There is religion in the North, here fanaticism. The Methodist sect predominates.

Q. What is the majority opinion in Alabama about the tariff?

A. The majority is strongly opposed to the tariff. But very attached to the Union. The nullificators of South Carolina find no support among us.

Q. What do you think of the use of the jury?

A. I think the jury useful in criminal cases. I think it is useful in civil cases when it is a question of facts clearly distinguished from law or appreciations of morality. I think for instance that all questions of damages or defamation ought to be tried by jury. But when it comes to civil matters properly so called, to questions of law, and to the examination of legal documents, I think the jury is detestable, and would much prefer the judges alone. One of the disadvantages of our juries is that they are drawn from too small areas (the counties). The jurors know about the matter before it is argued. It is judged before it is heard and judged in a tavern.

When we got to Montgomery, we heard that a man had just been killed by a pistol shot in the street.

*   *   *

Conversations with Mr. Poinsett,[1] (*from the 12th to the 17th January 1832*)

The United States has an immense future in seaborn trade.[2] We are certainly destined to become the leading maritime power in the world. The first reason for that is the crops our land grows. We have here a quantity of raw materials that all the world needs. We are the most natural carriers. Besides our national genius calls, us, like the English, to be the ship-brokers of foreign nations. See what is happening already; it is almost only Americans who carry the produce of America to Europe, and European goods come to America in American ships. Our ships fill the ports of Havre and Liverpool, but we hardly see an English or French ship in ours.

Q. One hears that American shippers have the lowest running costs. How does that happen?

A. From mental qualities and not from physical advantages. The cost of labour being very high in America, the ships cost more to build, and the seamen's wages are higher than in Europe. But the American sailor has an energy, thriftiness and an understanding of his own interests which belong to him alone. There is never an English or a French ship that crosses the

[1] Poinsett (1779–1851) had been on a diplomatic mission in South America, and had been Minister in Mexico from 1825 to '29. For his meetings with Tocqueville see also pocket notebook number 5, pp. 177–180.

[2] See notebook E, p. 237.

ocean in as short a time as ours, none that stays so short a time
in port. Thus we make up and more than make up for our disadvantages. Moreover the American, on sea as on land, has a
quality which makes him singularly adapted to succeed and
make his fortune. He is a highly civilised man thrown into a
society in formation, where trades have not had time to become
absolutely classified. As a result each man of us knows a little
of everything, and is accustomed from childhood to do a little
of everything. Our workmen make shoes, and their wives cloth
and carpets. There is a phrase which is always in our mouths in
face of any difficulty, and it gives our character perfectly: 'I
will try.'

Q. One hears that generally your ships do not last long?

A. One must distinguish between boats made to sell, and
those intended for our own use. There is a shipyard in the
North. The ships that come out of it do indeed have a short life.
But when we want to make a ship to use ourselves for as long
as possible, we find that our building timber, Florida evergreen
oak in particular, is the best in the world. One reason why our
ships do not last long is that our merchants often have little
capital at their disposal to begin with. It is a matter of calculation on their part. Provided that the ship lasts long enough to
bring them in a certain sum beyond their expenses, their aim is
attained. Besides there is a general feeling among us about
everything which prevents us aiming at permanence; there
reigns in America a popular and universal belief in the progress
of the human spirit. We are always expecting an improvement
to be found in everything. And in fact that is often correct. For
instance I asked our steamboat builders on the North Bank a
few years ago why they made their vessels so weak. They
answered that perhaps they might even last too long, because
the art of steam navigation was making daily progress. In fact
these boats which made 8 or 9 knots, could not, a little time
afterwards, compete with others whose construction allowed
them to make 12 to 15 knots.

Q. Do you not think that when the mass of the American
population will be established in the Mississippi valley, your sea
trade will suffer, capital being chiefly directed towards industry
and agriculture?

A. I believe exactly the opposite. It is just as important for the population of the Mississippi that the Union should have great sea power, as it is for the States on the Atlantic, since the greatest outlet for their crops is overseas. If we could not stop our ports from being blockaded, what would happen to our cotton, corn, sugar . . . .[1] which grow on the banks of the Mississippi, the Missouri and the Ohio, and which are carried every year to South America and to Europe? That is how I vigorously answered Mr. Clay in Congress, when he was speaking of the concessions made by the States of the West for the trade of the Atlantic States; I proved to him that what was called a concession was in the interests of the West itself.

Q. Do you not think that in the absence of coercive laws, such as the 'press gang' or *inscription maritime*, it will be difficult for the Union to find enough sailors in time of war?

A. No. First high wages will always bring us a crowd of foreign sailors, and besides, in time of war, trade will suffer and a multitude of unemployed sailors will ask for nothing better than to man the State's ships.

Q. What are the principles of the Union concerning trade and the law of the sea?

A. The most complete reciprocity in trade. We have observed that the particular advantages that we have obtained abroad, were by no means equivalent to the harm that resulted from the privileges that we had to grant in return. So not only do we never ask to be treated on a special footing in foreign ports, but we positively refuse privileges. That is what happened to me when I had the duty of negotiating a commercial treaty with the peoples of Southern America. As to our law of the sea, we claim that the flag covers the goods. I think that we are wrong there; in the first place I do not know if that privilege really exists in international law; but what is certain is that the opposite principle is very useful for peoples who dominate the sea. Now in a short space of time we are destined to find ourselves in that position. Then we shall have to disavow our principles, something which is always bad for a nation, as it is for a man. The principle that the flag covers the goods is only good for nations that can never hope to dominate the seas. France is in that position. France will always be a great sea-power. Never the first. It would not even be in her interest to aim at that.

[1] The dots are Tocqueville's.

Q. What do you think of tariffs in general and of that of the United States in particular?

A. I am no partisan for tariffs. I think that they tend to hold trade back rather than help it. As for the United States' tariff, I think that it has done neither great harm nor great good. Men with disappointed ambitions have made a pretext out of it. But I do not think it has had either the good or the bad effect attributed to it. Its supporters say that the immense progress our industry has made in the last fifteen years is due to it. I do not believe it. What did give the impulse to our industries was the war of 1812.[1] Prohibitions in time of peace are never adequate. Only war can really close access to a country. It is war that has forced us to become industrial; the impulse would have been maintained afterwards without the tariff. Even with the duty the quantity of English goods imported increases every year. But we have in our land, with or without a tariff, natural advantages that cannot be taken from us. The opponents of the tariff say that it ruins the South: I do not believe it. The only effect which it produces on the South does not seem to me to have been noticed yet. This is it: in refusing entry to English manufactured goods in our ports, we diminish the wealth of the English manufacturer. So as not to make a loss in his industry, he must do one of these two things: either diminish the cost of labour, or diminish the cost of the raw material. Now in England and even in the whole of Europe, it is *impossible* to reduce a workman's wages without sending him to the workhouse. He only earns just enough to live on. So the reduction must be born by the raw materials. The result of the tariff has then been to lower the price of our cotton. (*Note*: this seems to me to be in contradiction with the rest and to prove that the tariff is useful to the North.) I consider the usefulness of tariffs from one single point of view; if moderate, they are a form of tax that falls more fairly than many others.

Q. In America are morals really as good as is said?

A. There is laxity in the lower classes of society, but otherwise morals are excellent everywhere. I have never seen any-

[1] The controls which the English, at the time of the Napoleonic blockade of Europe, claimed to exercise over United States ships, had led the two powers into war (June 1812). Peace, on the basis of the *status quo*, was not signed until December 1814.

thing that one can compare to this state of affairs in any of my travels. There is nothing like it in England. The people and the upper classes in England are very disorderly in their morals; morality is only found in the middle classes. There is such a prodigious respect for the marriage tie among us, that the lover of a married woman disgraces himself even more surely than she who yields to him. The road to honours is shut to him; even that to wealth becomes difficult for him; he has to count himself very lucky if he dies otherwise than by assassination. The woman's relations often feel bound to revenge the honour of the family on the man.

Q. But to what, according to you, is this extreme chastity of morals due? I tell you frankly that I cannot look on you as a *virtuous* people.

A. Neither do I think that we are more virtuous than many other peoples. The chastity of our morals is due more to particular circumstances and especially to the complete absence of a class of men with the time and means to attack women's virtue. Besides I think that the race of women is very remarkable in America. I find them much superior to our men.

Q. Do you think this state of morals reacts on the political state of society?

A. Certainly, very much. It gives us habits of order and morality which serve powerfully to bridle our political passions.

Q. What do you think of the influence of religion on politics?

A. I think that the state of religion in America is one of the things that most powerfully helps us to maintain our republican institutions. The religious spirit exercises a direct power over political passions, and also an indirect power by sustaining morals. It is because many enlightened Americans are convinced of this truth that not only do they not show the doubts they may have about the reality of Christianity, but even hesitate to join new sects such as the Unitarians. They are afraid that they may lead indirectly to the destruction of the Christian religion, which would be an irreparable ill for humanity.

Q. What do they mean in the South by the procedure of nullification? It seems to me that that procedure amounts purely and simply to annulment of the Union.

A. No doubt it would come to that indirectly; but the *nullificators* deny that. They only claim that the separate States have the right to *suspend* the laws of Congress and to call for the convocation of a Convention.

Q. Does that doctrine make you afraid for the future of the Union?

A. No. The *nullificators* only form a party in South Carolina; even there their majority is doubtful. And even if they had the whole State with them, what can the 700,000 whites who live there do against the forces of the Union? This party, like so many others, owes its existence to the personal ambitions of a few citizens, particularly Mr. Calhoun[1] and Mr. Duke. The doctrine of nullification has in the past been preached without conviction; now it has believers. (Mr. Poinsett comes from South Carolina and is a member of the Legislature.)

Q. Is the difference as real as they say between the social state of the South and that of the North?

A. Yes. The difference is evident and all in favour of the North.

Q. What are the reasons for it?

A. The first is slavery; the second the climate. The South however is progressing, though it seems to go back because the North and West go so fast. Every ten years the South loses some proportion of its representation; the West and North on the other hand keep increasing their votes. Power is quickly shifting from these old centres. Soon the thirteen original States will not have the majority in Congress.

Q. It is impossible that this state of affairs should not create a state of *jealousy* and *suspicion* in the South. The weak do not generally believe in the fairness of the strong.

A. That is true.

Q. Has the South got ships to carry its produce?

A. It has none. It is the North that goes to fetch the produce of the South and carry it all over the world.

Q. How did this strange state of affairs arise?

A. Partly because in the South there is still no lower class. One would not know where to find a population of sailors.

Q. But why not employ the Negroes?

A. That would be taking a chance of losing them; they would desert. Besides there is no industry in the South.

---

[1] Calhoun (1782–1850) had already been Secretary of State and Vice-President of the Union, when in 1828 he rose violently against the new customs duty which he described as the 'tariff of abominations'.

Q. Do you see any means of getting rid of the slaves?

A. No. The plan which consists in buying them up at the expense of the State and transporting them elsewhere, seems to me extravagant. The wealth of the whole Union would not be enough. In proportion as the number of slaves diminished, their price would become exorbitant. Besides the need felt for them would lead to their being introduced again by the slave trade. I do not share the fears born of the increasing numbers of the blacks as far as the safety of the white race is concerned. A slave revolt would never succeed. If they ever became enlightened enough to combine their forces and form a formidable league, they would be wise enough to see that, placed as they are, they could never hope for final success.

Q. Do the half-castes make common cause with the blacks?

A. No. They treat them with disdain, and the latter hate them. They think they are much closer to the whites than to the blacks. The most dangerous men are the emancipated blacks. Their presence makes the slaves restless and long for freedom. I think it is indispensable to take away from the masters the right to free their slaves, and especially the right to free them by will. Washington gave a very bad example by freeing his slaves at his death. It is an extraordinary thing how far public opinion is becoming enlightened about slavery. The idea that it is a great evil and that one could do without it is gaining ground more and more. I hope that the natural course of things will rid us of the slaves. I know people still who have seen slavery in New England. In our time we have seen it abolished in the State of New York, then in Pennsylvania; it only holds on to a precarious existence in Maryland; there is already talk against it in the Legislature of Virginia. The black race is continually retreating towards the South, pushed by the emigration of men of the white race.

Q. Do you think that slaves are smuggled into the territory of the Union?

A. Hardly at all. But the slave trade nonetheless exists on an immense scale. Last year the English House of Commons made an inquiry into the matter, and I read myself in its report that the number of blacks carried off each year from Africa amounts to 300,000.

Q. What do you think of the Indians of the United States?

A. I think that it is a race which will perish without the wish to become civilised. One could only succeed in that with the help of the *half-castes*. Besides I think that the civilised man has the right to take the land of savages from which the latter do not know how to profit, and where the white man flourishes and increases rapidly.

Q. Do you think that the banking system in force in the United States has helped the prosperity of the country?

A. Yes. In a country where there is as little capital as there is here, banks are of immense usefulness, but I do not know if the same argument would apply to France or England. Of all the banks of the States, I think that of New Orleans was established on the best plan.

Q. Is it true that in the United States public opinion does not shun bankrupts with the rigour with which they are treated in Europe?

A. Yes. So long as there is not clear fraud on the merchant's part, opinion does not blame him. He can launch out on the most hazardous undertakings, begin without capital, risk borrowed money in all manner of ways, without materially damaging his reputation; he begins again the next day. Almost all our merchants play double or quits, and that is thought quite straightforward. One must admit that our commercial morality is very different from that of Europeans.

Q. How are the roads in America made and repaired?

A. It is a great constitutional question to know whether Congress has the right to make roads other than military ones. I am myself convinced that this right exists, but, being contested, it is so-to-say never used. It is often the States which undertake to open and keep up the roads that pass through them. But more often the roads are paid for by the counties. In general our roads are very badly kept up: we have no central authority that can force the counties to do their duty. Supervision being local, it is partial and without energy. Private individuals, it is true, have the right to sue a local authority which does not repair its roads properly; but no one wants to bring a case against a local authority. The only tolerable roads are the turnpikes. I think the system of turnpike roads is very good. But it needs time to become a national habit. It must be made to compete with the system of free roads. If the turnpike road is much better or shorter than the other, travellers will soon see that it is an economy for them to go that way.

Q. Does the election of the President rouse real political passions?

A. No. Those concerned get very excited. There is a great fuss in the papers. But the mass of the people stays indifferent. The President in fact has so little influence on their happiness! It is in very truth Congress that rules.

Q. Can you give me any information about Mexico?

A. All that I have seen of that beautiful country leads me to suppose that, before the Spaniards arrived, the inhabitants had reached a state of civilisation *at least* as high as theirs. But first superiority in the art of war and then oppression have destroyed everything.

Q. How is the Mexican population now composed?

A. Spaniards for whom a white skin is a sort of nobility, and poor and ignorant Indians who till the soil. They are free and in law equal with the Spaniards, but in fact they count for nothing in the political balance. There are hardly any Negroes or mulattoes.

Q. What do you think about the future of that country?

A. I hope that it will come to settle down on a solid basis. It is certain that it is progressing. One must not judge the Spaniards of the New World too severely. When the Revolution caught them, they were still living in the sixteenth century, but without the primitive virtues which the freedom of that time often gave to men then. I have often found that idea useful in my dealings. I have often asked myself what sixteenth-century men would have done in such circumstances and what they would have thought. Answering those questions enabled me with near certainty to foretell the future. You could not imagine a more complete unawareness of all the discoveries of modern civilisation. They began, as in South America, by wishing to establish a great undivided Republic. They did not succeed, and, for my part, I do not believe that a great republic can endure, at least unless it is a federation. The Mexicans have ended by adopting, bar some unimportant exceptions, the United States Constitution. But they are not yet advanced enough to use it as we do. It is a complicated and difficult instrument.

Q. Do you not think that the nations of Europe made a

clumsy mistake in thinking that the independence of the Spanish colonies would offer immense openings for them?

A. Yes, certainly. The wants which civilisation causes have not yet come to be felt in Spanish America. The time has not arrived yet, but it will come.

Q. What is the position of the clergy in Mexico?

A. It is daily losing its influence. Already it has hardly any support from the people. You see that this state of affairs bears no resemblance at all to that of Spain. But the Mexican clergy still has its property. That is immense wealth which no one has yet dared to touch. It was the clergy who, in Mexico, began the Revolution. They were afraid that the Spanish Cortes would confiscate their property, and they roused the people. They only wanted to make a half-revolution, but, the movement started, it was impossible to hold back.

I ended the conversation by asking Mr. Poinsett about moral standards in Spanish America. He answered laughing: That is not the pretty side of the picture. I have passed part of my life in Spanish America and can say that from Cape Horn to the 35th parallel of latitude North, I have not known a woman who was faithful to her husband. The ideas of right and wrong are so upside down on this point that a woman takes it as a disgrace not to have a lover.

*   *   *

(*24th January 1832*)

Mr. Everett (Edward),[1] told me today that of Members of Congress nine-tenths belonged to the lawyer class. The land-owners are in very small numbers there.

*   *   *

(*24th January 1832*)

Mr. Serurier[2] who was French Minister in the United States twenty years ago, told me that he found that a very great change had taken place when he came back. Men were of lesser stature; one saw no more great political abilities.

*   *   *

[1] Cf. Pierson, op. cit., in the index.   [2] Cf. Pierson, ibid., in the index.

(*24th January 1832*)

Mr. Trist,[1] a government official, a Virginian and a very talented man, said to me today: that Virginia was but a shadow of herself; that her great men and even her notable men had disappeared, and that one saw no more such rise in their places.

* * *

(*27th January 1832*)

Mr. Trist, a senior official in the State Department, said to us today: Everything is published in this country, but perhaps nowhere else is it so difficult to collect documents bearing on past events. Since nothing is stable, neither men nor things in our government offices, the evidence vanishes at an incredible rate. Nothing, for instance, is harder than to get a record of the proceedings of Congress. Recently Virginia wanted to print the proceedings of her Legislature since the Revolution. Never could a complete copy of the debates be found. The scheme had to be given up.

* * *

(*28th January 1832*)

I asked Mr. Adams[2] today why one accepted that difference between the social condition of the new States of the West and that of those of New England. He answered me: That is due almost entirely to the point of departure. New England has been peopled by a very enlightened and profoundly religious race of men. The West has been peopled by all the adventurers to be found in the Union. People for the most part without principles or morality, whom poverty or bad behaviour has driven from the old States, or who are only bent on enriching themselves.

[1] Cf. Pierson, ibid., in the index. [2] Cf. Pierson, ibid., index.

III

Pocket Notebook Number 1

The number of passengers arriving from Europe in New York from 1st January to 9th June 1831 is 4,000.

Courier and Enquirer, 10th June

Colony which the 'coloured men' founded at Wilberforce in upper Canada. It might be interesting to visit.

id.

The Annals of America from the discovery by Columbus in the year 1482 to the year 1826, by Abial Holmes, D.D., in 2 vol.

The author lives at New Haven or Cambridge.

Steamship.

Summer night.[1]

How to set about bringing in the children of the counties? Will not irreparable harm to their morality result?

What are the terms of the contract of hiring? See in the district.

The Northern Traveller with plates, 1 vol. A dictionary of all religions and religious denominations, Jewish, heathen, Mohammedan and Christian with an appendix containing a sketch of the present state of the world as a population. Religion . . .[2] by Hannan Adams, Boston, 1817.

Book recommended by M. Balestier.

The Swedish Stockbridge at 40 miles from Albany on the Boston road.

Law of inheritance.

Democracy.

Spirit of change.

[1] There are two addresses here in a handwriting other than Tocqueville's. The first cannot be read. The second is: Dr. Wainwright in rear of Grace Church.

[2] The dots are Tocqueville's; in English in manuscript.

[Here there is the plan of a house in the manuscript with the following details.]

Eleven windows in the two wings in the interior of the square.

From the kitchen to the wall at the bottom of the garden, sixty paces.

From the entrance gate to the first wall of the buildings, thirty-six paces.

From there to the external wall opposite, ninety paces.

From that wall to the first wall of the women's wing, twenty-two.

Length of the wings in the square, forty-six paces.

Length of   ,[1] fifty-two.

Act of the 20th Congress about Penitentiaries in the District of Columbia. Act of 2nd March 1831.

1620. The Jesuits planted the standard of the cross on the site of Detroit, the year in which the Puritans landed at New Plymouth.[2]

The customary law of Paris was in force there right up to 1810.

From *Detroit Courier*

They are not like the French Saint-Simonians, a strange assembly where the burlesque mixes with the serious. It is a philosophic sect whose manners are simple and strict, and who do not lay themselves open in the very least to laughter.

Thus the same cause, indifference, drives men in two opposite directions. Those whose spirit is ardent, imagination tender or lively, the unfortunates who have much to expect from the other life, stay [?] in the bosom of the most positive, the most imperious and the most powerful of all the religions. Cool and logical spirits, meditative and tranquil characters, men whose ways are intellectual or learned join, on the other hand, a purely philosophical sect which allows them to make an almost public profession of pure deism.

So the two great principles stand confronted in their simplest and most complete form. The argument is between authority and liberty in their ultimate extremes.

As to pecuniary loss (if any think of this) much less labour I should have bestowed on official business, well directed, will

[1] One word not read.   [2] In English in the manuscript.

easily procure something more than a bare subsistence, which all know is scarcely afforded by the salaries at Washington: I can have no cause of resentment therefore on that account.[1]

The Indians in the neighbourhood of Saint Louis have just crossed into American territory, putting everything to fire and sword. The new-settlers are retreating and forces concentrating at Saint Louis.

Journal of 4th July 1831

One might say that the European is to the other races of man what man in general is to the rest of animate nature. When he cannot bend them to his use or make them indirectly serve his well-being, he destroys them and makes them vanish little by little in front of him. The Indian races are melting in the presence of European civilisation like snow in the rays of the sun. The efforts they make to struggle against their destiny only hasten for them the destructive march of time. About every ten years (a) the Indian tribes who have been pushed back into the wilds of the West, see that they have gained nothing by retreating, and that the white race advances even faster than they go back. Angered by the very sense of their own impotence, or enraged by some new injury, they assemble and descend impetuously over the lands they once inhabited, where now the dwellings of Europeans are rising up, the rustic huts of the pioneers and, further on, the first villages. They rush through the country, burning dwellings, killing flocks and carrying off some scalps. Then civilisation goes back, but goes back like the tide of a rising sea. The United States take up the cause of the least of their colonists and declare (b) war on these wretched tribes. Then a regular army marches to meet them, and not only is American territory reconquered, but the white men, driving the savages before them, destroying their villages and carrying off their flocks, go and establish the further limit of their possessions a hundred leagues beyond what it was before. Deprived of their new adopted fatherland by what wise and enlightened Europe is pleased to call the *right* of war, the Indians start again on their

[1]From 'As to . . . account' in English in Tocqueville's manuscript.

(a) Note by Tocqueville: To be put aside.

(b) Variant: The American Federation declares that these wretched tribes have violated the law of nations.

march to the West until they come to a halt in new wilds where the white man's axe will not be slow to make itself heard again. In the land which they have recently plundered and which is now safe from invasion, there rise up smiling villages which soon (so at least the inhabitants are convinced) will be populous cities. Marching before the immense European family of whom he forms as it were the advance guard, the pioneer in his turn takes possession of the forests recently inhabited by the savages. There he builds his rustic hut and waits till the first chance of war opens his way to new wilds.

*   *   *

At Utica (6th July 1831)

Sunday school: 200 convicts 2 o'clock on Sunday.

30 teachers from the seminary.

Only to read. Rapid progress.

One must enquire from the controller at Albany to find out what the prisons cost under the old system. It is thought that that of New York cost 50,000 dollars a year.

Comb shop.

The contractor's representative is present.

He told me that the average of the pay for each prisoner is 25 cents. A good worker at liberty would be paid 1 dollar. Here there are some who are paid 4 shillings, but generally they are taken on without knowing the trade. Besides they never work as well as when at liberty.

He then contradicted himself: I think that they work as well as they can. Work is a consolation for them.

Stone-cutting shop.

No representative of the contractor. I think I understood that the work of these prisoners is used for State buildings. The keeper told me that his men worked well, perhaps better than when at liberty. A good workman at liberty earns 12 shillings.

Tool shop.

30 prisoners, one representative of the contractor.

Q. How much a day do you pay for the work of one prisoner?

A. An average of 30 cents.

Q. And how much would you pay the same man in freedom?

A. At least 20 dollars a month.

Q. What is the reason for the difference?

A. 1st. The contractor got very favourable terms because, at the time he made the deal, the State needed him. I think that without doing his business badly, he could have given 50 cents. 2nd. The contractor is obliged to keep the prisoners at work, even when the products of their labour cannot be sold. He cannot dismiss his workmen in proportion to the work. He must make up for that disadvantage by the price per day.

Q. Besides the prisoner works less than the man at liberty?

A. That is true for some days, but not for a year. I am convinced that in the course of a year one gets more work from a prisoner than from a free worker.

The Keeper seemed a man above the average.

Q. How do you get this sustained work from the prisoners?

A. From the fear they feel for the whip. I regard the punishment of the whip (the only one used at Auburn) as the only means of maintaining the discipline of the prison, and as the most humane punishment.

Shoe-maker shop. 62 convicts.

By the Keeper alone.

Q. How much are these men paid per day?

A. They are not paid by the day but by the piece. A pair of boots of first quality is paid 16 shillings, second quality 12 shillings, and a pair of shoes 5 shillings.

Q. What is the price of the same things at Auburn?

A. A pair of first quality boots 20 shillings, second 16 shillings, and a pair of shoes 1 dollar.

Q. Does the contractor live in Auburn?

A. Yes.

Q. Does he come here often?

A. Seldom more than once a week.

Q. Why is that?

A. He has less reason than another to come because he pays by the piece. Besides he refers to me.

Q. You then are a *professional man* ?[1]

A. Yes.

Q. How in a country where the professions are so well paid, does one find good workers who consent to become keepers?

A. There is great difficulty in finding them. It was my health that made me decide to come here.

Q. Do you think that there is an advantage in the keepers' being professional men?

A. Yes. A great one. When the keeper is not a professional man it is impossible for him to supervise the prisoners' work properly. One has to allow a contractor into the workshop, which has disadvantages for discipline. Formerly they were forbidden to go into the workshops. But it is difficult to find contractors on such conditions. The contract with the Shoemaker is in writing; it is the oldest one in the place. The contract was made by the piece to make the contractor's presence pointless.

Q. Do you often punish your men?

A. Very seldom. I have never seen, for the thirteen years I have been in the place, better discipline or fewer punishments.

Cooper Shop. 43 prisoners.
No representative of the contractor, but he often is there.
Keeper intelligent.

Q. What is the average for each man's work?

A. 25 cents.

Q. What would one pay a similar man at liberty?

A. About 83 cents.

Q. What is the reason for the difference?

A. 1st. The contractor is bound to pay the ignorant and clumsy prisoner the same as the capable one. 2nd. That he is not sure of selling all that he has made.

Q. Besides do you think that the prisoner works as well as the free man?

A. I do not doubt it.

Q. Do you often have occasion to punish?

A. Very seldom. They know that punishment is inevitable and strikes the offender on the spot. They do not risk it.

Q. Does the prisoner you want to punish rebel sometimes?

[1] In English in the manuscript.

A. That has happened very seldom. And, in such case, the other prisoners have immediately taken the side of the keeper.

Q. Are you obliged to show a record of punishments?

A. Yes. Every evening we give the Deputy Keeper a list of punishments, cause and number of strokes.

Weaver Shop. 105 prisoners.

No contractor, but he comes very often.

The Keeper does not seem to have as much intelligence as the others. He could only give me approximate answers.

The average is 25 cents per man; he does not know what he would earn at liberty.

Q. What were you doing before you came here?

A. I was a farmer.

Q. Are there any *professional men* among the Keepers?

A. There are two masons, a shoe-maker and a ruined trader.

Q. Does it often happen that there are difficulties between the Keeper and the Contractor who comes to visit the workshop?

A. Ordinarily they get on very well together. In the two years I have been here, I have only twice seen a quarrel between them; it was settled on the spot by money.

Q. Are you often obliged to punish?

A. I have not given a stroke here for six weeks.

Q. What do you think of the wooden gallery that goes round the workshop?

A. I think it is the most excellent invention one could have. It greatly lessens the need to punish.

Blacksmith Shop. 37 prisoners.

Keeper very intelligent and out of the ordinary.

Q. Are you often obliged to punish the men?

A. I have once gone four and a half months without giving a single stroke. Now it is two months and a half since I have given any. The secret gallery wonderfully helps us to maintain discipline. I came to the prison before it was begun. I remember just how difficult it was to reduce the men to silence. I remember seeing nineteen corrected in less than an hour.

Q. What do you think of the contract system?

A. I think that one could do without it, and that the way in which it is used here is very dangerous. This is the whole story: to begin with there were only keepers and prisoners in the prison. The prisoners worked on behalf of the State. To save time and get rid of a lot of detail, the agent introduced the contract system. But then the agent was not allowed to address a single word to the prisoners, not even to go to them. I can assure you that for three years the prisoners in my workshop did not even know who the contractor was. After some time the contractor was allowed to come himself into the workshop and supervise the work himself. After that, to give orders to the prisoners; then to send his representative. You see now that he is forever talking to the prisoners. We are being led little by little to the ruin of discipline. Now there are more strangers than keepers in the establishment.

Q. Do you think there are many prisoners who mend their ways?

A. I am talking to you as a man who wants to know the truth. What the books say about the extent of Reform is fiction. I am certain no one here does. . . .'[1]

Number of individuals reunited each year.

* * *

Journey to the West

Arirval at Albany.

Ceremony of 4th July. Mixture of impressions, some funny, some very serious. Militia on foot and on horse, speeches swollen with rhetoric, jug of water on the platform, hymn to liberty in a church. Something of French spirit.

Perfect order that prevails. Silence. No police. Authority nowhere. Festival of the people. Marshal of the day without restrictive power, and obeyed, free classification of industries, public prayer, presence of the flag and of old soldiers. Emotion real.

Departure from Albany in the night of 4th July. Valley of the Mohawk. Hills not high. Wooded the whole way up. A part of the valley wooded too. In general the whole country has the look of a wood in which clearings have been made. Much resemblance to Lower Normandy. Every sign of a new country.

[1] The text breaks off on the last but one page of the notebook. On the last page there are only two addresses not in Tocqueville's handwriting, the first hardly legible, the second: S. Warren, Ivory. The dots are Tocqueville's.

Man still making clearly ineffective efforts to master the forest. Tilled fields covered with shoots of trees; trunks in the middle of the corn. Nature vigorous and savage. Mixture in the same field of bushes and trees of a thousand different species, plants sown by man and various self-sown weeds. Brooks on all sides. New country peopled by an old people. Nothing untamed but the ground; dwellings clean and well cared for; shops in the middle of the forest; newspapers in isolated cabins. The women well turned out.

Not a trace of the Indians, the Mohawks, the most admired and the bravest of the confederate tribes of the Iroquois.

Road infernal. Carriage without springs and with curtains.

Calmness of the Americans about all these annoyances; they seem to put up with them as necessary and passing ills.

* * *

Arrival at Utica

Charming town of 10,000 inhabitants. Very pretty shops. Founded since the War of Independence. In the middle of a pretty plain.

* * *

Departure from Utica (*6th July*)

Country looks the same as the day before.

Met the first Indians at Oneida Castle, 116 miles from Albany. They were begging. [?]

* * *

Arrival at Syracuse

Placed in the middle of a rather unhealthy but thickly peopled plain. Junction of the two canals of Erie and Oswego. Visit to Mr. Elam Lynds. In his hardware store. He could not speak to us because he was busy selling. Conversation with him.[1] A man of vulgar exterior, full of intelligence and energy. Despotic tendencies show clearly in him.

[1] See non-alphabetic notebook 1, p. 23.

Pocket Notebook Number 1

(This is written on 'the Frenchman's island' in the middle of Lake Oneida.)

* * *

(*7th July*)

Leave Syracuse at 2 o'clock. On horseback. Umbrella, gun, game-bag. We plunge through new clearings. We arrived at 6 o'clock at Fort Brewerton. General look round. The forest in permanent contest with man. Birds killed. View of Lake Oneida. Stretches beyond the horizon to the East between little wooded hills. Not a house nor clearing in view. Monotonous, lonely look. We sleep in a detestable inn. Departure at 6 o'clock in the morning.

We plunge through an immense forest where the path is hardly traceable. Delicious freshness that reigns there. Sight wonderful and impossible to describe. Astonishing vegetation. Enormous trees of all species. Mass of foliage, grasses, plants, bushes. America in all her glory, waters (?) running on every side, huge pines uprooted by the wind, twisted among plants of every sort. In two hours we came to South Bay.

Conversation on Frenchman's island. They settled in these parts thirty-five [?] years ago. At that time the Frenchman's presence was already only a tradition. Had been in the island thirty-one [?] years ago. She remembers some flowers and an apple tree near which were the remains of a wooden house.

We embarked by ourselves in a little boat. With difficulty we reached the island. Emotion we felt on setting foot there. Different look of the country we had just been through. Land gone wild again. Traces of man. We force our way through a belt of immense trees. We arrive at a clearing where trees, already big, had clearly once been cut. Some old, rotting trunks, leaning among brambles, plants and branches. In the middle of the island we find an old apple-tree. Near there a vine, gone wild again, twining right up to the top of the neighbouring trees like a liana. The house was there. There is no trace left of it. We wrote our names on a plane tree. We set out again. Profound silence of the island only broken by the birds that live there free. We traversed the whole island without finding any trace of the two beings who had made it their universe. This expedition is

130

what has most vividly interested and moved me, not only since I have been in America, but since I have been travelling.[1]

*   *   *

Arrival at Auburn. Visit to the prison (*9th July*)
(*10th July*) Stay
(*11th July*) Stay

Visit to Governor Throop. Small farm. Cultivating his land. The function of governor is so badly paid that it is only by spending six months in the country that he can make ends meet. 'The great men' do not canvass at all for this too badly paid position (remark of Lynds).

[1] See journey to Lake Oneida, pp. 321–327.

IV

Pocket Notebook Number 2

Arrival on the 16th at Canandaigua. First visit to Mr. Spencer. Difficulty about sleeping accommodation and dinner. Long conversations with him.

Lake very picturesque. *Red-Jacket*.[1]

*　　*　　*

(*17th July*)

Anglican church. Visit to the Alms-house of the county. Walk. Very agreeable evening.

*　　*　　*

Departure from Canandaigua (*18th July*)

Appearance of the country peopled as far as Batavia. After that scattered houses. Marsh. Road of tree trunks. Arrival at Buffalo. Walk through the town. A crowd of savages in the streets (day of a payment) new idea which they suggest. Their ugliness. Their strange look. Their oily, bronzed skin. Their long, black, stiff hair. Their European clothes worn in savage fashion. Scene of a drunk Indian. Brutality of his fellow Indians and of the Indian woman who accompanies him. Population brutalised by our wines and spirits. More horrible than the equally brutalised populations of Europe. Besides, something of the wild beast. Contrast with the moral and civilised population in the midst of which they are found.

Second walk through Buffalo. Pretty shops. French goods. Refinement of European luxury. Second sight of Indians.

[1] Tocqueville gives a detailed account of his conversations with Mr. Spencer about Red-Jacket in alphabetic notebook A, Indians.

Impression less disagreeable than the day before. Some of them having more or less the looks of our peasants (but with a savage touch), colour of Sicilians. Not a passable Indian woman.

Departure for Detroit. Little steamboat. No one knew us. Notable change in the manners of the Americans towards us. Violent, contrary wind. The lake rough as a sea in a heavy storm.

* * *

(*20th July*)

At 9 o'clock in the morning we touched at Erie, founded by the French under the name of 'Presqu'île'. Now the lake has opened a passage between the mainland and the peninsula and made the latter into an island. Visit to Erie in a heavy downpour of rain. A canal is now under construction coming from Pittsburgh (formerly Fort-Duquesne), which will end at Erie. It will join the Mississippi to the North Coast, the Gulf of Mexico to the Atlantic Ocean.[1] We set out again on our way an hour later.

* * *

(*21st July*)

Quarrel with the captain. Arrival at Cleveland at 6 o'clock in the evening. Up to there the aspect of the lake had been uniform. Generally to the right the lake, like a sea, stretched its transparent waters to the horizon. We hugged close to the shore of Pennsylvania and Ohio on the left. That side, generally quite flat and sometimes a few feet high, was almost everywhere covered in primeval forest whose immense trees were reflected in the waters that bathed their roots. The very uniformity of the sight is impressive. One is tempted to think that the ship that bears one is the only one to trace a furrow in the waters of the lake and that the land one sees has not yet fallen under man's dominion. But that is all nothing. After coasting along for hours beside a dark forest that only ends where the lake begins, one suddenly sees a church tower, elegant houses, fine villages, with an appearance of wealth and industry. Nothing

[1] No doubt it is to the Erie-and-Ohio canal, which was effectively finished in 1832, that Tocqueville here refers: but it goes from Portsmouth to Cleveland, and not from Pittsburgh to Erie. As for the well-known Erie canal which joins Buffalo through the lake to the port of New York, that had been finished by 1825.

but nature is savage here; man fights against her everywhere armed with all the resources of civilisation. One goes without transition from the wilds into a city street, from the most savage scenes to the most smiling pictures of civilised life. If you are not caught by nightfall and forced to lodge at the foot of a tree, you are sure to come to a place where you will find everything, even French fashions and Palais Royal caricatures.

At 7 o'clock we left Cleveland. Lovely night. The moon lighting the forest and reflected in the waters of the lake.

* * *

(*22nd July*)

At sunrise we are sailing through the middle of the lake towards the North West, the shores are only to be seen in the distance, but a great many little islands surround us. We are passing beside the little island of 'Middle Sister' near which took place the naval battle in which the English were defeated.

Entry of the Detroit River. An island; two passages. We take the English channel. House of Fort Malden. French appearance of the village. Catholic Church. Cock on the church tower. Scottish soldier in full dress on the bank; on the other side two stark naked savages in a canoe, twisting as fast as a whirlpool round our boat. Rings hanging at the nose. Under the trees on the bank, huts of a sort with a fire in the middle. Naked children around. On one side extreme civilisation, on the other the extreme opposite.

We arrived at Detroit at 4 o'clock. A fine American village. Many French names on the houses; French bonnets. We went to see Mr. Richard,[1] the priest in charge of the Catholic church in Detroit. We found him busy teaching at school. His story: brought up by the Irish in Paris; studied theology at Saint Sulpice; ordained priest at the last ordination of 1791; went into exile; came to Detroit; a few years ago was Congress representative for the territory of Michigan. An old man whose religion seems to be ardent and sincere. Desultory conversation, but interesting. The Protestant population begins to be preponderant in Michigan on account of emigration. But Catholicism gains some converts among the most enlightened men.

[1] Cf. Pierson, op. cit., pp. 282 f.

Mr. Richard's opinion about the extreme coolness of the upper classes in America towards religion. One of the reasons for the extreme tolerance; anyhow tolerance complete. Nobody asks you *of what religion you are, but if you can do the job*. The greatest service one can do to religion is to separate it from temporal power. The slightest nuance of ill feeling towards popular government, intrigues and cabals; the elections are even made by the central government. United States systems for the new States. They are made to get accustomed by degrees to governing themselves. Colony of native Christians at Michilimackinac. Their zeal, their ardour, their education.

On leaving Mr. Richard our embarrassment about which way to set out. All the Americans wanted us to choose the best roads and oldest settlements. We wanted the wilderness and savages but did not like to say so too clearly.

Saginaw Bay was proposed and, to put an end to the argument, we decided on that.

* * *

(*23rd July*)

We bought pillows, a compass, brandy, sugar, and ammunition. We hired two horses.

Conversation with Mr. Biddle.[1]

We left at 11 o'clock. Our dress. Our way of travelling. Birds killed. Our joy at advancing at last into the wilds. Perfectly flat ground. One league without trees and under cultivation around Detroit. After that we enter a thick forest through which a fine road has been cut. From time to time a little cleared space. A circle of wonderful trees around, mixed with burnt trees; a field covered with trunks; in the middle a log-house, often without windows. No poverty. Peasants well-clothed. Cattle bells around. Air of prosperity near Troy, at the door of a log-house family drinking tea. Houses become more and more scattered. Immediately after them the forest starts again. We went through some delightful marches; like English gardens where nature has paid all the expenses. Dinner at Troy. French Canadian scene.

We arrived at Pontiac at 8 o'clock in the evening. We wanted to change horses. We were referred to a man living a mile out

[1] Cf. Pierson, op. cit., p. 240.

in the forest. We set out by ourselves. Night scene. Incredible silence of the forest. Effect of the moon through the trees. After half an hour we see a little clearing, a log-house. We jump over the fence, but we hear dogs and do not dare to go close. We arrive at last. We enter a room filling the whole extent of the house. Fire in a corner, tools of all sorts, an excellent bed in another corner, the man and woman lying in bed, the woman dressed like a lady. Strange mixture of prosperity and poverty. The Americans in their log houses have the air of rich folk who have temporarily gone to spend a season in a hunting-lodge.

* * *

(*24th July*)

On leaving Pontiac the road little by little loses its character of a main road. It begins to twist through the woods. Settlements become infinitely rarer. We had been given a letter of intro-duction to a Mr. Williams[1] whose trade is buying and selling to the Indians and who could give use useful information; pass-ing a settlement 4 miles from Pontiac we speak to an old man who is this very Mr. Williams. We show him where we want to go. We talk to him about the Indians. Praise of them. Nothing to fear from them. One can trust them more than the whites.

Cultivated fields seemed to stop all at once. At very long intervals some log-houses. Very picturesque country. Wooded hill. A multitude of lakes seen under the woods. At five miles from Little Spring a wonderful valley; slope of a hill covered with immense pines. Torrent that can be heard from the bottom of the ravine. We turn back to admire the sight. We notice an Indian who is following us running without making more noise than a wolf. Plaited hair, head bare, ear-rings, sort of blouse, red breeches without bottom. Moccasins. A powder-flask, long carbine and two birds in his hand. An involuntary start of terror. What Mr. Williams had said and the look of his face reassure us. We speak to him. He listens quietly and makes a sign that he does not understand English. We give him some brandy and buy his birds. We mount again. After some time we turn round. The Indian following our tracks. We slow down. He slows

[1] Cf. Pierson, op. cit., index.

down. We run. He runs without making the slightest noise. Strange impression made by this silent and mysterious being who seems to hover round us. A mile further we see another carbine in the woods. We fear a surprise. It is a white man, apart from his hat dressed pretty well like a savage. It is a European turned half savage. He shows his hut in the branches! He lives by hunting. He speaks to the Indian in his language (Chippewa). He talks to us in terms of great praise about the Indians whose nature and way of life he seems to love. He invites us to come and see on our return. We start off again at a fast trot. The Indian always on our tracks for two miles. Arrive at the small clearing of Little Spring. Travelling camp of Indians. Men, women and children round the fire, eating potatoes and half roasted corn. Expression of their faces pleasant enough when they smile; terrible when they are serious. Quite good-looking in profile;[1] ugly full face. Too prominent cheekbones. Good things they tell us of them. Not to be feared except when drunk. Otherwise honest and gentle. The proof of it is that the master of Little Spring had left his wife and six little children in the midst of this Indian horde, and this very morning had been out hunting.

Look of the country from Little Spring to Grand Bank. Very hilly ground. No copse. High full-grown trees well-spaced as if they had been planted by man. Ground beneath covered with tall plants, especially bracken. Hardly any more houses. From time to time a troupe of Indians walking through the plants under the trees, or a fire. Dinner at Grand Bank. A single shoe-smith. We start out again at 7 o'clock. We enter a forest of huge oaks. The copse begins again. The road turns into a path hard to follow. Night comes on. Our anxiety at not being able to reach Flint River. The wind subsides. Complete tranquillity. Deep darkness. Impressive silence of the woods, disturbed by the sound of our horses and the cries of a single bird which seemed to follow us. The moon at full rises. Wonderful effects. Beneath the trees, plants silvered by the moon like the waves of the sea, withered trunks that seem black lying on the ground in the middle. Strange effects on the immense trunks of the oaks, huge columns of white marble. Moon through a withered wood on the edge of a clearing. A little lake seen between the

[1] Tocqueville has drawn the profile of an Indian in the margin.

hills under the trees. Very far off, the fires of an Indian camp. Icy coolness. We get to the top of a hill. A clearing. A stream. We are not sure of the way. I go off alone to the houses I see far off in the clearing. I leap from tree to tree my gun in my hand. Immense oak on the ground. I cross the stream on some trees half squared out. Then I see in the moonlight that they have made a rough dike, and begun a building which is probably a saw-mill. Unfinished houses. No one. To find Beaumont again I am forced to shout terribly loud. I am afraid of attracting the Indians. Echoes in the wild. Silence that follows. We find each other. We go on walking for half an hour more. We hear the distant sound of dogs. We get to a clearing and see a light. Beaumont goes there. Woman alone, hides herself. Points to Mr. Todd.[1] He holds his dog in. His bear tied to the door. Munching its oats in the moonlight. He gives us a bed. I sleep on the ground.

*　　*　　*

(*25th July*)

We are provided with an Indian guide, a young man twenty years old. *Sagan Kuisko* of the tribe of *Saulters*.[2] Bare head, sort of blue smock fixed at the neck by a tin plaque. Ear-rings of tin. Blue trousers without bottom like the Indians. Moccasins. Leather belt. Tomahawk. Carbine. Not dirty. White teeth. Very pleasant smile. Savage look; dog like a wolf. Nothing resembling politeness. But attention to everything useful. He is accompanied by a child of twelve or thirteen. No weapon. They walk, or rather run in front of us with the lightness and silence of their race, without looking to see if we follow. First we pass the Flint river. There we enter a vast clearing. High plants. Indians running, stooping among them, looking for wild fruits. It is only after two or three miles that we get right into the virgin forest. Same scene more or less the whole day. Copse not very high; immense trees scattered among it. Oaks of immense thickness without branches almost up to the top; gigantic pines. As many trees on the ground as standing. Immense trees broken by the wind as they decay, forming something like vaults. Uprooted trees shaped like an immense shield.

[1] Cf. Pierson, op. cit., p. 259.
[2] Name given to part of the Chippewa tribe from Sault-Sainte-Marie.

Plants and ivy that grow on all the brash. Trees suspended in the air. Others thrown over streams. Marshy places riotous with vegetation; wonderful confused mass of foliage. The continuity of the sight is striking by its very duration. No more birds except an occasional bird of prey, and at long intervals some wood pigeons. Feeling of isolation, of abandon, greater even than on the ocean. Even more impossible to find one's way. Our Indians leap in front of us for four hours without stopping, never hesitating about which path to take, and seeming to know the ground even in its slightest details. One of them utters a sort of dull savage cry. He points out through the branches the highest tree; one of the well-known *Bible trees*. The picture they make. We go on again. Our Indians stop. They draw a line in the sand. Pointing to one end and shouting 'Flint', to the other and shouting 'Saginaw', and then indicating the middle to show that we have reached half way and ought to stop. We make a gesture of drinking to show that we want to stop by a spring. They start running again and lead us to a place where there is a pool of rainwater. We unsaddle from our horses and take our provisions. We could not find any bread at Flint. Our meat is bad and most of our eggs rotten. We only have some sugar and a few biscuits. A cloud of mosquitoes attracted by the water soon make the place intolerable for us. We start out again. At 5 o'clock we reach the bank of a swift stream, with steep sides, but not deep. We take breath, thinking we can see a settlement of white men. On the other bank, a field of corn and three abandoned wigwams. Delightful view; high forest trees to the right, to the left the stream flowing slowly between its lonely wooded banks.

The Indian points to the sun and makes a sign that it is too late for us to be able to reach Saginaw. He throws himself down on a tree-trunk to make us understand that night will overtake us, and to induce us to pass it where we are. We have not dined. We urge him to go on. He makes a sign that he is tired. We offer him the unbreakable bottle. Then he goes off like an arrow. Journey past high forest trees, from time to time the stream across our path. From time to time a hut of oak bark and the remains of a burnt out fire. We only meet one single being; a woman asleep with a child by a fire. Impassive look. We kill some game and then want to stop. The Indian makes a sign that now we must put an end [*sic*] to the undertaking. Night overtakes us. The whole time immense trees to leap over and marshes to cross. The Indian is clearly worn out with fatigue. He gets a terrible nose-bleed. We mount him behind. Odd sight. We give him our horses, guns and game-bag, and walk. Dampness and silence of the forest. A gun-shot in the distance. The whole party stops. Road almost impossible to find. Cloud of mosquitoes, torments that they make us suffer. At 8 o'clock in the evening we reach a meadow. Grass four feet high. Our two Indians utter three savage cries; an answer comes from the distance where we see a fire. Soon we come up to the banks of a river nearly as large as the Seine at Paris, the Saginaw, which the prairie grass had hidden. The last rays of sunset showed us a little Indian canoe, like a long black fish, coming towards us. In it crouched a man whom we took for an Indian. Dressed much like them. Moccasins, bare head. He spoke to them in their language. I wanted to get into the boat holding my horse by the bridle. 'You must take the saddle off,' the supposed Indian said to me, 'sometimes they get drowned.' Norman accent; French hard to understand. I take off my saddle, put it in the canoe, and get in beside it. The grown-up Indian gets in the end, holding the bridle. The French Canadian paddles, the horse swimming. Strangeness of the sight. I talk to the boatman; mixture of French and Indian blood; half savage. The Indian when he gets to the bank, feeling devoured by mosquitoes, wraps himself up completely in his blanket and throws himself on the ground. My anxiety about Beaumont. Soon I hear the sound of the canoe again. The moon comes up full. It casts its light on the forest, the stream and the whole scene. Impression impossible to describe. Two men address us in French; they are French Canadians and their language is that of our peasants. We are taken to one of the three houses that make up Saginaw. Terrible night. Mosquitoes. Forced to roll up like the Indian in my blanket and to sleep on the floor. Indians asleep at the door with their dogs.

* * *

(*26th July*)

Saginaw. An area of cultivation in the midst of savage tribes and impenetrable forest. Beauty of the lonely stream that runs

140

at its foot. We go to see Mr. Williams. He trades with the Indians. He shows us a quantity of little objects intended for their use, for which they pay with the money given to them by the United States as the price of their land and with furs. Clearly he robs them. What he and all the other Europeans say about the savages; excellent folk. Good and gentle. More reliable than the whites. Universal testimony. Coming back I go into the house of one of the French people. His wife like an Indian woman, working at a mat. A red child by her side. I ask her if she is French.—No.—English?—No.—What blood? She answers me lowering her head: *a savage.* The Frenchman was her husband and she had already given him several children. Extraordinary race; mixture of the savage and the civilised man; does not know any language well; speaks English, French and Indian. Has a taste for the wilds, but is still attached to the towns. A common case, they say, among the French. Go duck shooting with the young man in an Indian canoe. Ducking, we go up the Saginaw through impenetrable forests. Some savages come up to us. Envy of my gun which, they say, is fired by the rain. Where are guns like that made? In the land where the fathers of the French Canadians live. Beavers. Sort of insects. . . .

In the evening towards sunset we come back alone in the canoe, and go down a branch of the Saginaw. Such an evening as one hardly ever sees. Still air, cloudless sky. Our canoe glides without making the slightest noise. We paddle gently and enjoy the sight. Still, transparent water. Wonderful vegetation on the banks. Immense forests reflected in the water, setting sun shining through and casting its light on the undergrowth. In twenty years all this will be replaced by villages, a change in the near future which makes the present sight still more impressive. Echo of a gun shot. We come back at nightfall. Our efforts to keep safe from the mosquitoes.

*　　*　　*

(*27th July*)

We want to leave. We are prevented. We go down to the meadows along the Saginaw to shoot wild duck. A French Canadian guides us. Our conversation about the Indians. Their passion for strong waters is irresistible. An Indian drinks as much as he can drink, though he die of it. When sober, excellent people. Their hospitality. In the wilds, give their own food. Unfortunately it is no longer easy to deceive them about the value of goods. Have no religion. But believe in a God, the author of good, and a spirit the author of evil, and another world where one plays the whole time. We go into the prairie. Inexpressible torment caused by the mosquitoes. We see some long snakes. We ask the French Canadian why he does not follow us into the long grass. He is badly shod, says he, and is afraid of the rattle-snakes. So there are some. Many in the prairie. The Indians have a cure which stops them dying. We become more circum-spect. We see humming-birds for the first time. A storm that day. Beautiful sight. Calm preceding it. Buzzing of insects, burst of thunder, its almost endless echo in the solitudes that surround us.

* * *

(*28th July*)

After a sleepless night we leave Saginaw alone at 5 o'clock. Solemn feeling that we experienced when, after saying good-bye to our hosts, we went into the forest without a guide. I felt ill at ease. We easily found the river Cass again. We had breakfast there. Beauty and tranquillity of the place. Abandoned wigwam. Two roads. Doubt. We took the one to the right and crossed the stream. The track seemed little trodden. Unpleasant doubt for a long time. We look at the sun and the compass. Finally we arrive at the place where we had lunched. At 6 o'clock in the evening at last we got out of the forest in which we had not met a living creature except for some deer and birds. Memories of the 28th July 1830 in the forest.

* * *

(*29th July*)

We reached Pontiac by the same road without anything worth noting.

* * *

(*30th July*)

Visit to the little lakes of Orchard and Pine. Settlement of the year. Cabin of Doctor Burns.[1] Strange mixture of a very culti-

---

[1] Blank in the manuscript.

vated upbringing and present habits of another nature. Books. Look of poverty, slum; we found him raking his field. Details he gave us.

* * *

(*31st July*)

Arrival at Detroit. Walk in the evening along the quay. Meeting with one of our fellow passengers on the *Ohio*. He told us that the *Superior* had just arrived on its way to Green Bay. We immediately change our plans and decide to go to Green Bay.

* * *

(*1st August*)

We embark at 2 o'clock. Shore of Detroit. Land low and cultivated. Many houses. Lake Saint Clair. In the evening dancing on the bridge. American gaiety.

* * *

(*2nd August*)

The next day we are in sight of   ,¹ situated at the mouth of Lake Huron. We enter that immense lake. The wind turns contrary. We go on to the fort, and from there to Black River two miles further up to get wood. Visit to the fort. Bearing of officers and soldiers. Drill. Insubordination.

* * *

(*3rd August*)

At 1 o'clock I go shooting in the marshes on the other side of the river Saint Clair. First we go to the fort. In the forest on the way the sound of a savage drum. Some cries. We see coming eight savages stark naked except for a little loin-cloth. (6 children, 2 men). Besmeared with dyes from head to foot. Hair bristling, lots of ends falling in queue behind. A wooden club in hand, jumping like devils. Beautiful men. Dancing for fun and to get money. We give them a shilling. It is the War-dance. Horrible to see. What a degradation. Another dance on their knees, head to the ground. We do not know how to go on [?]. Some huts in the marsh on the other side. A canoe

¹ Probably Port Huron.

unfastens and comes. Alarming navigation. Good hunting in the marsh.

* * *

(*4th August*)

We leave at six o'clock in the morning. Day with absolutely nothing to note. Towards evening all land out of sight.

* * *

(*5th August*)

At 4 o'clock we get to the end of Lake Huron. We see some mountains in the distance. The end of the lake is strewn with an innumerable multitude of little islands which spring like groves from the surface of the lake. Perfect solitude. Forests on all sides. Not the least trace of man. Not a ship in sight. Coasting Saint Joseph island, the ruins of a fort of that name. Chimneys still standing. We enter the Sainte Marie river. Sometimes as wide as a lake. Sometimes shut in between islands and wooded projections of land. Perfect solitude. From time to time a family of Indians on the bank, sitting immobile by their fire. Their canoe drawn up on the beach. A big canoe manned by eight men comes towards us. The Indians fire off their guns and raise shouts of joy. They give us some pigeons. We give them some brandy. At sunset we enter a very narrow channel. Wonderful view. Delightful moment. The river water still and transparent. A superb forest reflected in it. In the distance blue mountains illuminated by the last rays of the sun. Fire of Indians burning through the trees. Our boat goes majestically on through this solitude, to the sound of fanfares which the echo from the wood returns from every side. At night we cast anchor. Dance on the bridge. Astonishment and wonder of the Indians at the sight of the first steam-boat *working in the water*.[1]

* * *

(*6th August*)

A year ago today we made a King.[2] Thick fog that prevents us leaving. It lifts disclosing little hills and everlasting forests. At

---

[1] The words in italics are in English in Tocqueville's manuscript.
[2] Louis-Philippe, King of the French (1830–1848).

9 o'clock arrival at Sault-Sainte-Marie. Delightful site. Wonderful weather. Sainte-Marie a palisaded square with a flagstaff and a huge American flag in the middle. Further on, two points of land covered with lovely trees, that shut the river in. Under the trees some wigwams. Between the points, rapids. Further on mountains and everlasting forests. At our arrival the whole population on the bank and on the roofs of houses. A boat like ours not seen more than once a year. Strange character of this population, mixture of all sorts of blood. The most numerous, the French Canadians, *bois-brulés*[1] or half-caste. Every gradation from European to savage. Faces streaked and painted. Hair fixed back with feathers. We take an Indian canoe to go to Lake Superior. Visit to an Indian traders' camp. (See below). Description of that canoe of painted bark. Sitting in the bottom eight (counting ourselves) solemn and impassive. At the two ends, a French Canadian, half a savage but who had kept all the gaiety of his fathers, singing and making jokes as he sent the canoe flying. Forwardness of the Indians towards Mr. Mullon.[2] Baptism in the ship's cabin. Odd feeling to us to hear French at the end of the world, and French with old turns of speech and a provincial accent: *laridondaine, laridondon.* From time to time; 'hou! ou', that is 'go on'. We come to the foreland with oaks. A little Indian village. Their hut [?]: twelve feet in diameter, six feet high. Their savage dogs. The chief asks to see my gun (percussion). Dress of the chief: red trousers, a blanket, hair tied back on the top of his head. Two feathers in it. I fire my gun for him. He admires it, and says that he had always heard it said that the French were a nation of great warriors. I ask the meaning of his feathers. He answers with a smile of pleasure that it is a sign that he has killed two *Sioux.* (He is a *Saulter*, a tribe always at war with the other.) I ask him for one of the feathers, telling him that I will carry it to the land of the great warriors, and people will admire it. He takes it out at once from his hair and gives it to me, then stretches out his hand and shakes mine.

We come back. Descent of the rapids. Incredible skill of the French Canadians. Pass like an arrow between the rocks. The

[1] A small band of the Chippewa tribe at Burnt Woods, on the *Bois Brulé* River, near the west end of Lake Superior, northern Wisconsin.
[2] See non-alphabetic notebook 1, pp. 32–35.

Johnson family (conversation forgotten) at the camp of the
Indian traders. A dry, cold, taciturn Englishman in the middle
of this crowd of French Canadians and savages whom he is
leading to trade with the Indians of Lake Superior. The French
Canadians surround us with the openness and goodwill of Frenchmen. They seem delighted to see French people. We ask them
for information about the Indians. All those whom they know,
and they go every year right to the end of the lake, wear the
same clothes as those we have seen. Not thieves. Willing and
hospitable. Friends of the Europeans who provide them with
things that have become indispensable to them. Wild beasts in
war. Kill all indiscriminately. Scalp and burn their prisoners.
The *Saulters* and the Sioux, the two rival nations. The chiefs
have only nominal authority. No justice. Blood-money or private
vengeance. No religion. Belief in God and in another world
where those who have lived badly will have to hunt in a forest
without game. The others in forests full of game. Antipathy of
the Indians for the English language, their liking for the
French: in the most distant wilds the Indians greet Europeans by
saying, *Bonjour*.

*   *   *

(*7th August*)

We leave at 5 o'clock in the morning. We cross the South-
West point of Lake Huron. Fleet of 22 Indian canoes. Going
in the opposite direction and returning home when they have
received the presents from the English.

At 3 o'clock we are skirting Bois-Blanc and Île Ronde and
arrive at Mackinac. Island three leagues round and fairly high.
At the top the white defence-works of an American fort. On
the shore some fifty houses, several of them rather pretty,
belonging to the American company. On the bank a great number
of Indian huts. They visit there, coming from distant parts, for
the sake of the presents. Two churches. We take a French
Canadian guide. We go to see the perforated rock. Picturesque.
From there the pyramid looks strange from its size and shape.
We come back at 5 o'clock. Beaumont goes to sketch the perforated grotto. As for me, I go roaming as is my habit. I go to
see the parish priest; he is not there. Madame Framboise.
Indian blood. Interesting details about her life. Woman much

to be respected. Letter from a young Indian woman. Indian book of prayers. A camp of French Canadians on the bank. A bivouac round the fire. A French Canadian with the look and manners of a Frenchman. Gay, open, energetic. Some half-caste. I sit by their fire and talk with them. Their chief, a half-caste, very intelligent man. Information he gives me about the savages. Better the further off they are from Europeans, unless they are Christians. In the depths of the wilds of the North West still armed with arrows. Happy there. Extraordinary abundance of animals. They always retreat a hundred leagues in advance of civilisation. Inability of the Indians to take in that the advance of the Europeans will catch them up sooner or later. They only take it in when it is too late to remedy it. Hereditary chiefs. Not the same as war-chiefs. Sort of justice. The murderer is handed over to the family who kills him or accepts his ransom. No robbers at all. Terrible in war. Iroquois and Hurons have almost disappeared. Hurons pretty well destroyed. Iroquois: the remnants dispersed among the other tribes on this side of the lakes. Many at Green Bay.

Catholic zeal. Eagerness to fight the Presbyterians. Mr. Mullon coming to take up a sort of challenge. Efforts of the poor French Canadians to support their church and establish a school. Visit to Mr.   .[1] Return to the boat at 11 o'clock. On the return journey glimpse of a hut of savages. Family singing a church hymn in Indian.

* * *

(*8th August*)

Day without incident passed on the water. From time to time, to right and to left, low ground covered with forests.

* * *

(*9th August*)

Arrival at 8 o'clock in the morning at Green Bay. Fort. Village on the bank in the middle of a prairie on the bank of a stream. Indian Iroquois village higher up. Large settlement. We do not know what to do; I go shooting alone. River crossed by swimming. Canoe. Plants at the bottom of the water. I get lost for a

[1] A gap in the manuscript.

moment; return to the place without realising it. After dinner go out with an Englishman to Ducks Creek: 4 miles. We go by canoe up a little lonely stream. Arrival at the house of an Indian woman. Grass. Pleasant jaunt. We come back.

* * *

(*11th August*)

Conversation with a civilised savage, dressed like one of our peasants. Speaks English well. The savages like the French better (said he): his ideas about civilised life: hopes that all the Indians will adapt themselves to it. Is not a Christian. Religion of the Indians. God, immortality of the soul. The Indian paradise. To obey his commandments.

Monotonous journey on the lake.

* * *

(*12th August*)

Arrival at 11 o'clock at Mackinac.

Pharo savage. European hat, black feather round it. Circle of tin round the top. Three *voltigeurs'*[1] feathers on the crown. Immense ear-rings. Nose pierced, a ring in it. Tie black. Smock blue. Large collar made of tin plates with animals engraved on them; tin rings on the legs; red garters with a quantity of little glass beads. Embroidered mocassins. A red cloak in which he drapes himself. View of an old French Canadian that they are more beautiful in their savage dress, entirely naked except for feathers in belt and on head. Long hair plaited often right down to their legs. The whole body painted. Pigeon shooting. Canadian pointer. Sermon of Mr. Mullon.

* * *

(*13th August*)

Leave Mackinac at 9 o'clock. Nothing of interest on the return journey. Arrive on the evening of Sunday, the 14th, at Detroit.

[1] The *voltigeurs*, who wore feathers in their caps, were crack troops.

V

Pocket Notebook Number 3

The two great social principles which seem to me to rule American society and to which one must always return to find the reason for all the laws and habits which govern it, are as follows:

1st. The majority may be mistaken on some points, but finally it is always right and there is no moral power above it.

2nd. Every individual, private person, society, community or nation, is the only lawful judge of its own interest, and, provided it does not harm the interests of others, nobody has the right to interfere.

I think that one must never lose sight of this point.

(30th September 1831)

A completely democratic government is so dangerous an instrument that, *even in America*, men have been obliged to take a host of precautions against the errors and passions of Democracy. The establishment of two chambers, the governor's veto, and above all the establishment of the judges. . . .

(30th September 1831)

*   *   *

Try to find out the number of criminal cases in which there is no prosecution and the number in which there is an acquittal.

Information important in order to compare criminal investigation methods here with our own.

To know if it often happens that from fear or selfishness people are unwilling to bear witness.

Look into divorce.

Another principle of American society of which one must never lose sight: every individual being the most competent judge of his own interest, society must not carry its solicitude on his behalf too far, for fear that in the end he might come to count on society, and so a duty might be laid on society which it is incapable of performing.

It is in virtue of this principle that the Americans claim that, without criminal investigation police, they succeed in uncovering more criminals than we. Since, when a crime is committed, the whole population takes part in uncovering it and pointing out the offenders, a task which no administrative department could ever fulfil in the same way.

But the useful mean between these theories is hard to grasp.

In America free morals have made free political institutions; in France it is for free political institutions to mould morals. That is the end towards which we must strive but without forgetting the point of departure.

England is weighed down by an enormous debt and intolerable taxes. Many people say that it is English aristocratic institutions that are to blame for this. That is partly true. But should one not take into consideration the political difficulties in which England has found herself placed, and from which a democratic government would have extricated her not at less expense, and, no doubt, with less prosperity and glory than the aristocracy?

Every religious doctrine has a political doctrine which, by affinity, is attached to it. That is an incontestable point in the sense that, where nothing runs contrary to that tendency, it is sure to show itself. But it does not follow that it is impossible to separate religious doctrines from all their political effects. On the contrary, in almost every country in the world one has seen material interests bring about this separation. The Catholics in Canada and in the United States are invariably the supporters of the democratic party. Does it follow that Catholicism leads to the democratic spirit? No. But the Catholics there are poor and almost all come from a country where the aristocracy is Protestant. *(1st October 1831)*

* * *

Put questions to Mr. Sullivan about the public prosecutor's office, and to Messrs Gray and Coolidge about the local and county systems.[1]

10 or 12 towns in a county. 3,000 inhabitants. 8 counties in Connecticut.

* * *

Today in the hospital for deaf-mutes at Hartford I saw a young girl who was deaf, mute and blind. She was able, however, to sew and to thread a needle. From time to time she smiled at her thoughts. It was a strange sight. How could anything funny or pleasant take place in a soul so walled in, what form does it take?

The director told me that she was gentle and very easy to handle. He added that her sense of smell was so perfect that in a heap of dirty linen, she could recognise her own by its smell. In the same way she knew what man or woman it was who came close to her.

They have already had two or three Negroes in the institution. I was assured that they could not see any difference in their intelligence from that of the whites.

* * *

(*7th October 1831*)

I have just had a conversation with Mr. *Huntington*,[2] a lawyer at Hartford and one of the commissioners for the Connecticut prison. He tried to explain to me the criminal investigation organisation in the State of Connecticut.

He said to me:

In each county we have a criminal justice department, and an Assize Court which is held once every three or four months as found needful in the chief town of the county.

When a crime has been committed, the accuser brings the case before one of the Grand Juries (what does a Grand Jury mean in Connecticut?). The Grand Jury then informs a Justice of the Peace who issues the *warrant* by which authority the

---

[1] These questions come in notebook F, p. 309.
[2] Cf. Pierson, op. cit., p. 442.

accused is arrested and brought before a judge who decides whether or not he is to be kept in custody.

Important matters come before a Grand Jury before they reach the ordinary jury. All cases that are not very serious, go straight before an ordinary jury. Our criminal procedure is very simple. We have still further simplified down the formalities of English criminal legislation. It is only the State of Connecticut that has thus rid itself of the formalities in force in the motherland.

* * *

(*8th October 1831*)

I have an inkling about two things in the constitution of the public prosecutor's department here. First, that there is no true hierarchy among the different officials of the department of public prosecution; that is to say that one has no right to give orders to another, nor even to supervise his work. But their duties are, and are considered, more or less important according to the status of the courts in reference to which they work; but each has a separate sphere of action. Secondly, in America the duties of bringing a case before the court and of conducting the prosecution in court are kept separate. Everything, or almost everything, to do with the preparation of the case, is not the concern of the public prosecutor, but it is he who prosecutes before the tribunals and appears in court.

All this needs to be confirmed.

There are 8 counties in the State of Connecticut which has 290,000 inhabitants. Average of about 36,000 people in a county. In each county there are 10 or 12 towns (the town is the ultimate *individual* in the American system); so there are about 3,000 people in each town. Wethersfield has 3,000 people.

* * *

(*7th October 1831*)

Mr. *Welles*, judge at Wethersfield, told me today: Our juries are chosen each year in each town by the Justice of the Peace and his *selectmen*, although every *freeholder* has the *right* to be a juror. They are careful to choose only the most competent people from among the *freeholders*. Generally speaking our juries are very well selected. I have known juries in which I would have felt as much confidence in every respect as in the judges. In the State of New York where the jury is chosen by lot, it is often a pitiable selection.

Mr. Dannery.[1] Observations about morals. Women's conversation among themselves. Crapulent tastes of the men. Dissoluteness of the lower classes before marriage.

* * *

(*11th October 1831*)

The jury is the most powerful and the most direct application of the dogma of the sovereignty of the people. Because the jury is nothing but the people made judge of what is allowed and of what it is forbidden to do against society.

From this point of view the jury is an eminently republican institution (democratic or aristocratic depending on the class from which the jurors are chosen). All governments which, in practice if not in theory, are not based on the sovereignty of the people, have been obliged to destroy the jury, or to modify it in such a way that it no longer represents public opinion.

That is, notably, what Bonaparte did.

One reason why the Restoration in France fell, is that it did not dare to base itself either on the ancient principle of divine right, or on the dogma of the sovereignty of the people, but tried to make two opposing elements pull in harness. In 1828 for instance, when M. de Peyronnet[2] made the choice of jurors entirely dependent on lot, he probably did not doubt but that he was helping us to take a great step forward towards a republic. But what men most lack is to know how to take a decided line. They are never either good enough or bad enough, sincere enough or crafty enough, sufficiently disinterested or sufficiently selfish; they want to combine all these things and are overcome by the effort.

* * *

(*12th October 1831*)

Mr. Duponceau[3] told us today: 'English and American legislation only know of two means of action: *imprisonment* and *bail*. They make a great abuse of them.'

[1] Cf. Pierson, op. cit., p. 476.
[2] Cf. S. Charléty, *La Restauration* (1815–1830), Paris 1921, pp. 259 f.
[3] See notebook F, p. 291; cf. Pierson, op. cit., p. 474.

Consequence of the principle that the jury must be examined; . . .[1] the jury went out at half past one o'clock. They stated that there was no possibility of their ever agreeing.

The court immediately informed them that they should return to their room until they agreed or would be discharged by the close of the term of the court. One of the jurors stated he had a violent headache, the Recorder replied that unless the illness was dangerous he should be locked up. Several other gentlemen of the jury stated that the jury room was extremely uncomfortable, in consequence of the want of fire—that they required food and other refreshments. The district-attorney stated to the court that the illness complained of by one of the jurors appeared to be a sufficient reason to warrant their discharge. The Recorder ordered officers to be sworn to convey the jurors to the jury room, and keep them safely until 11 o'clock in the morning of tomorrow, to which hour the Court stands adjourned.

His Honour, however stated that the jurors should be furnished with beds and refreshments in the tea-room where a comfortable fire should be prepared. The Court adjourned.

New York Morning Courier and Inquirer
(13th October 1831)

* * *

(14th October 1831)

[2]When the social state allows a people to choose its magistrates, the magistrates so elected can without disadvantage be clothed in a power which no despotic authority would dare to confer on them.

So it is that the selectmen in New England have the right to have the names of drunkards posted up in the public houses, and to impose a fine on the publican, or even on a third party, who should give them any wine. Such a power of censorship would be found revolting under the most absolute monarchy. People submit to it easily here. When once things are organised on that basis, the lower the qualification to vote and the shorter the

---

[1] The dots are Tocqueville's.
[2] The inspiration for these notes seems to have come from reading *Town Officer or Law of Massachusetts* by Isaac Goodwin, Worcester, 1829. See notebook F, p. 291.

time for which a magistrate holds office, by so much greater is the magistrate's power.

Nowhere is there more arbitrariness than in republics, because there is nothing to fear from arbitrariness there; but that is one of the reasons why, when a republic turns into a monarchy, it usually falls under so cruel a despotism. There the non-elected and irremovable magistrate keeps the powers of the elected and temporary one.

Association to punish a crime.

If I had to class human miseries, I should put them in this order:
1st. Illnesses.
2nd. Death.
3rd. Doubt.
Life is neither a pleasure nor a grief. It is a serious duty imposed on us, to be seen through to the end to our credit.

* * *

Philadelphia (25th October 1831)

When the detractors of popular governments claim that in many points of internal administration, the government of one man is better than the government of all, they are, in my view, incontestably right. It is in fact rare for a strong government not to show more consistency in its undertakings, more perseverance, more sense of the whole, more accuracy in detail, and more discretion even in the choice of men, than the multitude. So a republic is less well administered than an enlightened monarchy; republicans who deny that, miss the point; but if they said that it was not there that one must look for the advantages of democracy, they would win back the initiative. The wonderful effect of republican governments (where they can subsist) is not in presenting a picture of *regularity* and *methodical order* in a people's administration, but in the *way of life*. Liberty does not carry out each of its undertakings with the same perfection as an intelligent despotism, but in the long run it produces more than the latter. It does not always and in all circumstances give the

155

peoples a more skilful and faultless government; but it infuses throughout the body social an activity, a force and an energy which never exist without it, and which bring forth wonders.[1] It is there that one must look for its advantages.

* * *

(25th October 1831)

'The people is always right', that is the dogma of the republic just as, 'the king can do no wrong', is the religion of monarchic states. It is a great question to decide whether the one is more false than the other: but what is very sure is that neither the one nor the other is true.

Mr. *Washington Smith*[2] told me yesterday that almost all the crimes in America were due to the abuse of alcoholic drinks. 'But,' said I, 'why do you not put a duty on brandy?'

'Our legislators have often thought about it,' he answered. 'But are afraid of a revolt, and besides the members who voted a law like that would be very sure of not being re-elected, the drinkers being in a majority and temperance unpopular.'

Yesterday also another Mr. Smith, a very respected Quaker, told me: 'The Negroes have the right to vote at elections, but they cannot go to the Poll without being ill treated.'

'And why', said I, 'is the law not carried out on their behalf?'

He answered me: 'The laws have no force with us when public opinion does not support them. Now the people is imbued with very strong prejudices against the Negroes, and the magistrates feel that they have not the strength to enforce laws which are favourable to the latter.'

Since I have been in America I have almost got proof that all the enlightened classes are opposed to General Jackson, but the people holds to him and he has numbers in his favour.

Today, 24th October 1831,[3] I took part in a meeting held to commemorate Penn's landing on the American continent . . . [4] years ago.

* * *

[1] Var: and which throughout all time has made the greatest nations.

[2] Cf. Pierson, *op. cit.*, pp. 459 f. The same conversation is noted under the heading *Negroes* in alphabetic notebook 2, pp. 224–226.

[3] There is a contradiction between this date and that of 25th October given at the beginning of this section. [4] A gap in the manuscript.

Pocket Notebook Number 3

(28th October 1831)

One of the chief reasons that support morals in America among all above the simple people, is the spirit of equality which prevails there. Even with us, where morals are more relaxed, a man of the upper classes who dishonoured a girl of the same classes, or who, introduced into the family by the trust of the parents, debauched their daughter, that man would be lost in reputation. Now that upper class in America includes everyone who has something to live on and has had a decent education.

* * *

Baltimore (29th October 1831)

We arrived here yesterday. Today we attended the fourth and last horse-race that takes place at this time of year. The horses were fine, but the *jockeys* ridiculously dressed. There were many people in carriages and on horseback. But, all in all, it was not yet like one in Europe. A Negro having ventured to come on to the ground with some whites, one of those gave him a shower of blows with his cane without that causing any surprise to the crowd or to the Negro himself.

Yesterday we went to a large subscription ball given on account of the races; we as foreigners paid nothing, but the Americans paid 5 dollars each. The company was brilliant; the women were remarkably pretty, but dressed in an odd way.

This ball can give an idea of American society. Money is the only form of social distinction; but see how arrogantly it classifies individuals. In France one would scarcely have dared to put so high an entrance charge on a public meeting; it would have been felt as insolent pretension on the part of rich people to separate themselves from the rest.

I have seen here a book with the laws of the United States relating to trade. I must have that book.

* * *

(1st November 1831)

How can one be in doubt about the pernicious influence of military glory in a republic? What determines the people's choice

157

in favour of General Jackson who, as it would seem, is a very mediocre man? What still guarantees him the votes of the people in spite of the opposition of the enlightened classes? The battle of New Orleans. And yet that battle was a very ordinary feat of arms, and the people who so allows itself to be captivated is the most anti-military, the most prosaic and the least emotional that there is on earth.

Number and proportion of *commitments* and *acquittals* in the State of Pennsylvania and New York: see the letter written by Mr. Ed. Lewingston (? Livingston) to Roberts Vaux on . . .[1] 1828, page 12 *in fine*.

* * *

(*3rd November 1831*)

Birth has kept a certain influence in America. Men who bear names celebrated in the history of the colonies, or names made famous by the War of Independence, are rather freely called to great positions, especially positions of honour. So in Massachusetts the Governor is Mr. Lionel Lincoln, and the Lieutenant-Governor Mr. Winthrop, both of them descended from the first governors of the colony. In the State of New York the Lieutenant-Governor is Mr. Livingston, descended from the greatest family of the country. In Maryland the Governor is Mr. Howard, son of the well-known Colonel Howard, and the representative of one of the most ancient families. All these gentlemen are very ordinary individuals, and clearly owe their promotion to nothing but their names. The people is attracted by those intellectual distinctions from which it feels it has nothing to fear. Birth speaks to its imagination without arousing its envy. It does not feel the same about wealth. Rich men are seldom the people's candidates. It does not persecute them, but leaves them on one side.

* * *

Baltimore (*4th November 1831*)

Mr. Howard,[2] a very distinguished engineer of this country, told me today that he had been sent (I do not know whether by

---

[1] A gap in the manuscript.   [2] Cf. Pierson, op. cit., p. 508.

the government or by a company) to look into the possibility of joining the Great Lakes to the Mississippi by a canal. This was the result of his researches: from Lake Michigan to the point where the Illinois river is navigable for steamboats is a distance of 95 miles. The level of the Illinois river is 150 feet below that of Lake Michigan. To get the water to flow from Lake Michigan on that side, it is only necessary to cut through a hill 25 miles long, whose greatest height above the level of Michigan is only 13 feet. It is true that there is a stratum of stone to cut through. Nonetheless it is one of the earliest canal projects that could offer itself. If it is carried out one day, the Great Lakes which already have several channels of communication with the Atlantic, will also have easy communication with the Gulf of Mexico. From the bottom of the lake one could easily go down to New Orleans, travelling more than 1,500 leagues by inland navigation.

Today, 4th November, we saw in an Alms-house a Negro whose madness is extraordinary: there is at Baltimore a slave-trader who, it seems, is much feared by the black population. The Negro of whom I speak imagines that this man sticks close to him day and night and snatches away bits of his flesh. When we came into his cell, he was lying on the floor, rolled up in the blanket which was his only clothing. His eyes rolled in their orbits and his face expressed both terror and fury. From time to time he threw off his blanket, and raised himself on his hands shouting: 'Get out, get out, don't come near me.' It was a terrible sight. This man is one of the most beautiful Negroes I have ever seen, and he is in the prime of life.

* * *

(*4th November 1831*)

Mr. Cruse,[1] a very talented man and editor of one of the principal newspapers in Baltimore, told me today: With us there is no power external to the people; whatever it wants, one must submit. The militia itself is the people, and is of no avail when it shares or excuses the passions of the majority. We saw a terrible instance of this twenty years ago. It was the time of the war against England, a war which was very popular in the South. A journalist ventured violently to attack war

[1] Cf. Pierson, op. cit., p. 505.

feeling. The people assembled, broke his presses, and attacked the house where he and his friends (belonging to the first families in the town) had shut themselves up. An attempt was made to call out the militia; they refused to march against the rioters, and did not answer the call. The municipal authorities could only save the journalist and his friends by sending them to prison. The people did not feel itself satisfied. That night it assembled and marched against the prison. Again one tried to assemble the militia, but without being able to do so. The prison was taken by storm; one of the prisoners was killed on the spot and the rest left for dead; one wanted to make prosecutions, but the juries acquitted the offenders.

*   *   *

(*6th November 1831*)

As far as I can judge a republic does not seem to be as natural and appropriate a social state for the South as for the North of the United States. Does that depend on the difference in education existing between the North and the South, or on the physical constitution and the differences of character resulting therefrom in the two parts? Or rather that the enlightened classes, still little accustomed to the government of democracy in the South, more easily allow secrets to be revealed, which the same classes in the North would keep hidden? That is something which I still do not know. What is certain is that my impression is not the same in the two parts of the Union. The North presents me, externally at least, with the picture of a strong, regular, durable government, perfectly suited to the physical and moral state of things. In the South there is in the way things are run something feverish, disordered, revolutionary and passionate, which does not give the same sense of strength and durability.

Why, as civilisation spreads, do outstanding men become fewer? Why, when attainments are the lot of all, do great intellectual talents become rarer? Why, when there are no longer lower classes, are there no more upper classes? Why, when knowledge of how to rule reaches the masses, is there a lack of great abilities in the direction of society? America clearly poses these questions. But who can answer them?

Throughout the whole of this affair, the tone and language of Jackson was that of a heartless despot, alone intent on preserving his power. Ambition is his crime and will yet prove his curse.

Intrigue is his vocation, and will yet overthrow and confound him. Corruption is his element and will yet re-act upon him to his utter dismay and confusion. He has been a successful as well as a desperate political gangster, but the hour of retribution is at hand; he must disgorge his winnings, throw away his false dice, and seek the hermitage, there to blaspheme and execrate his folly, for to repent is not a virtue within the capacity of his heart to obtain.[1]

* * *

Vincennes Gazette (12th November 1831)

Today I met on the Ohio a great landowner from the State of Illinois. He painted me a wonderful picture of the prosperity of the country, and added that it was being peopled at a great rate. 'Do many Europeans go there?' I asked.

'No,' he answered, 'the greatest number of emigrants come from Ohio.'

Is not that fact characteristic of the nature of the country and the character of its inhabitants? It is only forty years ago that Ohio began to get peopled. The State Capital has only existed for thirty years, and already the new generation does not find enough opportunities of getting rich there, and is setting out on the march to lands newer still.

* * *

(21st–25th November 1831)

If nature has not given each people an indelible national character one must at least admit that physical or political causes have made a people's spirit adopt habits which are very difficult to eradicate, even though it is no longer subject to the influence of any of those causes. We have seen in Canada Frenchmen who have been living for seventy years under English rule, and remain exactly like their former compatriots in France. In the midst of them lives an English population which has lost nothing of its national character.

[1] The last two paragraphs are in English in the manuscript.

Not less than fifty years ago, colonies of Germans came to settle in Pennsylvania. They have kept intact the spirit and ways of their fatherland. Round them is all the agitation of a nomadic population, with whom the desire to get rich knows no limits, who are attached to no place, held back by no tie, but go off everywhere where the prospect of fortune beckons. Immobile in the midst of this general movement, the German limits his desires to bettering his position and that of his family little by little. He works unendingly, but leaves nothing to chance. He gets rich surely, but slowly; he sticks to his domestic hearth, encloses his happiness within his horizon and shows no curiosity to know what there is beyond his last furrow.

*   *   *

On the Ohio (*25th November 1831*)

Ohio, State without national character, mixture of Europe, of the North and the South and of the East of the United States. With even fewer prejudices than any other State. This is proved by the laws, civil, criminal and political.[1]

*   *   *

Cincinnati (*1st December 1831*)

Growth of Cincinnati. Its causes. Its appearance. Interest of the provinces of the West. Figure they ought to cut in the Union. Their future destinies. Difference made by slavery to prosperity and civilisation, illustrated by Kentucky and Ohio.[2]

Public education; care of the United States in forming new States.

Criminal laws.

Blacks *legally* driven out of Ohio, *in fact* living there.

Are there *political* innovations?

There are in *civil* and *criminal* matters.

*   *   *

[1] See notebook E, pp. 261–265.
[2] See non-alphabetic notebooks 2 and 3, p. 97; and notebook E, pp. 266–269.

Pocket Notebook Number 3

(4th December 1831)

Independently of several other causes, what gives such a similarity to all the parts of the Union, is the high degree of civilisation that prevails there. If ever the world comes to be completely civilised, the human race will in appearance form only one people. Reason, like virtue, does not bend at all in different climates, and does not vary with temperaments and the nature of places. It is one, it is inflexible. Everywhere it tends to the same end, and progresses by the same roads. All the peoples then that take reason for the guide of their actions, must have great points of resemblance: to think, to believe, to feel the same things in a whole lot of circumstances. On the other hand, when a people takes as its model a certain ideal perfection peculiar to it, when it is concerned to do as its fathers did and not to do the best possible, when it follows customs and not reasonings, it stays completely itself and time only adds to the differences that separate it from its neighbours. Does not the change that takes away from a people its originality and its physiognomy, also take away part of its nationality and its individual vigour? That is what seems to me to be in question.

*　*　*

(26th December)

I imagine that often what one calls the character of a people, is nothing but the character inherent in its social state.

So the English character might well be nothing but the aristocratic character. What tends to make me think that is the immense difference between the English and their descendants in America.

Political parties when they come to birth in a people, have for some time and in some respects the attributes of youth. Their passions and their excesses have something of generosity, of the extreme, and of devotion in them. But the political parties in a nation, long stirred by factions, take on a character of dishonourable selfishness, a sort of spirit of misanthropy, something in a word that tastes of disenchantment and cold passions, and belongs to old age.

(31st December 1831)

*　*　*

Pocket Notebook Number 3

A day at New Orleans (1st January 1832).

Arrival at New Orleans. Forest of ships. Mississippi 300 feet deep. External appearance of the town. Beautiful houses. Huts. Muddy, unpaved streets. Spanish architecture: flat roofs; English: bricks, little doors; French: massive carriage-entrances. Population just as mixed. Faces with every shade of colour. Language French, English, Spanish, Creole. General French look, but all the same notices and commercial announcements mostly in English. Industrial and commercial world *American*. Visit to Mr. Mazureau.[1] We fall into the midst of children, sweets and toys. To the theatre in the evening. *Le Maçon*.[2] Strange scene presented by the auditorium: dress circle, white; upper circle, grey. Coloured women very pretty. White ones among them, but a trace of African blood. Gallery black. Stalls: we felt we were in France; noisy, blustering, bustling, gossiping, and a thousand leagues from the United States. We left at 10 o'clock. Ball of the quadroons. Strange sight: all the men white, all the women coloured or at least with African blood.

Only link produced by immorality between the two races. A sort of bazaar. Coloured women destined in a way by the law to concubinage. Incredible laxity of morals. Mothers, young girls, children at the ball. Yet another fatal consequence of slavery. Multitude of coloured people at New Orleans. Small number in the North. Why?

Why of all the European races in the New World is the English race the one that has most preserved the purity of its blood, and has mixed the least with the native peoples? Apart from strong reasons depending on national character and temperament, there is a special cause for the difference. Spanish America was peopled by adventurers drawn by thirst for gold, who, transplanted alone to the other side of the Atlantic, found themselves in some sort forced to contract unions with the women of the people of the land where they were living. The English colonies were peopled by men who escaped from their country from reasons of religious zeal, and whose object in coming to the New World, was to live there cultivating the

[1] Tocqueville has given an account of this visit in pocket notebook number 4, pp. 171-173, and notes the conversation in non-alphabetic notebook 3, pp. 101 ff. See also Appendix, pp. 383–384.

[2] No doubt Auber's *Le Maçon*, first produced at the Opéra-comique in 1825.

land. They came with wives and children, and could form a complete society on the spot.

(*3rd January 1832*)

* * *

(*3rd January 1832*)

I found out today that in the course of the year 1828, 1,000 sailing ships and 770 steamships entered the port of New Orleans. The number increases every year.

Conversation with a lawyer whose name I have forgotten. 2nd January 1832.

Jury: effort of the Americans to introduce the jury in civil matters into the institutions of Louisiana. Difficulty in applying it to French laws. Has not yet become established as a habit. Dislike of being a juror. Resulting delay for the cases. Their habitual incompetence.

When a whole people proclaims that an institution is good, when all parties recognise its usefulness, and that not just at one time or in one place, but throughout long centuries and in all parts of the world where offshoots of that people have settled, and no matter what political laws they have adopted, it is difficult to admit that that institution might be vicious. That is what has happened about the use of a jury in civil cases.

* * *

Effect of direct and indirect election in America. Good choices, bad choices.

From Mobile to Berkeley	13m
from B. to Montgomery	180
from M. to Fort Mitchell	90
from F. to Milledgeville	150
from M. to Augusta	95
from A. to Charleston	150
	678

(*4th January 1832*)

Bad choices in little republics are partly accounted for by the fact that men of distinction do not canvass for honours or enter on a political career; this disadvantage seems to me more than compensated for by the absence of great excitement and the upheavals brought about by lust for power.

* * *

(*4th January 1832*)

The greatest merit of the government of the United States is that it is *powerless* and *passive*. In the actual state of things, in order to prosper America has no need of skilful direction, profound designs or great efforts. But need of liberty and still more liberty. It is to nobody's *interest to abuse it*. What point of comparison is there between such a state of affairs and our own?

* * *

[1]The cells full; ceaseless punishment needed; 11 blacks and 2 whites today in the cells.

494 convicts in all, men, women and children, mostly for more than one year. Some for less for the county of Philadelphia. Wash Street Prison, is a mixture of State and County Prison.

Men twenty-five years old in the dormitories.

For the last five years the prison has just covered its expenses.

Only 5 sick in the men's hospital.

6 women. Average of deaths: 6 per cent.

No contractor.

The trade of weaver is more productive than the guild of
.[2]

Average of detention punishments: 8 per week.

Baltimore. The dignity keepers [*sic*]:[3] one agent, one clerk, one physician.

Houses of Correction.

Interview with the Director.

Q. After what age is there little hope for reform?

A. For the boys fifteen years old. Fourteen for the girls.

---

[1] The following notes are in pencil at the end of the notebook; they are preceded by a drawing and some illegible lines.

[2] One word illegible.　　　　　　　　[3] The word in English in the manuscript.

Q. What is the principal cause that sends children to the house of correction?

A. Misfortune. The bad behaviour of parents.

Pittsburgh.
190 cells—convicts 64.
Costs 186,000 dollars.
Bad position. Far from the river.
Only 4 convicts converted.

Pocket Notebooks 4 and 5

Faith seems exhausted, but interest remains.

(*6th January 1832*) *Conversation with a lawyer from Montgomery*
Advantage of restricting the electoral qualification. Bad choice absorbed. *A kind of fatality for the leaders*.[1] Wrong idea spreading that the people is able to do everything.

Bad state of the judiciary in Kentucky, Tennessee, Mississippi, Alabama and Georgia. Bar slight exceptions the same institutions as in the North, but bad choice of men. Chosen by the legislature, advised [?] by the executive. Divided responsibility. Coterie of petty political leaders; civil commotions due to bad state of justice; first cause of the brutish manners in this part of the Union. No confidence in right; reign of force increasing at an alarming rate. Revealing expression of a man, important in his county, who has been punished. It is a jury taken from a small area, excellent jury for the criminal; for matters of moral appreciation should be bad, partial and of uneven justice.

The men of the South poorer, less persevering, less well educated. No schools. Half or two-thirds cannot read. Religious feeling not only certainly less strong, but runs more to fanaticism. Alabama Methodists against luxury are not so violent as South Carolina.

Mixture of civilisation and of barbarism. Characters of the States of the South. Refined institutions, brutish manners.

At Washington: ask about the past life and profession of all the members of Congress.

Population of adventurers from the *South*, one of the reasons for the brutishness of morals of the new States of the South.

There are in fact in political institutions two sorts of instabi-

[1] In English in the manuscript.

lity which must not be confused. The one affects secondary laws which change with the more or less changing will of the legislator. That can exist in an orderly and well established society. It is often even the necessary consequence of the political constitution of a people. The other affects the very bases of society and the *generating principles* of the laws. That cannot be without troubles and upheavals. The nation that suffers from that is in a state of violence and transition. America provides an instance of the first. For the last forty years we have been tormented by the second. By confusing them, many people form exaggerated fears and hopes, and make inaccurate comparisons.

Knoxville (*8th January 1832*)

* * *

I add that one does not see great political parties and dangerous factions appear except where the second exists. The first brings to birth coteries and not parties, discussions   [1] and not quarrels, noise and not war.

If you want to know whether a people is *settled*, and whether it can or cannot count on the future, consider it under this aspect. Near Montgomery in the State of Alabama, I saw a little sight that made me reflect: outside a planter's house was a charming little white girl (his daughter) whom a young Indian girl was holding in her arms as she lavished on her quite maternal caresses. To the side was a Negress who was amusing the child. The child's slightest movements showed a sense of the superiority which, in her young experience, lifted her already above the two companions whose care and caresses she accepted with a sort of feudal condescension. Crouched in front of her and watching her slightest gestures, the Negress seemed strangely divided between the love and the respectful fear which her young mistress inspired in her, whereas in the very lavishness of the Indian girl's tenderness there was something free, something even a little savage, which contrasted oddly with the submissive posture and humble manners of her companion. Something which I could not see having attracted her attention in the wood, she got up abruptly, pushed the child rather roughly on one side, and without saying anything dived into the undergrowth.

[1] A gap in the manuscript.

Universal suffrage, which has wonderful advantages, can only exist among a people for whom government, more especially good government, is only a secondary interest. I think that that government cannot be the regulator of society.

Instinct of the French for military glory. One of the pre-eminent characteristics of their race. Bonaparte in Canada and in Louisiana. His son, Flexibility. Inflexibility.

[1]What I call great political parties: those which are attached to the generating principles and not to their consequences, to general conceptions and not to particular cases, to ideas and not to men. Such parties generally have nobler features, more generous passions, clearer conventions, and a more frank look than the others. The private interest which always plays a great part in political passions, is there more skilfully concealed under the veil of public interest, and sometimes even succeeds in escaping the sight of those whom it animates and drives to action.

Little political parties are without the political faith of the others. On the contrary there is a character of selfishness which shows at every minute and comes ostensibly into operation in all their acts. Their language is violent and vague, their progress timid and uncertain. The means they employ are wretched, as are the ends they seek. The great political parties often make one feel pity for humanity, the little ones scorn. The former overturn society, the latter disturb society more than they shake it. But both, the one and the other, have one feature in common. They hardly ever employ, to reach their ends, means which reason completely approves. They make a show of strong bombastic passions.

There are men of integrity in almost all parties, but there is no party of integrity.

America has had great parties, but there are not any more now. There has been a great gain in happiness, but, in morality, I doubt it. In the whole world I do not see a more wretched and shameful sight than that presented by the different coteries (they do not deserve the name of parties) which now divide the Union. In broad daylight one sees all the petty, shameful passions disturbing them which generally one is careful to keep

[1] Cf. notebook E, pp. 238–239.

hidden at the bottom of the human heart. As for the interest of the country, no one thinks about it, and if one talks about it that is just for form's sake. The parties put it at the head of their deed of association, just as their fathers did, to conform to an old usage. It has no more to do with the rest of the work than the royal permission which our fathers printed on the first page of their books.

It is pitiful to see what a deluge of coarse insults, what petty slander and what gross calumnies, fill the newspapers that serve as organs for the parties, and with what shameful disregard of social decencies they daily drag before the tribunal of public opinion the honour of families and the secrets of the domestic hearth.

It is the representative of France. Honour to the flag whatever be its colours.

We had[1] if I am not mistaken, twenty-one letters for New Orleans. It would indeed be a difficult task to put all this formidable correspondence in order, and to classify each letter according to the importance of the person to whom it is addressed. But we are among those who think that, however much of a hurry one is in, one cannot make too many sacrifices in favour of logic. Having settled the order, we directed our steps towards the house of Mr. Mazureau who had been described to us as the eagle of the New Orleans bar, and who speaks French, an advantage we have come to appreciate during our travels. We had a thousand troubles and wasted endless time in finding his house, the houses being unnumbered, or the numbers not following at all; 2 came before 1 and 10 followed 90. That is an arithmetic in use by the corporation of New Orleans to which we were not yet accustomed. Besides that served to give us a true respect for the Consul; to be able actually to conceive of good government in a city where the stranger cannot find his way!

We arrived at last. The Negro who opened the door for us and of whom we asked if we could see Mr. Mazureau, looked fixedly at us at first without seeming to understand us. Finally he said to us:

'How! Sir, today?'

[1] Cf. Appendix.

'Yes, certainly fellow, why not?'

There was a fair amount of energy in our answer, but not a word of argument: but the slave seemed convinced, and lowering his head in a submissive way, opened the drawing-room door.

The eagle of New Orleans, wrapped up in his dressing-gown, and sitting beside what in Louisiana is called a French fire-place, and in France would be called a rustic one, was at that very moment receiving the congratulations of his family united around him. One could see his children, grandchildren, nephews, first cousins once removed, even cousins' children, sweets, jam, toys, the whole family picture complete. It was only left for us to register emotion, to cry even with feeling as all the eighteenth-century philosophers do in their books. Joy seemed to reign in every face, concord in every heart. We are such good friends on the day of new year gifts!

For ourselves, we stopped struck with astonishment at the sight. Finally a ray of light reached even us. We understood the embarrassment of the Consul, the astonishment of the Negroes, those good Negroes whom we had treated as churls. To bring a letter of introduction on New Year's Day! What unseemly behaviour! Alas! where is the happy time when I would sooner have forgotten my own name than the advent of the 1st of January!

At the sight of his unwelcome visitors, Mr. Mazureau got up quickly and came towards the door, enveloping in the eddies of his dressing-gown two grandchildren who, lost in the middle of this dark labyrinth, let out piercing cries in our direction. In our haste we upset I do not know how many of the toys that covered the floor and made a cardboard dog bark, which set a real pug barking and dashing for our legs. Finally we did meet in the middle of the sitting-room and expressed our mutual pleasure at making each other's acquaintance.

It is said that to make a State stable one must give influence to the rich and not to the poor, and that is right. But the reason is added that the rich have an interest in preserving their great fortunes which the poor have not. That in most cases is not true. Often a poor man has even more interest in keeping a little fortune on which he can live, than a rich man in keeping a large one which makes him enjoy life. It seems to me that if the former want to change the existing state, it is not because they are poor, it is because things are bad for them; if the latter like the *status quo*, it is not because they are rich, but because they are happy. Add that the poor have less hatred, and that they know it would be difficult for the rich to harm them.

Mandates legally imperative, great and fatal innovation in the West. The greatest advantage of *representative* republics, say the supporters of that form of government, is that the people are only called on to judge and appreciate a man, not to administer nor to rule. That in itself is not completely true; for the people in judging the man, is more or less called on to pronounce on the line of action which he should pursue. But they have no immediate responsibility there, and that already is a great point gained; but, if one were to choose a deputy of the people in order to impose on him a narrow obligation to act in such and such a way, the people puts itself in the place of its representative and one falls back into the chaos of the republics of antiquity.

(*12th January 1832*)

* * *

(*12th January 1832*)
About oaths.

The Americans make great use of oaths. There is no public official, however unimportant, who does not swear faithfully to fulfil the duties of his office. The oath is always accompanied by the English formula, 'and so help me God', which in some sense makes the divinity one of the contracting parties, and makes him guarantor of the execution of the contract. But no oath is required from the electors, such is the respect felt due to freedom of opinion in this great act of political life.

Note however that, as in America there is a legal and known means of reforming the Constitution, obedience to that Constitution, while it exists, is a strict obligation and one perfectly in accord with the dogma of the sovereignty of the people. As for imposing an oath of obedience to the Constitution on those who are assembled to choose a constituent body, that is an absurdity which a logical people such as the Americans would reject with scorn, besides in their opinion it would constitute

a tyranny imposed by one party on another, and they understand the theory of the sovereignty of the people too well to
permit that.

In France where the superior power of the Constitution is not
clearly defined and where the extraordinary means to remedy
its defects are not indicated, where the legislative body is of
necessity invested with the right to revise Constitutional laws
(a right which ought always to exist somewhere), in France, I
say, we are at each election in some sort both a *legislature* and a
convention, we insist on the oath which the Americans do not
require even for those who are appointing the legislature. That
is to say that we make a man swear obedience to a law, while
allowing him to appoint someone who could receive from him
the legal assignment to modify or abolish that law. But with us
the principles of liberty are still in their infancy, as badly understood by those who urge as by those who attack them.

The Americans allow proof by oath in civil cases where it is
not contrary to a written document. The men of law to whom
I have spoken, claim that this rule does not here lead to the
serious abuses that one might fear. I am inclined to believe that;
there is something in the complete confidence in the law which
leads men not to take advantage of it. Besides respect for truth
thus becomes a social necessity of the first importance, and one
felt by all. But when the legislator strikes depositions in certain
cases with a presumption of untruth, he diminishes their value
in all others. There is no better means of making men untrust-
worthy than showing them that one mistrusts them. I take it as a
very happy circumstance for a people when proof by witnesses
has come to be something accepted in its habits or morals.
But it would be very dangerous to introduce it anywhere where
it has not always existed. Besides it makes the function of a jury
in civil cases necessary. The English owe the preservation of
proof by witness, as of many other fine institutions, to customary
law, common law.[1]

* * *

(*12th January*)

The jury is the most direct application of the principle of the
sovereignty of the people. Everywhere where a power outside

[1] The last two words are in English in Tocqueville's manuscript.

the people wishes to establish it and to make it function in good faith, it will be destroyed by it. There is in fact no power outside the people except a powerful aristocracy which without ostensibly falsifying the institution of the jury, can exist concurrently with it, for it is only a powerful aristocracy which could hope to make itself master of the juries, and is composed of sufficient numbers itself to constitute the jury. Then the jury is the most terrible weapon of which tyranny could make use. I am sure that the juries in England are not selected, as in America, from all the classes. Bonaparte was very consistent in making the jury depend   ,[1] and very clever in not destroying it altogether. The jury would have ended by killing the Restoration. The great mistake of Louis XVIII was to want to make a crowd of irreconcilable principles work together.

Many people think that Bonaparte was the enemy of all forms of liberty. In that they do not do him justice. Bonaparte's great and enlightened mind saw clearly the advantages that spring from civil liberty, and he always showed himself liberal and generous in that respect. But at the same time he has always been seen as the greatest enemy of political liberty which hampered him in his doctrine. Bonaparte felt for liberty the thought-out hatred of an ambitious and dominating genius, and not the hostile reactions and blind activity of a pirate.

* * *

(*12th January*)

He knew very exactly what he could hope and fear from liberty. That in France for (? 200)[2] years we have had anarchy and despotism in all their forms, but never anything that looked like a republic.

If Royalists could see the internal functioning of a well-ordered republic, the deep respect professed there for acquired rights, the power of those rights over the crowds, the religion of law, the real, effective liberty enjoyed there, the true reign of the majority, the natural ease with which everything progresses, they would see that they were including under a single name diverse states that have nothing analogous between them.

---

[1] Illegible word.   [2] The figure is uncertain.

Our republicans on their side would feel that what we have called the republic, has never been anything but a monstrosity that one does not know how to classify, a   [1] covered in blood and filth [?], dressed in rags[2] to the noise of the quarrels of antiquity: and what does it matter to me whether tyranny is clothed in a royal mantle or in a Tribune's toga? If I feel its hand heavy on me? When Danton had wretched men whose only crime was not to think as he did, slaughtered in the prisons, was that liberty? When later Robespierre sent Danton to the scaffold because he had shown himself his rival, there was justice in that no doubt, but was that liberty? When the majority of the Convention proscribed the minority, when the arbitrary power of proconsuls took from citizens their goods, their children and their life, when an opinion was a crime, and a wish expressed in the sanctuary of the domestic hearth merited death, was that liberty? But, some one might say, I am looking into the blood-stained annals of the Terror. Let us pass over the time of *necessary* severities, shall I see liberty reign in the time when the Directory destroyed the newspapers, and sent the members of the majority that was going to overturn it, to die in the wilds of Guiana [*sic*]? When Bonaparte as Consul substituted the power, the tyranny of one man for the tyranny of factions? Again was that liberty, was that a republic? No, in France we have seen anarchy and despotism in all its forms, but nothing that looked like a republic.

*   *   *

(*13th January*)

[10 lines too fragmentary to be translated].

One of the most striking features of American institutions is that they form a perfectly logical chain. That is a merit to which very few peoples can aspire, and which, when one examines it close up, does not perhaps contribute as much to success as a crowd of *profoundly* superficial minds pretend. Logic and uniformity in laws are two things about which a great fuss is made, much less because of their excellence than because of the weakness, mediocre intellects have for discovering their absence, and the ease with which they find they can invent theories in which

---

[1] A gap in the manuscript.   [2] Variant: tinsel.

these two merits are found. The fact is that there are pretty few peoples who can be understood from one end to the other. The special reason that has put the Americans in a state to be understood, is that they have been able to build their social edifice from a clean start.

If it be true that each people has a special character independent of its political interest, just as each man has one independent of his social position, one might say that America gives the most perfect picture, for good and for ill, of the special character of the English race. The American is the Englishman left to himself. The picture follows of what I mean by the English character. . . .[1] All that is brilliant, generous, splendid, and magnificent in the British character, all that is aristocratic and not English.

Spirit coldly burning, serious, tenacious, selfish, cold, frozen imagination, having respect for money, industrious, proud and rationalist.

* * *

Conversation with Mr. Poinsett, 13th, 14th and 15th January 1832.[2]

Nullification: nullificators or rather their secret motives. Their inability to break the Union: doubtful majority in South Carolina, not forming a party at all in the other States. South Carolina musters 700,000 whites. Tariff oppressive in some respects, but imaginary cause of real passions. Difference between the social condition of the South and North: causes [3] and slaves. Almost every ten years the South loses representatives and the North gains them. Causes of jealousies and hatreds. But the South is progressing. Why it has no ships, no working class, slaves, bad reason for the manufactures. Slaves, evil which one cannot remedy. Transition impossible, enormous expense to which no one would ever agree, excessive. Useless tax on importation. Little danger in slavery; if sufficiently educated to cause a serious revolt, educated enough to see that it could not succeed. Mulatto not very dangerous as

[1] Dots in the manuscript.
[2] See non-alphabetic notebook 3, p. 89 and 110–119, and notebook E, pp. 236–237.
[3] Word illegible.

nearer white than black. Free black dangerous from example. Sense of the evils caused by slavery and of the possibility of doing without it, which is growing throughout the South. Slavery continually ebbing back towards the South. Hope of seeing it disappear altogether in some centuries. Slave trade. 300,000 blacks exported from Africa, read in the registers of the Chamber of Commerce last year.

Mexico. Remains of a civilisation perhaps more advanced than that of the Spaniards. Attempt at great republics made in South America and in Mexico, impossible. Necessity of federal system for great republics. That of Mexico copied from the United States. In progress, hope of success. One must not judge the Spaniards too severely. Coming out of the sixteenth century. Race much less mixed than people say. White skin, nobility. No blacks. Indians equal before the law. Race in fact ignorant and poor. The most beautiful and delightful country in the world. Mistake of the European powers in expecting an outlet, there must first be needs. Dispossession of the clergy. The people even more against them than the government, but began the Revolution to seize their goods.

Indians in the United States who cannot adapt themselves to civilisation, will disappear. Can only civilise themselves with the help of half-castes.

Banks very useful for the United States where capital is lacking. Bank of New Orleans. Lax view of bankruptcies at least where there has not been fraud. Industrial brigandage.

Roads. Doubt whether central government has the right. Sometimes by the States. More often by the counties. Badly kept up. Substantial loans in the localities. *Turnpikes* better system. Difficulty of getting a people used to them. Ineffectiveness of the law which allows help to counties.

President: agitation of newspapers and interests. Mass of the people indifferent. President without power. Congress which governs.

Penitentiary system: An attempt. Bad for the South. Very few white criminals. Crimes punished in the family. Impossibility for this reason of comparing the South and the North.

There is one class of man who scorns the black more than the white does, that is the mulatto. In that he behaves like the lackeys of great lords, who call the people scum.

There are a thousand reasons which go to support republican liberty in the United States, but few are enough to explain the problem.[1] Society there has been built from a clean slate. There is neither victor nor vanquished to be seen, neither working man nor noble, neither prejudices of birth nor of profession, but the whole of all America is in like case and a republic succeeds only in the United States.

The growth of the Union offers an immense field for human activity, continually diverts it from disturbing the State, and offers an easy prey for industry and work. But in what part of the world could one find more fertile lands, more wonderful wilds, more superb rivers, wealth more inexhaustible and untouched than in South America, and yet South America cannot maintain a republic.

The division of the Union into little States reconciles internal prosperity with national strength, it multiplies political interests, and weakens the spirit of party by dividing it. But Mexico forms a federal republic, and Mexico is still very far from prospering.

There is one great reason which dominates all the others and which, when one has weighed everything, alone sways the balance. The American people taken in mass is not only the most enlightened in the world, but—what I put much higher than that advantage—is the one whose practical political education is the most advanced. It is that truth in which I firmly believe that inspires in me my one hope for the future happiness of Europe.

But this insoluble question always remains: the material and special advantages of the United States would certainly not be enough for them without their high civilisation and experience. Would the latter be enough without the former?

* * *

(*14th January*)

Only an ambitious or a foolish man could, after seeing America, maintain that in the actual state of the world, American political institutions could be applied elsewhere than there. To be convinced of that it is enough to see the different ways in which republicanism is understood and functions in the various States of the Union according to the different degrees of [2]

---

[1] See notebook E, pp. 234–235. [2] One word illegible.

and experience found there. When I speak of their institutions, I mean taken as a whole. There is no people but could usefully adopt some parts of them.

Political liberty is a difficult food to digest. It is only the most robust constitutions that can take it. But when it has been digested, albeit with pain, it gives the whole body social a nerve and an energy which surprises even those who expected the most from it.

America created municipal liberty before it created public liberty. We have done and still do exactly the opposite. Cause of all our ills, we want to erect a column beginning with the capital; to be master-craftsmen before we are apprentices.

One of the causes which singularly militate in favour of the Union [?] is that all the outstanding men and all the great political passions have an interest in supporting it.

Fatal influence of the military spirit and military obedience on liberty.

The Americans do not have virtue (*vertu*), but principles.

VII

Alphabetic Notebook 1

Reasons for the social state and present government in America:

1st. *Their origin:* Excellent point of departure. Intimate mixture of the spirit of religion and liberty. Cold and rationalist race.

2nd. *Their geographical position:* no neighbours.

3rd. *Their commercial and industrial activity.* Everything, even their vices, is now favourable for them.

4th. *The material prosperity* which they enjoy.

5th. *The spirit of religion that prevails:* Republican and democratic religion.

6th. The diffusion of useful knowledge.

7th. Morals very chaste.

8th. Their division into little States. They prove nothing for a large one.

9th. The absence of a great capital where everything is concentrated. Care to avoid it.

10th. Commercial and provincial activity which means that everyone has something to do at home.

B

BANKRUPTCY

Try to find out the number of bankruptcies in the towns.

Bankruptcy: M.   ,[1] a distinguished Philadephia lawyer, told me today (27th October 1831)[2] that the number of declared bankrupts in Philadelphia was about 800 per year. It is true that in America people who are not traders, as well as traders, can go bankrupt.

He added: The need for a bankruptcy law is universally

---

[1] A gap in the manuscript.   [2] See non-alphabetic notebook 2, p. 69.

felt among the trading and manufacturing States of the Union. Several have already tried to establish one, but the Supreme Court of the United States having declared that such a law is unconstitutional, it has been necessary to wait for Congress to take the matter up, which it has not yet done. We formerly had a bankruptcy law, but being the work of a party, the party that succeeded it in power repealed it. It is one of the ills of our system of government that matters of general interest are made subservient to political passions, even when the subject in question is not of a nature to excite such passions. The actual state of our legislation in case of bankruptcy, is deplorable. We have no guarantee against fraud. The creditor is continually the victim of his debtor, the scandal of a bankrupt become rich again, without having paid his creditors, is continually repeated.

C

NATIONAL CHARACTER OF THE AMERICANS

Restlessness of character seems to me to be one of the distinctive traits of this people. The American is devoured by the longing to make his fortune; it is the unique passion of his life; he has no memory that attaches him to one place more than another, no inveterate habits, no spirit of routine; he is the daily witness of the swiftest changes of fortune, and is less afraid than any other inhabitant of the globe to risk what he has gained in the hope of a better future, for he knows that he can without trouble create new resources again. So he enters the great lottery of human fate with the assurance of a gambler who only risks his winnings. The same man, we were told, has often tried ten occupations. He has been seen successively a trader, lawyer, doctor and minister of the gospel. In one word, men do not have habits here, and what they see under their eyes prevents them from forming any: 1st. Many have come from Europe and have left behind their habits and their memories there.

2nd. Even those who have long been established in this country have kept this difference of habits. As yet there is no American outlook. Each takes from the association what suits him, and remains as he was.

He has inhabited twenty different places and has nowhere formed ties that hold him; and how could it not be so? Here laws are continually changing, and magistrates succeeding one another; systems of administration triumph turn by turn; nature herself changes more quickly than man.

By a strange inversion of the ordinary order of things, it is nature that changes, while man is unchanging. The same man may give his name to wilds that none has traversed before him; he has been able to fell the first tree in the forest, and build in the midst of the solitude a planter's house round which first a hamlet has formed, and which is now surrounded by a huge city. In the short space between birth and death he has seen all these changes, and a thousand others like him have been able to do so. In his youth he has lived among tribes who now live only in history; during his life rivers have changed or diminished their course, the climate is different from what it was before, and all that is still in his imagination only a first step in an endless career. Howsoever powerful and impetuous the course of history is here, imagination always goes in advance of it, and the picture is never large enough. There is not a country in the world where man more confidently takes charge of the future, or where he feels with more pride that he can fashion the universe to please himself. It is a movement of the mind which can only be compared with that which brought about the discovery of the New World three centuries ago. And in fact one might say that America has been discovered for the second time. And one must not imagine that such thoughts only take shape in a philosopher's head; the artisan thinks them as much as the speculator, the peasant as much as the town-dweller. They belong to every object. They form a part of all feelings; they are palpable, visible, felt and, in some sort, strike all the senses.

Often born under another sky, placed in the middle of an ever moving picture, driven himself by the irresistible torrent that carries all around him along, the American has no time to attach himself to anything, he is only accustomed to change and ends by looking on it as the natural state of man. Much more, he feels the need of it, he loves it, for instability instead of causing disasters for him, seems only to bring forth wonders around him. (The idea of a possible improvement, of a successive and continuous betterment of the social condition, that idea is ever before him in all its facets.)

* * *

Alphabetic Notebook 1

CANADA

(*25th August 1831*)[1]

External appearance: Canada is beyond comparison, of those parts of America which we have visited so far, that which bears the greatest analogy to Europe and, especially, to France. The banks of the Saint Lawrence are perfectly cultivated and covered with houses and villages in every respect like our own. All traces of the wilderness have disappeared; cultivated fields, church towers, and a population as numerous as in our provinces has replaced it.

The towns, Montreal in particular (we have not yet visited Quebec) bear a striking resemblance to our provincial towns. The basis of the population and the immense majority is everywhere French. But it is easy to see that the French are a conquered people. The rich classes mostly belong to the English race. Although French is the language almost universally spoken, the newspapers, the notices and even the shop-signs of French tradesmen are in English. Commercial undertakings are almost all in their hands. They are really the ruling class in Canada. I doubt if this will long be so. The clergy and a great part of the not rich but enlightened classes is French, and they begin to feel their secondary position acutely. The French newspapers that I have read, put up a constant and lively opposition against the English. Up to now the people having few needs and intellectual interests, and leading, in material things, a very comfortable life, has very imperfectly glimpsed its position as a conquered nation and furnished but feeble support to the enlightened classes. But a few years ago the House of Commons, which is almost all French Canadian, has taken measures for a wide extension of education. There is every sign that the new generation will be different from the present generation, and in a few years from now, if the English race is not prodigiously increased by emigration and does not succeed in shutting the French in in the area they now occupy, the two peoples will come up against one another. I do not think that they will ever merge, or that an indissoluble union can exist between them. I still hope

[1] These notes on Canada can be expanded by Tocqueville's conversations recorded in non-alphabetic notebook 1, under the dates of 24th, 26th and 27th August 1831, pp. 40–47.

that the French, in spite of the conquest, will one day form a fine empire on their own in the New World, more enlightened perhaps, more moral and happier than their fathers. At the present moment the division of the races singularly favours domination by England.

* * *

(*27th August 1831*)

The country between Montreal and Quebec seems to be as populous as our fine European provinces. Moreover the river is magnificent. Quebec is on a very picturesque site, surrounded by a rich and fertile countryside. Never in Europe have I seen a more lively picture than that presented by the surroundings of Quebec.

All[1] the working population of Quebec is French. One hears only French spoken in the streets. But all the shop-signs are English; there are only two theatres which are English. The inner part of the town is ugly, but has no analogy with American towns. It strikingly resembles the inner part of our provincial towns.

The villages we saw in the surroundings are extraordinarily like our beautiful villages. Only French is spoken there. The population seems happy and well-off. The race is notably more beautiful than in the United States. The race there is strong, and the women do not have that delicate, febrile look that characterises most of the women of America.

The Catholic religion there has none of those accessories which are attached to it in those countries of the South of Europe where its sway is strongest. There are no monasteries for men, the convents for women are directed towards useful purposes and give examples of charity warmly admired by the English themselves. One sees no Madonnas on the roads. No strange and ridiculous ornaments, no ex-votos in the churches. Religion is enlightened, and Catholicism here does not arouse the hatred or the sarcasms of the Protestants. I own for my part that it satisfies my spirit more than the Protestantism of the United States. The parish priest here is in very deed the shepherd of his flock: he is not at all an entrepreneur of a religious industry like the greater part of American ministers. One must

[1] Beaumont dates this note on 25th August. Cf. *Œuvres*, viii, 253.

either deny the usefulness of clergy, or have such as are in Canada.

I was in the reading-room today. Almost all the newspapers printed in Canada are in English. They are about the size of those of London. I have not read them yet. There is a Quebec paper called the *Gazette*, half-English, half-French; and a completely French paper called *Le Canadien*. These papers are about the size of our French papers. I have read several copies with care: they keep up a violent position against the government and even against everything English. *Le Canadien* has as its epigraph: *Our Religion, our language, our laws.* One could hardly be franker. The contents correspond to that title. Everything that could inflame little or great popular passions against the English is carefully emphasized in this paper. I read an article that said that Canada would never be happy until it had an administration of men of French Canadian birth, principles, ideas and even prejudices, and that if Canada escaped from England it would not be to become English. In the same paper there were some fairly pretty pieces of French verse. There were accounts of prize-givings where the pupils had played *Athalie, Zaire* or *la Mort de César*. In general the style of this paper is vulgar, peppered with Anglicisms and strange turns of phrase. It is very like the papers published in the Canton de Vaud in Switzerland. I have not yet seen in Canada any man of talent, nor any production that gives proof of the same. He who should touch the feelings of the French Canadians and rouse them against the English, is not yet born.

The English and the French merge so little that the latter exclusively keep the name of *Canadiens*, the others continuing to call themselves English.

* * *

Visit to one of the civil courts of Quebec

We came into a large hall divided into tiers crowded with people who seemed altogether French. The British arms were painted in full size on the end of the hall. Beneath them was the judge in robes and bands. The lawyers were ranked in front of him.

When we came into the hall a slander action was in progress. It was a question of fining a man who had called another *pendard* (gallows-bird) and *crasseux* (skinflint). The lawyer argued in English. *Pendard*, he said, pronouncing the word with a thoroughly English accent, 'meant a man who had been hanged.' No, the judge solemnly intervened, but who ought to be. At that, counsel for the defence got up indignantly and argued his case in French: his adversary answered in English. The argument waxed hot on both sides in the two languages, no doubt without their understanding each other perfectly. From time to time the Englishman forced himself to put his argument in French so as to follow his adversary more closely; the other did the same sometimes. The judge, sometimes speaking French, sometimes English, endeavoured to keep order. The crier of the court called for 'silence' giving the world alternatively its English and its French pronunciation. Calm re-established, witnesses were heard. Some kissed the silver Christ on the Bible and swore in French to tell the truth, the others swore the same oath in English and, as Protestants, kissed the other side of the Bible which was undecorated. The customs of Normandy were cited, reliance placed on Denisart,[1] and mention was made of the decrees of the Parliament of Paris and statutes of the reign of George III. After that the judge: 'Granted that the word *crasseux* implies that a man is without morality, ill-behaved and dishonourable, I order the defendant to pay a fine of ten louis or ten pounds sterling.'

The lawyers I saw there, who are said to be the best in Quebec, gave no proof of talent either in the substance or in the manner of what they said. They were conspicuously lacking in distinction, speaking French with a middle-class Norman accent. Their style is vulgar and mixed with odd idioms and English phrases. They say that a man is *chargé* of ten louis meaning that he is asked to pay ten louis. *Entrez dans la boîte*, they shout to a witness, meaning that he should take his plaec in the witness-box.

There is something odd, incoherent, even burlesque in the whole picture. But at bottom the impression made was one of

[1] Denisart (1712–65), procureur of the Châtelet and author of the well-known collection of *Décisions nouvelles et de notions relatives à la jurisprudence*, 6 vol., 1754–56.

sadness. Never have I felt more convinced than when coming
out from there, that the greatest and most irremediable ill for a
people is to be conquered.

* * *

(*28th August 1831*)

Mr. Neilson came to look for us today to take us to see the
country. (As for Mr. Neilson, his character and position, see the
conversation.)[1] This walk could not have given us a more
favourable impression of the French Canadian population. We
found well-cultivated fields and houses redolent of well-being.
We went into several. The main room is furnished with excellent beds; the walls are painted white. The furniture is very
clean. A little mirror, a cross or a few engravings of scriptural
subjects complete the whole. The peasant is strong, well-built,
well-clothed. His welcome has the frank cordiality which the
American lacks; he is polite without servility, and receives you
on a footing of equality but obligingly. Among those we visited
there was even something of distinction in their manners which
struck us. (It is true that we were taken to see the first families
in the village.) All in all this race of men seemed to us inferior
to the Americans in knowledge, but superior in qualities of the
heart. One had no sense here of that *mercantile* spirit which
obtrudes in all the actions and sayings of an American. The
French Canadian's power of reasoning is little cultivated, but
it is simple and straightforward; they undoubtedly have fewer
ideas than their neighbours, but their sensibility seems more
developed; theirs is a life of the heart, the others' of the head.

* * *

(*29th August*)

Today we went on horseback to visit the countryside without
a guide.

In the commune of Beaufort, two leagues from Quebec, we
saw the people coming out of church. Their dress indicated the
greatest well-being. Those who came from a distant hamlet
were returning there by carriage. We broke away into the paths
and gossiped with all the inhabitants whom we met, trying to

[1] Cf. above, pp. 41–47.

turn the talk to serious matters. This is what seemed to come out from these talks:

1st. Up to now great well-being prevails among them. The land in the neighbourhood of Quebec is sold extremely dearly, as dearly as in France, but it also brings great returns.

2nd. The ideas of this population still seem little developed. But they already feel very clearly that the English race is spreading round them in alarming fashion; that they are making a mistake in shutting themselves up in an area instead of spreading over the still free land. Their jealousy is acutely aroused by the daily arrival of newcomers from Europe. They feel that they will end up by being absorbed. One sees that all one says on this subject touches their feelings, but they do not see the remedy clearly. The French Canadians are too much afraid of going out of sight of their church tower; they are not shrewd enough. 'Oh! you are quite right, but what can one do?' That is how they answer. They clearly feel their position as a conquered people, not counting on the goodwill, I would not say of the government, but of the English. All their hopes are fixed on their representatives. They seem to have that exaggerated attachment to them, and especially to Mr. Neilson— 'But he is English,' they said to us, as if in astonishment or regret—which oppressed people generally have for their protector. Several of them seemed perfectly to understand the need for education, and to take lively pleasure in what had just been done to help it on. All in all we felt that this population could be led, although still incapable of leading itself. We are coming to the moment of crisis. If the French Canadians do not wake out of their apathy, in twenty years from now it will be too late to do so. Everything indicates that the awakening of this people is at hand. But if in this effort the middling and upper classes of the French Canadian population abandon the lower classes, and let themselves be carried in the swing with the English, the French race is lost in America. And that would truly be a pity, for there are here all the elements of a great people. The French of America are to the French of France as the Americans are to the English. They have preserved the greater part of the original traits of the national character, and have added more morality and more simplicity. They, like them, have broken free from a crowd of prejudices and false points of departure which cause and will cause all the miseries of Europe. In a word, they have in them all that is needed to create a great memory of France in the New World. But will they ever succeed in completely regaining their nationality? That is what is probable, but, unfortunately, not certain. A man of genius who understood and felt, and was capable of developing the national feeling of the people, would have a wonderful part to play here. He would soon become the most powerful man in the colony. But as yet I do not see him anywhere.

There is already in Quebec a class of men who make a transition between the French and the English: they are Englishmen related to French Canadians, Englishmen discontented with the administration, and Frenchmen in office. This class is represented in the periodicals by the *Gazette de Quebec*, a mixture of French and English, in the political assemblies by Mr. Neilson and probably several others whom we do not know. It is they who rouse my greatest fears for the future of the French Canadians. They rouse neither their jealousy nor their passions. On the contrary their interests are more French Canadian than English, because they are opposed to the government. At bottom, however, they are English in manners, ideas and language. If ever they take the place of the upper classes and of the enlightened classes among the French Canadians, the nationality of the latter will be lost without reprieve. They will vegetate like the people of Lower Britanny in France. Luckily religion puts an obstacle in the way of marriages between the two races, and creates in the clergy an enlightened class which has an interest in speaking French, and in nourishing itself on French literature and ideas.

We were able to notice in our talks with the people of this country, a basis of hatred and jealousy of the lords. But the lords have, so to say, no rights; they are, as much as one can be, of the people, and are almost all reduced to cultivating the soil. But the spirit of equality and democracy is alive there as in the United States, although it is not so rationalistic. I found again at the bottom of the hearts of those peasants the political passions which brought about the Revolution and which are still the cause of all our ills. Here they are inoffensive, or almost so, since nothing stands against them. We thought, too, that we noticed that the peasant did not see the clergy's right to levy the tithe without repugnance, and that he was not without envy in contemplating the wealth which this tax put into the hands of some ecclesiastics. If religion ever loses its sway in Canada, it will have been by that breach that the enemy has come in.

Like the Frenchman, the French Canadian has a gay and lively spirit; there is almost always something pungent in his answers. One day I asked a farmer why the French Canadians allowed themselves to be hemmed in in narrow fields, when they could find fertile, uncultivated lands at twenty leagues from home. 'Why', he answered, 'do you love your wife best, although your neighbour's has more beautiful eyes?' I thought there was real and profound feeling in that answer.

The French papers in Canada every day print little pieces of literature in prose or verse, a thing one would never find in the vast columns of the English papers. The verses are in the old style of French verse writing. It has a simple, naive turn, very far removed from our big words, and the emphasis and affected simplicity of our present-day literature, but revolves on small, old ideas.

* * *

(*31st August 1831*)

We went today with Mr. Neilson and with a French Canadian called M. Niger [?] along the left bank of the Saint Lawrence as far as the village of Saint Thomas 10 leagues from Quebec. That is where the Saint Lawrence widens out to 7 leagues, a width it keeps for 50 leagues. All the countryside we went through was wonderfully fertile; with the Saint Lawrence and the mountains to the North it formed the most complete and magnificent picture. The houses are *universally* well built. They are redolent of comfort and cleanliness. The churches are rich, but rich in very good taste. Their interior decoration would not seem out of place in our towns. Note that it is the commune itself that imposes its own taxes to keep up the church. In this part of Canada one hears no English. All the population is French, and yet when one comes to an inn or a shop, the sign is in English.

* * *

General remarks (1st September 1831)

We have noticed in the talks we have had with several French Canadians that their hatred is directed even more against the government than against the English race in general. The people's instincts are against the English. But many French Canadians of the enlightened classes are not animated, to the extent we had expected, by the wish to keep the trace of their origin intact, and to become a race completely apart. Several of them seemed to us to be near to merging with the English, provided the latter would treat the country's interests as their own. So it is to be feared that with time and especially with the emigration of Irish Catholics, this fusion may take place. And it could not work except to the detriment of the race, language and customs of the French.

But it is certain that:

(1) Lower Canada, luckily for the French race, forms a State apart. Now the French population in Lower Canada is in the proportion of ten to one to the English. It is compact. It has its government and its own Parliament. It really forms the body of a distinct nation. In a Parliament of eighty-four members, there are sixty-four French and twenty English.

(2) Up to now the English have always kept to themselves. They support the government against the mass of the people. All the French newspapers voice opposition, all the English ones support the ministry, with only one exception, *The Vindicator*, at Montreal, and that too was started by French Canadians.

(3) In the towns the English and the French Canadians form two societies. The English make a parade of great luxury; none of the French Canadians have more than very limited wealth; thence jealousy and small-town bickerings.

(4) The English have all the export trade and the main controls of internal trade in their hands. Yet another cause of jealousy.

(5) The English are daily getting possession of lands that the French Canadians regard as reserved for their race.

(6) Finally the English in Canada show all the traits of their character, and the French Canadians have kept all the traits of French character.

So the odds are strongly in favour of Lower Canada finishing up with an entirely French population. But they will never be a numerous people. Everything around them will become English. It will be a drop in the ocean. I am very much afraid that, as Mr. Neilson said in his frank, brisk way, fate has in fact pronounced and North America will be English.

* * *

(*2nd September 1831*)

We have seen a great many ecclesiastics since we have been in Canada. They clearly seem to us to be the leading class among the French Canadians. All those we have seen are knowledgeable, polite and well educated. They speak a pure French. In general they have more distinction than most of our French parish priests. One sees in their talk that they are *completely French Canadian*. They are united in heart and interest with the people and talk very sensibly about their needs. But they usually seemed to have feelings of *loyalty* towards the King of England and generally to support the principle of legitimacy. But one of them said to me: 'We have everything to hope now, the ministry is *democratic*.' Now they always put up opposition, and they would certainly rebel if the government became tyrannical. *All in all*, this people is prodigiously like the French people. Or rather these still are French people, trait for trait, and consequently entirely different from the English populations surrounding them. Gay, lively, joking, fond of glory and renown, intelligent, eminently sociable, their manners are gentle and their character obliging. The people are in general more moral, more hospitable and more religious than those in France. It is only in Canada that one can find what in France we call a *good child*. The Englishman and the American are either *coarse* or *icy*.

A peasant said to me: 'If ever one gets into a quarrel, the English are not white men.'[1]

* * *

[1] Beaumont, viii, 263, explains this phrase by completing it. 'They have also kept all the French idioms. One of them said to me: "If ever one gets into a quarrel, the English are not white men."'

(*2nd September 1831*)

Five or six years ago the English government wanted to unite the whole of Canada in one assembly. That was the measure best designed completely to break up the French Canadian nation, so the whole people rose at once and it is from that time that it knows its strength.

Several parish priests told me that in their parish there was not a single individual talking English. They themselves did not understand English at all, and used us as interpreters.

The appointment of militia officers is a function of government, but the House of Commons having decided that to be a militia officer it is necessary to reside in the place in question, the result has been to put the command of the armed force almost exclusively in the hands of French Canadians.

A French Canadian told me today that the debates in the House of Commons were lively and hot-headed, and that often hasty resolutions were taken of which one repented when heads had cooled. Might he not have been speaking about a French Chamber?

F

PUBLIC FUNCTIONS

Public functions, especially those that might tempt the ambitions of able and outstanding men, are very badly paid in America.

Evidence to prove that: Mr. Ingham was a member of the administration which General Jackson thought fit to dissolve at the beginning of 1831. (A measure for which there was no previous precedent.) Mr. Ingham claimed that he and several of his colleagues had been turned out of office because they did not wish to meet socially Mrs. Eaton (whose lover, he claimed, the General was), from which there followed a very scandalous quarrel between Mr. Ingham and Major Eaton. Following on these events and Mr. Ingham's return to his constituency, he was given a dinner by his friends there, and on that occasion made a speech claiming that he was glad to get back to obscurity, a claim to which incidentally the asperity and bitterness of his

style sufficiently gave the lie. He said among other things: 'As[1]
to pecuniary loss (if any think of this) much less labor [? than]
I should have bestowed on official business, well directed, will
easily procure something more than a bare subsistence, which,
all know, is scarcely afforded by the salaries at Washington—I
can have no cause of resentment therefore on that account.'

Daily New York Advertiser, 30th June 1930

* * *

Public Officials

They are absolutely on the same footing as the rest of the
citizens. They are dressed the same, stay at the same inn when
away from home, are accessible at every moment, and shake
everybody by the hand. They exercise a certain power defined
by the law; beyond that they are not at all above the rest. The
official and the man are never confused. The respect in which the
one is held, does not extend to the other; today there was a
letter in the paper from a Boston manufacturer offering General
Jackson a tortoise shell comb of American manufacture. He
addressed the President as 'Dear Sir.'

1st June 1831

* * *

We paid a visit today to the Governor of New York State.[2]
We found him living in a very small wooden farmhouse of one
story, and occupied in personally supervising the cultivation of
his fields. Mr. Elam Lynds was telling us that the position of
Governor was so badly paid (5,000 dollars) that if Mr. Throop
were not able to spend six months of the year on his farm, he
would be ruined. He criticised this parsimony which, he said,
prevented men of distinction from canvassing for so badly paid
a post, whereas with their ability they could make more *in some
business*. An idea characteristic both of the social state and of the
state of morals in the United States.

Auburn, 12th July 1831

---

[1] From 'as to . . . account' in English in manuscript.
[2] Governor Throop.

I

PUBLIC EDUCATION[1]

Everyone I have met up to now, to whatever rank of society they belong, has seemed incapable of imagining that one could doubt the value of education. They never fail to smile when told that this view is not universally accepted in Europe. They agree in thinking that the diffusion of knowledge, useful for all peoples, is absolutely necessary for a free people like their own, where there is no property qualification for voting or for standing for election. That seemed to be an idea taking root in every head. So the great expense for these States here has been the establishment of public education (Beaumont has the actual figures). I do not yet know what is thought here about the disadvantages of half knowledge which are so serious with us. In any case it seems to me that the strongest arguments urged in Europe against the excessive diffusion of knowledge, could not be relevant here. Because:

1st. Religious morality suffers less from that here than anywhere else. There is no hostility between religion and science.

2nd. There is less to fear here than anywhere else from the malaise caused to a State by a great number of people whose education lifts them above their standing and whose restlessness could disturb society. Here nature provides resources which are still so far beyond all human efforts to exhaust them, that there is no moral energy and no intellectual activity but finds ready fuel for its flames.

Mr. Power's opinion. See: Religion.[2]

Sing-Sing, 1st June 1831

INDIANS

Sometimes one sees even among those Indians who are encircled now by European possessions, men whose better intelligence foresees the destiny of the Indian race and whose savage energy still seeks to fight against a future from now on inevitable. Red-Jacket who died in 1829 in the village of Senecas near Buffalo, was one of those whom one might call the last of the Indians.

[1] In French: *Instruction publiques*.   [2] See below p. 206.

Mr. Spencer told me (18th July 1831) the following stories about him. Red-Jacket had been in our time in the New World the greatest enemy of the whites and, from hatred of them, of the Christian religion. Feeling that the time had passed for struggling with open force against the Europeans, he at least made use of all the moral power which he enjoyed among his compatriots to prevent them from becoming fused in the midst of us. Red-Jacket knew our ways and understood English; but he did not condescend to speak it. His influence over his compatriots was immense. It would be difficult, added Mr. Spencer, to imagine a man whose eloquence was more natural and captivating, or who could handle irony more skilfully. I remember that ten years ago an Indian from the neighbourhood of Buffalo was accused of having killed an American. He was arrested and brought before one of our juries. I was then district attorney and had to conduct the case against him. Red-Jacket appeared for the defence, and though he had to use an interpreter, he won his case. After the hearing he came up to me and said apparently with great simplicity, 'No doubt my brother', (he meant the accused) 'formerly did you a great injury.' I answered that before his crime I did not know that he existed. 'I understand,' Red-Jacket answered. 'The white man whom he killed was your brother, and you wanted to avenge him.' I tried again to get that idea out of his head and make him understand the nature of my duties. Red-Jacket after listening attentively to me, asked whether the Ancients of my people paid me for what I had just explained that I was doing. I said 'yes'. Then, pretending to be moved by the most lively indignation, he cried out: 'What! Not only do you want to kill my brother who has never done you any harm, but you have sold his blood in advance!'

I confess, Mr. Spencer added, that I stood aghast at that apostrophe. . . .[1]

Many years ago now the Presbyterians in Boston sent a missionary to the Mohawk Indians who then lived in the valley which still bears their name. Red-Jacket was among them. The tribe assembled to hear the missionary. After which, according to their custom, there was a general debate and Red-Jacket having obtained a decision to send back the Presbyterian

[1] The dots are Tocqueville's.

197

minister, was appointed to inform him of this resolution: 'My father has spoken well,' said Red-Jacket, 'but my brothers have a doubt which they wish cleared up. Our ancestors have told our fathers that they had seen the Great Spirit, and we believe our fathers. It is said that the white men believe a book which the Great Spirit has given them: but it is added that each of the innumerable tribes of white men puts a different meaning to this book. Have my brothers been given a false report?' The missionary was obliged to say that there was some truth in what Red-Jacket was saying, and the latter went on with an air of humility: 'If the white men to whom the Great Spirit has been at pains to open knowledge of everything, and to whom he has given this book, are not sure of understanding it, how can my father expect poor savages to succeed in that?' The missionary strove to explain that Christians only differed about certain points, and agreed about all the rest. Red-Jacket, having let him talk as much as he wanted, ended the interview by saying: 'These things are difficult for the red men to understand. But if my father would go and repeat them to our nearest neighbours the white men, and if the results of his preaching is to prevent the white men from stealing our land and our herds as they are doing every day, my father can come back to the red men and will find their ears more open.'

19th July 1831. On Lake Erie, on board the *Ohio*

* * *

First meeting with the Indians

The first Indians we met lived at Oneida Castle, a village about 270 miles from New York. They ran after our carriage asking for alms and we did not have leisure to observe them. But on arriving in the evening of 18th July at Buffalo, we came upon a considerable gathering of them. They came, we were told, to receive the price of the lands which they had ceded to the United States, and for which the latter were paying the rent.

Never, I think, have I suffered a more complete disappointment than in seeing these Indians. I was full of recollections of M. de Chateaubriand and of Cooper, and I was expecting to find the natives of America savages, but savages on whose face nature had stamped the marks of some of the proud virtues which liberty brings forth. I expected to find a race of men little different from Europeans, whose bodies had been developed by the strenuous exercise of hunting and of war, and who would lose nothing by being seen naked. Judge my amazement at seeing the picture that follows. The Indians whom I saw that evening were small in stature, their limbs, as far as one could tell under their clothes, were thin and not wiry, their skin, instead of being red as is generally thought, was dark bronze and such as at first sight seemed very like that of Negroes. Their black hair fell with singular stiffness on their neck and sometimes on their shoulders. Generally their mouths were disproportionately large, and the expression on their faces ignoble and mischievous. There was however a great deal of the European in their features, but one would have said that they came from the lowest mob of our great European cities. Their physiognomy told of that profound degradation which only long abuse of the benefits of civilisation can give, but yet they were still savages. Mixed with the vices which they got from us, was something barbarous and uncivilised which made them a hundred times more repulsive still. These Indians were covered in European clothes, but they did not use them in the same way as we do. (Some dressed themselves in blankets; the women with breeches and hats; the men in women's clothes.) One could see that they were not yet at all accustomed to wearing them and felt themselves imprisoned in their folds. To European ornaments they added the products of barbarian luxury, feathers, necklaces, enormous ear-rings. Their movements were quick and jerky, their voices shrill and discordant, their glances restless and savage. At first sight one might have been tempted to mistake each of them for some wild beast of the forest to whom education had been able to give some slight look of a human being, but who nonetheless remained an animal.

Having wandered to some distance from the town, we ran into a crowd of Indians who were returning to their village. Most of them were more or less drunk. An Indian woman was rolling in the dust of the road, uttering savage cries. Close to the last houses we saw an Indian lying at the edge of the road. It was a young man. He was motionless and, we thought, dead. Some stifled groans that painfully broke from his breast showed that he was still alive and struggling against one of those dangerous fits of drunkenness brought on by brandy. The sun had already sunk, and the ground was damp. Everything indicated that the wretched man would breathe his last sigh there, if he was not helped. From time to time a group of Indians came past. They came up, roughly turned their compatriot's body over, felt his heart to see if he was still alive, and then continued on their way without condescending even to answer our questions. All my life I shall remember a young Indian woman who seemed at first to come up to him with interest; I thought it was the wife or sister of the dying man. She looked at him attentively, called his name aloud, felt his heart and being assured that he was alive, tried to shake him out of his lethargy. But seeing that her efforts were useless, she burst out in fury against the inanimate body lying in front of her; she struck his head against the ground, twisted his face in her hands, and kicked him with her feet. As she gave herself over to these acts of ferocity, she uttered inarticulate and savage cries which I think I can still hear echoing in my ears at the moment I am writing these lines. Finally we thought we must intervene, and peremptorily ordered her to be off. We heard her as she went away uttering bursts of barbarous laughter.

When we got back to the town, we told several people about the young Indian whose body was stretched on the road. We spoke of the imminent danger to which he was exposed; we even offered to pay the expense of an inn. All that was useless: we could not persuade anyone to budge. Some said to us: 'Those men are used to drink to excess and sleep on the ground; they never die from accidents like that.' Others recognised that the Indian would probably die, but one could read on their lips this half-expressed thought: 'What is the life of an Indian?' The fact is that that was the basis of the general feeling. In the midst of this American society, so well policed, so sententious, so charitable, a cold selfishness and complete insensibility prevails when it is a question of the natives of the country. The Americans of the United States do not let their dogs hunt the Indians as do the Spaniards in Mexico, but at bottom it is the same pitiless feeling which here, as everywhere else, animates the European race. This world here belongs to us, they tell themselves every day: the Indian race is destined for final destruction which one

cannot prevent and which it is not desirable to delay. Heaven
has not made them to become civilised; it is necessary that they
die. Besides I do not at all want to get mixed up in it. I will not
do anything against them: I will limit myself to providing everything that will hasten their ruin. In time I will have their lands
and will be innocent of their death. Satisfied with his reasoning,
the American goes to the church where he hears the minister
of the gospel repeat every day that all men are brothers, and
that the Eternal Being who has made them all in like image,
has given them all the duty to help one another.

20th July 1831

* * *

Mr. Neilson said to us today in speaking about the Indians:
That people will disappear completely, but they will fall victims
to the pride of their spirit. The least among them thinks himself
at least equal to the Governor of Quebec. They never will adapt
themselves to civilisation, not because they are incapable of
behaving like us, but because they scorn our way of living and
consider themselves our superiors.

Quebec, 31st August 1831

G

Reprieves[1]

Mr. Ingersoll, a lawyer and former member of the Philadelphia
legislature, told us today (14th October 1831): 'The right of
granting reprieves is subject to much greater abuse in republics
than under monarchies. One notices that in comparing what
happens with us with what happens in France. Here experience
has shown that it is a delusion to condemn a man to perpetual
imprisonment, because sooner or later he will be reprieved.
With us the ruler changes endlessly, and every change opens
new chances for the condemned man. Besides there is no inter-
mediary between him and the relations or friends of the prisoner.
He ceaselessly finds himself attacked in some sort hand to hand.
It is not in human nature that he should always resist. Under
monarchies, on the contrary, it is almost impossible to get
access straight to the sovereign, and his ministers can easily
avoid importunities by saying that the king refuses.

[1] In French: *Grâce.*

Note: I have read in the registers of Sing-Sing prison that in the year 1824 (I think) of 180 prisoners who had been set at liberty, 95 had been reprieved. I have ascertained that many recidivist crimes were committed by men who had been reprieved. Since that time the abuse has diminished a great deal.

M

MARINE

The English merchant fleet numbers an effective of 19,110 ships with a tonnage of 2,199,959.

The French merchant fleet has 14,600 ships. But they only amount to 700,000 tons.

Revue britannique of November 1830

MASSACHUSETTS

We have gone through the State of Massachusetts at its widest point, going from Albany to Boston;[1] we found its aspect entirely different from that of New York State. There are no more log-houses, no more burnt trees, no more trunks abandoned in the middle of the fields; in a word, no more traces of the wilderness. The fields are well cultivated. The country has an old-established look. Almost all the houses are charming (especially in the villages), and there prevails a height of cleanliness which is something astonishing. The countryside itself is more picturesque; there are many mountains.

20th September 1831. *Boston* is a pretty town in a picturesque site on several hills in the middle of the waters.

What we have seen of the inhabitants up to now is completely different from those of New York. Society, at least that to which we have been introduced, and I think it is the best, is almost exactly like that of the upper classes in Europe. Luxury and refinement prevail there. Almost all the women speak French well, and all the men we have met up till now have been in Europe. Their manners are distinguished and their conversation turns on intellectual subjects; one feels one has escaped from those commercial habits and that money-conscious spirit

[1] From the 7th to the 9th September 1831.

which makes New York society so vulgar. In Boston there are already a certain number of people who, having nothing to do, seek out the pleasures of the mind. There are some people who write. We have already seen three or four very nice libraries, all literary. (I ought also to note that we hardly see anyone except people of distinction. But they are of a different sort from the men of distinction in New York.) Besides it would seem that the prejudice against people who do nothing (by and large a useful prejudice) is still strong at Boston. As in all the States that we have been through up to now, at Boston intellectual work is especially directed to religious subjects. Out of twenty-five semi-periodical works or magazines that we found in the Athenaeum there were twelve that were more or less concerned with religious matters.

P

Penitentiaries

The penitentiary system such as is established at Sing-Sing, seems to me dangerous to apply. This is the reason: beyond question the discipline at Sing-Sing is infinitely better than anything comparable one can see in France. Its effects are:

1st. The health of the prisoners.

2nd. Their extreme concentration on work.

3rd. The revenue the State gets from their work.

4th. *Perhaps* the moral reform of a certain number.

How are these effects produced? By the complete *silence* which isolates the prisoners from one another, and the continual *work* which occupies their physical and moral faculties. How is a sufficient degree of *silence* and *work* obtained? By the power of inflicting corporal punishment given arbitrarily to all the guards.

But how do the guards use this power in a way to produce the two effects of which I speak? That, in my view, is the main question and the one on which all the others depend. The power of giving strokes is granted to the guards of the gangs, and it often happens that they use it badly (too much or too little). Certainly, at least, it does not produce the same effect. To get this never-flagging attention from the guards, and to compel them to be at the same time pitiless and just, the Americans have made prison discipline the most pressing interest of each of the guards. The prisoners are free; they are armed,[1] have no chains and are kept in by no walls. An act of simultaneous determination on their part would infallibly set them at liberty. The preservation of discipline is the only tie that holds them. Every moment the guard tells himself that his life depends on the care with which he prevents plots, maintains assiduous work, and also avoids exasperating by unjust treatment an irascible character whose sudden influence might lead all the rest to follow him. Therefore he will be severe and just, and he will be so not from sense of duty or fear, but from self-interest. So then it is by putting themselves in the midst of danger, by braving it face to face, that the Americans seem to me to have succeeded in conquering it. And it is in that that I find their example dangerous to follow. As long as the machinery is in good order, the discipline prevailing in their prisons will be a thousand times better than that of any of Europe. But there cannot be a half-revolt there. So the system at Sing-Sing seems in some sense like the steamships which the Americans use so much. Nothing is more comfortable, quick and, in a word, perfect in the ordinary run of things. But if some bit of the apparatus gets out of order, the boat, the passengers and the cargo fly into the air.

Sing-Sing, 29th May 1831

* * *

Observations of fact to add to what has gone before

Three years ago a man who was pointed out to us, suddenly left the workshop, hatchet in hand, and called on his work-mates to revolt. They hesitated, and the man in question was arrested. It is clear that on that day the life of the guards at Sing-Sing hung on a thread. If by the negligence of one of them, five or six prisoners had come to an understanding and made a plot, no doubt they would have formed a nucleus and carried the others with them.

The same day

* * *

[1] Their working tools are meant.

Another observation

We saw 250 prisoners working in a shed cutting stone. These men, put under quite special supervision, had all committed acts of violence marking them as characters particularly to be feared. Each had to left and right a stonecutter's hatchet. Three unarmed guards walked about the shed. Their eyes were ever restless.

The same day—30th May 1831—in a quarry we saw several hundred prisoners working the stone under a burning sun (it was one of the hottest days of the year), they seemed to be working as energetically as workmen paid for the job.

Mr. Prince, minister at Sing-Sing and master of a boarding-school at the same place, told us that, all considered, he looked on the prison guards as men exposed to great danger, and felt that experience to date of the obedience of the prisoners was too recent to be absolutely decisive. He compared the director of the establishment to a man who had tamed a tiger which, one day or another, might eat him up. Mr. Prince seemed to me an intelligent man and in a position to have an opinion. He did not believe in any great moral *reform* effected by the Sing-Sing system.

Mr. Cartwright[1] seemed to us to think the same, but no one can know anything about it, as authentic statistics are lacking. I think that they would be more favourable to the system than the Americans seem to believe.

31st May 1831

* * *

Up to now we have met a great many people who have studied the matter much, and are doubtful whether one could succeed in *reforming* criminals.

10th June 1831

* * *

We have more and more reason to make the same comment.

1st August 1831

[1] Cf. Pierson, op. cit., in the index.

Q

QUAKERS

Mr. W. Smith told me today (25th October 1831) that the Quakers did not number more than 2,400 in Philadelphia. Their trouble is that they purge themselves all the time.

R

RELIGION

The gospel mission seems to us here more an industrial undertaking than a matter of zeal and conviction. Mr. Cartwright told us that it was almost impossible to get *chaplains* of ability for the penitentiaries because they were paid too little.

Sing-Sing, 30th May 1831

Several people have told us that clergymen endlessly change their positions.

* * * As above

There are 35,000 Catholics in New York. There were not 30 fifty years ago. Mr. Power (Vicar-general) claims that the number is daily increasing by conversions. They already form the most numerous *community*.

What has struck me most in Mr. Power's conversation is:

1st. That he seems to have no prejudice against republican institutions.

2nd. That he regards enlightenment as favourable to the moral and religious spirit.

Conversation of 9th June 1831

Mr. Richard, parish priest at Detroit (Michigan), has been sent by a largely Protestant electorate to Congress, of which for three years he has been one of the most respected members.

As above

The offerings given by the Catholics are enough to pay for the support of the ministers and the upkeep of the churches.

As above

Alphabetic Notebook 1

Conversation with Mr. Wainwright,[1] an Anglican clergyman

Mr. Wainwright seems a man of sense. He has (a rare thing in America) the manners of the best society and does the duty for the most fashionable church in New York.

Q. Is there any point of contact here between religious ideas and political doctrines?

A. None. They are like two worlds entirely apart in each of which one lives in peace.

Q. How does that state of affairs arise?

A. Because the ministers of the different sects have never interfered in politics, and have never been, nor claimed to be, a political power. We feel that we do our standing harm if we meddle with any political matter. A great many of us even abstain from voting at the elections. That is what I, for my part, am always careful to do.

Mr. Smith, chaplain of Auburn prison, told me the same thing. He added: 'I am convinced that if it was suggested to the body of Presbyterian Ministers that their members should be given some political importance, they would turn down the suggestion without hesitation.' Mr. Smith is a young Presbyterian Minister of a fairly ordinary turn of mind, but full of zeal and good intentions.

Auburn, 12th July 1831

* * *

'I do not believe that a republic can exist without morals, and I do not believe that a people can have morals when it has no religion. I judge then that the maintenance of the religious spirit is one of our greatest political interests.'

That is a literal resumé of a conversation we have just had with Mr. Richard, the head of the Presbyterian seminary at Auburn. Mr. Richard is an old man whose piety seemed to us sincere and even *ardent* (a rare thing in America). We had asked him whether, in his opinion, the religious principle were not losing its power. 'Perhaps in the large towns, not in the small ones and in the countryside. I think, on the contrary, that during

[1] Cf. Pierson, op. cit., in the index.

207

the last thirty years we have made headway.' (I am much afraid that he deludes himself.)

Auburn, 13th July 1831

* * *

Mr. Richard, a Catholic priest, has been sent to Congress by a Protestant electorate. Mr. Neilson, a Protestant, has been sent to the Commons in Canada by a Catholic electorate. Do these facts prove that religion is better understood or that its power is enervated? They prove, I believe, both one and the other.

27th August

* * *

Sing-Sing

There is an old man at Sing-Sing who can remember seeing the Indians established in this place. The name itself of Sing-Sing is taken from the name of an Indian chief.

Sing-Sing, 29th May 1831

We were shown a house where a descendant of Oliver Cromwell lives.

As above

* * *

Penitentiary system

Every prisoner on the hulks in England costs 91 francs 7 centimes a year.

To keep him on the Bermuda islands costs 117 francs 11 centimes all expenses included.

Revue Britannique of November 1830

Persons who believe in the moral reform of adult prisoners.	Persons who do not believe in it	Persons who are doubtful
	Maxwell N.Y. *Willsee*, agent at Sing-Sing, except in so far as the prisoners learn to earn their living. *Woodruff*, agent at Blackwell's island.	Over Kent Riker } seem almost sure that there is no reform.

T

Virgin lands:[1] way of cultivating them

When a new-settler arrives, he goes to live with a neighbour, if there is one. If there is not, he puts up a tent. The first operation is to clear the field, which he does with the help of labourers. The expense of this work is estimated at about 3 dollars per acre of land (including the clearing and erection of fences). When the land is thus prepared, the new-settler sows an acre of potatoes, and sows wheat or corn in the rest according to the nature of the soil. Corn will do in the dampest soil because it is sown in spring. The new-settler has to bring provisions for at least six months. Two barrels of corn for himself and his family, and one barrel of salted pork will be enough: the latter item costs 14 dollars. Tea does for drink. It is generally calculated that to establish a new settlement one must start with 150 to 200 dollars in hand. You spend 100 dollars on buying the land, and get 80 acres for that sum; the rest is needed for the expenses of the initial settlement and incidentals. With that money the new-settler also buys animals which do not cost much to feed. They are let loose in the woods with a bell, and graze freely. A labourer costs one dollar when he is not fed, 6 shillings when he is. Oxen are used on the work costing 12 shillings a day.
Information given us on 30th July 1831 near
Pontiac by a young Scotch doctor, a new-settler.

*   *   *

The rod measures 16½ feet (English), the acre measures 20 rods in length by 8 in breadth (smaller than the arpent).
In the neighbourhood of Syracuse and Lake Oneida uncultivated land is sold for 5 or 6 dollars an acre, and cultivated land for 15 to 20 dollars (8th July 1831).
At Canandaigua cultivated land is sold for 18 to 20 dollars, and the best for 25 dollars an acre; same price at Buffalo. In the territory of Michigan uncultivated land is always sold at 10 shillings an acre. One is bound to pay the whole price on the spot. The same applies to all the land sold by the State. (It is a

---

[1] In French: *terres incultes*.

general measure adopted because of the difficulty of collecting the money due.)

The State finds it to its own and the public's interest to sell cheaper but without delay in payment.

Buying the land is considered the easiest part of the undertaking when one wants to clear land. The real expense is getting it under cultivation. That costs 5 to 10 dollars per acre (cutting the trees, carrying them away, making fences and clearing the ground), the yearly income from an acre so prepared is 2 to 4 dollars. The rate for a day's work is 50 cents, not including food. If the day labourer is not fed, it is 6 shillings (this is in contradiction to a lot of information according to which the cost of a day's labour without food is 8 shillings or a dollar).

Information obtained on 22nd July, on Lake Erie from an inhabitant of Detroit.

*   *   *

One can put the income from an acre of cultivated soil at 2 dollars and very often even more. Buying the land is nothing; the real expense is getting it ready, on account of the cost of labour.

This is how one must set about making a profit, when one does not cultivate the land oneself (a very infrequent case). I get a man to clear 20 acres. I give him 5 dollars per acre, and I provide the cart and the oxen for the work. Besides I give him the seed, and then we share between us the first year's harvest. If the harvest is good, the half that goes to me more than pays the outlay of the 5 dollars. The subsequent harvests all belong to me.

Information provided by our host at Pontiac[1] on
25th July 1831

*   *   *

General questions

The principle of the republics of antiquity was to sacrifice private interests to the general good. In that sense one could say that they were *virtuous*. The principle of this one seems to be to make private interests harmonize with the general interest. A

[1] According to pocket notebook 2 Tocqueville left Pontiac on the 24th July after having arrived the night before.

sort of refined and intelligent selfishness seems to be the pivot on which the whole machine turns. These people here do not trouble themselves to find out whether public virtue is good, but they do claim to prove that it is useful. If the latter point is true, as I think it is in part, this society can pass as enlightened, but not as virtuous. But up to what extent can the two principles of individual well-being and the general good in fact be merged? How far can a conscience, which one might say was based on reflection and calculation, master those political passions which are not yet born, but which certainly will be born? That is something which only the future will show.

Sing-Sing, 29th May 1831

*   *   *

When one reflects on the nature of this society here, one sees to some extent the explanation of what I have just written; American society is composed of a thousand different elements recently assembled.

The men who live under its laws are still English, French, German and Dutch. They have neither religion, morals nor ideas in common; up to the present one cannot say that there is an American character, at least unless it is the very fact of not having any. There is no common memory, no national attachments here. What then can be the only bond that unites the different parts of this huge body? *Interest.*

Sing-Sing, 29th May 1831

VIII
Alphabetic Notebook 2

A

ASSOCIATION[1]

The power of the association has reached its highest degree in America. Associations are made for purposes of trade, and for political, literary and religious interests. It is never by recourse to a higher authority that one seeks success, but by an appeal to individual powers working in concert.

The last word in the way of an association seems to me to be the temperance societies, that is to say an association of men who mutually agree to abstain from a vice, and find in collective power an aid in resisting what is most intimate and personal to each man, his own inclinations. The effect of temperance societies is one of the most notable things in this country.

10th October 1831

* * *

When a great crime arouses public attention, the inhabitants of the place where it was committed come together, appoint a commission of men charged with the duty of discovering the criminals, and raise a fund to cover the expenses. I have seen some examples. This fact both proves the weakness of the criminal investigation police in America and shows that people know how to use association in such a case.

15th October 1831

* * *

[1] Other notes about association are to be found in notebook E, pp. 252–253.

At Baltimore the Washington memorial which is 160 feet high and cost, I think, a million francs, was erected partly by association.

Baltimore, 30th October 1831

At Baltimore it is an association that provides the prizes at the races, established the race-course and manages the race-meetings.

Baltimore, [30] October 1831

*   *   *

Association. See *Economy.*[1]

C

CENTRALIZATION

Defects resulting from the lack of centralization in America. Mr. Tuckerman[2] told me today (27th September 1831) that the State of Massachusetts lacked any central authority with power to visit the schools, and to inspect them and publish each year, as is done in the State of New York, reports describing the state in which they are found, the number of children taught. . . .[3]

CONVENTION

The right to assemble in Convention is the most extreme consequence of the dogma of the sovereignty of the people. Example of a convention which I saw in America and which will, better than any other, serve to make clear what a *political* convention is; for there are conventions concerned with every subject.

One knows how greatly the question of tariff or free trade has stirred men's minds in the United States. One might say that the tariff question arouses the only political passions that there are in the Union, because tariffs favour or harm, not opinions only, but very powerful material interests. The North attributes part of its prosperity, and the South almost all its troubles to them.

[1] Cf. p. 219, below.   [2] Cf. Pierson, op. cit., pp. 394 f.
[3] Dots in the manuscript.

About two months ago Mr. Sedgwick, the brother of Miss Sedgwick the authoress, who also lives in the little village of Stockbridge in Massachusetts where I saw him, thought of proposing by publicity in papers to all the opponents of tariffs that they should send deputies to Philadelphia and appoint a convention to advise on the best means whereby to achieve the freeing of trade. This idea, which spread in a few days by the power of the press from Maine to New Orleans, was favourably taken up by all the States whose interests were concerned for or against. The opponents of tariffs got stirring on all sides and appointed deputies to make representations to Congress. These deputies were almost all very distinguished men; one saw among them the names of Gallatin, Berian [?] and many men known in the South; the Carolinas alone sent 60 deputies. On 1st October 1831 the assembly, which consisted of more than 200 members, was constituted in Philadelphia. The discussions were public, and from the first day took on a thoroughly legislative character. Thus there was a general argument about the extent of the power of Congress, the principle of the theory of free trade, and finally the provisions in practice of the different tariff regulations of 1828. After ten days the assembly adjourned indefinitely, after they had drafted an address to the American people. This address set forth that:

1st. Congress has not the right to impose a tariff, and the existing tariff was unconstitutional.

2nd. It is not in the interest of peoples, and in particular of the American people, that freedom of trade should be restricted.

Of all that I have seen in America it was that Convention which most struck me as being for us a dangerous and impracticable consequence of the sovereignty of the people.

14th October 1831

* * *

(*14th October 1831*)

Today I was at the house of Mr. Ingersoll, a lawyer and former member of the legislature, and expressed the views I have just written down. He answered me: 'The dangers which alarm you are, in my view, less to be feared; as long as men have freedom to talk, it is odds against their taking to action. Besides, note carefully, the object of the Convention is not to act, but to persuade; it represents an opinion, an interest, and does not set out to represent the nation which is there, all complete, in Congress. The Convention, on the contrary, starts from the assumption that it does not represent the majority, but wishes to act on public opinion and change the persuasion of the majority.' 'But', said I, 'the opinion and interest of which you speak, could present their arguments any day by means of the press.'

'You realise,' replied Mr. Ingersoll, 'the immensely greater power of an assembly compared to an obscure journalist, or the individual efforts of a man of parts. For my part I regard the right to assemble in convention as the rational consequence of the dogma of the sovereignty of the majority. There are some opinions which, although they are shared by a minority, would forever be suppressed by the majority, unless, besides the public assemblies which express the all-powerful wishes of the majority, there were not meetings (thus reinforced by the moral power given by numbers) which argued for the interests of the minority, and which acted not by laws, but by speeches designed to win over the majority itself.'

'Very well,' I answered, 'certainly nothing is more logical, but I should not need other examples to show to what extent the immutable laws of logic are inapplicable to the affairs of this world. Imagine a people not entirely accustomed to the rule of laws and the reign of persuasion; grant it passions and great political interests; allow that besides the majority that makes the laws, there arises a minority which is only concerned with the preamble and stops short at the recital, and you will see what happens to public order. Do you not see that in the minds of almost all men there is but a step, and the easiest step of all to take, between proving that a thing is good—and carrying it out? Besides are there not certain political questions where the majority is so uncertain that each party can claim that it is the majority? So you allow the creation besides the directing power of a power whose moral authority is as great and which nonetheless, feeling that it has the strength to struggle against the established order, will respect it on account of this metaphysical consideration that the Convention's function is to enlighten opinion and not to coerce it, to counsel and not to act.'

Mr. Ingersoll admitted that he had spoken only with reference to the United States, and only with reference to the present time. 'As we can without danger conform to our principles,' he said, 'we do well to do so. Besides my view has always been that one should make the laws for the peoples, and not the peoples according to the laws. I conceive that an assembly like the Philadelphia Convention could entail great dangers in France. However it seems to me that association against the outsider has some analogy with our use of Conventions. What renders Conventions so dangerous for you is the concentration of the whole of France in Paris. I conceive that a factious assembly held in Paris could have a destructive power over the whole State. There is nothing like that in America. Speaking generally, I am firmly persuaded that as long as you do not grant a strong individuality to your provinces, you will never be sure of remaining free.'

* * *

Centralization

The Americans have such a fear of centralization and of the power of capitals, that they almost always take care to put the seat of legislative and executive power far from the capitals. Thus the seat of the legislature and government of the State of New York is at Albany; the seat of the government of Pennsylvania is at Arisban,[1] a little town in the interior of the country, and not at Philadelphia; that of Maryland at Annapolis and not at Baltimore.

In what concerns criminal justice, roads, prisons and generally for all undertakings that demand rapidity of execution or continuity of conception, the lack of centralization makes itself felt in America.

25th October 1831

D

DUELLING

The duel based on extreme susceptibility to points of honour, the monarchic duel, is almost unknown in America. The laws which

[1] [?] Harrisburg.

oblige a man to fight in some parts of Europe in certain defined cases, do not exist at all. Duels however do take place, but they are no more than a means outside the law of satisfying the most violent and implacable passions. In Europe one hardly ever fights a duel except in order to be able to say that one has done so; the offence is generally a sort of mental stain which one wants to wash out, and which most often is washed out at small expense. In America one only fights to kill; one fights because one sees no hope of getting one's adversary condemned to death. There are very few duels, but they almost always end in death. All this does not apply more than partially to the South.

Philadelphia, 22 October 1831

E

EQUALITY

(*17th September 1831*)

An incredible *external* authority prevails in America. All classes endlessly meet, and there does not seem the slightest indication of different social positions. Everyone shakes hands. At Canandiagua I saw a district attorney shake hands with a prisoner. Inequality born of wealth and education is certainly found in private life. Generally speaking the wealthiest and most well educated people live in a closed circle. But for an outsider these inequalities are not noticeable, and they are in fact, I think, less felt than anywhere else. I do not think that there is any *calling* which of itself lowers the standing of the man who exercises it. One keeps on seeing in the papers this phrase of a man, 'he keeps a respectable tavern in such [a] place'.[1] It is clear that white servants regard themselves as their masters' equals. They gossip on familiar terms. On the steamboats at first we wanted to give a tip to the *steward*. We were stopped from doing so by being told that that would humiliate him. In the inns I have seen him sit down at table by our side when everyone had been placed and served. Besides it is almost impossible to find servants in America. They say that they are giving 'the help'[2] (the word is characteristic) and want to be treated as neighbours

[1] From 'he' to 'place' in English in Tocqueville's manuscript.
[2] Tocqueville uses the English term.

who come temporarily to give their neighbours a hand. They must eat with their masters.

Anecdote to support what is said above about there being no way of earning money, *within the law*, which public opinion regards as *degrading*.

I found myself in a drawing-room in Boston behind two respectable gentlemen who seemed to be discussing an important subject with interest:

'How much will that bring you in?' said the one.

'It is quite a good business,' replied the other, 'one gets about a hundred dollars for each.'

'Indeed,' the other answered, 'that is, as you say, good business.'

Now they were talking of nothing less than two pirates who were going to be hanged the next day. One of the speakers, who was the City-Marshal, was obliged by his office to be present at the execution and to see that everything was properly carried out. The law allowed him for performing this duty a hundred dollars for each man hanged, and he spoke of these two victims as if they were a pair of oxen that he wanted to sell the next day at the market.

Told by the Consul

*   *   *

In all the journeys I have made in the United States I have never seen one single person in his own carriage or with his own horses. The wealthiest people travel in public conveyances without servants. A hundred times have I seen women alone with their husband or mother, without a serving woman and almost without luggage. Generally speaking they never complain about anything and adapt themselves to all the discomforts of travel in a way that shows that their education is different from that received by women of the best circles in Europe.

*   *   *

(*14th October 1831*)

Mr. Ingersoll, a distinguished lawyer and former member of the legislature of Philadelphia, told me today: I believe that there is more social equality with you than with us. With you, I believe, talent and fortune are exactly on the same footing. Here, talent opens every door, but fortune gives a decided pre-eminence.

* * *

Slavery

See the conversation of 30th October 1831 with Mr. Latrobe.[1]

The law lends its power to the slave's master. He can have him imprisoned as long as he wants provided he pays the expenses.

Baltimore, 3rd November 1831

ECONOMY

Today (26th November 1831) going down the Ohio below Pittsburgh, we passed by the colony of Economy. The town of Economy is situated on the banks of the Ohio in a fertile plain. It now has a thousand inhabitants who live there in great prosperity and are rapidly increasing their communal capital every year. This society is one of the most remarkable in existence. The Founder is the leader not answerable for the undertaking. He directs the common efforts and presents no accounts. All the other members of the society are only agents who have but a possible claim to the common fund, if the association is broken up. But until that event they only get enough to live on in comfort. If some of them want to withdraw, they can, but they leave their stake. If the whole society should wish to be dissolved, it can do it. But it has not yet wanted to, and its affairs prosper incredibly. It already owns an immense tract of land.

I

EDUCATION

Mr. Tuckerman,[2] a very zealous Presbyterian minister who is particularly concerned with such matters, said to me today

[1] Above, non-alphabetic notebook 2, pp. 72–78.
[2] Cf. Pierson, op. cit., in the index.

(27th September 1831): *For God's sake,*[1] in France don't raise a fund destined for the schools, or at least make it insufficient so that it only serves to encourage. We have observed that when the communities know that the government provides all the money for education, they become rather indifferent about their schools. But when they are putting their own money into them, they take a great interest in seeing that it is well employed. It is to that cause that we attribute the superiority of the schools in Massachusetts over those in Connecticut.

We had previously been told the same thing by Mr. Spencer at Canandaigua. He even claimed to have noticed that the same applied to every sort of communal and district interest.

Education

In New England the law obliges all towns having 80 families or landowners to provide a school where reading, writing, English grammar, geography and arithmetic are taught for at least six months in the year.

All towns with 500 families must have a school where one learns the history of the United States, surveying, geometry and algebra.

Finally in all towns with 4,000 inhabitants, the schoolmaster will be capable of teaching Latin, Greek and foreign history.

One sees the importance given to primary education or elementary knowledge. It is immense. Everywhere the history of the country and geography are compulsory subjects of instruction.

*   *   *

(*4th November 1831*)

In Maryland and, I think, throughout the South there was no law about public education four or five years ago. The people refused to be educated, so as not to have to pay the tax for the schools. It is only since that time that efforts have begun to be made. But I do not think that up to the present there is a general law in Maryland about the matter; ignorance there is still very great.

[1] In English in Tocqueville's manuscript.

J

JURY

V. vol. 2. conv. [?] Gray, 21st September 1831.[1]

(*22nd September 1831*)

The jury is a political institution even when it is used in civil cases. That is the fundamental conception of which one must never lose sight; it is the point of departure for judging it.

Today I was present at a hearing in the Circuit Court.[2] The case was as follows: a ship had been insured; it was lost. The insurer claimed that the ship was not seaworthy. The case was brought before a jury whose verdict established that the ship was in fit state to sail at the time of the agreement. Appeal from the decision of the jury before the Court of Circuits. This Court, presided over by a judge of the Supreme Court of the United States, could not decide the matter itself, but could well send it back to another jury.

Counsel for the insured—Mr. Fletcher, a very good Boston lawyer—began by answering several complaints that had been made against the jury that had given the verdict in his favour. The jury were capable men. They had given their sustained attention to the case. Then dealing with the point of law, he maintained that if the judges were given discretionary power to annul the different verdicts of the juries, the institution of the jury would become a mere show without power. He admitted nonetheless that in cases where a jury had been moved by passion, or had made a palpable and clear mistake, there was occasion to quash the verdict. But he maintained that, apart from these extraordinary cases, in all cases where, when a matter was doubtful, the jury had only followed an opinion not shared by the judge, the latter had not the right to reshape the *verdict* He went on from that to argue the facts.

We could not be there to hear the answer, but during the interval we were talking to one of the judges, and he said to

---

[1] See non-alphabetic notebook 2, pp. 52–54. See also conversations and remarks on this subject in notebook F, pp. 290, 295.

[2] The Circuit Courts are the federal courts of first instance, competent, for example, when one of the States is a party to a case, or when citizens of different States are suing one another.

us: 'I see that what you have just heard surprises you; you cannot form a clear idea of the limits within which the functions of jury and judge are performed. Such limits are effectively fixed more by practice than by theory. We have in fact the right to quash the jury's verdict for any reason whatsoever, and send the case back before another lot of men. But it is a right that we only use in the last extremity, and when the mistake or the passion could not escape anybody's notice. The people attaches great importance to decision by juries, even in civil matters; it keeps a very jealous eye open to see that nothing is done to undermine the moral authority of the jury. When a judge quashes a verdict, he takes on himself an immense responsibility. For my part I do not think that I have quashed more than ten in my life, and when I see that a jury has come to a decision for reasons which, without convincing me, nonetheless have some weight, I leave the appreciation entirely to them and respect their opinion. 99 appeals in 100 fail. And out of 50 plaintiffs there is perhaps only one who appeals to us. It is in this way that the institution of the jury, which one could make almost illusory by following theories, regains all its power in practice.

M

MORALS[1]

American morals are, I think, the most chaste that exist in any nation, a fact which can, it seems to me, be attributed to five chief causes:

1st. Physical constitution. They belong to a Northern race, although they almost all live in a climate hotter than that of England.

2nd. Religion still holds great sway over their souls. They have even retained some of the traditions of the strictest religious sects.

3rd. They are entirely absorbed by their preoccupation with making a fortune. There are no idle ones among them. They have the *settled* habits of people who work the whole time.

4th. There is no trace of the prejudices of birth which prevail in Europe, and it is so easy to make a fortune that poverty is never

[1] *Moeurs* in French.

an obstacle to a marriage. As a result the individuals of both sexes are early joined in marriage, only marry because they are attracted one to the other, and they find themselves tied at a time of life when a man is almost always more sensible of the pleasures of the heart than of the senses. It is rare for a man not to be married at twenty-one.

5th. The women generally receive a rational education (perhaps even a somewhat rationalistic one). The reasons listed above make it possible without great drawbacks to allow them extreme freedom; the transition from the status of girl to married woman has no dangers for them.

* * *

Boston (21st September 1831)

Mr. Clay who apparently is busy making statistical researches in this matter, told Beaumont that in Boston there were about 2,000 prostitutes. (I have great difficulty in believing it.) They are recruited from the country girls who, having been seduced, have to escape from their neighbourhood and family and find themselves without resources. It seems that the young men of the town frequent them. But the fact is hidden with extreme care and the evil is limited to that, without ever passing the domestic threshold or disturbing family life. A man who was not convicted, but suspected, of carrying on an *intrigue*, would immediately be excluded from society. All doors would be shut against him. Mr. Dwight told me that a venereal disease was a mark of infamy which it was very hard to wash off.

Moreover, the police does not interfere in any way with prostitutes. The Americans say that it would legitimatize the evil if such a remedy were used against it. Mr. Dwight told us (a thing we had already had occasion to notice in the prison reports) that of all prisoners those who were most seldom found to reform were the women of loose morals.

Mr. Wood[1] told me today (24th October 1831) that there were many natural children in Philadelphia. The English law is followed here, and when a girl of the people is pregnant, the overseer of the poor interrogates her and gets her to tell him the

[1] Cf. Pierson, op. cit., pp. 460 f.

name of the child's father, so that the local authority can bring an action against him, and prevent the bastard from being a charge on him. In that there is a terrible brake against immorality.[1]

MARYLAND

See the conversation of 30th October 1831 with Mr. Latrobe.[2]

Population of Maryland in 1830: 446,912 souls, 291,102 whites, 52,942 free blacks, 102,878 slaves.

N

NEGROES

In Massachusetts the blacks have citizens' rights. They can vote at elections . . .[3] but the prejudice is so strong against them that their children cannot be received in the schools.

(*27th September 1831*)

* * *

Many people in America, and the most enlightened people, have maintained to me that the Negroes belong to an inferior species. Many others have maintained the contrary thesis. The latter quote in support of their view the aptitude of Negro children in their schools, and the example of some Negroes who, despite all obstacles, have made an independent fortune. Mr. Wood of Philadelphia quoted among others the case of a Negro of that town who had made an enormous fortune and owned several ships whose crew and captains were black.

Philadelphia (22nd October 1831)

* * *

Mr. Smith, a very well-informed and able Quaker of Philadelphia, told us today (24th October 1831) that he was perfectly

[1] Tocqueville changed his mind much later on about this. Cf. my edition of his *Journeys to England and Ireland*, London and New Haven, 1958, p. 62 f.

[2] See above p. 72.   [3] The dots are Tocqueville's.

convinced that the Negroes were of the same race as us, just as a black cow is of the same race as a white one. The Negro children show as much intelligence as the white ones; often they learn faster. We asked him if the blacks had citizens' rights. He answered:'Yes, in law, but they cannot present themselves at the poll.' 'Why so?' 'They would be ill-treated.' 'And what happens to the rule of law in that case?' 'The law with us is nothing when it is not supported by public opinion.' Slavery is abolished in Pennsylvania. We asked him what in his opinion was the only means of saving the South from the ills which he foresaw. He answered that it was to bind the Negroes to the soil like the serfs in the Middle Ages. 'Serfdom is a bad institution,' he added, 'but it is infinitely better than slavery properly so called. It will serve as a transition towards the state of complete freedom. But I am perfectly certain that the Americans of the South, like other despots, will not ever agree to give up the least part of their powers, and will wait to have them snatched from them.'[1]

In the prison of Walnut Street in Philadelphia I have just noticed that the blacks were separated from the whites even for their meals.

(*25th October 1831*)

*　　*　　*

At Philadelphia the blacks are not buried in the same cemetery as the whites.

*　　*　　*

(*4th November 1831*)

In Maryland the free Negroes pay the same school-tax as the whites, but they cannot send their children there.

(*4th November 1831*)

Mr. Latrobe said to me today: I am very much afraid that the in-coming Legislature may pass unjust and oppressive laws against the blacks. People want to make it intolerable for them to remain in Maryland. One must not hide it from oneself; the white population and the black population are in a state of war.

---

[1] The same conversation is noted down in pocket notebook number 3, p. 156.

They will never mix. It must be that one of the two will sur-render the ground to the other.

R

RELIGION IN POLITICAL INSTITUTIONS

Massachusetts has a law imposing fairly heavy fines for swear-ing. This law is preceded by this preamble:

Whereas the horrible practice of profane cursing and swear-ing is inconsistent with the dignity and rational cultivation of the human mind, with a due reverence to the Supreme Being and his Providence, and has a natural tendency to weaken the solemn-ity and obligation of oaths lawfully taken in the administration of justice; to promote falsehood, perjuries, blasphemies and dis-soluteness of manners and to loosen the bonds of civil society . . .[1] this law must be read and posted up every year at the great town meeting. (See *Town Officer* p. 259).

2nd. Sunday observance is a civil law. There are fines to enforce it and various officials, called constables, *tythingmen* and others whose special duty it is to see to this. The latter among other things have the right to interrogate people who are travelling on Sunday, and to condemn them to a fine if they do not give good reasons. (*See Town Officer*, page 277.)

Mr. Hyde of Neuville told me that he had been stopped in this way, and could not continue on his way without establishing the necessity of his journey. I think however that this last regulation is not strictly observed. There are some public conveyances on Sunday and the post goes; but many people are indignant at that and would like to stop it. Boston on Sunday has, literally, the appearance of a deserted town.

3rd. On the 17th October 1831, the Governor of Massa-chusetts (by the advice and consent of the council)[2] made a pro-clamation inviting all the inhabitants of the Republic to assemble in their respective churches on the 1st December 1831 to offer thanks to God for the benefits granted to the Republic during the year, and prayers for the confirmation of these benefits. See this remarkable report in the *Boston Courier* for 19th October 1831.

[1] Until 'society' quoted in English.
[2] The passage in parentheses is in English in Tocqueville's manuscript.

T

TOLERANCE

It is above all the Catholics who were the first, after the foundation of Maryland, to establish practical tolerance in matters of religion. Up to that time all the sects had claimed it for themselves without granting it to others. The Quakers were burnt in England. They took refuge among the Presbyterians of Boston who themselves had fled from persecution in the motherland. And there they were hanged.'[1]

Philadelphia, 28th October 1831

W

WASHINGTON

Mr. Sparks, a learned Bostonian, who has already published the correspondence of all the ambassadors and notable men of the time of the American Revolution, and who is at the moment working on a life of Washington,[2] showed me today (17th September 1831) several volumes full of accounts and copies of letters in Washington's handwriting. They are business letters, and account-books referring either to his military administration or the management of his property. The whole is executed with a care, neatness, accuracy and detail which would do credit to a *clerk*. The handwriting is beautiful, tranquil and perfectly uniform throughout all the pages. He signs everything, even copies of letters, and each signature looks just like a facsimile. It is difficult to conceive how a man whose ideas were so wide-ranging could condescend to such details.

---

[1] This note seems inspired by a conversation of Tocqueville's with Brown which is to be found in non-alphabetic notebook 2, pp. 71 ff.

[2] Sparks did in fact publish successively: *Writings of George Washington with a Life of the Author. Notes and Illustrations*, (1834–7) and *The Life of Washington* (1843).

IX

Notes on Kent[1]

Commentaries

The Senate in the United States is at the same time a judicial, legislative and, in certain circumstances, administrative body. It plays a part in treaties, in the appointment of officials. . . .[2] Argument to determine whether, in time of war, the President has the right to order the militia to march and to take command of it.

[Kent: *Commentaries* 1], 246

Advantage of the two Houses proved by reasons and examples; utility of leaving the execution of the law to a single agent.

[K. *C.* vol 1], p. 254

The fittest men, Kent says frankly in speaking of the judges, would probably have too much reservedness of manners and severity of morals, to secure an election resting on universal suffrage.

[K. *C.* vol. i], p. 272

In monarchical governments, the independence of the judiciary is essential to [guard] the rights of the subject from the injustice

---

[1] James Kent (1763–1847), great American jurist, Professor of Law at Columbia College in 1796, Judge of the Supreme Court of New York in 1804, Chancellor of the State of New York in 1814. His *Commentaries on American Law* (1826–30) was a work that made him famous both for the extent of his knowledge and for the acuteness of his mind. Tocqueville met Kent in New York in June 1830, and the great man sent him his *Commentaries* (cf. Pierson, op. cit). See also J. Duer, *Discourse on the Life, Character and Public Services of James Kent* (1848); W. Kent, *Memoirs and Letters of Chancellor Kent*, Boston (1894); J. T. Horton, *James Kent: a Study in Conservatism*, New York and London, 1939. A comparative study of Kent's and de Tocqueville's sociology of jurisprudence has yet to be made. Other notes on Kent's *Commentaries* are to be found in notebook E, pp. 245, 249–254.

[2] The dots are Tocqueville's.

of the crown; but in republics it is equally salutary in protecting the constitution and laws from the encroachments and tyranny of factions.

[K. C. vol. i], p. 275

The act of September 1789 is the one which established the whole basis of federal judicial order.

The *States Courts* could judge all the matters ordinarily decided by the *Federal Courts* (subject to appeal), provided:

1st. That Congress had not ordained otherwise.

2nd. That they were competent to judge these matters before the Constitution, Congress being able to *restrict* but not to *extinguish* the jurisdiction of the States Courts (judicial review). That is an aid to the dispatch of business and reduces cases of *competence*. But it multiplies cases of *appeal*.

[K. C., vol i], p. 376

The Common Law is followed by the Federal Courts in civil matters. They have announced that this is not so in criminal cases.

One of the most peculiar attributes of the Federal Courts is that resulting from the article in the Constitution which says that the different *States* cannot make a *law impairing the obligations of contracts*.[1] So when the States do make such laws, one appeals to the Court of the United States.

One can see that such cases could arise in many forms. There is hardly any political measure which does not harm acquired rights and consequently leaves room for appeal. The granting of such jurisdiction raised a very strong barrier against local passions and the injustices following therefrom. But immense power has been put into the hands of the federal judges.

[K. C., vol i], p. 387

*   *   *

Reflection

I see clearly that the Court of the United States should have the effect of forcing each State to submit to the laws of the Union, but only when it is seized of a case. But when there is a violation of the laws of the Union and no one complains, what happens

[1] The passage in italics in English in Tocqueville's manuscript.

then? Can the State be cited criminally before the Court? Is there a department of public prosecution whose duties cover such cases?

*   *   *

Intolerance

A law passed at the end of the last century in the State of New York declares that a Catholic priest who does not leave the State within a fixed time, shall be imprisoned for life and condemned to death if he comes back. Smith, the historian, who was writing in 1756, declares that this law was worthy to last forever.

[K. C., vol. ii], p. 63

Possibility of marrying at fourteen years old for men and twelve for women.

[K. C., vol. ii], p. 67

The parents' consent is not necessary at any age.

[K. C., vol. ii], pp. 73 ff.

Marriage is a civil contract.

[K. C., vol ii], p. 74

In many States it is not restricted to any special form. It is the intention of the parties which makes the substance of the matter.

*   *   *

On Divorce

The Courts in Massachusetts are authorised by statute to grant divorces causa impotentiae.[1]

[K. C.], vol ii, p. 81

One notes a great variety between the different States in the causes of divorce and the way it is obtained.

Several States show a strong tendency to restrict the number of divorces. Kent seems doubtful of the usefulness of divorce. He says: 'I have had occasion to believe, in the exercise of a judicial cognizance of numerous cases of divorce, that the sin

---

[1] Tocqueville quotes this in English.

of adultery was sometimes committed on the part of the husband, for the very purpose of the divorce.'

[K. *C.*], vol. ii, p. 88, note 2

Execution of judgments of foreign courts. Long discussion by Kent.

[K. *C*], vol. ii, p. 100 ff.

Besides divorce there is also separation.

[Ibid.], p. 106

*   *   *

Public education

Kent claims that in Connecticut the Selectmen have the right to take children away from their parents when the former do not give them any education, in order to give it to them. 'This law', said the late Chief Justice Reeve, 'has produced very astonishing effects, and to it is to be attributed the knowledge of reading and writing, so universal among the people of that state.'

Kent adds: 'During the twenty-seven years in which that distinguished lawyer was in extensive practice of the law, he informs us that he never found but one person in Connecticut, that could not write.'[1]

[Ibid.], p. 165

History of the funds destined for education in the State of New York. Very curious.

[Ibid.], p. 166

The first emigrants to Massachusetts made a son's disobedience to his father's orders a capital crime in imitation of the Jews.

[Ibid.], p. 172

*   *   *

Illegitimate children

English law does not permit legitimation by subsequent marriage. Eleven [States] of the United States (the newest ones) have nonetheless adopted it.

[Ibid.], p. 173

[1]Both quotations are in English in Tocqueville's text.

Notes on Kent

By a strange oddity, the old laws allow search for paternity, and many of them give no right of inheritance to the illegitimate child, even over his mother's property.

[K. C.], vol. ii, p. 175

* * *

Contract of marriage

Kent expresses the opinion that English Common Law is simpler, more natural and infinitely less complicated concerning the contract of marriage than Roman Law or our own.

[K. C.], vol ii, p. 153

* * *

Slaves

In Massachusetts where slavery does not exist, a marriage between a white and a coloured person is void.

[K. C.], vol. ii, p. 205

Legislative history of slavery in the State of New York. Atrocity of the first laws. Rapid changes beginning after the Revolution. Very curious.

[K. C.] vol. ii, pp. 205 ff.

The number of Charters of incorporation is increasing in the United States with a rapidity that seems to frighten Kent.

[K. C.], vol. ii, p. 219

In England, corporations are created, and exist, by prescription, by royal charter and by act of Parliament. With us, they are created by authority of the legislature, and not otherwise.[1]

[K. C.], vol. ii, p. 223

We are multiplying in this country, to an unparalleled extent, the institution of corporations and giving them a flexibility and variety of purpose, unknown to the Roman or the English law.[2]

[K. C.], vol. ii, p. 227

[1] Tocqueville quotes in English.   [2] Again quotation in English.

Notes on Kent

In England associations cannot acquire any land without the permission of the King. In America this power can only be limited in the Charter of incorporation.

[K. C.], vol. ii, p. 228

Power of the judges to declare laws unconstitutional.

[K. C.], vol. i, p. 420

Difficulties in understanding Common Law: 648 volumes necessary. Very curious passage in Kent.

[K. C.], vol. i, p. 441

Right of constituents to impose their will on their representative. Disputed. Important point.

[K. C.], vol. ii, p. 6

In cases of defamation the English do not allow proof of the truth of the defamatory facts.

[K. C.], vol. ii, p. 15

Controversial question in America. Strong tendency to permit proof. Freedom of the press too unlimited, breaking all bounds. Curious.

[K. C.], vol. ii, p. 19

Writ of Habeas Corpus.[1]

[K. C.], vol. ii, p. 22

Question of jurisdiction: what happens when two courts claim to be seized of the same case?
Who decides competence?

---

[1] Quotation in English.

X

Notebook E[1]

Miscellaneous papers which cannot be easily classified. Notes Reflections. Ideas.

10. Policy of the United States towards the Indians.

11. Arbitrariness; characteristic of Republics.

What maintains the Republic in the United States.[2]

There are a thousand reasons which concur to support republican liberty in the United States, but a few are enough to explain the problem.

In the United States, it is said, society has been built from a clean slate. One sees neither victor nor vanquished, neither plebeian nor noble, neither prejudices of birth nor prejudices of profession.

But the whole of South America is in this position, and a republic only succeeds in the United States.

The territory of the Union offers an immense field to human activity; it offers inexhaustible nourishment for industry and work; there love of well-being and of wealth perpetually offer an alternative to political ambition.

But in what part of the world could one find more fertile lands, more wonderful wildernesses, more superb rivers, more inexhaustible or more untouched riches than in South America? But yet South America cannot maintain a republic.

The division of the Union into little States reconciles internal

---

[1] The text of the notebooks E and F is based on copies to be found in the Yale Tocqueville Collection; the originals must be regarded as lost.

The transcriptions of these texts are occasionally faulty as Tocqueville's handwriting presented, particularly in his American travel diaries, considerable difficulties. We have corrected the copyist wherever meaning and context justified such a procedure. A few passages, however, remain obscure or unintelligible.

[2] See pocket notebook number 5, p. 179. Cf. *De la Démocratie en Amérique*, I, 1, p. 290 in our French edition.

prosperity and national strength; it multiplies political interests, and weakens party spirit by breaking it up; but Mexico forms a federal republic; it has adopted the constitution of the United States almost without alteration, and yet Mexico is still far from prospering. Lower Canada is surrounded, as is New England, by fertile and limitless lands. Yet, up to our days, the French population of Canada, unstirred by enlightenment, remains cupped in in a space much too narrow for it, and the price of land is almost as high in the neighbourhood of Quebec as in that of Paris, while close by land costs 10 francs per arpent.[1]

There is one great reason which dominates all the others and which, when one has weighed every consideration, by itself sways the balance: the American people, taken in mass, is not only the most enlightened in the world, but, what I rank as much more important than that advantage, *it is the people whose practical political education is the most advanced.*

It is this truth in which I firmly believe, that inspires in me the only hope I have for the future happiness of Europe.

But there always remains this great insoluble question: the special material advantages of the United States would not be enough at all without their high civilisation and experience, but would this high civilisation and this experience be enough without the former?

14th January 1832

FUTURE OF THE UNION[2]

One of the greatest dangers that the Union runs, which seems to result from its very prosperity: the speed with which the new nations are arising in the West and South-West certainly subjects it to a severe test.

The first result of this disproportionate growth is violently to change the balance of forces and of political influence. Powerful States become weak; nameless territories become powerful States. Wealth as well as population changes place. These changes cannot take place without bruising interests, or without arousing violent passions. The speed with which they come about renders them a hundred times more dangerous yet.

[1] About an acre and a half.
[2] Cf. *De la Démocratie en Amérique*, I, 1, p. 380 of our French edition.

That is not all. A society of nations, like a society of individuals, is a difficult thing to maintain. The more members there are in the society, the greater the difficulty becomes; moreover it is essential that each of them should bring moderation and wisdom to the common councils.

Now, not only do the new States of the Union, by the simple fact of their existence, increase the difficulty of maintaining the federal bond, but they also provide much slighter guarantees of wisdom and moderation than do the old States. The new States are generally made up of adventurers. The progress of society is so rapid, one might say so impetuous, that everything there is still in disorder. Nothing there in morals, ideas or laws betrays an appearance of order or stability. In a word, they have the half-savage, uncultivated minds which are characteristic of the first inhabitants of wildernesses, combined with the power which generally only belongs to old societies.

31st January 1832

One of the things that singularly militates in favour of the Union is that all the powerful men and all the great political passions have an interest in maintaining it.

INTEREST ON MONEY

There is not a State in the Union where interest on money is left to fix itself.

In South Carolina it was proposed to abolish the law about interest; this proposal was abandoned as likely to create too great an upheaval in society by changing the interest on previously incurred debts.

The rate of interest at New Orleans is 8%, in Massachusetts 6%.

Mr. Poinsett,[1] 27th January 1832

ON UNIVERSAL SUFFRAGE

Universal suffrage, which has wonderful advantages, can only exist among people for whom government, and especially good

---

[1] Cf. Pierson, op. cit., p. 644. The date of 27th January is probably a mistake: the last conversation with Mr. Poinsett was dated 17th January. See non-alphabetic notebook 3, pp. 110–119.

government, is a secondary interest. By *government* I mean the regulating power over society. Universal suffrage makes the absence of government easier in that it reduces the number of the discontented; but it reduces the obstacles that can oppose the action of the rulers, and it fills official positions with the men least capable of holding them. Witness all the States of the West and Louisiana.

There are two social states that can be clearly conceived: in the one, the people is enlightened enough and finds itself in such circumstances that it can govern itself. In that case society acts on itself. In the other, a power external to society acts on it, and compels it to go in a certain direction. These two principles are clear, and the consequences can be deduced easily and with logical strictness.

But there is a third social state in which power is divided, being at the same time both in society and external to it; that is difficult to understand in theory, and only exists with pain and labour in practice.

The United States has the first, England and more especially France, the third. Causes of malaise for these two powers; but it does not always depend on the peoples to arrive at the first state, and often, by wishing for it, they fall into the second. This should take a fairly high place in a collection of word-puzzles.

16th January 1832

TRADE[1]

How can one doubt that the Union will one day, and that day is drawing near, become the leading maritime power in the world? By herself alone, and for herself alone, she is already trading on a huge scale, and is destined to do so on a much greater scale still; moreover it is to enrich her that Spanish America is getting civilised.

It is easy to foresee that all the imports and exports of the new republics will be carried in American ships. One is all the more convinced of that when one reflects that the South of the United States has no trade. It is the North of the Union that

[1] For the conversation with Mr. Poinsett that suggested these reflections, see non-alphabetic notebook 3, pp. 110 ff., and pocket notebook 5, pp. 177–180.

undertakes the carriage of the produce of the South. And yet the race is English in the South as in the North. Can one believe that the Spaniards in the tropics and on the equator would ever have more industries than the English on the thirty-fifth parallel?

England will be the only rival of the United States as supplier of Spanish America (when the latter feels the needs of a civilised people). But the Americans will easily win, because they are nearer and sail their ships more cheaply.

This commercial movement will for America still further delay the moment of *plenitude*, which is so much to be feared, and will put off the century of revolutions.[1]

16th January

For a people there are three elements necessary for extensive maritime trade.

1st. *Raw* materials or *manufactured goods* to export.

2nd. Needs which the land cannot satisfy.

3rd. A shipping industry without which the other two are insufficient.

A nation can be very rich and very happy without sea trade, but sea trade is a great element in wealth; there is also a political element in that it gives natural nourishment and activity to many spirits and to passions that might have disturbed society.

On Great and Small Parties[2]

What I call great political parties, those concerned with principles and not their consequences, with general questions and not with particular cases, with ideas and not with men, those

[1] Opposite this paragraph on *Trade*, Tocqueville has written in the margin:

Merchant marine. Prodigious increase, first cause quantity of exportable products. Reasons for cheapness. Activity, general knowledge. (*a*) Willtry [*sic*] otherwise dearer. Labour force. American ships transporting everything from England and France. Wood for building. Three sorts. New England. New York. live out [*sic*] (*b*) One can manage without *inscription maritime*. Commercial interests. Slave trade. The union.

Theory of reciprocal trade. Flag covers the goods. Wrongly. No privileges. Tariff. General ideas applied to the United States. Almost indifferent. In what way harmful to the south. Conclusive questions to have manufactures. Morals, oaths, written law.

(*a*) Incomprehensible.

(*b*) Equally incomprehensible. Error in transcription.

[2] See pocket notebook number 4, pp. 170–171. *De la Démocratie en Amérique*, I, 1, p. 179 in our French edition.

parties generally have nobler traits, more generous passions, more real convictions and a look of more frankness and boldness than the others. Private interest which always plays a great part in political passions, is here more skilfully concealed under the veil of public interest; sometimes it even succeeds in escaping the sight of those whom it animates and drives to action.

The little political parties on the other hand are generally without political faith; their characters are consistent and stamped with a blatant selfishness shown in all their acts; their anger is cold. Their language is violent, their progress timid and uncertain. The means they employ are wretched, as is the end they seek; great parties overturn society, the little ones pester more than they disturb it; the first often make one pity humanity, the second despise it; both, the one and the other, have one feature in common: they hardly ever employ to reach their ends means which conscience completely approves. There are men of integrity in almost all parties, but there is no party of integrity.

America has had great parties, but they exist no longer; there has been a great gain in happiness, but, in morality, I doubt it. I cannot conceive a more wretched sight in the world than that presented by the different coteries (they do not deserve the name of parties) which now divide the Union. In broad daylight one sees in their breasts the excitement of all the little shameful passions which ordinarily are careful to keep themselves hidden at the bottom of the human heart.

As for the country's interest, no one thinks about it, and if it is referred to, that is for form's sake. The parties put it at the head of their deed of association, just as our fathers printed 'by royal permission' on the first page of their books.

It is a shame to see what coarse insults, what petty slanders and what impudent calumnies fill the papers that serve as their mouthpieces, and with what unashamed disregard of all the social decencies they daily arraign before the tribunal of public opinion the honour of families and the secrets of the domestic hearth.

14th January 1832

Notebook E

PROFITS FROM THE PLANTATION IN LOUISIANA

Today, 31st December 1831, I went to see a fine sugar plantation 50 leagues from New Orleans on the Mississippi. It employed 70 slaves; the profit, I was told, is about 5 or 6,000 dollars a year, all expenses paid, or 25 to 30,000 francs.

INDIANS

Conversation with Mr. Houston[1] on 31st December 1831. This man has an extraordinary history. After a stormy and troubled youth, he finally settled in the State of Tennessee. There his natural talents and no doubt also his obscure origin won him the people's votes. He had been elected Governor of the State.

At this time he had trouble inside his own family. He complained about his wife; others said that he behaved very badly to her. What is certain is that he left Tennessee, crossed the Mississippi, and withdrew among the Creeks in the district of Arkansas. There he was adopted by one of the chiefs and, it is said, married his daughter. Since then he has lived in the midst of the wilderness, half European, half savage.

We met him on the 27th December at the mouth of White River, where we had stopped to let the Choctaws get off. He was mounted on a superb stallion which had been caught in the prairies between Mexico and the United States. These immense wildernesses are grazing grounds for innumerable herds of wild horses, some of which are captured by the Spaniards or the Indians. Their origin is Andalusian, the horse, as is known, not being an animal native to America. Mr. Houston boarded our boat to go to New Orleans. Mr. Houston is a man about forty-five years old; the sorrows and troubles of all sorts by which his existence has been beset, have as yet left but slight trace on his features; his figure is athletic; everything about him indicates physical and moral energy.

We asked him a great many questions about the Indians, of which these are some:

Q. Have the Indians a religion?

A. Some of them have no belief in the immortality of the

[1] Cf. Pierson, op. cit., pp. 610 ff.

soul. But generally the Indians believe in a God who punishes or rewards the deeds of this life in the other world.

Q. Have they any form of worship?

A. The Osages, who live on the frontier of Mexico, pray every morning to the rising sun. The Creeks have no worship. It is only in times of great calamity, or before undertaking some great enterprise, that they devote themselves to public manifestations of worship.

Q. Have you often seen Indian Christians?

A. Seldom. My view is that it is a very bad plan for civilising the Indians to send missionaries among them. Christianity is the religion of an enlightened and intellectual people; it is above the intellectual level of a people as little advanced in civilisation, and so much the slaves of mere material instincts as the Indians. In my view, one should first try to win the Indians away from their wandering life, and persuade them to cultivate the soil. The introduction of the Christian religion would follow naturally on the change that had taken place in their social condition. I have noticed that only Catholicism has been able to succeed in making a durable impression on the Indians. It strikes their senses and speaks to their imagination.

Q. What sort of government have the Indians whom you have seen?

A. Generally a patriarchal government. Birth makes the chiefs. Among the tribes which contact with Europeans has made more enlightened, they are elected.

Q. Have they any law?

A. There is an idea deeply rooted in the minds of all the Indians, which for many tribes makes the only penal code. It is that blood should be avenged by blood; in a word, the law of retaliation; so when a man has killed, he is consigned to the vengeance of the relations of the dead man, to whom he is handed over.

Q. Does the law of *compensation* exist among the tribes you have seen?

A. No. The Indians of the South think it a disgrace to accept money as the price of the life of one of their brothers.

Q. The notions of justice of which you speak, are very rough. Besides, they only apply to murder. What happens in the case of theft?

A. Theft was absolutely unknown to the Indians before the Europeans introduced among them objects calculated likely to tempt their cupidity. Since then it has been necessary to make laws to prevent theft. Among the Creeks who are beginning to get civilised and have a written penal code, theft is punished by strokes of the whip. It is the chiefs who pronounce the sentence. Adultery by a woman is punished in the same way. Besides, generally the guilty woman's nose and ears are cut. The law of the Creeks punishes fornication equally.

Q. What is the status of women among the Indians?

A. A complete servitude. The women have to do all the unpleasant tasks, and live in great degradation.

Q. Is polygamy allowed?

A. Yes. One can have as many wives as one can feed. Divorce too is allowed.

Q. Do you think that the Indians have great natural intelligence?

A. Yes. I do not think they yield to any other race of men on that account. Besides, I am equally of the opinion that it is the same in the case of the Negroes. The difference one notices between the Indian and the Negro seems to me to result solely from the different education they have received. The Indian is born free; he makes use of this freedom from his first steps in life. He is left to look after himself as soon as he can act; even a father's power is an imperceptible bond for him. Surrounded by dangers, pressed by necessities, and unable to count on anyone, thus his mind must be ever active to find means to ward off such troubles and to maintain his existence. This necessity imposed on the Indian gives his intelligence a degree of development and ingenuity which are often wonderful. The ordinary Negro has been a slave before he was born. Without pleasures as without needs, and useless to himself, the first notions of existence which he receives, make him understand that he is the property of another, that care for his own future is no concern of his, and that the very power of thought is for him a useless gift of providence.

Q. Is it true that the valley of the Mississippi shows signs of the passage of a race of men more civilised than those who inhabit it today?

A. Yes. I have often come across fortified works which bear

evidence of the existence of a people who had reached a fairly high state of civilisation. Whence did that people come? Whither did it vanish? There is a mystery there. But one cannot doubt that it existed, and nothing indicates that the Indians of our day are the remnants thereof. The most probable view seems to me that they were Mexicans who in old days came and settled in the valley of the Mississippi.

Q. Could you give me any information about the line the American Government takes with the Indian tribes?

A. Yes. Very easily. There were and there still are within the Southern parts of the United States, several half-civilised Indian nations whose position vis-à-vis the governors of those States is equivocal, and who hold up the development that might take place in that part of the Union. Congress therefore, as much in the interests of the States of the South as those of the Indians themselves, has conceived the project of transporting them, with their consent, to country which should always remain essentially Indian land. Its choice fell on the upper part of the district of Arkansas. The territory which should be inhabited by the Indian nations, begins at an imaginary line that you can draw on the map from Louisiana to Missouri, and stretches right up to the frontiers of Mexico and to the vast prairies inhabited by the wandering hordes of the Osages. The United States have bound themselves by the most solemn oaths never to sell the lands contained within those limits, and never in any form to allow the introduction of a white population there.[1] There are already 10,000 Indians in the territory. I think that in time there will be 50,000; the country is healthy and the soil extremely fertile.

Q. Do you think that by this means the Indian race can be saved from the disappearance that seems to threaten it? Do you think that this arrangement will not still be only provisional, and that the Indians will not soon be forced to retreat?

A. No. I think that the Indian tribes of the South will find a refuge there, and that they will civilise themselves, if the government is willing to take trouble to encourage civilisation among them. Note that the isolated position in which the Indian

---

[1] Note by Tocqueville in the margin:

There is a law forbidding a white to buy an Indian's land. The United States does not recognise the Indians' right to alienate their land except in their capacity as a people, and when the purchaser is the United States itself.

tribes will be settled, will make it possible to take effective measures to prevent the introduction of strong drink among them. Brandy is the main cause of the destruction of the natives of America.

Q. But do you not think that the tribes foreign to one another will carry on continual internecine war?

A. The United States will man posts among them to prevent it.

Q. Do you believe in the possibility of saving the Indians?

A. Yes, surely. Twenty-five years of skilful handling by the government would certainly bring this result about. Several of the tribes of the South are already half-civilised.

Q. What degrees of civilisation do you find among these people?

A. At the head of all come the *Cherokees*. The *Cherokees* live entirely by cultivating the soil. They are the only Indian tribe that has a written language.

After the *Cherokees* come the *Creeks*. The *Creeks* subsist partly from hunting and partly from cultivating some land. They have some definite penal laws and a form of government.

Next I place the *Chickasaws* and the *Choctaws*. One cannot yet say that they have begun to get civilised, but they have begun to lose many of the traits of their savage nature.

The *Osages* come last of all; they live in continually moving hordes, are almost naked, hardly use firearms at all, and know no Europeans except the fur traders.[1]

The *Osages* are the last tribe of the South-West which has a treaty with the United States.

Q. But that reserve in Arkansas of which we were speaking just now, is only intended to receive the Indians of the South. What line has been taken about those of the West and North?

A. The Indians of the West and North do not find themselves surrounded, as do those of the South, by white populations. They border the United States, and are pushed back before them as the latter advance.

---

[1] Tocqueville has written in the margin opposite this: Story of Cooper. The Letters.

Notebook E

BANKRUPTCY

Congress has the right to make a general law about bankruptcy, but that law has never been made.

[K. C.], vol. ii, p. 321[1]

The great number of insolvencies and bankruptcies which take place every year in the different States of the Union, and more especially the indifference shown by public opinion about this matter, are one of the greatest stains on the American character.

People who should know told me that at Philadelphia the number of insolvencies amounts to about 800 in the year.

The Americans are renowned for their skill in business and their spirit of enterprise. But in general they are considered bad debtors.

When one considers the chastity of their morals, the simplicity of their manners, their habits of work and the religious and settled spirit which prevails in the United States, one is tempted to believe that the Americans are a virtuous people; but when one considers the commercial fervour which seems to devour the whole of society, the thirst for gain, the respect for money and the bad faith in business which appears on every side, one is soon led to think that this pretended virtue is only the absence of certain vices, and if the number of human passions seems restricted here, it is because they have all been absorbed in just one: the love of wealth.

29th December 1831

UNION: CENTRAL GOVERNMENT

The imperfection of the first American Union. Abasement of the State resulting from it; on this point see *The Federalist*, number 15, p. 60.[2] All this matter is very ably discussed.

The main characteristic which distinguishes the new American Union from the old one is this:

[1] Cf. James Kent. *Commentaries on American Law*, New York, 1827, p. 321, federal law on bankruptcy dates from 1898.

[2] *The Federalist or the New Constitution*, by A. Hamilton, J. Jay and J. Madison, 1788. This passage appears on pp. 66 ff. of the Everyman edition.

Notebook E

The old Union governed *the States*, not *the individuals*. It formed as it were a foreign power submitting inferior powers to its laws. The new federal government is in very truth the government of the Union in all things within its competence; it addresses, not the *States*, but *individuals*; its orders are addressed to each of the American citizens, whether he is born in Massachusetts or in Georgia, and not to Massachusetts or to Georgia. It has its own means of forcing each of these individuals to obey it without recourse to other authority than its own.

Example to show the difference: the federal government imposes a tax; in the old Union each State had the duty of collecting the tax and putting it in the coffers of the central government.

The new federal power not only imposes the tax, but has its own officials to collect it, independently of all other authority, from each American, and courts of its own to make sure that the money is paid; in a word, it governs in the fullest sense of the term. All the rights of sovereignty are transferred to it; but still it governs in a restricted circle beyond which it is not allowed to go.

The practical differences resulting from this new state of things, differences which are not at all obvious at first in theory, are however immense.

In that case as in the other the federal power has the right to impose laws on all the members of the Union and the right to force them to obedience. The only difference is in the means, but that difference is immense. When the government addresses itself to a State and notifies it of an order whose execution is unpleasant or difficult, it inevitably finds great difficulty in making itself obeyed: it discovers that its subject is an adversary with an interest in resisting it and strong means to succeed therein. If a State does not wish to come into open conflict, there are a thousand ways of avoiding the order given to it; it does not make itself obeyed, it enjoys its powerlessness and tolerates unpunished resistance to its laws; so civil war or anarchy is the ordinary consequence of such a state of affairs.

But when, on the contrary, the central government not only imposes laws but really governs within the circle of its powers, every time it issues an order, it is no longer a question for the States but for individuals, each one of whom finding that he confronts the Union alone and isolated, cannot contemplate resistance. The action of the central power on each individual in the case where it controls all the rights of sovereignty in matters that fall within its duties, is direct and not indirect. Its way of proceeding is simple, not complicated. It has no need to ask the support of anybody and discovers in itself all the power that it needs.

No doubt the national spirit, collective passions and provincial prejudices of each State tend singularly to diminish the extent of the central power so constituted, and to create centres of resistance to its wishes; restricted in its sovereignty, it cannot be as strong as a government whose sovereignty is complete, but that is an ill inevitable in confederations. What one can say is this, that in this state of affairs each State has far fewer occasions and temptations to want to resist and that, if the thought comes into its head, it cannot put it into execution without openly violating the laws of the Union, and interrupting the normal course of justice, and raising the standard of revolt, in a word suddenly taking up an extreme position, a thing which men always hesitate long to do.

It is to ignorance of this principle that all confederations, ancient and modern, have owed their dissolution and their ruin; so much influence, whatever one may say, have laws by themselves on the destiny of peoples (though many people say that laws are only the image of peoples).

It is an axiom of American public law that every power must be given full authority in its own sphere which must be defined in a way that prevents it stepping beyond it: that is a great principle, and one worth thinking about. This idea is expressed in the following sentence from *The Federalist* (number 23, p. 97); 'If the circumstances of a country are such as to demand a compound instead of a simple, a confederate instead of a sole, government, the essential point which will remain to be adjusted will be to discriminate *the objects*, as far as it can be done, which shall appertain to the different provinces of departments of power; allowing to each the most ample authority for fulfilling those which may be committed to its charge.'[1]

28th December 1831

---

[1] Tocqueville has not reproduced the exact wording of the last part of this quotation, which is, 'for fulfilling the objects committed to its charge'. Cf. *The Federalist*, Everyman edition, p. 112.

Notebook E

This much can be stated, that it is only a very enlightened people that could invent the federal constitution of the United States, and that only a very enlightened people and one peculiarly accustomed to the representative system, could make such complicated machinery work, and know how to maintain the different powers within their own spheres, powers which, without this continual care, would not fail to come into violent collision. The constitution of the United States is an admirable work, nevertheless one may believe that its founders would not have succeeded, had not the previous 150 years given the different States of the Union the *taste for, and practice of, provincial governments*, and if a high civilisation had not at the same time put them in a *position to maintain a strong, though limited, central government*. The federal constitution of the United States seems to me the best, perhaps the only, arrangement that could allow the establishment of a vast republic, and yet to imitate it is absolutely impracticable without the pre-existing conditions of which I was speaking above.

One thing that favoured the establishment of the constitution in America was that the different States, still young and little accustomed to independence, had not yet cherished to a high degree that individual pride and those national prejudices which make it so painful for old societies to give up the smallest parts of their sovereignty.

Examples of federal unions in antiquity and in modern history:
1st. The Amphictyonic council.
2nd. The Achaean league.
3rd. The Germanic body. [i.e. Holy Roman Empire.]
4th. United Provinces of the Low Countries.
5th. Switzerland.

All these confederations have suffered from the defect of the first American Union; they did not at all make a single people out of the different provinces united by establishing a central power and sovereignty in matters that concerned the union. They all came to suffer from civil war, or disintegration and anarchy, but none of them was sufficiently enlightened, as was the American Union, to see the remedy at the same time as it felt the ill and to correct its laws.

For the history of these confederations see the able résumé

made by Mr. Madison in *The Federalist*, numbers 18 and others, p. 72.[1]

29th December 1831

CONFISCATION

Many States of the Union have kept confiscation, even in cases of felony. But it has been abolished in political matters in the laws of the Union. See the law of 20th April 1790, ch. ix, section 24.

Public opinion is in general against confiscation.

[K. C.], vol. ii, p. 318

FINANCES

The financial resources of the United States consist only in revenue from indirect taxes. There are two obstacles which have long prevented Congress from imposing direct taxes:

The first is the extreme repugnance of the people against that form of tax.

The second is the difficulty of assessing them in a country like America.

This second cause is particularly well expressed in the following sentence from *The Federalist* (number 21): 'In every country it is a herculean task to obtain a valuation of the land; in a country *imperfectly settled and progressive in improvement* the difficulties are increased almost to impracticability.'[2]

29th December 1831

SOVEREIGNTY OF THE PEOPLE

The principle of the sovereignty of the people often gives the nations that adopt it an energy that the others lack. However the people does not always know how to impose the necessary sacrifices on itself. '*It is evident*', says Hamilton in *The Federalist*, '*from the state of the country, from the habits of the people, from the experience we have had on the point itself, that it is impracticable to raise any very considerable sums by direct taxation.*

---

[1] Cf. *The Federalist*, Everyman edition, pp. 83 ff.

[2] *The Federalist*, Everyman edition, p. 102. The underlining is Tocqueville's.

Tax laws have in vain been multiplied, new methods to enforce the collection have in vain been tried, the public expectations have been uniformly disappointed, and the treasuries of the States have remained empty. The popular system of administration, inherent in the nature of popular government, coinciding with the real scarcity of money incident to a languid and mutilated state of trade, has hitherto defeated every experiment for extensive collections, and has at length taught the different legislatures the folly of attempting them.'

(*The Federalist*,[1] p. 50)

In several places I have already noticed similar examples. It is difficult to make disagreeable laws, even when they are useful. However, taking everything into account, free peoples, I believe, sacrifice much more money than the others do for social purposes. But that is especially true in the case of aristocratic peoples; democracies live from day to day and are much less able to impose painful exertions on themselves for the sake of the future.

27th December 1831

One cannot know exactly how much energy and how great power of self-control American democracy could show in time of crisis. So far it has not experienced a crisis.

What is certain is that every time the central government has tried to impose direct taxes, it has not succeeded, and that even in the fervour of political passions stirred by the Revolution, it was never without the greatest difficulty that it succeeded in collecting men or money; even then always in insufficient quantity.

So then one must wait for the time when the nation will have recourse to *conscription* and to *heavy taxes* to be able to judge what sacrifices democracies can impose on themselves.

Patent Rights

Acts of Congress of 21st February 1793 and 17th April 1800.

It is Congress that has the duty of granting patent rights. It

[1] Cf. *The Federalist*, Everyman edition, p. 55. Tocqueville quotes in English.

is the Courts that decide the legal questions that can arise concerning patent rights.

It was a necessity to leave this matter to Congress, for it would be useless to obtain patent rights in one State, if that did not confer exclusive rights in another. In Germany where similar powers have not been granted to the central government, the exclusive right is in fact reduced almost to nothing, although very extensive in theory.

The exclusive right can last for fourteen years.

Besides, Kent points out that the questions that can arise out of patent rights, the question for instance of deciding how far it is a true invention or change, are very difficult to decide.

More than 4,000 patents had already been obtained in 1827.

English law is almost exactly the same.

The article contains extracts from the laws of several other nations on this subject.

[K. C.], vol ii, p. 299

COPYRIGHT

In England a statute of the 54th year of George III gives authors exclusive copyright for the duration of their lives.

In America the exclusive right, subject to the fulfilment of certain formalities on the part of the author, only lasts for fourteen years; it may be doubled if the author is alive at the end of that time.

Kent declares that 'the present law of Congress affords only a scanty and inadequate protection and does not rise to a level with the liberal spirit of the age.'

This matter is controlled by the Acts of 31st May 1790 and 29th April 1802.

[K. C.], vol. ii, p. 306

TAXATION: IMPOSITIONS

Troubles and injustices that result from taxation imposed by the localities themselves. Many absentees over-taxed. See the details given by Kent in his commentaries.

[K. C.], vol. ii, p. 268

Notebook E

English Laws

Barbarousness and absurdity of certain English laws still in force.

When a ship is wrecked on the coast, the ship and the cargo belong to the King according to Common Law; but a statute of the time of Edward I declares that it shall be otherwise if there is saved man or animal, 'dog or cat'.[1]

[K. C.], vol. ii, p. 259

It was only forty-six years ago that they gave up dating English laws from the first day of the session of Parliament; thanks to that provision, a man could be condemned to death for an act that was not considered a crime at the time when it was committed.

The generative principle of the English constitution is that Parliament is the source of all powers, and can do what it wishes.

The principle of the different American constitutions is diametrically opposite. In America the source of all powers is found in the constitution, a law pre-existent to all the others, and which can only be changed by the authority from which it emanates, the people. The legislature, far from being the source of powers, is subjected like all the rest to this law of laws from which it cannot for a moment depart without violating the first of its duties.

Associations[2]

The spirit of association, as I have already remarked elsewhere, is one of the distinctive characteristics of America; it is by this means that a country where capital is scarce and where absolutely democratic laws and habits hinder the accumulation of wealth in the hands of a few individuals, has already succeeded in carrying out undertakings and accomplishing works which the most absolute kings and the most opulent aristocracies would certainly not have been able to undertake and finish in the same time.

[1] The last three words are in English in Tocqueville's text.
[2] See also 'Association' in alphabetic notebook 2.

The number of charters of incorporation increases in the United States with a rapidity that appears to alarm Kent, I do not know why; his fears even seem to have been shared in 1823 by the legislature of New York; it seems that the Romans were afraid of associations.

[K. C.], vol. ii, p. 219

'We are multiplying in this country, to an imparalleled [*sic*] extent, the institution of corporations, and giving to them a flexibility and variety of purpose, unknown to the Roman and the English law.'[1]

[K. C.], vol. ii, p. 227

'In England corporations are created and exist, by prescription, by royal charter, and by act of Parliament. With us they are created by authority of the legislature and not otherwise.'[2]

[K. C.], vol. ii, p. 223

In England associations can never acquire land without the King's permission (*Mortmain law*). In America this power cannot be given limits except in the charter of incorporation.

[K. C.], vol. ii, p. 228

A legal association is formed by a contract between the people associating and the government, which cannot be revoked at the good pleasure of the legislature.

That does not apply to political corporations such as towns, counties and villages, whose powers the State can always increase, suppress or vary.

[K. C.], vol. ii, p. 246

SLAVES

Legislation about them.

In Massachusetts, where slavery does not exist at all, nonetheless a marriage contracted between a white and a person of

---

[1] This passage has already been quoted by Tocqueville in his notes on Kent, p. 232.

[2] Tocqueville quotes in English.

colour is void in law, such care has the English race in America taken to preserve the purity of its European blood.

[K. C.], vol. ii, p. 205

Legislative history of slavery in New York State: atrocity of the first laws; rapid changes introduced beginning from the time of the Revolution. Very curious.

Ibid., p. 205 ff.

When voting rights are *universal*, and deputies are paid by the State, it is a strange thing how low the people's choice can descend and how far it can be mistaken.

Two years ago the inhabitants of the district of which Memphis is the capital, sent to the House of Representatives of Congress an individual called David Crockett, who had received no education, could read only with difficulty, had no property, no fixed dwelling, but spent his time hunting, selling his game for a living, and spending his whole life in the woods. His competitor, who failed, was a fairly rich and able man.

Memphis, 20th December 1831

*   *   *

On the Mississippi (27th December 1831)

Just now we are travelling with a man called Mr. Houston.[1] This man has been governor of Tennessee. Afterwards he left his wife, having before that, it is said, subjected her to very bad treatment. He took refuge with the Indians, married one of them and became one of their chiefs. I asked what could have commended him to the people's choice. 'That he came from them', I was told, 'and had risen by his own exertions.'

I was again assured today that in the new States of the West the people generally make very bad choices. Full of pride and without enlightenment, the voters wish to be represented by people of their own sort. Moreover, to gain votes, one must descend to manoeuvres that disgust men of distinction. One must haunt the taverns, drink and argue with the mob; that is what is called *Electioneering* in America.

[1] See above, pp. 240–244.

' *The fittest men* ', Kent says frankly in speaking of the judges,
' *would probably have too much reservedness of manners and severity
of morals, to secure an election resting on universal suffrage.* '[1]

[K. C.], vol. i, p. 273

In several constitutions in the United States, the right of
the electors to force their representatives to vote in a certain
way has been recognised. The principle is contested by the
best minds.

[K. C.], vol. ii, p. 6

If it was generally adopted, it would deal a deadly blow at the
representative system, that great discovery of modern times,
which seems destined to exercise so great an influence over the
fate of humanity. It would then be the people itself that acted,
the deputies becoming its mere passive agents.

PATERNAL POWER

Paternal power which was so prominent a feature of the republics
of antiquity that some writers have seen in it the source of their
greatness and their duration, is reduced almost to nothing in
American institutions. American laws seem to look with as
jealous and suspicious an eye on the power of a father as on all
other powers that can interfere with human liberty.

Customs, morals and opinion are, in this, in harmony with
the laws. Paternal power is an aristocratic institution. It makes
old men into a privileged and governing class. It gives them a
sort of patronage by making their descendants depend on them,
all things antipathetic to democracy.

27th December 1831

Mr. [Richards], mayor of Philadelphia, told me that generally
when a father refused to give his consent to his daughter's marriage (a consent which is not required by the laws of many
States), and when in consequence she escaped from the paternal
roof and married her lover, public opinion almost always pronounced in favour of the daughter against her father, and forced

[1] Tocqueville has already quoted this passage on p. 228 above.

the latter to grant his pardon. For it to be otherwise, the young girl's choice must have fallen on a man absolutely unworthy of her.

31st December 1831

HISTORICAL

The imitation of Jewish laws and customs was carried to such a length by the first emigrants to Massachusetts, that they made the disobedience of a son to his father's orders a capital crime.

[K. C.], vol. ii, p. 172

PUBLIC EDUCATION

Kent, in his *Commentaries*, makes out that in Connecticut, when parents do not give education to their children, the Selectmen have the right to take them away from them in order to procure the instruction which they lack. '*This law*', said the late Chief Justice Reeve, '*has produced very astonishing effects and to it is to be attributed the knowledge of reading and writing, so universal among the people of that State.*' Kent adds: '*during the 27 years in which that distinguished lawyer* [Reeve] *was in extensive practice of the law, he informs us he never found but one person in Connecticut that could not write.*'[1]

[K. C.], vol. ii, p. 165

History of the funds destined for education in the State of New York. Curious.[2]

[K. C.], vol. ii, p. 166

INTOLERANCE

It is something incredible with what rapidity religious tolerance has made progress in America.

A law of the end of the last century in the State of New York declares that every Catholic priest who does not leave the territory of the colony within a fixed time, shall be imprisoned for

[1] Tocqueville has already quoted this passage on p. 231, above.
[2] Quoted already on p. 231 above.

life and condemned to death if he returns. The historian Smith, who was writing in 1756, declares that this law was worthy to last for ever.[1]

[K. C.], vol. ii, p. 63

I am convinced, Mr. Poinsett said to me today (16th January 1832)[2], that even nowadays in America the Lutherans would burn the Calvinists, the latter the Unitarians, and the Catholics all the others, if the civil power was given to any of those persuasions. There is always deep hatred between them.

EXPENSES OF A STEAMSHIP ON THE MISSISSIPPI

The *Louisville* on which we are sailing, weighs about 400 tons. It cost 50,000 dollars to build; it is not expected to last more than four years. The fresh water navigation, the snags and all the other dangers of the Mississippi reduce the life of ships that ply on this river to that short period (on the average).

The price of wood (average) on the banks of the Mississippi is 2 dollars a cord. The boat consumes 30 cords a day. That makes the expense reach 60 dollars.

Provisions and wages for the crew and passengers amount to about the same sum, which brings the expense of a ship of this size up to 120 dollars a day.

Information provided by the Captain of the *Louisville* on 26th December 1831.

There is one thing which America demonstrates invincibly, and of which I had been in doubt up till now: it is that the middle classes can govern a state. I do not know if they would come out with credit from thoroughly difficult political situations. But they are adequate for the ordinary run of society. In spite of their petty passions, their incomplete education and their vulgar manners, they clearly can provide practical intelligence, and that is found to be enough.

In France the middle classes have very narrow prejudices against the upper classes, but perhaps the upper classes, too, have

[1] Cf. above p. 230.
[2] See conversations with Mr. Poinsett in non-alphabetic notebook 3, pp. 110–119.

much too strong an unfavourable impression based on the vulgarity which they note in the others' manners and the turn of their thoughts. They deduce from that incontestible fact conclusions about political incapacity which are not justified, at least not to the extent that is supposed.

Another point which America demonstrates is that virtue is not, as has long been claimed, the only thing that maintains republics, but that enlightenment, more than any other thing, makes this social condition easy. The Americans are scarcely more virtuous than others; but they are infinitely more enlightened (I speak of the masses) than any other people I know; I do not only want to say that there are more people there who know how to read and write (a matter to which perhaps more importance is attached than is due), but the body of people who have understanding of public affairs, knowledge of the laws and of precedents, feeling for the well-understood interests of the nation and the faculty to understand them, is greater there than in any other place in the world.

30th November 1831

In America it is extremely interesting to observe the inclinations and instincts of democracy left to itself, and to see to what social state it must of necessity lead the society it dominates. Such a study is particularly interesting for us, the French, who are going perhaps towards despotism, perhaps towards a republic, but certainly towards a democracy without limits.

id.

About Equality in America

The relationship between the different social positions in America is rather difficult to understand, and foreigners make one or the other of these two mistakes: either they suppose that in the United States there is no distinction between man and man except that of personal merit, or else, struck by the high standing accorded to wealth here, they come to think that in several of our European monarchies, in France for instance, we enjoy a more real and more complete equality than that of the American republics. I hold, as I said above, that both these ways of seeing the matter are exaggerated.

First let us get the ground clear: equality before the law is not at the moment in question, for that is complete in America; it is not only a right, but a fact. One might even say that for whatever inequality exists elsewhere, the world of politics makes ample compensation in favour of the middle and lower classes who, with the inheritors of historic names, hold almost all the elected offices.

I am talking of equality in the exchanges of social life; the equality which draws certain individuals to come together in the same places, to share their views and their pleasures, and to join their families in marriage. It is in that that one must make distinctions between France and America. The differences turn out to be essential.

In France, whatever one says, prejudices of birth still hold very great sway. Birth still puts an almost insurmountable barrier between men. In France the profession a man exercises still to a certain extent places him socially. These prejudices are the most fatal of all to equality, because they make permanent and almost indelible distinctions, even when wealth and time are against them. Such prejudices do not exist at all in America. Birth is a distinction, but it does not in the least place a man socially; it carries with it no right and no disability, no obligation towards the world or towards oneself; class structure by professions is also almost unknown; it certainly does make a definite difference to the position of individuals, a difference of wealth rather than of standing, but it does not create any radical inequality, for it by no means prevents the intermarriage of families (that is the great touchstone).

However one must not suppose that in America all classes of society mix in the same drawing-rooms; that is not so. People in the same profession, with the same views and the same education, seek each other out by a sort of instinct and come together to the exclusion of others. The difference is that no arbitrary inflexible rule prescribes this arrangement. So there is little offensive in it. There is nothing final about it for anybody, and no one can be hurt by it. So in America less than anywhere else does one see that burning desire of one class to share not only the political rights but also the pleasures of the others.

That is the difference for the better between American society and our own.

This is the difference for the worse:

The first of all social distinctions in America is *money*.

Money makes a real privileged class in society, which keeps itself apart and rudely makes the rest conscious of its pre-eminence.

This pre-eminence of wealth in society has less fatal consequences for equality than those which spring from prejudices of birth and profession. It is not at all permanent; it is within the reach of all. It is not radical, but it is perhaps even more offensive still; it is paraded in America much more impudently than with us; talent, merit, which in France decidedly outweigh it when the two are in competition, are here obliged to give place to it. One can give several reasons for this state of affairs.

In France, inequality of rank was extreme. To compensate for imaginary distinctions it was necessary to have recourse to the only reasonable distinction, that of merit. In France, intellectual pleasures and gifts of the mind have always been held in high esteem.

In America, in the absence of all material and external distinctions, wealth appeared as the natural test to measure men's merit. Besides, the Americans are a people with very little feeling for the pleasures of the mind. Exclusively occupied in making their fortunes they must naturally have a sort of veneration for wealth. It arouses their envy, but tacitly they recognise it as the chief advantage.

To summarise then, men in America, as with us, are ranked according to certain categories by the give and take of social life; common habits, education and especially wealth establish these classifications; but these rules are neither absolute, nor inflexible, nor permanent. They establish passing distinctions and by no means form classes properly so called; they give no superiority, even in thought, to one man over another. So that although two men may never see each other in the same drawing-rooms, if they meet outside, they meet without pride on one side or envy on the other. At bottom they feel themselves to be, and they are, equal.

When one wants to judge the equality between the different classes of a people, one always comes to the question how marriages are made. That is the root of the matter. A certain equality, the result of necessity, politeness, or policy, can appear to exist and deceive the eye. But when one wants to take practical advantage of this equality for the intermarriage of families, then one puts one's finger on the wound.

Оніо

(*2nd December 1831*)[1]

Ohio was admitted into the Confederation in 1802. It then had a population of 40 to 50 thousand souls. Today, it has a million. This population is composed of some Europeans, a certain number of people from the South and the East, and of many adventurers from New England, who are already beginning to emigrate towards the less peopled States. Ohio could, without becoming more densely populated than many provinces of Europe, have ten million inhabitants. The fertility of the country seems inexhaustible. It is wonderfully watered by three or four little streams, tributaries of the Ohio, which run back towards the Great Lakes.

As to one's general impression of the State of Ohio, one can say that morally as well as physically it is a being in growth which has not yet any decided character. Its population is composed of too heterogeneous elements for it to be possible up to now, to identify any particular spirit in it or any special way of life. This is the country with the least national character. It is also the one with the fewest national prejudices; in these two respects it is both inferior and superior to the other parts of the Union. Its civil legislation shows how far it is free from precedents in criminal legislation; the State of Ohio has opened up a new line for itself. In civil law, it has amazingly simplified English legislation, and seems, as far as I can judge up to the present, to have freed itself pretty completely from the domination of tradition; I suppose it is the same in the world of *politics*. Laws about the blacks. *Political innovation, bold and decisive progress.*

More than any of the other parts of the Union, Ohio presents the spectacle of a society absolutely occupied with its affairs, and, in the matter of work, growing rapidly. It is there above

[1] See non-alphabetic notebook 3, p. 89 f. and pocket notebook number 3, p. 162.

all that one must go to have an idea of this social state, so different from our own; in Boston, in New York, in Philadelphia, in all the great towns of the coast, there is already a class which has acquired property and which has adopted sedentary habits and wants to enjoy wealth, not to make it. In Ohio everyone has come to make money. No one has been born there; no one wants to stay there; there is not a *single*, absolutely not a *single* man of leisure, not a single speculative mind. Everyone has his work, to which he devotes himself ardently. As yet people just don't know what upper classes are; the pell mell is complete. The whole of society is an industry. More than anywhere else, in Ohio there are no general ideas; ranks are mixed up there; even rules of behaviour still seem uncertain there; no one has had the time to gain a position, a political or social standing there; the people escape from all influences. Democracy there is without limits. Altogether, Ohio gives an impression of prosperity, but not of stability. It is a youthful being, strong and vigorous, but with whom the very speed of growth gives the impression of something transitory and temporary.

One of the most interesting things in Ohio is to see democracy there carried to extreme limits such as it seldom reaches. In those same States of the Union where we saw it most extended, where neither nobility nor wealth dispose of patronage, there are still some local influences: here it is a name which revives some great historical memory and speaks to the people's imagination; there it is the prestige of some great ability; in yet another place, services rendered. In many places it is the moral power exercised over a people's spirit by the memory of a whole life spent before its eyes in doing good. The democracy of Ohio is free even from these feeble influences. The inhabitants of Ohio arrived only yesterday in the place where they live. They have come without knowing one another, and with different morals and conceptions. The greater part of them have not come to stay. No common tie binds them together. There is not one among them who could talk about his life to people who would understand him. No one has had the time to establish a way of life, to win a reputation, or to establish an influence of any permanence on the strength of his services or his virtues. The result is that democracy in Ohio is even more chancy and capricious in its choices than any other that I know. The first comer flatters the people and often wins its vote which is controlled by nothing, *and yet society prospers.* But does it prosper because of democracy or despite of it? That is the point.

The new States of the West, that of Ohio in particular, seem to me to stand in the same relationship to the old States of the Union, as do the latter towards Europe. To explain myself:

The Americans in coming to America, brought with them all that was most democratic in Europe. When they arrived, they left behind on the other side of the Atlantic the greater part of the national prejudices in which they had been brought up. They became a new nation which adopted customs and new morals, and something of a national character. Today a new emigration has begun producing the same effects. The new emigrants bring to their adopted country principles of democracy even more disengaged from any ties, habits even less stamped by convention, and minds even freer than the former ones. It is interesting to trace in the laws the progress of this intellectual and physical movement. A faulty English law (and there are many such) is brought into America by the first emigrants. They modify it, adapting it more or less well to their social condition, but they still have a superstitious respect for it; they cannot get rid of it entirely. The second emigration takes place; the same men again force their way into the wilderness. This time the law is so modified that it has almost lost the trace of its origin. But a third emigration is still needed to bring its existence to an end. And when one bears in mind that this law was probably given to the English by the Saxons, one cannot but be astonished at the influence which the point of departure has on the good or ill destiny of peoples.

Another very remarkable thing in Ohio is this: Ohio is perhaps the State of the Union in which it is easiest to see, in a striking way and close up, the effects of slavery and of liberty on the social state of a people. The State of Ohio is separated from Kentucky just by one river; on either side of it the soil is equally fertile, and the situation equally favourable, and yet everything is different. Here a population devoured by feverish activity, trying every means to make its fortune; the population seems poor to look at, for they work with their hands, but that work is the source of riches. There are people who make others work for them and show little compassion, a people without energy, mettle or the spirit of enterprise. On one side of the stream, work is honoured and leads to all else, on the other it is despised as the mark of servitude. Those who are forced to work to live, cross over into Ohio where they can make money without disgrace. The population of Kentucky, which has been peopled for nearly a century, grows slowly. Ohio only joined the Confederation thirty years ago and has a million inhabitants. Within those thirty years Ohio has become the entrepôt for the wealth that goes up and down the Mississippi; it has opened two canals and joined the Gulf of Mexico to the North Coast; meanwhile Kentucky, older and perhaps better placed, stood still. These differences cannot be attributed to any other cause but slavery. It degrades the black population and enervates the white. Its fatal effects are recognised, and yet it is preserved and will be preserved for a long time more. Slavery threatens the future of those who maintain it, and it ruins the State; but it has become part of the habits and prejudices of the colonist, and his immediate interest is at war with the interest of his own future and the even stronger interest of the country.

So nothing shows more clearly than the comparison I have just made, that human prosperity depends much more on the institutions and the will of man than on the external circumstances that surround him. Man is not made for slavery; *that truth is perhaps even better proved by the master than by the slave.*

Information about Ohio

Civil and criminal law. See under the heading Law.

Banks: there are only two banks left in Cincinnati. Ten years ago all the banks in Ohio went bankrupt as the result of an excessive issue of notes.

Political Condition

Everyone that we have met so far has seemed to us to think that the principle of democracy is carried much too far in Ohio, and that the people generally make bad choices.

Notebook E

Canals

The State of Ohio has already made seventy miles of canals. The rivers are hard to navigate and the roads bad; in a year's time the canal joining the Ohio with Lake Erie will be finished; by its means one will be able to go down from New York to New Orleans without setting foot on land.

Blacks

According to the law, slavery is no longer allowed in Ohio. Free blacks are not even allowed to live there unless they give bail. But this last part of the law has never been put in force. Besides, it is said that there are no more than three thousand blacks in the State of Ohio.

CINCINNATI[1]

Cincinnati presents an odd spectacle. A town which seems to want to get built too quickly to have things done in order. Large buildings, huts, streets blocked by rubble, houses under construction; no names to the streets, no numbers on the houses, no external luxury, but a picture of industry and work that strikes one at every step.

It is always difficult to know exactly what causes the birth and growth of towns. Chance almost always plays a part. Cincinnati is situated in one of the most fertile plains of the New World. This advantage began to draw population to its neighbourhood. Factories were established there; they provided for that population and soon for part of the West. The success of industry there brought in new industries, and the movement is stronger than ever. Besides, Cincinnati has been and I think still is in part the entrepôt of the valleys of the Mississippi and the Missouri with Europe through New York, and of the States of the North with Louisiana. But in this last context it is probable that Louisville which is much better placed, will soon have the advantage.

---

[1] Tocqueville spent the 1st to 4th December 1831 there. See pocket notebook number 3 p. 162. Cf. Pierson, op. cit., chap. XLI.

Notebook E

We passed through the whole breadth of Kentucky, going from Louisville to Nashville.[1] We also passed through the greater part of Tennessee, going from Nashville to Memphis on the banks of the Mississippi. These two States seemed to us very like one another in many respects.

The country is covered with hills and shallow valleys through which a multitude of little streams flow; it is a land of natural, but uniform, beauty.

In both States the ground seemed still almost entirely covered by forest. At distant intervals a line of fencing, some burnt trees, a field of corn, some animals, a cabin made of roughly shaped tree trunks put on top of one another, indicated some denizen's isolated home. One hardly sees any villages. The cultivators' houses are scattered in the midst of the woods.

Nothing is more unusual than to see a brick house in Kentucky; we did not see ten of them in Tennessee. Except for Nashville.

The peasant's cabin in Kentucky or Tenessee is generally divided into two parts as shown in the margin.[2] All round there are a certain number of huts that serve as stables.

The interior of these dwellings show up the master's laziness even more than his poverty. There one finds a fairly clean bed, some chairs, a good gun, often some books and almost always a newspaper, but the walls are so open to the day that the outside air comes in on every side.

One is scarcely better protected than one would be in a shelter made of leafy branches. Nothing would be easier than to protect oneself against bad weather and stop the cracks, but the master of the place is incapable of taking such trouble. In the North there is a look of cleanliness and thoughtfulness in the ordering of the smallest houses; here everything seems sketched out, everything left to chance; one would say that the inmate lived from day to day with the most complete carelessness of the future.

In the parts of Kentucky and Tennessee through which we

[1] Tocqueville and Beaumont were at Louisville on 9th December 1831 and left Nashville on 11th December. See non-alphabetic notebook 3, the conversation with Mr. McIlvaine, pp. 99–100.

[2] Tocqueville has made a sketch of this cabin in the margin.

passed the men are big and strong; they have a national physiognomy, and an energetic look. By no means like the inhabitants of Ohio, who are a confused mass, a mixture of all the American races, they on the contrary all come from a common stock and belong to the great Virginian family. So, too, they have much more than any other Americans we have yet met, that instinctive love of country, a love mixed up with exaggeration and prejudices, and something entirely different from the reasoned feeling and the refined egotism which bears the name of patriotism in almost all the States of the Union.

Almost all the farmers we saw, even the poorest, had some slaves.

These are clothed in rags, but generally seem strong and healthy. [A few lines of the manuscript are damaged here.]

After passing over a fence of roughly shaped wood, not without the risk of being devoured by the owner's dogs, one reaches a cabin through whose walls a fire can be seen crackling on the hearth; one pushes open a door hung on leather thongs and having no lock; one enters a sort of savage hut which seems the refuge of every misery; there one finds a poor family living with the leisure of the rich. As you come in, the master of the house gets up, and receives you with pressing hospitality, but he is careful not to go himself to get what you need; in his mind it would be degrading to him to serve you. It is a slave who pokes the fire to warm the traveller; it is a slave who gets his clothes dried and brings him the food he needs. The master watches and his gestures direct his servants' work; he does nothing himself. If he opens his mouth, it is to call his dogs or to tell of some of their bold feats. There is no farmer in Kentucky or Tennessee so poor but can represent a fine example of the country gentleman of old Europe.

Nothing in Kentucky or Tennessee gives the impression of such a finished society; in that respect these two States are essentially different from those newly peopled by the Americans of the North, in which one finds the germs of the high civilisation of New England. In Kentucky or Tennessee one sees few churches and no schools. Society, like the individuals, seems to foresee nothing.

But yet they are by no means still rustic folk; there is none of that simplicity bred of ignorance and prejudices and   . . .

[one word missing] which distinguish agricultural peoples in the least accessible places. These men nonetheless belong to one of the most civilised and rational peoples in the world. Their manners have nothing of rustic naïveté. The philosophic and argumentative spirit of the English is found there as in all America. There is an astonishing circulation of letters and newspapers among these savage woods. We travelled with the mail. From time to time we stopped at what is called the post-office; almost always it was an isolated house in the depths of a wood. There we dropped a large parcel from which no doubt each inhabitant of the neighbourhood came to take his share. I do not think that in the most enlightened rural districts of France, there is intellectual movement either so rapid or on such a scale as in this wilderness.

In Kentucky and Tennessee slavery has immense effects on the character and habits of the masters: it halts the industry of the inhabitants, and prevents emigrants from outside from contributing theirs. But it presents no threat to the future of the colonists.

The black population is much smaller than the white, and it always will be so more and more. That is due to natural causes which can easily be demonstrated.

In Kentucky and Tennessee no crop requiring a very great number of slaves is cultivated; [the manuscript is damaged here; the gist is that the land does not produce any very valuable cash crop and is divided up into quite small holdings]; on each small holding lives a white family with a very small number of slaves; one does not see, as in the South, hundreds of slaves cultivating the land of one white man. Moreover Kentucky and Tennessee were peopled by poor emigrants who could not have assembled a great number of slaves on any one property even if the type of cultivation had made it easy to do so. In Kentucky and in Tennessee the masters live all the year round on their land. They direct their slaves' work and the poorest work with them themselves.

That then shows that it would be possible to do without slavery. Public opinion in these two States seems entirely to support this view. But slavery is an evil whose roots go so deep that it is almost as impossible to get free from it after its fatal influence has been noticed as before it was appreciated.

Notebook E

It would be absurd to want to pass judgement on a whole people after spending a week or ten days among them. So I can only trust to hearsay.

The inhabitants of Kentucky and Tennessee are well known throughout the Union for the violence of their behaviour; if what we were told in the country is true, they seem to deserve that reputation; they say that quarrels often lead to bloodshed, and that elections seldom pass off without knife-blows given and received.

Various reasons which are not impossible to define, must have combined to give the inhabitants of Kentucky and Tennessee the character attributed to them.

The first is the climate; passions have always been hotter in the South than in the North.

The second is slavery, a common factor for all the inhabitants of the South and one that modifies their national character in the same way. The habit of uninhibited command gives men a certain feeling of superiority which makes them impatient of opposition and irritated at the sight of obstacles. Slavery makes work a dishonour; it makes the whole white race a leisured class for whom money loses a part of its value and who seek their pleasures elsewhere in the resources of society and the pleasures of pride, a sort of aristocracy which is not guided at all by the sort of legal honesty of trading peoples, but which has its values of convention, its fine feelings and its point of honour. The Americans of the South are brave, comparatively ignorant, hospitable, generous, easy to irritate, violent in their resentments, without industry or the spirit of enterprise.

Take these same men to a new land, put them in a wild country where they must fight daily against all the miseries of life, and you will make their passions still more irritable and violent and further removed from society. The slightest tiresome contact with it will be painful to them; less civilised, they will have learnt even less to master themselves.

That is the whole story of the inhabitants of Kentucky and of Tennessee. They are men of the South, masters of slaves, but rendered half savage by solitude and hardened by the miseries of life.

Means of Increasing Public Prosperity

Almost all political precepts have in the way they are announced something so generalized, so theoretical and so vague, that it is difficult to derive the least advantage from them in practice. There are almost always so many remedies whose usefulness depends even more on the temperament of the patient than on the nature of the illness.

I only know of one means of increasing the prosperity of a people, whose application is infallible and on which I think one can count in all countries and in all places.

That means is none other than increasing the facility of communication between men.

On this point what can be seen in America is both strange and instructive.

The roads, the canals and the post play a prodigious part in the prosperity of the Union. It is good to examine their effects, the value attached to them and the way they are obtained.

America, which is the country which enjoys the greatest sum of prosperity that has ever yet been vouchsafed to any nation, is also that which, in proportion to its age and means, has made the greatest effort to supply itself with the free communications of which I was speaking above.

In France there are a great number of very crowded centres of population through which no road passes, in such a way that they are more separated from the rest of the nation than half the world has been in time past. I have no doubt that it would take longer and be more expensive to have ten sacks of wheat sent from some village in Lower Brittany to Paris than to have all the sugar of the colonies sent to the same place.

In America one of the first things done in a new State is to make the post go there; in the forests of Michigan there is no cabin so isolated, no valley so wild but that letters and newspapers arrive at least once a week; we have seen that. It is especially in these conditions that I felt the difference between our own social state and that of the American people. There are few rural districts in France, in which, proportionately speaking, as many letters and newspapers are received as in these still savage lands where man still fights against all the miseries of life and only has glimpses of society at long intervals.

Notebook E

When it seems that the population is turning towards a certain part of the country, there is a hurry to open a road thither. The road almost always comes before those whom it is intended to serve, but it encourages them to move; we have several times seen main roads opened up literally in the middle of the wilderness.

America has undertaken and finished the construction of some immense canals. It already has more railways than France; no one fails to see that the discovery of steam has incredibly increased the power and prosperity of the Union; and that is because it facilitates speedy communications between the different parts of that immense land. The States of the South, where communications are less convenient, are those which languish compared to the rest.

Of all the countries in the world America is that in which the spread of ideas and of human industry is most continual and most rapid. There is not an American but knows the resources of all the parts of the vast land that he inhabits; all the able men in the Union know each other by reputation, many of them personally. I have often been struck by astonishment to find how far that is the case. I can say that it has never happened to me to speak to an American about one of his compatriots without finding that he was up-to-date in knowing both how he was now placed and the story of his life.

I know that this intense industrial and intellectual movement is particularly encouraged by education, by the sort of government America enjoys, and by the altogether special situation in which the Americans find themselves. In America populations are not at all sedentary even in the old-established parts; almost all of them are real industrial entrepreneurs who feel the need for means of communication with a liveliness and use them with a zeal which one could never expect from the routine and lazy spirit of our peasants. The effect of a road or a canal is therefore more noticeable and above all more immediate in America than it would be in France.

So we ought to act as the Americans do in the new districts of the West; open the road before the travellers in the certainty that they will come along sooner or later to use it.

As to the means employed to open up communications in America, this is what I have noticed about the matter.

Notebook E

It is generally believed in Europe that the great maxim of government in America is that of laisser-faire, of standing by as a simple spectator of the progress of society, of which individual interest is the prime mover; that is a mistake.

The American government does not interfere in everything, it is true, as ours does. It makes no claim to foresee everything and carry everything out; it gives no subsidies, does not encourage trade, and does not patronize literature or the arts. But where great works of public utility are concerned, it but seldom leaves them to the care of private persons; it is the State itself that carries them out; the great canal joining the Hudson to Lake Erie was made at the expense of the State of New York; that joining Lake Erie to the Mississippi is the work of the State of Ohio; the canal joining the Delaware to Chesapeake Bay is an undertaking of the State. The main roads which lead to distant places are usually planned and carried out by the States and not by companies.

But it is important to observe that there is no rule about the matter. The activity of companies, of parishes and of private people is in a thousand ways in competition with that of the State. All undertakings of moderate extent or limited interest are the work of parishes or companies. Turnpikes or toll-roads often run parallel to those of the State. In some parts of the country, railways built by companies fulfil the functions of the canals as main thoroughfares. The local roads are maintained by the districts through which they pass. So then no exclusive system is followed; in nothing does America exemplify a system of that uniformity that delights the superficial and metaphysical minds of our age.

In institutions, laws, government of society and everyday life, everything, on the contrary, is different and various.

Everything adapts itself to the nature of men and places, without any pretension to bend them to the strictness of an inflexible rule. From this variety springs a universal prosperity spread throughout the whole nation and over each of its parts.

To return to roads and all the other means of bringing the achievements of industry or of thought quickly from one place to another, I make no claim to have discovered that they contributed to the prosperity of a people; it is a truth universally felt and recognised. I only say that America illustrates this truth most palpably, makes it stand out more clearly than any other country in the world, and that it is impossible to travel through this Union without being convinced, not by argument, but by the evidence of all the senses, that the most powerful and the most infallible means of increasing the prosperity of a country is in every possible way to encourage easy exchanges between those who live there.

AMERICAN MORES

The greatest equality seems to prevail between those who occupy very different positions in society.

The authorities seem extraordinarily approachable.

On the 13th of May, Mr. Morse,[1] a judge at Cherry Valley, introduced us to the Governor of New York, who was living in a boarding-house and received us in the parlour without any sort of ceremony whatsoever. Mr. Morse assured us that everyone could always do the same as we.

E

PARTY SPIRIT IN AMERICA

Mr. Schermerhorn[2] told me that there were no parties in America like those we have; the nation is no longer divided by two opposing principles that serve to keep it apart.

That state of affairs came to an end with the extinction of the two parties of *federalists* and *non-federalists*. Now there are scarcely more than those who defend and those who attack the measures of government in order to gain office and bring public opinion over to their side.

April 1831

EQUALITY

See American manners.

[1] Cf. Pierson, op. cit., p. 63.　　　　　[2] Cf. Pierson, op. cit., p. 49.

Notebook E

I

IMPRESSIONS

First Impressions

Up to now we have formed the impression that the Americans carry national pride to an altogether excessive length. I doubt if one could extract from them the smallest truth unfavourable to their country. Most of them boast about it without discrimination, and with an impertinence disagreeable to strangers that bears witness to but slight enlightenment. Generally speaking there is a lot of *small-town* pettiness in their make-up, and they make much of things in the way common to people unacquainted with great matters. But we have not yet met a really outstanding man.

By and large they seem to be a religious people. It is clear that no one thinks of ridiculing religious practices, and that the goodness and even the truth of religion is universally admitted *in theory*. How far is their life regulated by their doctrine? What is the real power of religious principle over their soul? How can the variety of sects not breed indifference, if not externally, then at least within? That is what remains to be known.

Up to now it seems to me that this country illustrates the most complete external development of the middle classes, or rather that the whole of society seems to have turned into one middle class. No one seems to have the elegant manners and refined politeness of the upper classes in Europe. On the contrary one is at once struck by something vulgar, and a disagreeable casualness of behaviour. But also no one has what we should call *mauvais ton* in France. All the Americans that we have yet met, right down to the simple shop-assistant, seem to have had, or to wish to appear to have had, a good education. Their manners are sober, poised and reserved, and they all wear the same clothes.

All the customs of life illustrate this mixture of the two classes which in Europe are at such pains to keep separate. The women dress for the whole day from seven o'clock in the morning. At nine o'clock one can already pay some calls. By mid-day one is received everywhere. All bears the stamp of a very busy life. We have not met any *fashionables* yet. I have even got the idea that chaste morals here are less completely due to strict principles than to the impossibility for all the young people of thinking of matters of love and of being seriously occupied with them.

15th May 1831

Pioneer.
Help given to religion by Congress.
[A few words incomprehensible.]
Truths that one cannot tell to the people.
Slavery. Way of fighting it. Experience and cruelty.
Piece work of public prosecutor.
Means of making canals, roads and post prosper.
Ways of becoming a lawyer in Ohio.
Reason for not committing crimes, impossibility of comparing America and Europe in this respect.
Different sorts of patriotism.
Sociability of the Americans.
Slavery quite different from that of the Ancients.
Newspapers. Character, effects of newspapers.
Influence of small States on the happiness of humanity.
About the power of the judges to declare laws unconstitutional. Consequences.
About confederation. Why the legists are so against it. Wonderful eulogy of the *Common Law*; its influence on the English spirit.
Lack of uniformity. Its advantages. What ought to be the limit to that.
Fatal influences of military spirit and habits in Republics.
About the dogma of the sovereignty of the people and the way it is understood in America.
Of the reasons which make democracy natural for America.
About the tendency to weaken the federal link.

In Washington ask for general information such as:
1st. The interests of the different States;
2nd. Future of the Union, causes of division;
3rd. Nullification in the South;
4th. What means has the Union to make itself obeyed?

5th. Ask if it is useful for the State to undertake enterprises;

6th. What are the principles of the United States in commercial questions?

7th. Composition of Congress, its spirit, its progress, its capacity, its enlightenment.

8th. What gives the Americans the commercial superiority which they have and makes it possible for them to navigate so inexpensively?

9th. Are educational establishments subject to any inspection?

Jealousy of democracy.

Interests of the provinces of the West.

Time when the Constitution was made.

Democratic country.

No rules.

Slavery in Kentucky.

Religion.

Blacks.

Corruption.

Fears to be entertained for the Union.

Lands to sell.

Jealousy against the central government.

XI

Notebook F

CIVIL AND CRIMINAL LAW IN AMERICA

Philadelphia (*15th November 1831*)

I have just had a conversation more than four hours long about judicial questions with Gilpin,[1] a very intelligent young lawyer of this town. Here is a resumé of what I learnt:

To understand American law, it is necessary to be acquainted with the judicial organisation and the principles of English legislation.

(1) The most ancient and the principal source of English laws is what is called *Common Law*. The Common Law is composed of two elements: (1) of the traditional customs which have never been collected into a body as has been done in France from the time of Beaumanoir,[2] but whose principles are found stated in the *Records* of the judges who have succeeded one another through several centuries; (2) of Statutes, or laws of the Parliaments. The Statutes are later in date than the customs, which latter come from the first years of the monarchy; they have modified and weakened them. They form with them the incoherent and undefined body of legislation which one calls *Common Law*. We will go on to see what further legal growths have come to be imposed on that.

(2) The temporal power of the clergy in England began with the Norman Conquest. The clergy in England, as on the Continent, was not slow to claim for itself jurisdiction in certain

---

[1] Cf. Pierson, op. cit., pp. 529 f.

[2] Philippe de Beauvaisis, author of *Les Coutumes de Clermont en Beaumanoir* which date from appr. 1280. Cf. F. Olivier-Martin, *Histoire du Droit français des Origines à la Révolution*, Paris, 1948, p. 117 f.

cases concerning conscience. All cases which concerned the execution of contracts which had some relationship to a sacrament, such as marriage and wills. The Church in claiming to give judgment in such cases, did not confine itself to the rules of one country more than another. It recognized the universality of Roman Law and discarded the Jury. In this way, Roman Law was introduced under the mantle of the Church into the English legal system. It occupied a limited position there, but a very important one. In the course of time, ecclesiastics gave up pronouncing judgment, but the ecclesiastical tribunals continued to exist, and they still exist in our day, under the name of Doctors Commons.

(3) It was only in the beginning of the reign of the Tudors that the inadequacy of customs or of the Common Law began to make itself felt. Society had become markedly civilised. Transactions between people had become more numerous and the need for a more developed law had followed on the growth of wealth and enlightenment. This change made itself felt at the time when royal power was at its apogee. It was then natural that plaintiffs should address themselves to the King's representative for judicial matters to obtain what the law could not give them. From that was born the court of the Chancellor, *Chancery or Equity Court*. That was the remedy the English found to amend the vices of their laws without changing them. They preferred to throw themselves on the mercy of arbitrariness and to create a sort of judicial dictatorship rather than undertake the reorganisation of their ancient institutions. In the matters that fell within their jurisdiction, these Chancellors created an entirely new law. They drew their principles sometimes from the Common Law, sometimes from Roman Law, sometimes from their own selves, and time established their jurisprudence.

One can list under four headings the cases over which the Courts of Equity claimed jurisdiction:

1st. What is called *Specific Performance of Contracts*.[1] Under the Common Law when a man who had made an agreement with another, refused to carry it out, the latter could only ask the jury for damages; that was only an incomplete form of justice, for I who entered into the contract, might have need of the thing promised and not of the money offered in its place. A society

[1] Tocqueville uses the English terms.

which had made some little advance in civilisation, could not put up with so rough a conception of equity.

So one turned to the Chancellor to find a remedy for the deficiency of the law. He accepted jurisdiction in cases of this type without the aid of a jury, and obliged the man who had undertaken the obligation to perform the actual terms of the contract. Note well that this applied only to *contracts* and not to cases concerning *real property properly so called*. A man buys some land; he pays for it. The property is transferred by the former owner who refuses to give it up; in that case there was no need to have recourse to the Chancellor. The jury could order that the real owner be put in possession. In that sense, to speak accurately, the contract had already been executed, and the matter was reduced to an ordinary question of ownership.

2nd. The second category of jurisdiction is what are called *Trust Estates*.[1] One man gives another some land but stipulates at the same time for the payment of a life annuity. The payment of that rent is no matter for the Common Law; it was difficult for the plaintiff to start an action. The matter raised a complicated question which went beyond what the Common Law had foreseen. There was, in fact, no question of claiming back what had been given. That really was the property of the recipient; it was only desired that the recipient should perform an act posterior to the sale but which nevertheless had been foreseen by the contracting parties. When cases of this type began to become common people turned to the Chancellor, who provided the remedy.

3rd. The third category of the Chancellor's jurisdiction is *bankruptcies*. The order in which creditors should rank; means of forcing the debtor to pay; all these rules could not get themselves settled in the framework of the semi-barbarous society of the Middle Ages. The need soon made itself felt, and the Chancellor took on the duty of filling up the gap in the law on this point.

4th. Everything relating to minors, guardianship of them and their property. That fell under the jurisdiction of the Chancellor, as the result of feudal conceptions. The lord, according to feudal laws, was the natural guardian of his vassals when minors. The King in that sense, was the guardian of his subjects when minors.

[1] Again: Tocqueville uses the English term.

When the royal power had grown still greater out of the ruins of that of the lords, it was the King, who through his Chancellor, took on the duty of regulating everything which concerned guardianships and to judge all the cases where the interests of minors were concerned.

It seems that when the defendant refused to obey the Chancellor's judgement, the latter had him arrested until he submitted, a procedure which is still enforced.

Such is a sketch of English law. It was necessary to talk about it in order to understand what had been taken over from it in Pennsylvania.

Gilpin's Explanation (continued)

First, it is desirable to understand the organisation of the Courts in Pennsylvania.

Pennyslvania is divided into one hundred counties, and these counties make up twelve *circuits*; there are twelve judges called *judges of the inferior court*.[1] Every three months they must hold a session in each of the counties that make up their circuit, not alone, but supported by two assessors who live in the county and who are not *lawyers*;[2] as a result of this, everything depends on the judge.

That court has jurisdiction over all cases where the sum in dispute is uncertain, and all those where the sum in dispute is known and does not exceed five hundred dollars.

Above that court comes the *Superior Court*.[3] It is composed of five judges. There are only five circuits in Pennsylvania. To provide for this second court, the five judges make their circuit every three months just as the inferior judges do. They have two categories of jurisdiction;

1st. They decide cases involving a known amount of over five hundred dollars;

2nd. They hear what we in French incorrectly call appeals; we will see later what an appeal signifies in English and American law.

Q. But I don't see in all that either Chancellor's Court or Ecclesiastical Court.

[1] In English in manuscript.
[2] In the margin Tocqueville writes 'I am not sure of this reply.'
[3] In English in manuscript.

Notebook F

A. These courts have never existed in Pennsylvania.

Q. To whom have their functions been attributed?

A. *Partly to the judges and partly to the jury*. In many cases they have abstained *entirely from doing what those courts used to do*.

Q. Elucidate those three ideas by examples.

A. Suppose that some case between a married couple (Ecclesiastical Court Doctors Commons)[1] involves a question of fact and a question of law. The English Court judges everything. Here, the judge only decides the question of law and leaves the question of fact to the jury by a special delegation which is called an *issue*.[2]

Q. Why do you not simply say that in that case you have merged the ecclesiastical jurisdiction with that of the *common pleas*?[2] The case you have described is a case of common pleas.

A. No, in a case of common pleas in common law, the jury is judge both of law and of fact. It follows the direction of the judge but it is not the judge who decides. In this case the jury only acts by delegation; it decides a special question and does not judge the case.

In almost all the matters that concern the jurisdiction of the *courts of chancery*, the jurisdiction of the chancellor has been purely and simply merged in the jurisdiction of the *common pleas*. Questions of law are subject to the *direction* of the judges following the precedents of the courts of equity, and the questions of fact are decided by the jury which gives the judgment.

There are, however, many aspects of the jurisdiction of the Chancellor which we have not adopted. Thus in Pennsylvania a litigant cannot be questioned by way of depositions taken in writing (*Sur faits et articles*).[3] So in Pennsylvania a man who enters into a contract in bad faith cannot be forced to carry out his engagement; and one is obliged to condemn him to pay excessive damages so as to force him indirectly to do what the Court of Chancery would have made him perform under threat of prison. Many people, struck by these gaps, have wished to

[1] Tocqueville has written in the margin: 'I am not certain about this answer.'
[2] English term used by Tocqueville.
[3] Tocqueville refers here to a procedure in French civil law, called *interrogatoire sur faits et articles* which did not exist in Pennsylvanian legal procedure. Cf. *Grande Encyclopédie*, vol. XII, p. 17 f. See also Blackstone, *Commentaries* III, London, 1803, pp. 437 f.

institute a Court of Chancery here; but public opinion has always stood out against it. You see that we have nothing here of what I called above the *specific performance of the contracts*.

Q. I begin to see what is the jurisdiction of the court of *common pleas* with you; it brings almost everything under its scope. But what I do not properly understand is the way in which it proceeds, the functions that are proper to the judge and to the jury, and the way in which the latter works.

A. To understand it thoroughly you must see it in action; but I will try to explain how it works in practice.

The court being composed of judges and jury, the plaintiff explains his claim, and produces his documents and his witnesses. The defendant disputes the documents, and calls other witnesses or cross-questions those called by his adversary; the judge speaks; he sums up the evidence for the facts, and states the law in the different hypotheses. The jury retires and brings in a unanimous verdict which, in the form of a clear-cut decision, embraces both fact and law. Suppose, for instance, that a man claims the ownership of an inheritance; his adversary counter-claims twenty years prescription; the judge having heard argument, says to the jurors: 'The plaintiff has an incontestable right to the property, but the defendant counter-claims prescription which, *under the terms of such a law*, should make him lose his case; it is for you to decide whether the defendant has proved that he did in fact enjoy the twenty years of possession of which he speaks.'

The jury confines itself to deciding that the property in question shall not be returned to the plaintiff. By that decision it establishes all at once: 1st. That the defendant enjoyed twenty years of possession. 2nd. That the law gives him the right to rebut the case that has been brought against him.

Q. But are reasons never given for the jury's verdict?

A. No, never. That is a result of the institution of the jury. Only *Records* are kept of the legal reasons given by the judge in his direction to the jury and they can be used by the appellant.

Q. Do you leave the examination of written evidence to the jury?

A. Yes. The jury decides all questions of fact, whether it be a simple fact such as some definite action, or a complicated fact such as the intention of the parties as shown by the documents produced by them.

Q. But how can a jury manage questions that require so much experience and sagacity?

A. It manages with the help of the judge who sums up the pleadings and examines the documents; besides you will see later on all the ways of recourse provided by the law.

Q. I used to imagine that the jury could only order the payment of a sum of money. But am I to understand that it can order that a man be put in possession of land?

A. Yes. Certainly; the jury orders that the true owner be restored to possession of his property.

Q. But in enforcing such a judgment incidents may arise. Who judges them, as the Court does not exist five minutes after it has pronounced judgment?

A. What you speak about seldom happens. In general the parties are not allowed to plead unless they do agree on the bases of the case perfectly, the extent and the limits of the field of litigation for example. If by chance the execution of such a judgment does give rise to an incident, that incident results in a new case which is judged by a new jury.

Q. The jury, no doubt, has nothing to do with the execution of its judgments?

A. No. As soon as the verdict is pronounced, the judge dismisses the jury which never has anything more to do with the case.

Q. When it is a case requiring expert evidence, how are things arranged?

A. The parties who have anticipated the need for such proof, call experts to give evidence before the jury, and they are cross-questioned like the other witnesses.

Q. Are written depositions read in the presence of the jury?

A. It *can* be done when the parties agree to that. It *must* be done when the witnesses live in another State. Then the judge sends a sort of judicial commission to the State where the witnesses are. They are heard, and the record of the hearing is given to the jury to read.

Q. Do you allow proof by witnesses for every sort of matter?

A. Yes. But we do not allow it against the clear sense of a document.

Q. So in France one is not allowed to prove by witnesses what *could* be proved by written evidence; in Pennsylvania, what is proved by written evidence. There the possibility, here the fact itself.

A. Exactly.

Q. I begin to understand the procedure in your civil cases; I clearly see that the jury must continually make great mistakes, both in law and in questions of fact, when the facts of a case are complicated. Tell me now what are the remedies?

A. The remedy lies in the power of the judges, an immense and arbitrary power, but one whose limits have been so fixed by custom and by public opinion that it is difficult to make ill use of it.

We do not have in Pennsylvania what are properly called judgments on appeal,[1] that is to say judgments pronounced by a superior Court which quash, modify or uphold the judgment pronounced by the first judges. Our system of recourse is absolutely different from yours; I will show by stages the means provided to remedy the faults that result from the institution of the jury.

The judge who presides over the *common pleas, always has the right, during the hearing in court, to annul the verdict of the jury and to send it back to reconsider the case.* That is the abstract principle; but the verdict, one knows, includes law and fact. Here there is a distinction that must be made in practice. For a judge to quash a verdict as unjust *in fact*, the injustice must be blatant; were it otherwise, the judge would expose himself to an immense moral responsibility. For, though the English do not have the same superstitious respect as the French for *the verdict of the jury on matters of fact*, they nevertheless agree in principle that it must not be interfered with except in the last extremity. If on the other hand the judge thinks that the jury have made a mistake of law, it is almost a duty for him to quash the verdict, and he does in fact quash it very frequently.

You see then that, however things may appear, it is the judge, with you as with us, who is master of the point of law, and that he also exercises an influence over the decision of the point of

[1] Tocqueville has noted in the margin: It does appear however that in the case of a judgment pronounced by an inferior court acting as an *ecclesiastical court*, there is occasion for an appeal, and a judgment on appeal such as we understand it, but that is an exception.

fact. That is a first guarantee against the incapacity of the jury. And here is a second against both the incapacity of the jury and that of the judge. It is what is called a *writ of error*,[1] or a demand for a new judgment.

That demand can be made in two ways:

1st. It is addressed by the loser to the judges of the same inferior tribunal that has already given judgment, to which the President of the Court of Common Pleas belongs.

The loser explains to this full court that the jury by its verdict has violated the law or committed an injustice. He produces new evidence, brings forward new witnesses, and argues the case again. The judge who has already given judgment is present with his colleagues and gives judgment, as they do, on this appeal.

If the court thinks that the jury has committed a plain injustice, or if it thinks it has made a mistake in law, whether it followed the judge's instructions or departed from them, it quashes the verdict, but without pronouncing judgment itself, sends the case back to the same judge and another jury.

If the jury persists, a fresh appeal can be made to the full court, which can again grant a *new trial*; theoretically speaking this could go on for ever, but in practice it would seem that after a second attempt the court of *Common pleas* ends by giving way.

2nd. That is one method of appeal open to the loser. But instead of addressing himself to the judges of the inferior court, he may (*I think at his option*) address himself to those of the superior court who, on taking cognizance of the case, proceed in the same way as the inferior judges, and send the case back, as the others do, if they quash it, to the same judge with another jury.

You see that strictly speaking, with us, there are not *two degrees*, but in some sort an appeal from the judge to himself. Our superior court is not devised to correct the judgments of the inferior judges, but to judge more important matters; it has a superiority in learning rather than a superiority in hierarchic position.

Q. Do you realise that the power of your judges is immense? It is altogether much greater than that with which we entrust them in France.

---

[1] English term used.

Notebook F

A. Yes. Their power is immense, but their responsibility is no less. In France the judges are irremovable; here they can always be removed for *bad behaviour*.[1] Everything is interlocked in a legal system.

Q. But what do you understand by *bad behaviour*? Is it necessary that the judge should have committed a crime or an offence anticipated by the law; or may it be a question of incapacity, partiality, passion, negligence, in a word all the *faults* (not *offences*) for which a magistrate may be blamed, but which the law cannot and will not define?

A. The expression *bad behaviour* is not at all defined. Although it is restricted within certain limits by precedents and public opinion, *bad behaviour* only applies to things done in a professional capacity, but it can be of a great many sorts.

Q. But are you not afraid that in this way the magistracy may fall little by little under the yoke of political opinions, and that it may lose the neutral and unchanging character proper to it?

A. I do not know what will happen in the future, but up to now those defects have not made themselves felt. Put the power of controlling the judges where you like, it must always for the public good be put somewhere. The complete independence of the magistracy seems to me a dangerous principle.

Q. So far we have been discussing the details concerning the institution of the jury in civil cases; now let us look at the institution from a general point of view. Tell me what you think about it?

A. As far as the correct decision in each case is concerned, it seems to me that the superiority of the jury as an institution can be contested,[2] though in this respect I am still inclined to think it better than permanent tribunals. I think that trial by jury costs the State more than the other. But I find that the institution of the jury has immense advantages that no other system could offer:

1st. It makes justice respected: not only can the jury not be corrupted, but one cannot suspect that it could be corrupted. So respect for the judgment given is very great.

2nd. The jury gives men a great experience of equity in practice. Each man, in giving judgment, feels that he might be

---

[1] The last two words in English in Tocqueville's manuscript.

[2] Tocqueville has noted in the margin: See in the *Federalist*, pp. 356–7, a very interesting opinion expressed by Hamilton on the institution of the jury. Cf. *The Federalist*, Everyman edition, pp. 423 f.

judged in his turn, and in absolutely similar circumstances.

3rd. It militates against that individual egotism which is the ruin of societies, and teaches men to concern themselves with something other than their own affairs, to take responsibility, and to play a public part.

4th. It helps incredibly to form the judgment and to increase the enlightenment of the people; that, in my opinion, is its greatest advantage; the jury is a school where the people come to learn their rights, where they come into contact with the most learned and enlightened of the upper classes, where the laws are taught in a practical way and one within the scope of their intelligence, by the most intelligent minds. In this respect I think the jury in civil cases is more important than the jury in criminal cases;[1] it has perhaps a more indirect influence on the politics of a people, but one that is even stronger.

Where the jury is established, even in civil cases, despotism is impracticable.

Q. But do you think one could establish it among a people who have not been long accustomed to it?

A. Yes, in making the jury, little by little, decide questions of fact separated from questions of law, and beginning with the facts in civil cases that have the closest analogy to the facts in *criminal* ones.

* * *

Conversation with the Recorder[2] of Philadelphia, an extremely intelligent and able young man

Q. Who compose your jury?

A. One must make a distinction between the right to be a

---

[1] Tocqueville has noted in the margin: I regard the jury in criminal cases as the strongest safeguard against tyranny, and it is especially for that reason that I value it in civil cases. This is how I have reached this opinion; laws are always unsteady so long as they are not based for support on morals. Morals are the only tough and durable power among a people.

So it is by grappling with civil suits that the jury, becoming an ever-active institution, and one which affects all interests, and to which everyone constantly has resort, it is in grappling with these suits that the institution of the jury truly penetrates into habits, fashions the human mind to its forms, and finally comes to be merged into the whole conception of justice.

Once it has entered in this way into morals, it cannot be removed from the laws in criminal matters.

Cf. *De La Démocratie en Amérique*, Ibid, p. 282 ff.

[2] Under the charter of 1691 the Recorder of Philadelphia is under the authority of the Mayor.

juror and the use of that right. Every citizen of Philadelphia *twenty-one years old* and paying taxes *can* be a juror. But in fact it is only about two-thirds of them who fulfil that function.

Every year the *assessors*[1] (those who fix the taxes) make a list of those whom they judge able to perform this social duty. They eliminate men who are notoriously *incapable* or *unworthy* and put the names of the others into a box from which 48 names are drawn at each session.

Q. Is this choice of the *assessors* arbitrary?

A. Yes.

Q. Does it happen that people appeal against their decision?

A. No. Jury service is an obligation that one is very glad to avoid, and besides the *assessor* changes every year and is elected, which is a great guarantee that he does not act lightly, and makes it easier to back up his decision.

Q. Are the jurors paid?

A. Yes, in criminal as in civil cases. They receive a dollar a day apart from travel allowance. This indemnity is paid by the State, never by the parties. This indemnity is almost always insufficient to cover the cost of travel and the waste of time involved.

Q. From how far off do the jurors come to the place of trial?

A. 8 or 10 miles at the most.

I then explained to the Recorder how things were done in France; my explanation seemed to surprise him very much; he emphasized the need to pay the jurors, adding that perhaps trial by jury was more expensive than another method.

Q. But do you really think it useful in practice?

A. By and large, yes. Trial by jury makes justice respected; it gives the people a practical knowledge of the laws and the valuable habit of arguing and hearing argument. But I think that one could introduce great improvements into the institution of the jury. One could leave questions of law entirely to the judge. Complicated questions of fact, such as those depending on the examination of documents, can also not be well judged by the jury.

Q. Do you think that the jury could be introduced in civil cases into the legislation of a country which has not had it?

A. Yes, with modifications and if one is careful to separate

[1] English term used.

and define the questions of simple fact which I think the jurors are more apt to decide rightly than the judges.

Q. In criminal cases does not the judge have a great influence over the jury?

A. Yes, when he knows how to handle it skilfully. There are some magistrates who seem to think it their business to secure a conviction and who charge the accused. They fail. A skilful judge should show himself perfectly impartial if he wants to direct the jury, which it is desirable that he should do, for the jury often makes great mistakes.

* * *

Philadelphia (13th November 1831)

Today I was present at one of the hearings in the States' Court: a man was being tried for making forged notes of the Bank of the United States.

One of the lines taken by the defence was that the man had only done so in order to discover the real forgers. Charles Mitchell (that was his name) was a former convict; he had long been paid by the police to make secret enquiries into crimes and, although he had not been paid this time, it was the police that he wanted to serve; such was the lawyer's argument, and what came out most clearly for me is that there is a secret police in America.

Mr. Dallas,[1] the attorney general, showed us all the exhibits in the case; they consisted in: 1st. The piece of forged money seized; 2nd. the circumstantial evidence; 3rd. The list of witnesses.

There are no interrogatories, nor written hearing; expert witnesses are listened to at the hearing as witnesses.

Id. Mr. Richards,[2] Mayor of Philadelphia, told us today that some judges press for a conviction but that nonetheless in general they show themselves impartial and even kind towards the accused, and exercise a great influence over the jury. That was not always the case with the attorneys general.

What gives the judges such immense power over the jury in criminal cases, is the immense influence they are necessarily in the habit of wielding in civil cases: *important*.

[1] Cf. Pierson, op. cit., p. 528 f.   [2] Cf. Pierson, op. cit., index.

The judge is definitely master of the law in civil cases. Why then are the questions not divided? Why not give him the *ostensible* direction of the legal part of the case? I see two good reasons for it: 1st. There is an advantage in having the verdict pronounced by the jury; it has more effect on public opinion; 2nd. It is almost impossible, and we find that ourselves in criminal cases (except the simplest ones) always to make a clear division between questions of law and questions of fact. The nature of things has often made an indissoluble link between them.

Besides, apart from rational motives, the strongest reason that one can give for the English procedure in this matter is that it was instituted at a time when there were, so to say, no questions of law to be resolved.

JURY

Boston (30th Semptember 1831)

It appears from a conversation that I have just had with Mr. Coolidge[1] that the jury here is composed from all who vote at elections; now the property qualification to be an elector is fixed so low that one can say that the whole population is on call for jury service.

Q. Do you observe any disadvantages from having the jurors taken like that from all the classes?

A. No. But our people are the most enlightened that there is in the world.

Q. Is jury service an oppressive duty?

A. No. The lot seldom falls on one.

Q. You acquiesce readily in it?

A. Yes. But nonetheless one regards it as a very disagreeable circumstance to have to form part of a jury.

Q. Do the jurors receive an indemnity?

A. Yes; they receive a small indemnity.

Q. Do you think that the rule of *unanimity* is a good one?

A. I have not thought in advance how to answer that question; but I am inclined to think that it is bad, and what leads me to think so is that it often happens that the jurors cannot agree, and then others have to be called.

[1] See non-alphabetic notebook 2, pp. 59–60. Cf. Pierson, op. cit., p. 366.

Note: two facts come out from this conversation, whose importance is very great:

The first, that the number of jurors is immense;

The *second*, that their functions are not unpaid.

* * *

Conversation with Mr. Duponceau[1]

Mr. Duponceau is a Frenchman who has been settled for fifty years in America, practising as a lawyer there.

He. There are certain cases in which the jury seems to me an excellent institution. Those for instance in which it is a case of fixing damages or unravelling the dishonesty of one of the parties. The jury then, not relying, as the judges do, on artificial and unsubstantial arguments, but following rather the instincts of honesty, more often spots bad faith.

In all other cases the usefulness of a jury in civil cases is, to me, a doubtful point.

English law only knows two means of action: *imprisonment* and *bail*; it makes monstrous abuse of them.

* * *

(*14th October 1831*)

I have just found in the book called *Town Officer*,[2] the following details about juries in New England.

The jurors are chosen every three years by the *Selectmen*.

They must be under seventy years old and have the right to vote to choose the national representatives.

The following are exempt from jury service: the Governor, the Lieutenant-Governor, the judges, the clerks of the common law court, secretary and treasurer of the commonwealth, Loan officers, Revenue officers, Judges and Registrars of Probate, Registrars of deeds, settled Ministers of the Gospel, Officers of any college, Preceptors of incorporated Academies,

---

[1] It was on the 12th October that Tocqueville met Mr. Duponceau. See pocket notebook 3, pp. 153 f. Cf. Pierson, op. cit., p. 474.

[2] In the margin: p. 200. The work in question is: *Town Officer or Laws of Massachusetts*, by Isaac Goodwin, Worcester 1829. See also pocket notebook 3, p. 154.

Physicians and *Surgeons*, Cashiers of incorporated banks, Sheriffs and their deputies, Marshals and their deputies, *Counsellors and attorneys at law*, justices of the Court of Session, Constables.[1]

No one may be a juror more than once in three years.

The jurors receive 1 dollar 25 cents a day and 6 cents a mile there and back.

Those who fail to present themselves for the jury are condemned by the court to a fine which cannot exceed 20 dollars.

Note: I observe that jurors are summoned to estimate the damage caused by a flood: id. occasioned by the bad state of a road; id. occasioned by an objectionable establishment.

* * *

Conversation with Mr. Curtis,[2] *a distinguished Boston laywer, about civil legislation (27th September 1831)*

Q. I have often before collected information about matters concerning civil law; but since these notions have not been acquired methodically, they are in confusion in my mind. This time, if you will allow it, we will take things in their logical order.

When a man wants to start a case against another, what is the first act in the procedure?

A. In each county there is an officer called the *Sheriff*. The sheriff is the agent of the civil power and the enforcer of its judgments.

When a man wants to begin a case against another, he goes to find this official. The sheriff's order makes this summons known to his adversary.

In New England every man who claims to be a creditor and brings an action for the recovery of the debt, has the right to have his adversary imprisoned, or to force him to give bail. In other States of the Union, to gain the power to imprison his adversary (in the case when he does not give bail), it is necessary to affirm on oath the reality of the debt. It is not like that here; the creditor, without even fulfilling this formality, can set the sheriff in motion and have his debtor imprisoned.

---

[1] Enumeration is in English in Tocqueville's manuscript.
[2] Cf. Pierson, op. cit., p.385.

On the day fixed by the summons, the defendant or his lawyer appears before the tribunal and, if he is not ready, asks for an adjournment.[1]

Q. I now understand the procedure for coming before the tribunal. Tell me now to which tribunals one can go.[2]

A. The plaintiff pays for that at his risk and peril.

Q. Has every judge the right to disclaim jurisdiction?

A. Yes. But the parties can appeal from his judgment disclaiming jurisdiction.

[N.B. These answers seem not to follow straight on from the text, and perhaps it is just a mistake of the copyist.]

A. When less than 20 dollars are in dispute, one goes to the Justice of the Peace who gives judgment without the intervention of a jury.

2nd. When it is a question of inheritance, when, for instance, an heir brings a case or a legatee wishes to claim his right, he goes to a judge (the judge of probate).[3] This judge has both *administrative* and *judicial* functions. He does not allow the heir or the legatee to take his share until he has given bail into his hands for the value of the personal property.

When a case arises out of the inheritance, he judges it without the help of jurors. But the litigants can appeal to a higher court.

3rd. The third court of first instance before which one can bring one's case, is the court of *common pleas*. One can say that that is ordinarily the competent court, and that all the others are established for cases that are an exception.

The court of *common pleas* is made up of a judge and twelve jurors: it is held four times a year; that is what are called terms.

Its jurisdiction extends to all cases to do with the boundaries of land, and all those that can be reduced to a question of damages.

This is how matters are conducted before that court: the lawyers on one side and the other produce evidence, depositions written or verbal. They plead.[4] The President sums up; he explains the point of law and states the questions of fact. The

---

[1] In a note in the margin: Can he demand evidence?

[2] In the margin: And first who decides the competence?

[3] English term used.

[4] Note by Tocqueville in the margin: Proof by witnesses is allowed for all sorts of matters, except for four or five cases foreseen by the law; that is the general principle.

jury retire to their room, and then pronounce a verdict which at one and the same time gives judgment on the point of fact and the point of law. But this verdict is divisible. The part that concerns the facts cannot be questioned (except before a higher court); the part that concerns the law can be annulled on the spot by the judge or quashed later by him, if the litigants claim and prove that the law has been violated.[1]

Moreover, as a verdict never creates a precedent, if the parties do not complain, the judge leaves the *verdict* as it has been given, even if it be contrary to the law. (It is the judge who decides whether a question is one of fact or of law.)

The jurors are never entrusted with the interpretation of a document.

One cannot cross-question the opposite party in front of the jury. Only the Court of Chancery has the right to undertake such an examination.

I recently saw a case that lasted for nine days on end in front of the same jurors. But such an event is very rare.

4th. The fourth and last court of first instance is the Court of Chancery.

The Court of Chancery is an English institution. It is only thirty years ago that we introduced it into Massachusetts; it still has a more limited jurisdiction than in England or in the rest of the United States. We have no Chancellor. Before it was introduced here, its place was filled by giving part of its jurisdiction to other courts.

I regard the Court of Chancery as a necessary institution, when the jury is used in civil cases.

Its jurisdiction is of two sorts:

1st. It takes provisional decisions about all matters of urgency; broils and fights; it gives summary judgment and acts as umpire; the arrangement is that it has no terms, but is in session all the year.

2nd. It judges all questions of conscience, all cases where the good faith of the parties is put in question, and all those which, since they cannot be solved by the payment of a sum of money, give occasion for judgments whose execution is difficult and contested.

It is the jurisdiction of the Court of Chancery which is the

[1] In the margin: Must judgment then be given on the point of law alone?

most difficult part of our law for a foreigner. It is determined by *nuances* rather than by fixed rules; to feel at home in this subject one needs a sensitivity acquired by experience.

In Massachusetts one is always free to bring a case before the *common pleas*, even when it is of a type that ought to go to chancery, always provided that one reduces it to a question of damages.

REFLECTIONS[1]

This is what seems to me to stand out most clearly from the preceding conversation.

It is clear that the whole of English, and, in consequence, American law is an ancient fabric made out of elements brought in at different periods, and in which we must look neither for any new idea, nor deduction from principle, nor methodical order.

It seems to me *so far* certain that in the beginning judgment by jury was applied to everything. That indeed was the only judicial principle of our fathers, the Germans; but that judicial form can only subsist in the context of a society in its infancy, and one in which cases are based on the appreciation of a fact.

In proportion as European societies became more civilised, the difficulty of confining oneself to the jury was more and more felt. On the continent and especially in France, where the advantages of a new state of affairs have always struck men's minds more than those of the old state, the jury was made to vanish in order to establish permanent tribunals.

In England, on the contrary, where the human mind makes slower progress, where the need for logic is not such a preoccupation as it is with us, and where people are much more guided by everyday facts and held back by the fear of any complete change, in England, instead of destroying the jury, untold efforts were made to keep a place for it in the legal system.

Each century, as new progress was made in the social condition, demonstrated the impossibility of having such-and-such a type of case decided by a jury. Keeping pace with these difficulties as they presented themselves, ever new expedients were devised to get round them.

Thus it came about that the multiplication of cases (and they

[1] On the jury see that word in alphabetic notebook 2, pp. 221–222. Cf. *De La Démocratie en Amérique*, I. 1, p. 282 ff.

increase in proportion to the growth of a society in enlightenment and wealth) made felt the impossibility of using trial by jury to decide everything. So a minimum was fixed below which the jury would not be consulted.

When the legal system had developed, the need was felt for a standing tribunal to interpose between the parties and prevent them from doing anything, while they were waiting for a decision, to prejudice their rights; and it was necessary to create that tribunal.

When people began to see more clearly the *interests* involved in cases, it was felt that but half justice was provided by reducing all cases to questions of damages, and it was also seen that, as soon as a court ordered something to be *done*, there could be argument about the meaning of the judgment, and the difficulties involved in carrying out such a judgment could only be resolved by turning to the judge who had made it. Now the jury is a judge chosen for the case and one who vanishes as soon as he has given judgment. Nonetheless the institution of the jury was not given up, but a tribunal was created alongside of it to determine questions of that sort.

Finally, even in actions where there was only a question of money, it was increasingly felt, as the law became more complicated, that fact and law were forever getting involved and could hardly be sorted out from one another. Even then they did not despair of preserving the jury, but its *verdict* was made divisible. The judge remained responsible for questions of law and the interpretation of documents: the jury found its function concentrated, not in appearance but in reality, on the questions of fact.

The conclusion[1] from all of that is that the jury in civil cases

[1] Long note by Tocqueville in the margin, opposite the paragraph beginning 'The conclusion . . .':

Besides I cannot believe that one could safely entrust a permanent judicial body with the right to decide the *constitutionality* of the laws if the jury did not exist.

Now this power of the judges is one of the greatest remedies for the faults of democracy.

The judges forming a body absolutely apart would be dangerous for liberty or would soon lose their power.

The jury introduces a habit of argument and experience of public affairs to a great many people.

It teaches a people to become involved in public business and to think of the business of society as being its own.

is by its very nature an institution appropriate to the needs of a nascent society and not for the exigencies of an enlightened and developed legal system. The English laws show the near impossibility of adapting it completely to an advanced social state and leave one in great doubt whether it is useful to *justice* in the position that has been kept for it; but its political *usefulness* is immense and it is from that point of view that one must consider it.

* * *

Continuing the conversation with Mr. Curtis

Q. Don't you think that many parts of your procedure could be simplified and could you give me a satisfactory reason for all the rules that control you?

A. No. Our legal system has been formed in stages. It has been bequeathed to us by our fathers. Custom has made us understand its spirit and familiarized us with its practices. But it would be impossible to apply it as we have it to another people. There is nothing of logical deduction about it.

Q. Do you think that after all the jury is useful in civil cases?

A. For my part, and many people think like me, I think that in almost all cases, and even when it is a question of fact, one can place more reliance on the ability of the judges than of the jurors.

Nonetheless, the people is astonishingly attached to trial by jury even in civil cases, and it would be absolutely impossible to get rid of it.

Common Law

English common law[1]

It is a great subject to deal with, that of common law, its advantages, its disadvantages and its influence. Here I only want to throw out a few suggestions.

It gives a great outward strength to justice, it prevents the magistracy from becoming a body outside the people and gives it immense and almost always useful power in political questions.

Established in civil affairs as in criminal ones, it gets such a grip on customs and enters so far into ideas and morals that it becomes impossible to abolish it in criminal cases. Now one cannot conceive a people in which a jury is solidly established which is not a free people.

[1] Note in margin: 31st December. On the Mississippi. The ideas in this note are incoherent and ill digested, but it contains many things which I can use.

English common law has never been written down as certain of our customs have been; it is strictly the knowledge of the past, the understanding of precedents. In English common law, there are examples but there is no law.

As time goes on, examples from the past become more numerous; the subject matter, the documents recording them increase. (Kent, *Commentaries*, vol. i, p. 441, asserts that at the moment there are no less than 648 books required to make the library of a man of law.)

It is necessary to distinguish between the points of law which the common law leaves in eternal doubt (theoretically speaking) and the judicial institutions, the conservative principles which it has created and which have often become real laws, such as the jury, the cross examination of witnesses. . . . . [1]

Such a way of ordering justice seems absolutely barbarous to those who are used to a codified system.

However I am not far from believing that in the hands of an equally enlightened people the two systems reach almost the same result.

I think that men's respect for jurisprudence increases in proportion to the scarcity of written laws.

Vagueness in a legal system is a social ill so palpable and so generally felt that, where there is no law, a sort of instinct of preservation attaches magistrates to precedents and triumphs in their hearts over the urge to use their power and make innovations. So for all the great principles of law about which jurisprudence has had a thousand occasions to pronounce, the judge finds himself truly bound, not in theory, but in practice; it does not even occur to him to wander from the path trod and retrod so many times: there are only infrequent questions, not very important matters and new cases in which argument is open and the judge feels himself in a position to have an opinion of his own.

How strange it is! In the country where the judges have the right to refuse to apply the laws of the State because they are unconstitutional, they are bound in the smallest cases by the opinion of their predecessors and submit their reason to that of another. The Common Law seems to increase the importance of the magistrate by raising him almost to the rank of a legislator. The truth, however, is that it lowers him: under the Common

[1] Dots in the manuscript.

Law the judge obeys his predecessors; under written law, the law.

Is not this more or less what happens among the nations that have the best codes? Can the most skilful legislator foresee all cases; is anything more required than the establishment of general principles which, in their application, give rise continally to disputes?

There are no doubt more points left vague under the Common Law than under a written law; but the cases that are left in doubt by a written code are harder to judge and more slowly settled than those which arise under the Common Law, since, where the law is written down, jurisprudence has less power. So then the two systems in the hands of enlightened peoples balance out more or less.

But the partisans of the Common Law go further, and think that it should be given the preference. It is that which I do not think can be sustained.

The Common Law which was born in times of ignorance, and which has been added to at different times and by different hands, cannot present a whole so complete, so rational and so linked together as the written law resulting from the labours of an assembly or a man in an age of sanity.

All, or almost all, of the advantages of the Common Law are shared by it with written law, and written law has besides some advantages of its own.

The greatest is to make the law in its important points and its general principles open to all. Under the Common Law it is only a man of law who knows what is allowed and what forbidden.

The second advantage is that for the man of law it makes a sane, fixed and not variable law, which is less expensive to study and easier to remember.

The Common Law is a dangerous weapon in the hands of a people with little enlightenment.

One can say that the Common Law is a cause which results from its effect, a law which springs from a judgment instead of forming the basis for it. So then if the judicial body is ill composed and if it is not continuously controlled by an enlightened public opinion, the legal system can fall into a state of almost complete barbarity.

I see a special and limited advantage for the Common Law

under Monarchies, and especially under absolute Monarchies. It is to make the people take part in the formation *clandestinely* of the law. Under the Common Law the judge is in some sort a legislator, especially in new cases.

Now the judge is a man of his century; public opinion surrounds him, and he shares a feeling for the national needs of his age with all his generation.

That is even more true yet if the judge is always working in the presence of a jury; he will then without noticing it himself put his ideas and those of his generation into his judgments, that is to say into the law. In his hands the law will undergo unfailing changes which will make it the interpreter of the opinions and the needs of each century. But this advantage of the Common Law will not be felt in States where the people take a part in law-making. There, there is no need to proceed by indirect means.

It is to that flexibility of the Common Law as much as to its feudal origin that one should attribute the character of independence which distinguishes it from written law.

It is fairly generally admitted that Roman Law is more complete, less tied up, more provident and competent than the Common Law, but it is maintained, and with reason, that there prevails in the latter a respect for political rights, and a spirit of liberty absolutely unknown to Roman Law. That applies to Roman Law, but will not do as an argument against written law in general. Kent expresses this idea in his *Commentaries*, vol. i, p. 507, in these terms: 'The value of the civil law is not to be found in questions which relate to the connexion between the government and the people, or in provisions for personal security in criminal cases. In every thing which concerns civil and political liberty, it cannot be compared with the free spirit of the English and American common law. But upon subjects relating to private rights and personal contracts, and the duties which flow from them, there is no system of law in which principles are investigated with more good sense, or declared and enforced with more accurate and impartial justice.'[1]

Born among the Barbarians the Common Law is, like the civilisation that brought it forth, defective, but it breathes the spirit of independence of the centuries in which it began to

[1] Quotation from Kent in English in manuscript.

flourish. I should not feel any doubt about deciding in the negative the question whether today it is preferable to written law. But its abolition on the continent of Europe has been a great misfortune. I believe that, on the other hand, its maintenance in England has singularly helped to feed ideas and principles of liberty and indirectly, by that means, has served, in spite of its defects, towards the progress of civilisation in that island, whereas the introduction of written law on the continent, though it is a law more complete, more competent and more civilised, if one may put it so, has helped to establish despotism in Europe, and, by that, has harmed the cause of civilisation which it seemed to serve.

Apart from the political consequences which the preservation of the Common Law has had in England, I believe that its existence has, besides, singularly helped to give a certain turn to the English spirit.

It has created in that nation what one might call the spirit of precedents, that is to say a certain turn of mind that leads men to look not for what is reasonable in itself, but for what is done, not for what is right, but ancient, not for general theories but for particular facts. I have no doubt that experience of the Common Law and the part that the men of law and the judges have at all times taken in argument about political matters, have proved a powerful auxiliary for aristocratic institutions, and, in conjunction with them, have greatly helped to give the English that superstitious respect for the works of their fathers and that hatred of innovation which distinguish them.

In the United States where the laws as well as morals tend towards a democracy without limits, one nevertheless still finds this tendency which the Common Law gives to the human spirit. One notices it in the unruffled state in the whole of society but it is among the men of law that one sees its evident mark. The men of law in the United States are the enemies of change, the men of precedents: that is not precisely their character in France. The mania for generalizing everything is what distinguishes our lawyers; the absence of general ideas is notable in America among the men of law.

Generally American men of law emphatically sing the praises of the Common Law. They oppose codification with all their powers, which is to be explained in this way:

1st. If a code of laws was made, they would have to begin their studies again.

2nd. The law becoming accessible to the common herd, they would lose a part of their importance. They would no longer be like the Egyptian priests, the sole interpreters of an occult science.

Some distinguished men in America, even outside the bar, are opposed to codification, among others Mr. Poinsett. Mr. E. Livingston on the contrary is very much in favour of it. He told me straight out today that the lawyers who were of an opposite opinion had an interest in the matter.

The fact is that unwritten constitutions often give rise to less argument than those that are written down.

It is easier to prove an antecedent fact than to discern the intention of a legislator and the spirit of the written law.

CONSTITUTIONS COMPARED

Massachusetts 1779

Legislative Power

1st. Two branches, together bearing the name of the General Court of Massachusetts.

The Senate

Composed of 40 persons elected for *one* year.

Conditions for being Electors of the Senate

To be twenty-one years old, three pounds of revenue or sixty pounds of capital (*estate*).

The senators are chosen by each district.

Conditions of Eligibility

To be elected senator a man must be 'seized in his own right of a freehold within the commonwealth of the value of three hundred pounds at least or possessed of personal estate to the value of six hundred pounds, or of both to [?] the amount of the same sum.'[1]

[1] Tocqueville quotes in English.

2nd. To be an inhabitant of the district for which one is chosen.

3rd. An inhabitant of the Republic for five years.

House of Representatives

The number of the members is in proportion to the population and varies with it.

Conditions for being an elector: the same as above.

Conditions of Eligibility

1st. To have lived for a year in the district which nominates him.

2nd. Having been seized in his own right of a freehold of the value of one hundred pounds or any rateable estate to the value of two hundred pounds.[1]

Particular Rights of the House

1st. To impeach before the Senate.

2nd. To vote subsidies.

3rd. To be paid journeys there and back.

Executive power

Chosen by whom?—The electors of the senators and the representatives.

For how long? One year.

What conditions? 1st. Seven years of residence in the Republic; 2nd. Being seized in his own right of a freehold of the value of one thousand pounds; 3rd. That he professes the Christian religion.

Extent of his power

1st. He prorogues the legislature.

2nd. He is commander of the forces by sea and land.

3rd. He has the right to grant pardons (on the advice of his Council), except in case of impeachment by the House of Representatives.

4th. He appoints the officers of justice, the attorney general and the solicitor general.

[1] Tocqueville quotes in English.

Notebook F

DIRECTOR OF PUBLIC PROSECUTIONS IN THE UNITED STATES

He is in some ways above, in some ways below ours.

He is below in that: he does not have such a high standing in society; he has no status in civil cases; he performs no permanent functions; in some States his salary depends on the judge, in others on the conviction of the accused.

The official of the department of public prosecution is in no sense a magistrate. He does not have the whole of society under his supervision. He is not the guardian of criminal justice. A criminal case begins without his co-operation; he does not direct it at all and only plays an indirect part. The criminal investigation police is divided between several hands instead of being united in his own.

He is above in that: his power in certain aspects is almost unlimited. He cannot be set in action by a private person; he is the absolute and uncontrolled master of public action.

He does not prosecute if he does not want to, and he can prevent the jury from pronouncing judgment by *declaring that he withdraws*.

All this side of the American legal system seems ill-digested and lacking in logic. It is a mixture of *arbitrariness* and *weakness*. I think the constitution of our department of public prosecution is preferable.

CRIMINAL PROCEDURE

One can divide it into three steps or summary inquiries:

1st. Before a Justice of the Peace to put him in a position to know if he ought to issue a summons and insist on bail.

2nd. Before a grand jury to see if an accusation should be brought.

3rd. Before a petty jury to see if a conviction is justified.

These three points are very summary.

If the accused pleads *guilty,* the jury is not consulted; the court sometimes hears witnesses to find what the extent of the punishment should be, and pronounces judgment.

Judicial Organisation

1st. Of what officials is the department of public prosecution composed?

2nd. What is the extent of its duties in theory and in practice? Does it need to be set in motion?

3rd. What is its responsibility and to whom is it accountable?

4th. Who becomes an official of the department of public prosecution?

5th. What social position has it?

5th bis. Has it any political functions?

6th. What is in fact the theory of the power granted to the jury? Does it judge fact and law?

7th. Are all crimes judged by a jury?

8th. Can the decision of the jury be quashed?

9th. Does it often happen that the jurors are divided?

10th. How is the hearing conducted before them?

11th. What, on the average, is the duration of each case?

12th. Is the jury differently composed in criminal and in civil cases?

13th. Are the jurors chosen ever taken far from where they live and retained for a long time?

14th. Where are the assizes held?

15th. Who presides over them?

16th. What part does the presiding judge play?

Civil Side

Is there a justice of the peace? What are his functions? Conciliatory mission.

Criminal Sides

Investigation of Crimes.

(1) When a crime is committed, to whom does one apply in each locality?

(2) Who has the right to lay the first information?

(3) Who has the right to have the accused arrested?

(4) What are the means of information? Are searches made? Does one question witnesses?

(5) Who brings the matter before the grand jury?

(6) On what evidence does the grand jury decide?

(7) What are the delays in the procedure? Does it depend on anyone to make them more or less long? If on the director of public prosecutions, to whom is he responsible?

(8) Who pays the witnesses before the petty jury?

(9) Who sees that the judgement is carried out?

Department of Public Prosecution in Massachusetts

The department of public prosecution in Massachusetts is composed of two parts:

(1) There is a district attorney in each county, who appears before the court of common pleas, prosecutes the smallest offences, and appears in the name of the State in small affairs.

(2) There is a general attorney who follows the Court of *Oyer and Terminer*,[1] prosecutes great crimes and has the direction of important matters where the interests of the State are involved.

There is no precedence in the hierarchy between these two officers; they are completely independent in *their spheres* (which appears to be the constitutive conception of the English department of public prosecution). As a result many States have felt how useless it is to multiply the branches of the department of public prosecution in this way.

In Connecticut and in Ohio for instance there are only the district attorneys.

Cincinnati, Walker,[2] 2nd December 1831

Department of Public Prosecution in Ohio

There are only district attorneys, no general attorney. The district attorneys are nominated by the judges and receive no regular salaries. It is the judges who, each year, decide the salary they ought to receive. That of the district attorney in Cincinnati hardly ever amounts to more than five or six hundred dollars. This complete dependence of the department of public prosecution on the judges is regarded as a great evil.

[1] Criminal trial under the writ of *oyer* and *terminer* or commission to circuit judges to hold court (from *audire* and *terminare*).

[2] See conversation with Mr. Walker, non-alphabetical notebook 3, pp. 90–93 and 94–98. Cf. Pierson, op cit., p. 554.

Nevertheless, his position is even so more tolerable than that in New England where he is paid a certain sum (three dollars, I believe!) for each conviction, being given nothing if the man is acquitted. In Ohio the department of public prosecution has the official right to prosecute every sort of offence, has also the right not to prosecute any, without being forcibly set in action by a private person. In general he does not officially prosecute crimes other than those punishable by imprisonment.

He alone can take action before the grand jury.

In Ohio the judges have authority to order the accuser to pay the costs, but it is a power that they use almost never.

Mr. Ware, Cincinnati, 4th December

Mr. Dallas.[1]

Quid felony and others.

Crimes

Quid? No bills were found or were not prosecuted. What precisely is the right of the department of public prosecution to stop a case? What rule does it follow? What happens to cases not pursued?

Quid executent a mare committed.[2] [*sic.*]

Criminal and Civil laws of Ohio

The criminal laws of Ohio are very original. They deserve careful study. They are the most gentle that there are. Nevertheless Mr. MacIlvaine,[3] a judge of the Supreme Court of the United States, assured us that under their sway crimes have not increased (a point to verify).

It takes into consideration categories of criminality quite different from ours. Thus the *value* of the object stolen and the *result* of the attempt modify the extent of the punishment.

Their most fundamental defect seems to me that they do not punish *recidivism* at all. The harm in such a state of affairs

[1] Cf. Pierson, op. cit., p. 528f.

[2] The quotation is wrong and probably should read: 'Quid exsequentur a mare commissum.' How pursue a thing entrusted to the sea. In the context that must mean that you cannot go back on a case that has been dropped.

[3] Tocqueville's conversation with Mr. MacIlvaine on 9th December 1831 is recorded in non-alphabetic notebook 3, pp. 99–101. Cf. Pierson, op. cit., p. 530 f.

already shows up emphatically in the facts; one continually sees the same men re-appearing at assizes for little offences the slight penalty for which they know will not be increased because of their relapse, to the great damage of individuals and of society. We heard general complaints about that.

The penal law of Ohio classes the sexual act with a child under ten years old, even with consent, as *rape* (a wise and moral law).

It punishes fornication, that is to say the cohabitation of an unmarried man and woman even though they are both free. That law is shared by most of the States of the Union; although it confuses conceptions of vice and of crime, of sin against God with offence against society, it does not shock anyone; it is supported by the strictness of morals, and besides it is a consequence of the Presbyterian customs that the Americans derive from their origin. In Ohio fornication is prosecuted *officially*; but I think that such prosecutions are rare.

The department of public prosecution can officially prosecute adultery.

Civil Legislation

Ohio seems to me to have escaped more completely than any of the States of the Union we have visited so far from English precedents and memories.

Thus it has not only suppressed the exceptional jurisdictions of the Ecclesiastical Courts and the Courts of Equity, but has once for all given the powers of these Courts to the Courts of *Common Pleas* and the *Superior Court*.

In Pennsylvania, from failure to take this step which seems so simple and reasonable, justice suffers from being defective and obscure. There are a great many useful procedures which cannot be followed because, according to the *Common Law*, their powers belong to exceptional tribunals that no longer exist.

It appears that in Ohio a *new trial* cannot be granted more than twice. Today I attended the Court of *Common Pleas* at Cincinnati. The jury seemed to us to be composed of people coming from the lowest class of the population.

Lawyers in Ohio

There is not yet a school of law in the West. To become a lawyer one must have spent two years in a lawyer's office and have undergone an examination before a commission appointed by the judges.

A copy of the following given on 1st October 1831 to Mr. Sullivan[1] in Boston:

1st. Of what officials is the department of public prosecution composed?

2nd. Who chooses its members?

3rd. Are they chosen from the lawyers?

4th. Can they be dismissed at will and by whom?

5th. Does one central authority control all the members of the department of public prosecution? In other words are the Attorney General or the Solicitor General in correspondence with the district attorneys and other officials of the same sort? Are they considered their superiors in the hierarchy and have they the right to control their conduct?

6th. What precisely are the functions of the department of public prosecution?

7th. Do these functions often have points of contact with politics?

Has the department of public prosecution for instance the right to prosecute towns, districts or counties that refuse or omit to perform some of their political obligations?

8th. What standing does the department of public prosecution have in public opinion?

Juries

1st. What precisely are the functions of the grand jury? Does it not have at the same time administrative, political and judicial functions?

2nd. Who are the people who compose the grand and the petty jury, and how are they chosen?

3rd. Have you not noticed disadvantages in choosing jurors from the lower ranks of society?

4th. Do the same individuals often serve as jurors? What recompense are they given? How much time, on each occasion, are they obliged to sacrifice for the functions of the jury?

5th. Do people dislike performing these functions? Do the upper classes try to get out of them?

[1] See pocket notebook 3, p. 151. Cf. Pierson, op. cit., p. 405.

6th. Do you not think that the jury in civil cases is useful more from the political than from the judicial point of view; in other words do you not think that civil cases would almost always be as well or better decided by the judges alone? In that case would not the advantage of the jury be to give more moral force to the judgment, to accustom the people to business, and to make them look on the affairs of society as their own?

7th. Do you think, everything well considered, that the rule of unanimity has a real usefulness? How, in practice, does one succeed in applying it?

The Judges

1st. Can the judges be dismissed, by whom and in what circumstances? Does it often happen that judges are dismissed?

Has that sometimes been done for political reasons?

2nd. Have you never noticed disadvantages resulting from the right given to the judges to declare laws unconstitutional?

3rd. Are the judges always chosen from the lawyers? Is great trust felt in them? Do they, in general, enjoy popular favour?

4th. Do they not sometimes show too much compliance with prevailing opinion, even when they do not share it themselves?

Justices of the Peace

1st. What are the duties of a Justice of the Peace?

2nd. Does the institution of Justices of the Peace form, as in England, a public institution?

How do your Justices of the Peace differ from those in England?

3rd. By whom are they chosen? By whom dismissed and in what circumstances?

4th. From what class of society are they usually chosen?

5th. Do the upper classes willingly undertake the duties of a Justice of the Peace?

Do not such duties involve tiresome disputes that put them off?

6th. Do the Justices of the Peace receive any recompense whatsoever?

Notebook F

1st. I have heard it said that the results from your ways of proceeding against criminals are at least as good as our own, that is to say that there are perhaps fewer crimes left unpunished with you than with us; do you think it would be absolutely impossible to get authentic statistics in this respect? Could one, for example, find out through the district if many crimes are committed whose authors remain unidentified, and from the *clerk* of the court of assizes the proportion of acquittals to convictions? Without such knowledge, one cannot attempt any reform in our criminal laws?

2nd. What is the system of costs in criminal cases?

If the accused calls witnesses, is he obliged to pay them?

When the department of public prosecution calls witnesses, by whom are they paid?

When a man who has suffered from a crime prosecutes the other, must he pay the costs?

Are the costs in criminal cases considerable?

*　　*　　*

(*10th October 1831*)

Mr. Riker,[1] Recorder of New York, told me: In the State of Pennsylvania it is a principle that the guilty man in a criminal case pays the costs. It is, in my opinion, a salutary principle, but we have not introduced it here. With us it is an axiom that he who pays with his body owes no more to justice.

In Connecticut there is no State Attorney properly so called, but each county has an official who fulfils his duties.

Mr. Coxe,[2] a judge at Philadelphia, told me today, 13th October 1831: 'I am very much in favour of the mitigation of punishments; I believe and I have noticed in my experience that a less severe but more certain punishment is a stronger restraint than a terrible punishment, but one that, for that very reason, is always in doubt.

'But on the other hand I am positively opposed to the general abolition of the death penalty; I think that it is indispensable for giving criminals an interest in not going beyond a certain

[1] Cf. Pierson, op. cit., p. 535.   [2] Cf. Pierson, op. cit., p. 461.

limit, for example, for preventing their adding murder to theft; a thing to which they would necessarily be driven by the fear of discovery.

'So I think that the death penalty should be maintained in the laws, but that it should only be used in the last extremity. I have always seen that an *execution* had a bad effect on the public.

'In my whole life I have only known of four people executed in Philadelphia (for *State crime*). The jurors generally have a strong repugnance against bringing in a verdict that sends a man to death. They choose the second degree.'

Note: In the general legislation of Philadelphia there is (for a first crime) nothing in between death and only twelve years imprisonment. In my view that is a very unsatisfactory state of affairs. For recidivism there is imprisonment for life.

*　　*　　*

(*16th October 1831*)

Mr. Barclay,[1] a lawyer in Philadelphia and secretary of the Society for prisons, told me today: 'Every man in Pennsylvania has the right to be judged by a jury; however there are a few petty offences which are judged by what we call the Mayor's Court, however one can always appeal against the sentence of that court to the Court of Session. It is only instituted for the benefit of offenders and to prevent them staying in prison in the interval between sessions.'

Q. What difference is there between the Court of *Oyer and Terminer* and the Court of *Quarterly Sessions*?

A. Those are two criminal courts independent of one another and placed on the same footing. The Court of Oyer and Terminer judges the most serious cases.

He added: Before the grand jury one only hears witnesses for the prosecution.

Q. Before the petty jury, are witnesses paid?

A. Yes, for those for the prosecution; no, for those for the defence.

Q. Is it true that when the witnesses for the prosecution cannot give bail for their appearance before the court, they are put in prison?

[1] C. Pierson, op. cit., p. 459.

A. Yes, professionally I have come across a deplorable example of that.

A young Irish girl was killed in Philadelphia in the middle of a public dance. Two of her companions who saw the crime committed and who could not give bail, were arrested. At the moment when the crime was committed, the session was coming to an end; it had to wait three months; at the end of that time the case was adjourned. In that way these young girls stayed more than six months in prison, although no one accused them of any offence.

Mr. Coxe, who for a long time was Attorney General, told me that in America, where the department of public prosecution has a much lower standing than in France, in one respect, however, it has been granted an immense power; that of withdrawing from a case, even after the verdict of the grand jury, and so preventing the prosecution from continuing; it is, as Mr. Coxe said, a much greater power than that of granting pardon.

The department of public prosecution always speaks last in America. It is remarked that that is bad.

The judges are appointed until *ill behaviour*, that is to say that to stop being a judge, one must oneself be judged. The form of this sort of criminal case is as follows: the man who complains about a judge makes a petition to the legislature. If the latter, after having heard its commission's report, believes that there is reason for a prosecution, it pronounces an *impeachment* and appoints commissioners to pursue the matter before the Senate who judge it.

There are no special offences enumerated in advance by the law. The provisions concerning the powers of the judges are among the most interesting features of American constitutions.

The department of public prosecution has the right to prosecute all sorts of offences (in Maryland) without the need to be set in motion. But in fact it only prosecutes the most serious offences in this way. Otherwise the department of public prosecution does not play so great a part in prosecuting cases as in France. When a crime is committed, one brings a complaint before a Justice of the Peace who alone issues the warrants and questions the witnesses. A summary of the proceedings is sent to the clerk of the court of sessions; it is only then that the department of public prosecution begins to play a part. On the basis of the evidence of which I have been speaking, it draws up an act of accusation, called an indictment, and communicates it to the grand jury. It is its responsibility to summon the witnesses for the prosecution before the grand jury.

If the grand jury brings in a *bill of ignoramus*,[1] it has the man set at liberty. If the grand jury brings in a *true bill*, the department of public prosecution has the case set down for the assizes, summons the witnesses for the prosecution and argues the case before the jury.

The president of the court has an immense influence over the jury. Often, however, he abuses it. In Maryland it is observed as in France that men accustomed to judge, end by no longer believing in innocence, and make it their business to secure a conviction.

The theory, however, is that the president is an impartial being who should only state points of law and, as far as fact is concerned, not influence the view of the jury. But it often happens that on the contrary the president *argues* for the prosecution.

In Maryland when the grand jury has pronounced a *bill of ignoramus*, it is impossible to go back on its decision. But this infallibility is accorded to juries of both degrees.

When the petty jury acquits, the invariable principle is that there is no appeal.

When it convicts, its decision is liable to correction in two ways: the *judge* can quash the verdict on the spot if he is completely convinced that the accused is innocent or that the jury has violated the law. If he does not do that, one can obtain a *writ of error*.[2] That is an appeal to a superior court (this last point must be gone into more deeply).

In Maryland the Governor can grant pardon after the judgment.

Mr. Williamson,[3] *Baltimore* (*3rd November 1831*)

* * *

Commitment[1] is the act by which a judge has a man imprisoned.

A man can be prosecuted under several *indictments*; that is to say that a man who has committed six insignificant little thefts, can be condemned to twenty years in prison.

---

[1] Tocqueville uses the English terms. [2] English term in manuscript.
[3] Cf. Pierson, op. cit., index.

Notebook F

Some questions about judicial procedure in the United States of America, specially about the jury in civil cases.

There does exist a central judicial authority that resides, I believe, in the Supreme Court of the United States. What exactly comes within the cognizance of the Supreme Court? I have a clear impression that it has nothing in common with our *Cour de cassation*, that it does not have to act as censor over the administration of justice by the individual States who themselves *judge finally*, and that it is only concerned with exceptional cases, as for instance law suits that may arise between the citizens of two different States. But it is essential to get an exact idea of the extent of its cognizance.

Then I must examine the judicial organisation in each State, at least in the most important ones, and those that are pointed out as showing the most notable points of difference from the most important ones.

Is there an institution in the United States which corresponds, either in name or in fact, with the Justices of the Peace, in France or in England? Are there officers of justice entrusted, as those are, with a function of conciliation?

Are there several grades of jurisdiction? Do these two or more grades exist habitually or only exceptionally?

Is there an authority in the individual States analogous to our *Cour de cassation*, that is to say one not at all concerned with questions of fact, but only with violations or false applications of the law? If such an authority exists, are the appeals that can be addressed to it formulated by the parties and in their interest, and in that case are they a bar to subsequent proceedings? Or else can they only be formulated in the interests of the law?

Extent of the power of the jury:

The jury only takes cognizance of certain matters; but what are the rules that determine its competence?

Is that competence basic or by exception, that is to say does it extend to all matters that are not disposed of by a special law, or, on the contrary, is it restricted to matters in which special laws have given it cognizance?

Competence of the jury:

What is the judicial authority that decides the competence of the jury? Is it the court itself in which the jury exercises its duties, or is it an independent judicial authority whose sole, or at least whose principal, function is the determination of this competence?

Should there not be a judicial authority having the widest jurisdiction and before whom all cases should be brought, except for exceptional cases in which this court itself could refuse jurisdiction? Or, alternatively, should it be, as in France, for the plaintiff himself to predetermine the question of competence, and at his own risk and peril to bring the case before the judicial authority to whose decision he thinks the case should be submitted?

Is the jury totally excluded from cognizance of points of law? Has it not (as in England, at least in criminal cases) the power of giving a *general verdict*, that is to say one covering fact and law together? Or else cannot the judges, in certain cases, confer this power on it?

As to fact, is the jury always competent to decide the matters cognizance over which is, in general, granted to it?

There are judicial facts whose appreciation is simple and easy: there are others whose appreciation is complicated and hard.

In general purely *material* facts belong to the first class; as when it is a case of deciding the fact of possession, an act of violence, or the fact of the return of a sum of money or an object of personal property.

Mental facts are in general much less easy to appreciate. They are generally either the sort of question that may qualify a perfectly definite act, or questions about the interpretation of clauses in an agreement: thus, in taking possession of land did a man have a positive title to do so, or was he merely permitted to do so? When such-and-such a sum of money or such-and-such an object of personal property was handed over, was it done as a loan or as a free gift? Argument about the extent and the effects of conditions of a sale or a donation.

If the jury takes cognizance of all the facts without exception (always within the scope of the matter referred to it for decision), how can it be in a position to appraise questions demanding knowledge beyond its compass and legal conceptions? In fact most judicial *mental* facts are so intimately tied up with questions of law that it seems impossible to separate them.

But if on the other hand the jury is excluded from cognizance of certain facts, those especially which are complicated by *legal* aspects, by what rule is this exclusion regulated?

Are there in this respect general principles and agreed categories of questions, of which the jury cannot take cognizance?

Or, on the other hand, is there some sort of judicial authority invested with discretionary powers to take away from the jury, as circumstances suggest, cognizance of questions whose solution appears beyond its compass?

This last hypothesis seems very improbable. This discretionary power would in truth be much more simple and easy to apply than general principles; but that would be putting the jury in a state of dependence on the magistracy, and permitting the magistracy so to say to confiscate the power of the jury and the profit of its own power, and it is unbelievable that American institutions would authorise such a substantial delegation of the rights of the people to the benefit of any permanent authority whatsoever.

I have just stated the terms of one of the problems to be solved.

And here is another:

It is not enough to decide which of the parties has good law on its side; it is necessary to decide the way of executing the judgment.

Execution of judgment:

Is it the judge who controls the way of executing it?

One can see in that way that everything will go without hindrance, but the judge would come out as master of even more power perhaps than it is in the spirit of the institutions to give him.

Thus the English who are evidently afraid of entrusting too much power in this way to the judge and who, on the other hand, do not disguise from themselves that the decision about the way of executing judgement might in many cases go beyond the capacity of the jury, have cut the Gordian knot instead of undoing it.

If I believe the information contained in a book on the administration of justice in England (Mr. Cotter),[1] in all cases

[1] Mistake of the copyist: the book in question is Charles Cottu's *De l'administration de la justice criminelle en Angleterre et de l'esprit du gouvernement anglais*, 2nd ed., Paris, 1822: cf. pp. 124 f. Cf. also the English edition of this work, so

submitted to a jury, the execution of all agreements is always reduced to a matter of damages, that is to say an indemnity of a fixed sum.

That is buying the advantage of extending the competence of the jury a little dear, since by that the violation of almost all agreements is made legitimate.

In truth, there are some purely personal matters whose performance no judicial system can ever directly order. Thus, if a Scribe promises a musical comedy to the director of the Gymnasium and refuses to write it, he can only be forced to pay damages; and that is what happens everywhere and has always happened; *nemo potest precise legi ad factum*,[1] said Roman Law.

But there are a great many other promised acts whose literal and enforced execution can be, and every day is, ordered by courts of justice. Thus, if an individual has promised to sell me his country house and refuses to execute the conveyance, the judgment orders him to do so, and ordains, that if he does not do so, the judgment itself has the force of a sale. If my neighbour undertakes to carry out works to bring water to my land from a spring on his, the judgment orders him to do the work, and, in default, authorises me to have them done at his expense.

Ah well! It would seem that in England, in both the first and second of these cases, I should only get damages representing the harm I was deemed to have suffered as a result of their breaking their promises.

It has always seemed to me that there is in that a half-denial of justice. For it can be very important to me that the agreement should be carried out literally; the money indemnity which I am forced to accept in exchange, may not at all make up for the harm I have suffered; in a word, the contract is capable of enforced literal execution; I ask for that, and it is important for me; to refuse me that is to do me an injustice. That certainly is a radical defect in English judicial organisation.

important for Tocqueville's comprehension of English law: *On the Administration of Criminal Justice in England and the Spirit of the English Government* by Ch. Cottu, London, 1822.

[1] Incorrect quotation. No doubt it should be the maxim: 'Nemo praecise cogi potest ad factum,' which can be found in Bartolus's commentary on the law. 1. Digest *De actionibus empti.*' Bartolus uses it as a basis for distinction between law-suits 'to be executed *manu militari*' and those 'not to be executed *manu militari*'; it is found too in Vinnius and Pothier who limit it to suits that can lead to bodily compulsion. See also art. 1142 in the French Civil Code.

Moreover I have difficulty in believing that the breaking down of all agreements into a matter of damages, can be as general and as absolute as that author makes out. But it is a matter of great interest to know what is done in this respect in the United States.

Appeal against the decision of the jury:

Is the decision of the jury subject to any appeal? Is this appeal confined to points of law in cases where the jury is called on to decide them?

Extent of power to prove by witnesses:

Is proof by witnesses allowed to establish all facts? Are the prohibitions against that as wide and as rigorous as in France?

If proof by witnesses cannot be accepted in certain cases, is it for the judges to determine those cases? Or is it for the jury in matters within its cognizance?

In a case where proof by witnesses is heard, it is much better that those who determine the facts, be it the judge or the jurors, should decide (as in France) according to their conviction alone, and without being hobbled by legal proof. However, one must make sure that there are not any exceptions to this principle, especially in cases where the judges take cognizance of fact.

These last questions even touch on the state of civilisation or morality of a country. The prohibition against proof by witnesses shows distrust of the good faith of people as witnesses. The establishment of the system of legal proofs shows mistrust of the conscience or the understanding of men as judges or jurors.

Composition of the jury:

How and in accordance with what rules is the jury made up? Are property qualifications or other guarantees of capacity required? Do men of high social position feel the same repugnance as in France against performing these duties and do they seek to avoid them by as many subterfuges?

Enquiry into these last points might throw light even on the extent of competence of the jury and explain its greater or less capacity to perform certain parts of its duties.

Is the jury chosen by lot or appointed as in England by the sheriff's choice?

What are the general bases of the organization of the personnel of the magistracy?

The judges are appointed by the executive power, I believe, but are they taken from a list of candidates chosen by the people?

Are they appointed for life or temporarily, and in the latter case, for how long a time?[1]

---

[1] There follows the copy of a letter in English from Tocqueville to Mr. Ryker dated 15th November 1831 and beginning: 'Sir, at our late passage through New York . . .' The letter will be found in the editor's French edition of the *Correspondance générale*.

XII

Journey to Lake Oneida[1]

At sunrise on the 8th of July 1831 we left the little village of Fort Brewerton and began to make our way towards the northeast.

At about a mile and a half from our host's house there was a path opening into the forest; we went down it at once. It was beginning to get too hot for comfort. A stormy night had been followed by a heavy day. Soon we found protection from the sun in the middle of one of those deep forests of the New World whose sombre savage majesty strikes the imagination and fills the soul with a sort of religious terror.

How can one paint such a sight? On marshy land where a thousand streams not yet hemmed in by the hand of man flow and are lost in liberty, nature has sown pell-mell in incredible profusion the seeds of almost all the plants that creep over the ground or climb above the soil.

Over our heads stretched a vast dome of vegetation. Below this thick veil and amid the damp depths of the forest, there lay one vast confusion; a sort of chaos. Trees of all ages, foliage of all colours, plants, fruits and flowers of a thousand species, entangled and intertwined. Generations of trees have succeeded one another there through uninterrupted centuries and the ground is covered with their debris. Some seem to have fallen yesterday;

[1] Beaumont published the journey to Lake Oneida in the first volume of the *Œuvres et Correspondance inédites* which was afterwards published as Volume 5 of his edition of the *Œuvres Complètes* (pp. 161–71). The Tocqueville archives contain a copy in Madame de Tocqueville's handwriting and corrected by Tocqueville himself.

A very short sketch of the story appears in pocket notebook 1, pp. 130–131.

The journey has previously been translated by Mrs. Simpson, Nassau Senior's daughter. Cf. *Memoirs, Letters and Remains of Alexis de Toqueville*, London, 1861, l, 131 ff.

others already half sunk into the ground have but a hollow surface without depth, others are finally reduced to dust and serve to fertilize their last offshoots. Amid them a thousand different plants press in their turn towards the light. They glide between these immobile corpses, creep over their surface and under their decaying bark raise and disperse their powdered debris. It is like a fight between death and life. Sometimes we happened to come on an immense tree that the wind had torn up by the roots, but the ranks are so crowded in the forest that often despite its weight it had not been able to make its way right down to the ground. Its withered branches still balanced in the air.

A solemn silence reigned in the midst of this solitude; one saw few or no living creatures; man was missing from the scene, but yet this was no desert. On the contrary, everything in nature showed a creative force unknown elsewhere; everything was in movement, the air seemed impregnated with the smell of vegetation. It was as if one heard an inner sound that betrayed the work of creation and could see the sap and life circulating through ever open channels.

We walked on for several hours through these imposing solitudes in the light of an unsettled day, without hearing other sound than that of our horses' hooves rustling the piled up leaves of several winters, or forcing their way through the withered branches that blocked the path. We, too, kept silent, our souls filled with the grandeur and the novelty of the sight. At last we heard the echoes of an axe-stroke, the first distant announcement of the presence of a European. Some trees cut down, trunks burnt and charred, and a few plants useful to the life of man sown in the midst of the confusion of a hundred shapes of debris, led us to the pioneer's dwelling. In the centre of the rather restricted clearing made by axe and fire around it, rose the rough dwelling of the precursor of European civilisation. It was like an oasis in the desert.

We stayed a few moments conversing with the man who lived there, and then continued on our way and half an hour later reached a fisherman's hut built on the very edge of the lake that we had come to visit.

Lake Oneida is placed among low hills and in the middle of still virgin forest. A belt of thick greenery surrounds it on all sides, and its waters lap the roots of trees reflected on its still, transparent surface. Only a fisherman's isolated hut rose on its banks. Beyond that, no sail appeared on all the lake, and no smoke was seen to rise over the forest, for the European, though he has not completely taken possession of these banks, has already come near enough to drive away the numerous and war-like tribe who of old gave the place its name.

About a mile out from the bank where we stood were two oval-shaped islands of equal length. They were covered by woods so thick that they entirely covered the ground on which they grew; two copses, one would say, floating peacefully on the surface of the lake.

No road passes by this place; in these parts one sees no great industrial establishments, and no places celebrated for their picturesque beauty. But it was not chance that led us to this solitary lake. For it was the end and object of our journey.

Many years before, a book called *Journey to Lake Oneida* had fallen into my hands. The author there tells how a young Frenchman and his wife, driven from their country by the storms of our first revolution, came to take refuge in one of the islands enfolded by the waters of the lake. There, cut off from the whole world, far from the storms of Europe and rejected by the society that saw them born, these two unfortunates lived for one another, each consoling the other for their unlucky fate.

The book left a deep and lasting impression on my mind. I cannot say whether the effect on me was due to the author's talents, to the inherent charm of the story, or to my impression-able age; but the recollection of the two French people in Lake Oneida had always remained in my memory. How often have I envied them the tranquil joys of their solitude. Domestic hap-piness, the charms of conjugal union, and even love itself came to be merged in my mind with the picture of the solitary island where my imagination had created a new Eden. When I told my travelling companion this story, he too was deeply moved by it. We often talked about it, and always ended by saying, sometimes laughing, sometimes sadly, 'The only happiness in the world is on the shores of Lake Oneida.' When events that could not have been foreseen took us both to America, this recollection returned to us more forcefully. We promised our-selves that we would go and see our two French people, if they were still alive, or at least visit their home. Consider how strange is the power of imagination over the human mind; these savage parts, this silent, immobile lake and these islands covered with greenery, did not strike us at all as something new; on the contrary we seemed to be revisiting a place where we had passed part of our youth.

We went straight to enter the fisherman's hut. The man was in the forest. An old woman was living there alone. She came limping to receive us on the threshold of her dwelling. 'What do you call that green island a mile off rising out of the lake?' we asked her. 'It is called the Frenchman's island.' she replied. 'Do you know what gave it that name?'—'I have been told that it is called after a Frenchman who many years ago came to settle there.'—'Was he alone?'—'No, he had brought his young wife with him.'—'Do they still live in this place?'—'Twenty-one years ago, when I came to settle in this part, the Frenchman was no longer in the island. I remember having the curiosity to visit it. It was still a lovely place then, that island that from here seems so wild to you; the interior of it had been carefully cultivated; the French people's house was placed in the middle of an orchard, surrounded by fruits and flowers. A great vine ramped over the walls and by then covered them on every side; but the house was already falling into decay for want of an inhabitant.'—'What then became of the French people?'—'The woman died, and the man left the island and it is not known what happened to him afterwards.'—'Would you lend us the boat moored by your door, to cross the lake to the island?'—'Very willingly. But it is a long way to row and hard work for those who are not accustomed to it, and besides what could you find interesting in a place that has run wild again?'

As we went straight on, without answering, to push the boat into the water: 'I see what it is,' she said. 'You want to buy that island; the soil is good, and land is not expensive yet in our district.' We answered that we were travellers. 'Then,' she went on, 'no doubt you are related to the Frenchman and he has instructed you to visit his property.'—'That even less.' We answered. 'We do not even know his name.' The good woman shook her head incredulously, and we, getting to work with the oars, began to move rapidly towards the Frenchman's island.

During that short crossing we remained in deep silence, our hearts filled with gentle and sad emotions. The nearer we got, the less understandable did it seem that that island could once have been inhabited, so wild did its banks seem. We almost thought that we had been made the sport of a lying tale. Finally we got to the bank, and gliding under the huge branches of the trees projecting over the lake, we began to force our way further forward. First we crossed a circle of trees hundreds of years old that seemed to defend the approaches to the place; once through that rampart of greenery, we immediately came on a different sight. Scattered copse and young forest trees filled all the interior of the island. In the forests through which we had passed in the morning, we had often seen man struggling with nature hand to hand, and succeeding, albeit with difficulty, in robbing it of its forceful, wild character to bend it to his laws, Here, by contrast, we saw the forest regaining its sway, setting out again to conquer the wild, defying man and quickly making the traces of his passing victory disappear.

It was easy to see that some industrious hand had once cleared the ground in the centre of the island now occupied by the new generation of trees of which I have spoken. One met no old trunks there stretched over the debris. Everything, on the contrary, seemed young. It was clear that the surrounding trees had sent out off-shoots into abandoned fields; weeds grew where once the exile's harvest ripened; brambles and parasitic plants had come to take back possession of their former domain. One could hardly, at far intervals, discern the trace of enclosure or the mark of a field. For an hour we searched in vain through the undergrowth of the wood and the brambles encumbering the ground for any sign of the abandoned dwelling. That rustic luxury which the fisherman's wife had just described to us, the lawn, the flower-beds, the flowers, the fruits, those products of civilisation which loving care had nourished in the depths of the wild, all that had vanished with the beings who lived there. We were just going to give up our attempt, when we saw an apple tree half dead with old age; that began to put us on the track. Nearby a plant, which we first took for a liana, climbed up the highest trees, twining round their tall trunks or hanging like a leafy garland from their branches. Looking more closely at it, we recognised that it was a vine. Then we knew for sure that we were on the very place chosen forty years before as their last asylum by our two unhappy compatriots. By scooping away the thick bed of leaves covering the ground, we were barely able to find some debris falling into dust, which in a short time would have ceased to exist. As for the remains of her who was not afraid to exchange the delights of a civilised life for a tomb on a deserted island in the New World, it was impossible for us to find any trace. Did the exile leave his precious burden in his wilderness? Or did he instead carry it to the place where he, too, was destined to end his life? That is something no one could tell us.

Perhaps those who read these lines will not understand the feelings they record, and will treat them as exaggerated or chimerical. Nonetheless I will say that it was with hearts full of emotion, racked by fear and hope, and inspired by some sort of a religious feeling, that we began our meticulous searches and followed up the traces of those two beings whose name and family and part of whose story was unknown to us; a story whose only claim on our attention was that they in this very place had suffered griefs and joys that touch all men's hearts, because they have their origin in all hearts.

Is there wretchedness greater than that of this man!

Here is an unfortunate whom human society has shunned: his fellows have rejected him, banished him, and forced him to renounce their intercourse and flee into the wilds. Only one being has remained attached to him, followed him into solitude, and come to dress the wounds of his soul and to give him, in exchange for the joys of the world, the more pervading emotions of the heart. There he is reconciled to his fate. He has forgotten revolutions, parties, cities, his family, his rank and his fortune; he breathes again. His wife dies. Death comes to strike her and spares him. Poor wretch! What can become of him? Will he stay alone in the wilds, or will he go back to society where he has long been forgotten? He is no longer adapted either for solitude or for the world; he does not know how to live either with men or without them; he is neither a savage nor a civilised man: he is nothing but a piece of debris, like those trees in the American forests which the wind has had the power to uproot, but not to blow down. He stands erect, but he lives no more.

When we had passed through the island in every direction, visited its smallest ruins, and listened to the icy silence that now reigns in its shadows, we took our way back to the mainland.

I was sad as I saw this vast rampart of greenery retreating into the distance. It had for long years defended these two exiles from the European's bullet and the savage's arrow, but it could not protect their cottage from the invisible blows of death.

XIII

A Fortnight in the Wilds[1]

Written on the Steamboat 'The Superior'. *Begun on* (*1st August 1831*)

One of the things that pricked our most lively curiosity in going to America, was the chance of visiting the utmost limits of European civilisation, and even, if time allowed, visiting some of those Indian tribes who have chosen to retreat into the wildest open spaces rather than adapt themselves to what the whites call the delights of social life. But it is harder than one would have thought to get to the wilds nowadays. Leaving New York, the further we got to the northwest, the further did the end of our journey seem to flee before us. We passed through places celebrated in the history of the Indians; we found valleys that they had named; we crossed rivers still bearing the names of their tribes, but everywhere the savage's hut had given way to the civilised man's house. The forest was felled; solitude turned to life.

But still we seemed to be following the tracks of the natives. Ten years ago, we were told, they were here; there, five years; there, two years. In the place where you see the prettiest village church, a man would tell us, 'I cut down the first tree of the forest.' 'Here,' another told us, 'the grand council of the Confederation of the Iroquois used to be held.'—'And what has become of the Indians,' said I?—'The Indians,' our host replied,

[1] 'A Fortnight in the Wilds' was first published by Beaumont in the *Revue des Deux Mondes* of 1st December 1860, before appearing in the 1st volume of *Œuvres et Correspondance inédites* which subsequently made up volume 5 of his *Œuvres Complètes* (pp. 173–258). The Tocqueville archives have an autograph manuscript and a copy of the same revised and corrected by Tocqueville himself. It is that copy which is used here; Tocqueville had only changed some details of style in his original draft.

The journey took place between the 18th and 29th July 1831. There is a first version of the story in the diary for that time in pocket notebook 2, pp. 132–143.

Cf. also *Memoirs, Letters, and Remains of Alexis de Tocqueville*, 1, 140 ff.

'are I do not quite know where, beyond the Great Lakes. It is a race that is dying out; they are not made for civilisation; it kills them.'

Man gets accustomed to everything. To death on the field of battle; to death in hospital; to kill and to suffer. He gets used to every sight. An ancient people, the first and legitimate master of the American continent, is vanishing daily like the snow in sunshine, and disappearing from view over the land. In the same spots and in its place another race is increasing at a rate that is even more astonishing. It fells the forests and drains the marshes; lakes as large as seas and huge rivers resist its triumphant march in vain. The wilds become villages, and the villages towns. The American, the daily witness of such wonders, does not see anything astonishing in all this. This incredible destruction, this even more surprising growth, seem to him the usual progress of things in this world. He gets accustomed to it as to the unalterable order of nature.

In this way, always looking for the savages and the wilds, we covered the 360 miles between New York and Buffalo.

The first sight that struck us was a great number of Indians, who had assembled that day in Buffalo to collect the rent for the lands they had handed over to the United States.

I do not think I have ever suffered a more complete disappointment than the sight of those Indians. I was full of memories of M. de Chateaubriand and of Cooper, and I had expected to find in the natives of America savages in whose features nature had left the trace of some of those proud virtues that are born of liberty. I expected to find them men whose bodies had been developed by hunting and war, and who would lose nothing by being seen nude. You can guess my astonishment as I got close to the sight described here:

The Indians that I saw that evening were small in stature; their limbs, as far as could be seen under their clothes, were thin and far from muscular; their skin, instead of being of the copper-red colour that is generally supposed, was dark bronze so that at first sight it seemed very like that of mulattoes. Their shiny, black hair fell with a peculiar stiffness over neck and shoulders. Their mouths were generally disproportionately large, and the expression of their faces ignoble and vicious. Their physiognomy told of that profound degradation that can only be reached by a long abuse of the benefits of civilisation. One would have said they were men from the lowest mob of our great European cities. And yet they were still savages. Mixed up with the vices they got from us, was something barbarous and uncivilised that made them a hundred times more repulsive still. These Indians carried no arms; they wore European clothes; but they did not use them in the same way as we do. One could see that they were not at all made for their use, and they found themselves imprisoned in their folds. To European ornaments they added articles of barbarian luxury, feathers, enormous ear-rings and necklaces of shells. These men's movements were quick and jerky, their voices shrill and discordant, their glances restless and savage. At first sight one was tempted to think that each of them was but a beast from the forest, to whom education had given the appearance of a man, but who had nonetheless remained an animal. These weak, depraved beings belonged however to one of the most renowned tribes of the ancient American world. We had before us, it is sad to say it, the last remnants of that famous Confederation of the Iroquois, who were no less well-known for manly wisdom than for courage, and who long held the balance between the two greatest European nations.

But one would be wrong to try and judge the Indian race by this shapeless sample, this straying sucker from a savage tree that has grown up in the mud of our cities. That would be to repeat the mistake that we ourselves commit and of which I shall have occasion to speak later.

We went out from the town that evening and, not far from the last houses, we saw an Indian lying at the edge of the road. He was a young man. He made no movement and we thought him dead. Some stifled sighs that hardly forced their way from his breast made us realise that he was still alive and struggling against one of those dangerous forms of drunkenness that are brought on by brandy. The sun had already gone down and the ground was getting more and more damp. There was every indication that the wretched man would breathe out his last sigh there, at least unless he was helped. It was the time at which the Indians were leaving Buffalo to return to their village; from time to time a group of them came and passed close by us. They came up, roughly turned their compatriot's body over to see who he was, and then went on their way without deigning to answer our questions. Most of these men were themselves drunk. Finally a young Indian woman arrived, who at first seemed to come up with some interest. I thought that it was the wife or sister of the dying man. She looked at him attentively, called him aloud by his name, felt his heart and, being sure that he was alive, tried to rouse him from his lethargy. But when her efforts were in vain, we saw her burst out in fury against his inanimate body lying in front of her. She struck his head, twisted his face with her hands, and trampled on him. While she applied herself to these ferocious acts, she uttered such inarticulate and savage cries that, at this moment, they still seem to vibrate in my ears. Finally we felt we must intervene and peremptorily ordered her to draw back. She obeyed, but as she went off, we heard her burst into a barbarous laugh.

When we got back to the town, we told several people about the young Indian. We spoke of the imminent danger to which he was exposed; we even offered to pay his expenses at an inn. All that was useless. We could not persuade anyone to bother about it. Some told us: these men are accustomed to drink to excess and sleep on the ground. They certainly will not die from such accidents. Others admitted that the Indian probably would die; but one could read on their lips this half expressed thought: 'What is the life of an Indian?' That indeed was the basis of the general feeling. In the midst of this society, so well-policed, so prudish, and so pedantic about morality and virtue, one comes across a complete insensibility, a sort of cold and implacable egotism where the natives of America are concerned. The inhabitants of the United States do not hunt the Indians with hue and cry as did the Spaniards of Mexico. But it is the same pitiless feeling that animates the whole European race here as everywhere else.

How many times during our travels have we not met honest citizens who said to us of an evening, sitting peacefully by their fire: the number of the Indians is decreasing daily. However it is not that we often make war on them but the brandy that we sell them cheap every year carries off more than our arms could kill. This world here belongs to us, they add. God in refusing the first inhabitants the capacity to become civilised, has destined them in advance to inevitable destruction. The true owners of this continent are those who know how to take advantage of its riches.

Satisfied with this reasoning the American goes to the church where he hears a minister of the gospel repeat to him that men are brothers and that the Eternal Being who has made them all in the same mould has imposed on them the duty to help one another.

At ten o'clock in the morning of the 19th July we boarded the steamboat *Ohio* going towards Detroit. A strong breeze was blowing from the northwest and gave the waters of Lake Erie the very look of the waves of a stormy ocean. To the right stretched a limitless horizon. To the left we hugged the southern shores of the lake so close that we often came within earshot of it. These shores were perfectly level and different from those of all the lakes I have ever chanced to visit in Europe. Neither were they any more like the shores of the sea. Immense forests shaded them and formed round the lake as it were a thick belt that was seldom broken. From time to time, however, the country suddenly changes its look. Just round a wood one sees the elegant spire of a clock tower, houses striking in their whiteness and cleanness, and shops. Two paces further on, the primeval and apparently impenetrable forest reclaims its dominion and again reflects its foliage in the waters of the lake.

Those who have passed through the United States will find in this picture a striking emblem of American society. Everything there is abrupt and unexpected; everywhere, extreme civilisation borders and in some sense confronts nature left to run riot. That is something that one cannot conceive in France. As for me, in my traveller's illusions—and what class of man has not its own— I was imagining something quite different. I had noticed in Europe that the more or less withdrawn position in which a province or town is placed, its wealth or its poverty, its smallness or its extent, exercised an immense influence on the ideas, the morals, the whole civilisation of its inhabitants, and often caused a difference of several centuries between the various parts of the same area.

I supposed that it was like that, but to a even greater extent. in the New World, and that a country peopled as is America in an incomplete and partial fashion ought to show all conditions of existence and provide a picture of society in all its ages. America, according to me, was then the only country where one could follow step by step all the transformations which social conditions have brought about for man and where it was possible to discover something like a vast chain descending ring by ring from the opulent patrician of the town right down to the savage in the wilds. It was there, in a word, that I counted on finding the history of the whole of humanity framed within a few degrees of longitude.

Nothing is true in this picture. Of all the countries of the world America is the least adapted to provide the sight that I went to seek. In America, even more than in Europe, there is one society only. It may be rich or poor, humble or brilliant, trading or agricultural, but it is made up everywhere of the same elements; it has been levelled out by an egalitarian civilisation. The man you left behind in the streets of New York, you will find him again in the midst of almost impenetrable solitude: same dress, same spirit, same language, same habits and the same pleasures. Nothing rustic, nothing naive, nothing that smells of the wilds, nothing even that resembles our villages. The reason for this peculiar state of affairs is easy to understand. The parts of the territories which have been longest and most completely peopled have reached a high degree of civilisation. Education has been lavishly and profusely bestowed. The spirit of equality has stamped a peculiarly uniform pattern on the habits of private life. Now, note this well, it is precisely these same men who yearly go to people the wilds.⸱ In Europe each man lives and dies on the ground where he was born. In America nowhere does one meet the representatives of a race that has multiplied in isolation having long lived there unknown to the world and left to its own devices. Those who dwell in isolated places arrived there yesterday. They came bringing with them the morals, the ideas and the needs of civilisation. They only compound with savage life to the extent that the nature of things makes absolutely necessary. Hence the oddest contrasts. One goes without transition from the wilds into the street of a city, from the most savage scenes to the most smiling aspects of civilisation. If night overtaking you does not force you to take shelter under a tree, you have a good chance of reaching a village where you will find everything down to French fashions and poor copies of boulevards. The merchant of Buffalo or of Detroit is as well stocked as the one of New York; the factories of Lyon work for the one as for the other. When you leave the main roads you force your way down barely trodden paths. Finally, you see a field cleared, a cabin made from half-shaped tree trunks admitting the light through one narrow window only. You think that you have at last reached the home of the American peasant. Mistake. You make your way into this cabin that seems the asylum of all wretchedness but the owner of this place is dressed in the same clothes as yours and he speaks the language of towns. On his rough table are books and newspapers; he himself is anxious to take you on one side to know exactly what is happening in old Europe and asks you to tell him what has most struck you in his country. He will scribble on the paper a plan of campaign for the Belgians, and will solemnly tell you what still needs to be done to make France prosperous. One might think one was meeting a rich landowner who had come to spend just a few nights in a hunting lodge. And in fact the log cabin is only a temporary shelter for the American, a concession circumstances have forced on him for the moment. When the fields that surround him are in full production, and the new owner has time to concern himself with the amenities of life, a more spacious dwelling and one better adapted to his needs will replace the log-house and make a home for those numerous children who will also go out one day to make themselves a dwelling in the wilds.

But to come back to our journey. We sailed slowly along the whole day in sight of the shores of Pennsylvania, and later of Ohio. We stopped for a moment at Presqu'Ile, now called Erie. It is there that the Pittsburgh canal will end. By means of this undertaking the whole execution of which is, they say, easy and now assured, the Mississippi will be connected to the river of the north, and the wealth of Europe will flow freely along the five hundred leagues of land that lie between the Gulf of Mexico and the Atlantic Ocean.

In the evening, the weather having turned favourable, we moved quickly towards Detroit across the middle of the lake. On the following morning we were in sight of the little island called *Middle Sister*, near to which Commodore Perry won a celebrated naval victory over the English.[1]

[1] Battle of Lake Erie (10th September 1814) in the war between the United States and Great Britain. Cf. above p. 113, note 1.

A Fortnight in the Wilds

Soon afterwards the level coast of Canada seemed to be moving quickly towards us, and we saw the Detroit River opening in front of us and the houses of Fort Malden in the distance. This place, founded by the French, still bears many traces of its origin. The houses are placed and shaped like those of our peasants. The Catholic bell-tower with a cock on top rises in the middle of the hamlet. One might think it a village near Caen or Evreux. A strange sight turned our attention away from these sentimental reminders of France: on the bank to our right was a Scotch soldier mounting guard in full uniform. It was the uniform made so famous by the field of Waterloo. Feather in cap, jacket, all complete; his clothes and arms glinted in the sunlight. To our left, as if on purpose to point the contrast, two stark naked Indians, their bodies streaked with dyes, rings in their noses, came up at the same moment from the opposite bank. They were in a little bark canoe with a coverlet for sail. Letting their frail boat run with wind and current, they shot like an arrow towards our ship and in an instant had turned round it. Then they went off quietly to fish near the English soldier who, still glinting and unmoving, seemed put there as the symbol of the high civilisation of Europe in arms.

We reached Detroit at three o'clock. Detroit is a little town of two or three thousand souls, founded by the Jesuits in the middle of the forest in 1710, and still having a great number of French families.

By this time we had crossed the whole State of New York, and gone a hundred leagues over Lake Erie; by now we were touching the limits of civilisation, but we had no idea whatsoever whither to wend our way next. To get information was not as easy as one might have thought. To break through almost impenetrable forests, to cross deep rivers, to brave pestilential marshes, to sleep out in the damp woods, those are exertions that the American readily contemplates, if it is a question of earning a guinea; for that is the point. But that one should do such things from curiosity is more than his mind can take in. Besides, living in the wilds, he only prizes the works of man. He will gladly send you off to see a road, a bridge or a fine village. But that one should appreciate great trees and the beauties of solitude, that possibility completely passes him by.

So nothing is harder than to find anyone able to understand

what you want. You want to see forests, our hosts said smiling, go straight ahead and you will find what you want. They are there all right around the new roads and well-trod paths. As for Indians, you will see only too many in our public places and in the streets; there is no need to go very far for that. Those here are at least beginning to get civilised and have a less savage look. We were not slow to realize that we should not get the truth out of them by a frontal attack and that it was necessary to *manoeuvre*.

So we went to call on the official appointed by the United States to see to the sale of the still uninhabited land that covers the district of Michigan; we represented ourselves to him as people who, without any very decided intention of settling in the country, might yet have distant interest in knowing what land cost and how it was situated. Major Biddle, that was his name, this time understood wonderfully well what we wanted to do, and entered at once into a mass of details to which we paid avid attention. 'This part here', he said to us, pointing out on the map the St. Joseph River which, after many a bend, flows into Lake Michigan, 'seems to me the best suited for your scheme; the soil is good there; there are already some fine villages established there, and the road leading thither is so well maintained that public conveyances traverse it daily.' 'Good'! we said to ourselves. 'Now we know where not to go, at least unless we want to visit the wilds in a mail van.' We thanked Mr. Biddle for his advice, and asked him with an air of casualness and a pretended scorn, what part of the district had so far least attracted the attention of emigrants. 'In this direction', he told us without attaching more importance to his answer than we to our question, 'towards the northwest. As far as Pontiac and in the neighbourhood of that village some fairly good settlements have been established. But you must not think of settling further on; the ground is covered by almost impenetrable forest which stretches endlessly to the northwest, where one only finds wild beasts and Indians. The United States are always considering opening up a road; but so far it has barely been begun and stops at Pontiac. I say again, that is a part you should not think about.' We thanked Mr. Biddle again for his good advice, and left determined to take it in just the contrary sense. We could not contain ourselves for joy at having at last discovered a place to which the torrent of European civilisation had not yet come.

On the next day, the 23rd July, we hastened to hire two horses. As we contemplated keeping them for ten days or so, we wanted to leave a sum of money with their owner; but he refused to take it, saying that we could pay on our return. He showed no alarm. Michigan is surrounded on all sides by lakes and wilds; he let us in to a sort of riding-school of which he held the door. When we had bought a compass as well as provisions, we set out on our way, rifle on shoulder, as thoughtless of the future and happy as a pair of schoolboys leaving college to spend their holidays at their father's house.

If we had indeed only wanted to see forests, our hosts in Detroit would have been right in telling us that we need not go very far, for, a mile out of the town, the road goes into the forest and never comes out of it. The land it passes over is completely flat and often marshy. From time to time along the road one comes to new clearings. As all these settlements are exactly like one another, whether they are in the depths of Michigan or just close to New York, I will try and describe them here once and for all.

The bells which the pioneer is careful to hang round his beasts' necks so as to find them again in the dense forest, give warning in the far distance that one is getting near a clearing. Soon one hears the echoes of the axe that is cutting down the forest trees, and as one gets closer, signs of destruction make man's presence ever more evident. Severed branches cover the road, and trunks half scorched by fire or cut about by the axe, yet stand still erect in your path. As you go on your way, you come to a wood where all the trees seem to have been struck by sudden death. In full summer their withered branches seem the image of winter. Looking at them close-up, you see that a deep circle has been cut in their bark, which, by preventing the circulation of the sap, has brought them to a speedy death. That in fact is usually the planter's first beginning. As he cannot, in the first year, cut all the trees that adorn his new property, he sows corn under their branches and, by striking them to death, prevents them from shading his crop. After this field which is an unfinished sketch, a first step of civilisation in the wilds, one suddenly sees the owner's cabin. It is generally placed in the middle of some land more carefully cultivated than the rest, but where man is yet sustaining an unequal fight against nature. There the trees have been cut but not grubbed up; their trunks still cover and block the land they used to shade. Round this withered debris, wheat, shoots of oak, plants of all kinds, and weeds of all sorts are scattered pell-mell and grow up together in the untamed and still half-wild ground. It is in the middle of this vigorous and variegated growth of vegetation that the planter's dwelling or, as it is called in this country, his log-house rises. Just like the field around it, this rustic dwelling shows every sign of new and hurried work. It is seldom more than 30 feet long. It is 20 feet wide and 15 high. Both its walls and its roof are made of unsquared tree-trunks between which moss and earth have been rammed to keep the cold and rain out from the inside of the house. The closer the traveller gets, the more animated the scene becomes. As they hear his footsteps, the children, playing in the surrounding debris, get up in a hurry and run for shelter to their father's house, as if they were frightened at the sight of a man, while two great half-wild dogs with ears pricked and long muzzles, come out of the cabin and growling cover their young masters' retreat.

It is then that the pioneer himself appears at the door of his dwelling; he takes a good look at the new arrival; signs to his dogs to go back under cover and himself hastens to give them the example without a sign of curiosity or anxiety.

When he gets to the threshold of the log-house, the European cannot help casting an astonished glance round the sight before him.

Such a cabin generally has but one window, at which perhaps a muslin curtain is hanging; for in these parts where necessities are not seldom lacking, superfluities often abound. A resinous fire crackles on the hearth of beaten earth, and, better than the daylight, lights up the inside of the place. Over this rustic fire one sees trophies of war or hunt: a long rifle, a deerskin, some eagle's feathers. To the right of the chimney a map of the United States is often stretched, and the draught that blows through the gaps in the wall keeps raising and fluttering it. By it on a single shelf of ill-squared planks are a few tattered books; there one finds a Bible with its cloth and boards already worn out by the piety of two generations, a prayerbook and, sometimes, a poem of Milton or a tragedy of Shakespeare. Along the wall are some rough seats, made by the hands of the owner himself; some trunks instead of cupboards, some agricultural implements and samples of the harvest. In the middle of the room is a rickety table whose legs, still sprouting foliage, seem to have grown by themselves on the ground they cover. It is there that the whole family assembles every day to take their meals. One also sees an English china teapot, some spoons usually of wood, some cracked cups and newpapers.

The looks of the master of this dwelling is no less remarkable than the place that gives him shelter.

His angular muscles and thin limbs make one recognise at first glance the inhabitant of New England. This man has not been born in the solitude where he lives. His temperament alone makes that clear. His first years were passed in a society used to thought and argument. It is the strength of his will that has taken him to do work in the wilds to which he seems little adapted. But if his physical powers seem too slight for this undertaking, his features lined by the cares of life bespeak a practical intelligence, and a cold, persevering energy that strike one at first sight. His movements are slow and stiff, his words measured and his appearance austere. Habit and still more pride have given his features that Stoic stiffness that his deeds belie: it is true that the pioneer scorns things that often move men's hearts most violently; his goods and life will never depend on the chance of a throw of dice, or the fate of a woman; but to win affluence he has braved exile, the solitude and innumerable wretchednesses of life in the wilds, he has slept on the bare ground and risked fever in the forest and the Indian's tomahawk. He has one day made that effort, and renewed it through the years; perhaps he will carry on with it for twenty years more without discouragement or complaint. Can a man capable of such sacrifices be a cold, unfeeling being? Should one not rather recognise that he is consumed by some burning, tenacious, implacable passion of the mind? Concentrating on the single object of making his fortune, the emigrant has ended by making an altogether exceptional mode of existence. Even his feelings for his family have become merged in a vast egotism, and one cannot be sure whether he regards his wife and children as anything more than a detached part of himself. Deprived of the usual contacts with his fellow men, he has learnt to make solitude a pleasure. When one presents oneself on the threshold of his isolated dwelling, the pioneer comes forward to meet you; he shakes hands as custom provides, but his features express neither good will nor pleasure. He only starts talking to ask you questions, satisfying a need of the head rather than of the heart, and, as soon as he has found out the news he wanted to learn from you, he relapses into silence. One might think one was meeting a man who had come back home in the evening tired by the importunities and noise of the world. Ask him questions in your turn, and he will give you the information you lack intelligently, he will even provide for your needs and he will take care of your safety as long as you are under his roof. But there is so much of constraint and pride in all he does, and one is aware of such a profound indifference even about the result of his own efforts, that gratitude is frozen. But the pioneer is hospitable in his way, only his hospitality has nothing about it that touches you, for you feel that he himself in doing what he does, is submitting to an unpleasant obligation of life in the wilds. He sees it as a duty which his situation imposes, not as a pleasure. This unknown man is the representative of a race to whom the future of the New World belongs, a restless, calculating, adventurous race which sets coldly about deeds that can only be explained by the fire of passion, and which trades in everything, not excluding even morality and religion.

A nation of conquerors that submits to living the life of a savage without ever letting itself be carried away by its charms, that only cherishes those parts of civilisation and enlightenment which are useful for well-being, and which shuts itself up in the solitudes of America with an axe and a newspaper; a people who, like all great peoples, has but one thought, and presses forward to the acquisition of riches, the single end of its labours, with a perseverance and a scorn of life which one could call heroic, if that word were properly used of anything but the strivings of virtue. It is a wandering people whom rivers and lakes cannot hold back, before whom forests fall and prairies are covered in shade; and who, when they have reached the Pacific Ocean, will come back on its tracks to trouble and destroy the societies which it will have formed behind it.

In speaking of the pioneer one cannot forget the companion

of his trials and dangers. Look at that young woman at the other side of the hearth who as she sees to cooking the meal rocks her youngest son on her knees. Like the emigrant this woman is in the flower of her age; like him, she can remember the affluence of her first years. Her dress still shows an ill-suppressed taste for clothes but time has pressed heavily on her. By her features worn before their time, by her wasted limbs it is easy to see that existence has been a heavy burden for her.

In fact this frail creature has already had to face incredible trials. Scarcely embarked on life, she has had to tear herself away from her mother's tenderness and those dear fraternal links which no young girl gives up without a tear, even when she leaves them to share the opulent home of a new husband. The pioneer's wife carried off in an instant and without hope of return from her innocent cradle of youth has exchanged the charms of society and the joys of the domestic hearth for the solitude of the forest. Her nuptial couch was on the bare ground of the wilds. To devote herself to austere duties, to submit to privations once unknown to her, to embrace an existence for which she was not made, such has been the work of the best years of her life, such for her have been the delights of conjugal union. Want, suffering and boredom have changed her fragile frame but not broken down her courage. Amid the deep sadness engraved on her delicate features it is easy to see something of religious resignation, a profound peace and I cannot say what natural firmness and tranquillity that faces all the trials of life without fear or boast.

Half-naked children bursting with health, thoughtless of the morrow, true sons of the wilds, press round this woman. Their mother looks from time to time at them half in sadness half in joy. To see their strength and her weakness one would say that she has drained herself to give them life and does not regret what they have cost her.

The dwelling in which the emigrants live has no internal division and no storehouse. The whole family comes to seek shelter of an evening in the single room which it contains. This dwelling forms as it were a little world of its own. It is an ark of civilisation lost in the middle of an ocean of leaves, it is a sort of oasis in the desert. A hundred paces beyond it the everlasting forest stretches its shades around it and solitude begins again.

A Fortnight in the Wilds

It was only in the evening and after the sun was gone down that we arrived at Pontiac. Twenty very clean and very pretty houses making up as many well-furnished shops, a transparent stream, a clearing of a quarter of a league square and the ever-lasting forest all around: that is a true picture of the village of Pontiac which in twenty years perhaps, will be a town. The sight of this place reminded me of what M. Gallatin had said to me a month before in New York: that there is no village in America, at least in the sense which we give to that word. Here the houses of the cultivators are scattered in the middle of the fields. People only assemble in a place to establish a sort of market for the use of the surrounding population. In these so-called villages one only finds lawyers, printers or traders.

We had ourselves taken to the best hotel in Pontiac (for there are two) and were as usual ushered in to what is called the bar-room. That is a room where drinks are served, and in which the humblest labourer and the richest tradesman in the place come to smoke, drink and talk politics together on a basis, so far as externals go, of the most complete equality. The master of the house, or the landlord, was, I will not say a solid peasant, for there are no peasants in America, but anyhow a very solid gentle-man whose features had that openness and simplicity one asso-ciates with the people of the maquis in Normandy. He was a man who for fear of frightening you, never looked you in the face when he was talking to you, but waited until you were talking to some-one else to look at you at leisure. For the rest, a deep politician and, as the American habit is, a pitiless questioner. This worthy citizen, in common with the others there, at first looked at us with astonishment. Our travelling clothes and rifles made us not look like business men, and to travel to see the sights was something completely unwonted. To make short work of expla-nations, we said straightway that we had come to buy land. Hardly had we said it than we found that, to escape one evil, we had fallen into a much more formidable one.

It is true that they stopped treating us as extraordinary beings, but each of them wanted to do a deal with us; to get rid of them and their farms, we told our host that before striking any bargain, we wanted useful information from him about the price of land and means of cultivation. He took us at once into another room, slowly and deliberately spread out a map of

Michigan on the oak table which stood in the middle of the room, and putting a candle between us three, waited in impassive silence for what we had to tell him. The reader, without sharing our desire to settle in the open spaces of America, may yet be interested to know how so many thousands of Europeans and Americans who come every year to seek a new home, deal with the matter. So I will note down here the information with which our host at Pontiac provided us. We were often afterwards able to verify how perfectly correct it was.

'It is not like France here,' said our host, when he had quietly listened to all our questions and snuffed the candle; 'With you labour is cheap and land is dear; here buying the land is nothing, and men's labour is beyond price. I say that in order to make you understand that to settle in America, as in Europe, one needs some capital although one uses it differently. For my part I should not advise anyone to come and seek his fortune in our wilds, without at least having at his disposal a sum of 150–200 dollars. An acre in Michigan never costs more than 10 shillings when the land is still uncultivated. That is about the price of a day's labour. So a labourer can earn enough in a day to buy an acre. But the purchase made, the difficulty begins. This is how one generally sets about dealing with it. The pioneer comes to the place he has just bought with a few animals, a salted pig, two barrels of flour and some tea. If there is a cabin near, he goes there and is given temporary hospitality. If there is none, he puts up a tent in the middle of the wood that is to be his field. His first job is to cut down the nearest trees to build quickly a rough dwelling of the type you have already seen. With us, feeding the animals scarcely costs anything. The emigrant puts an iron bell on them and lets them run in the forest. It is very unusual for the animals left like that to themselves to leave the neighbourhood of their home. The greatest expense is the clearing. If the pioneer comes into the wilds with a family able to help in the first work, his task is fairly easy. But that is generally not so. Usually the emigrant is young, and if he already has children, they are in infancy. Then he must either see to all the first needs of his family himself, or hire the services of his neighbours. It will cost 4–5 dollars to clear one acre. When the land is ready, the new owner puts down an acre under potatoes, and the rest under wheat and corn. Corn is providential in the wilds; it grows in the water of our marshes and pushes up under the foliage of the forests better than in the heat of the sun. It is corn that saves the emigrant's family from inevitable destruction, if poverty, sickness or carelessness prevent him from making an adequate clearing in the first year. Nothing is harder to survive than the first years after the working of clearing. Later comes comfort and then wealth.'

That is what our host said, and we listened to these simple details with almost as much interest as if we ourselves had wished to profit from them. When he had stopped talking, we asked:

'Generally the ground in all the forest left to itself is marshy and unhealthy; does the emigrant exposed to all the wretchedness of solitude not also have reason to fear for his life?' 'Every clearing is a dangerous undertaking,' replied the American, 'and it hardly ever happens that the emigrant and his family escape from forest fever in the first year. Often when one is travelling in the autumn, one finds all the people in a cabin from the emigrant to his youngest son down with fever!'—'And what happens to these unfortunates when Providence strikes them like that?'—'They resign themselves and wait for a better future.'—'But can they hope for any help from their fellows?'— 'Hardly any.'—'But can they at least get the help of medicine?' —'The nearest doctor often lives 60 miles away. They do as do the Indians. They die or get well as God wills.' We went on: 'Does the voice of religion sometimes reach them?'—'Very seldom; we have not yet been able to *organize* any provision for public worship in our forests. Almost every summer, it is true, some Methodist clergymen come and do a tour of the new settlements. The news of their coming spreads incredibly quickly from cabin to cabin; it is the day's great news. At the time fixed the emigrant, his wife and their children make their way through the almost untrodden paths of the forest to the agreed rendezvous. People come from 50 miles around. It is in no church that the faithful meet, but in the open air under the trees. A pulpit made of ill-shaped trunks and great trees cut down to serve as seats are all the ornaments of this rustic church. The pioneers and their familes camp in the surrounding woods; there for three days and three nights the crowd devotes itself to religious observances with but rare intervals. One needs to see how ardently they pray and with what attention they listen to the solemn voice of the priest. It is in the wilds that men are seen to hunger after religion.'—'One last question. It is generally believed in Europe that the wilds of America are being peopled with the help of emigration from Europe. How then does it happen that since we have been in the forest we have not met a single European?' A smile of condescension and satisfied pride spread over our host's face as he heard this question: 'It is only Americans', he answered emphatically, 'who could have the courage to submit to such trials and who know how to purchase comfort at such a price. The emigrant from Europe stops at the great cities of the coast or in their neighbourhood. There he becomes a craftsman, a farm labourer or a valet. He leads an easier life than in Europe and feels satisfied to leave the same heritage to his children. The American, on the other hand, gets hold of some land and seeks by that means to carve himself a great future.'

When he had said those last words our host stopped. He blew out a huge column of smoke from his mouth and seemed ready to hear what we had to tell him about our plans.

First we thanked him for his valuable information and wise advice from which we said that we would certainly profit one day, and we added: 'Before settling in your district, my dear host, we intend to visit Saginaw and want to consult you about that.' At the mention of Saginaw there was a strange and sudden change in the American's expression; it would seem that we were dragging him off violently from the real world into the realms of imagination; his eyes grew wide and his mouth opened and every feature indicated the greatest astonishment: 'You want to go to Saginaw,' he cried out, 'to Saginaw Bay! Two rational men, two well educated foreigners want to go to Saginaw Bay? The story is hardly credible.'—'And why not then?' we replied. 'But do you really understand,' our host replied, 'what you are undertaking? Do you know that Saginaw is the last inhabited point until you come to the Pacific Ocean? Do you know that from here to Saginaw you find hardly anything but wilds and untrod solitudes? Have you thought that the woods are full of Indians and mosquitoes? That anyhow you will have to sleep at least one night in the damp forest shade? Have you thought about fever? Will you be able to manage for yourselves in the wilds and recognize your path in the labyrinth of our forests?' After that tirade he paused to judge the impression he had made. We answered: 'All that may be true. But we are leaving tomorrow morning for Saginaw Bay.' Our host reflected a moment, shook his head and said in slow, decided tones: 'Only some great advantage could lead two foreigners into such an undertaking; no doubt you have calculated, very mistakenly, that it is best to settle in the most distant place far from any competition.' We did not answer at all. He went on: 'Perhaps also the Canadian fur company has asked you to establish contacts with the Indian tribes on their frontier?' Silence again. Our host had come to the end of his guesses and kept silent, but continued in deep meditation on the strangeness of our plan.

'Have you then never been at Saginaw?' we asked. 'I,' he answered, 'for my sins I have been there five or six times, but I had something to gain by doing it and I cannot discover that you have anything to gain.'—'But do not forget, my worthy host, that we are not asking you whether we ought to go to Saginaw, but only how we can most easily do so.' Brought back like that to the question, our American regained all his sang-froid and clarity of vision. In few words and with admirable practical good sense he explained how we should set about crossing the wilds, went into the smallest details and anticipated even unlikely accidents. When he had come to an end of his recommendations, he again paused to see if we would finally disclose the mystery of our journey, and seeing that neither of us had any more to say, he took the candle up again, showed us to a room and, when we had very democratically shaken hands, he went back to finish the evening in the public room.

We got up at daybreak and got ready to go. Our host too was soon up. The night had not helped him to discover what made us behave in a way so extraordinary in his eyes. However, as we seemed completely decided to act against his advice, he did not like to return to the charge, but kept continually fussing around us. From time to time he would mutter under his breath: '*I find it hard to understand* what could induce two foreigners to go to Saginaw.' He repeated that phrase several times, until at last I said as I put my foot into the stirrup: 'There are a great many reasons that take us there, my dear host.' He stopped short on hearing those words and, looking me in the face for the first time, seemed to get ready to hear the revelation of a great mystery. But I, quietly mounting my horse, ended the matter with no more than a gesture of friendship and went off at a fast trot. When I turned my head fifty paces on, I saw him planted like a stack of hay in front of his door. A little afterwards he went into his house shaking his head. I suppose he was still saying: 'I can hardly understand what two foreigners are going to do at Saginaw.'

We had been advised to call on a Mr. Williams who since he had long been trading with the Chippewa Indians and had a son settled at Saginaw, could give us useful information. When we had already gone several miles into the forest, and were beginning to be afraid that we might have missed our man's house, we met an old man busy working in a small garden. We went up to him. It was Mr. Williams himself. He received us with great kindness and gave us a letter for his son. We asked him if we had anything to fear from the Indian tribes whose territory we were going to cross. Mr. Williams rejected that suggestion with something like indignation: 'No! no!' he said, 'you can go forward without fear. For my part I should sleep more soundly surrounded by Indians than by whites.' I note this as the first favourable view of the Indians that I have heard since coming to America. In thickly populated parts of the country men only speak of them with a mixture of fear and scorn, and I think that there they do in fact give cause for these two feelings. One can see above what I thought myself when I met the first of them at Buffalo. As you go on in this diary and follow me going among the European population on the frontiers and among the Indian tribes themselves, you will get both a more worthy and a fairer conception of the first inhabitants of America.

When we had left Mr. Williams we went on our way through the forests. From time to time a little lake (the district is full of them) appeared like a silver sheet beneath the leaves of the forest. It is difficult to conceive the charm pervading these pretty places where man has not yet come to live and where profound uninterrupted silence reigns. I have been through terrifying solitudes in the Alps where nature rejects the work of man, and where even in its very horror the sheer grandeur of the scene has something that transports one's soul with excitement. Here the solitude is as profound but does not bring the same sensations to birth. All that one feels in passing through these flowery wildernesses where everything, as in Milton's *Paradise*, is ready to receive man, is a quiet admiration, a gentle melancholy sense, and a vague distaste for civilised life; a sort of primitive instinct that makes one think with sadness that soon this delightful solitude will have changed its looks. In fact already the white race is advancing across the forest that surrounds it, and in but few years the European will have cut the trees that are now reflected in the limpid waters of the lake, and forced the animals that live on its banks to retreat to new wildernesses.

Always keeping on our way, we came to a district of a different aspect. The ground was no longer level, but cut by hills and valleys. Some of these hills have the wildest possible look. It was in one of these picturesque spots, when we had suddenly turned round to admire the imposing sight behind us, that we saw to our great surprise close to our horses' crupper an Indian who seemed to be following on our tracks. He was a man of about thirty, large and wonderfully well proportioned as they almost all are. His shining black hair fell along his shoulders except for two tresses fixed on top of his head. His face was striped with black and red. He was dressed in a sort of very short blue blouse. He wore red *mittas*: they are a sort of trousers that only come to the thighs, and his feet were clad in moccasins. A knife hung at his side. In his right hand he held a long carbine, and in his left two birds that he had just killed. The first sight of this Indian made no agreeable impression on us. The place was ill-chosen to resist an attack: on our right a pine forest rose to immense heights, and on our left a deep ravine led down to a stream that flowed over rocks hidden by the dense foliage, towards which we were descending like blind men! It was the matter of a moment to put our hands on our rifles, turn round and face the Indian across the road. He stopped, too. We stayed half a minute in silence. His face had all the characteristic traits that distinguish the Indian race from all others. In his black eyes shone that savage fire which still lights up the eyes of half-castes and is not lost until the second or third generation of white blood. His nose was arched in the middle and slightly blunt at the tip; his cheekbones were very high and his well defined mouth exposed two rows of shining white teeth which proved well enough that the savage, cleaner than his American neighbour, did not spend his day chewing tobacco leaves. I have said that when we turned and put our rifles at the ready, the Indian had halted. As we quickly looked him over, he remained completely impassive, with steady, unmoved gaze. When he saw that we had no hostile feeling on our side, he began to smile; probably he saw that he had frightened us. That was the first time that I had seen how completely gaiety changes the physiognomy of these savage men. I have later noticed the same a hundred times. An Indian in serious mood and an Indian smiling, are two entirely different beings. There is something of savage majesty in the immobility of the former which, against one's will, inspires fear. When the same man breaks into a smile, his whole face assumes an expression of naïveté and goodwill that gives it real charm.

When we saw our man had cheered up, we spoke to him in English. He let us talk on undisturbed, and then made a sign that he did not understand a word. We offered him a little brandy which he accepted at once and without thanks. Still talking in sign language we asked for his birds which he gave in exchange for a small piece of money. Having made his acquaintance like that, we gave him a wave and went off at a fast trot. After a quarter of an hour's rapid going, when I turned again, I was amazed to see the Indian. He moved with the agility of a wild animal without uttering a single word or seeming to quicken his pace. We stopped, he stopped. We went on again, he went on again. We broke into a full gallop. Our horses brought up in the wilderness went over all obstacles. The Indian broke into a double; I saw him sometimes to the right, sometimes to the left of my horse, leaping over the bushes and landing again noiselessly. One would say it was one of those wolves of Northern Europe who follow riders in the hope that they will fall from their horses and be the more easily devoured. The sight of this unchanging figure who, sometimes lost in the darkness of the forest, sometimes appearing in broad daylight, seemed to hover at our side, ended by getting on our nerves. As we could not think what could induce this man to follow us at such a rate—and perhaps he had been doing so for a very long time before we first noticed him—it came into our heads that he might be leading us into an ambush.

While worrying about that idea, we saw in the wood in front of us the muzzle of another carbine. Soon we came up to the man who carried it. At first we took him for an Indian. He was dressed in a sort of short frock-coat which, fastened round his loins, outlined an upright, well made body; his neck was bare and there were moccasins on his feet. When we got near and he raised his head, we saw at once that he was a European, and we stopped. He came up to us: shook hands warmly, and entered into conversation: 'Do you live in the wilderness?'—'Yes, there is my house', he pointed through the leaves to a hut much more wretched than ordinary log-houses. 'Alone?'—'Alone.'—'And what then are you doing here?'—'I go through the forest and kill the game I meet to right and left of my path, but one does not get good shots now.'—'And you like this sort of life?'—'More than any other.'—'But are you not afraid of the Indians?' —'Afraid of the Indians! I would rather live among them than in the society of the whites. No! no! I am not afraid of the Indians. They are worth more than we, provided we have not brutalized them with our strong drinks, the poor creatures!' We then pointed out to our new acquaintance the man who was following us so persistently and who then had stopped a few paces from us and stood as still as a milestone. 'He is a Chippewa,' said he, 'or as the French call them a *Sauteur*. I bet he is coming back from Canada where he has received the yearly presents from the English. His family should not be far from here.' This said, the American made a sign to the Indian to come up, and began to talk very fluently to him in his language. It was strange to see what pleasure these two men, so different in birth and manners, took in exchanging ideas with one another. Clearly they were discussing the respective merits of their weapons. The white, having looked at the savage's rifle very carefully: 'There is a fine carbine,' said he. 'No doubt the English have given it to him to use against us, and he will not fail to do so as soon as there is a war. That is how the Indians draw on their heads all the ills that weigh them down. But they know no better, the poor fellows.'—'Are the Indians skilled in using these long, heavy rifles?'—'There are no shots like the Indians,' our new friend answered warmly in tones of the greatest admiration. 'Look at the little birds he sold to you, sir. They are pierced by a single bullet and I am very sure that he only fired two shots to get them. Oh!' he added, 'there is nothing happier than an Indian in the country from which we have not yet driven the game. But the big animals sense our coming more than three hundred miles off, and as they retreat they make as it were a desert in front of us, in which the poor Indians cannot live unless they cultivate the ground.'

As we started on our way again: 'When you pass this way again,' our new friend called out, 'knock on my door. It is a pleasure to see white faces in these parts.'

I have recorded this conversation which in itself has nothing remarkable in it, to introduce the reader to a type of man whom we met very frequently thereafter on the verge of the inhabited land. They are Europeans who despite the habits of their youth, have ended up by finding inexpressible charm in the freedom of the wilderness. Taste and passion draw them to the solitudes of America, while their religion, principles and ideas attach them to Europe, so that they combine love of the savage life with the pride of civilisation, and prefer the Indians to their compatriots without however looking on them as their equals.

So we went on our way again, and still making the same rapid progress, in half an hour we reached a pioneer's house. An Indian family had established their temporary dwelling in front of this cabin. An old woman, two young girls and several children were crouched round a fire by whose heat the remains of a whole roebuck were cooking. On the grass a few paces away a stark naked Indian was basking in the sun, while a small child rolled in the dust near him. It was that that brought our silent companion to a halt; he left us without saying good-bye, and went to sit sedately down by his compatriots. What can have induced that man to follow our horses' tracks like that for two leagues? That is something we never could guess. After we had lunched in that place, we mounted our horses and went on our way through high but not dense forest trees. The copse had been burnt sometime before, as one could see by the charred remains of some trees lying on the ground. The soil is now covered with ferns which stretched away as far as one could see under the foliage of the forest.

A few leagues further on my horse cast a shoe, which caused us keen anxiety. Luckily near there we found a planter who succeeded in shoeing it again. Had it not been for that meeting, I doubt if we could have gone any further, as we were nearing the end of the clearings. This same man who thus enabled us to go on our way, advised us to press our pace, as the sun was beginning to sink and there were two good leagues between us and Flint River where we intended to pass the night.

Soon, in fact, we began to be enveloped in deep darkness. We *had to keep going*. The night was clear but freezing. So deep a silence, so complete a calm, prevailed in these forests that one might say that all the forces of nature were, as it were, paralysed. One could only hear the unwelcome buzz of mosquitoes and the noise of our horses' hoofs. From time to time one could see an Indian fire with an austere, unmoving profile outlined against the smoke. At the end of an hour we came to a place where the road forked. Two paths opened there. Which to choose? The choice was crucial. One of them led to a stream the depth of which we did not know, the other to a glade. The moon which was then coming up showed us a valley full of debris. Further on we saw two houses. It was so important not to lose our way in such a place at such an hour, that we decided to make inquiries before going any further. My companion stayed to look after the horses, and I, throwing my rifle over my shoulder, went down the valley. Soon I realized that I was coming into quite a recent clearing; immense trees with their branches still on them covered the ground. Jumping from one to another I succeeded in getting fairly quickly close to the houses, but the same stream we had seen before came between me and them. Luckily its course was blocked at this spot by huge oaks felled, no doubt, by the pioneer's axe. I managed to slide along these trees and reach the other bank at last. I moved cautiously up to the two houses, being afraid that they might be Indian wigwams. They were still not yet finished, I found the doors open and no one answered my voice. I came back to the banks of the stream and could not forbear stopping a few minutes in admiration of the sublime horror of the scene. This valley was shaped like an immense arena and, like a black drapery, the foliage of the woods surrounded it on all sides, while in the middle the moonlight breaking through formed the shadows into a thousand fantastic shapes dancing in silence over the brash of the forest. No other sound whatsoever, no breath of life broke the silence of this solitude. At length I thought about my companion, and called him at the top of my voice to tell him the result of my search, and get him to cross the stream and come and join me. My voice long re-echoed in the surrounding solitudes. But I got no answer. I shouted again and listened again. The same silence of the dead reigned in the forest. I became anxious and ran along the stream to find the way across it lower down. When I got there I heard the horses' hoofs in the distance and soon after Beaumont himself appeared. Surprised at my long absence, he had decided to come down to the stream; he had already got into the shallows when I called him. My voice could not reach him then. He told me that he too had made every effort to make himself heard, and, like me, had got frightened at not receiving any answer. Without the ford that served as a meeting place, perhaps we should have spent a great part of the night looking for one another. We set out once more on our way promising each other firmly that we would not separate again, and three-quarters of an hour on from there at last we saw a clearing, two or three cabins, and what gave us greatest pleasure, a light. The stream that ran like a violet thread along the bottom of the valley, sufficed to prove that we had arrived at Flint River. Soon the barking of dogs echoed through the wood and we found ourselves opposite a log-house and only separated from it by a fence. Just as we were getting ready to get over it, the moon revealed a great black bear on the other side, which standing upright on its haunches and dragging its chain, made as clear as it could its intention of giving us a fraternal welcome. 'What a devil of a country is this,' I said, 'where one has bears for watch dogs.'—'We must call out,' said my companion. 'If we try to pass the fence, we shall have difficulty in making the porter listen to reason.' So we shouted our heads off so successfully that at last a man appeared at the window. Having looked at us in the moonlight he said, 'Come in, gentlemen. Trinc, go to bed. To your kennel I tell you. Those are not robbers.' The bear went waddling back, and we went in. We were half dead with fatigue. We asked our host if we could have some oats. 'Certainly,' he answered; and at once started mowing the nearest field with complete American calm, and just as if he was doing it in the very middle of the day. In the meanwhile we dismounted and for want of stables tied our horses to the fence over which we had just passed. Having thus taken thought for the companions of our journey, we thought about our own sleeping arrangements. There was only one bed in the house. Beaumont having won the toss for it, I wrapped myself in my cloak and lying down on the floor, fell into the deep sleep befitting a man who has done fifteen leagues on horseback.

On the next day, the 25th July, our first care was to ask for a guide. Fifteen leagues of wilderness came between Flint Rock and Saginaw, and the road leading there is a narrow path that the eye can hardly see. Our host approved our plan, and soon brought along two Indians in whom, he assured us, we could place entire trust. One was a child thirteen or fourteen years old. The other a young man of eighteen. The latter's body, though it had not yet acquired the full vigour of ripe manhood, nonetheless gave an impression of agility combined with strength. He was of medium height, his body was upright and slender, his limbs supple and well proportioned. Long tresses fell from his bare head. Besides he had been at pains to paint his face as symmetrically as possible with black and red lines. A ring through his nose, a necklace and ear-rings completed his attire. His war-like gear was equally remarkable. At one side a battle axe, one of the celebrated tomahawks; at the other a long sharp knife with which the savages cut off the scalps of the defeated. Round his neck was hung a bull's horn that served him as powder-flask and he held a rifle in his right hand. As is usual with most Indians his gaze was fierce and his smile kind. By his side, to complete the picture, went a dog with ears pricked up and a long muzzle, more like a fox than any other sort of animal, and whose fierce appearance was in perfect harmony with the countenance of his leader. When we had looked at our new companion with an attention which he did not for a moment seem to notice, we asked him how much he wanted to be paid for the service he was going to do for us. The Indian answered a few words in his language, and the American quickly said that what the savage asked could be valued at two dollars. 'As these poor Indians,' our host kindly added, 'do not know the value of money, you give me the dollars and I will gladly see to getting him the equivalent.' I was curious to see what the good man considered the equivalent of two dollars and quietly followed him to the place where the deal was done. I saw him give our guide a pair of moccasins and a pocket handkerchief, objects whose total value certainly did not amount to half that sum. The Indian went back thoroughly satisfied, and I escaped noiselessly, saying to myself like La Fontaine: 'Ah! if lions knew how to paint!'

Besides it is not only the Indians whom the pioneers make their dupes. We ourselves were daily victims of their extreme greediness for gain. It is very true that they do not rob at all. They are too enlightened to do anything so imprudent, but otherwise I have never seen a hotel-keeper in a great city overcharge more impudently than these dwellers in the wilderness among whom I expected to find the primitive honesty and simplicity of a patriarchal way of life.

Everything was ready; we mounted and passing by a ford across the stream that forms the ultimate boundary between civilisation and the wilderness, we went in earnest into solitude.

Our two guides walked or rather jumped like wild cats over all the obstacles in the way. If we came across a tree blown over, a stream or a marsh, they pointed a finger to show the best path, went across and never turned to see how we got through the difficult place; accustomed to rely on himself, the Indian finds it hard to conceive that anyone needs help. If needs be, he knows how to do you a service, but no one has yet taught him to add to its value by obligingness and taking trouble. At other times we would have protested on our side at this way of behaving, but it was impossible for us to make our companions understand a single word. And besides! we felt ourselves completely in their power. There in fact the order was reversed; plunged into deep darkness, reduced to his own resources the civilised man walked like the blind, incapable not only of being his own guide in the labyrinth that surrounded him, but even of finding the means to sustain life. It is in the heart of the same difficulties that the savage triumphs; for him the forest obscured nothing; he felt at home there; he walked with his head high, guided by an instinct more sure than the navigator's compass. In the tops of the highest trees, under the densest foliage, his eye could see the prey close to which the European had passed and repassed a hundred times in vain.

From time to time our Indians halted; they put their fingers to their lips to show that we must keep silence and signalled to us to get off our horses. Led by them we came to a place where one could see the game. It was a strange sight to see the scornful smile with which they took us by the hand like children and led us at last close to the object that they had seen a long time ago.

Now as we advanced further the last signs of man disappeared. Soon there was nothing even to indicate the presence of savages, and we had before us the spectacle which we had been so long pursuing, the depths of a virgin forest.

Through undergrowth that was not thick and across which one could see objects at a considerable distance, the high forest rose straightway, composed entirely of pines and oaks. Forced to grow in a narrowly limited area and almost entirely hidden from the light of the sun, each tree grows quickly upwards looking for air and light. Straight as a ship's mast, it soon rises above everything surrounding it. It is then when it gets into this higher region that it quietly spreads its branches and envelopes itself in their shade. Others soon follow it in this high sphere, and they all, interlacing their branches, form as it were a huge dais above the ground that bears them. Below this damp and unmoving vault the look of things changes and the scene takes on a new character. Majestic order reigns above your head. But near the ground there is a general picture of confusion and chaos. Trunks that can no longer support the weight of their branches, are split half-way up and left with pointed and torn tops. Others, long shaken by the wind, have been thrown all complete on the ground; torn out of the soil, their roots form so many natural ramparts behind which several men could easily take cover. Immense trees, held up by the surrounding branches, stay suspended in the air, and fall to dust without touching the ground. With us there is no district so thinly populated and no forest so completely left to itself, that the trees, when they have quietly come to an end of their days, fall at last from decay. It is man who strikes them down in the vigour of their maturity, and rids the forest of their debris. In the solitudes of America nature in all her strength is the only instrument of ruin and also the only creative force. As in forests subject to man's control, death strikes continually here; but no one is concerned to clear the debris away. Every day adds to the number; they fall and pile up one on top of the other; time cannot reduce them quickly enough to dust and make fresh places ready. There many generations of the dead lie side by side. Some that have come to the last stage of dissolution, show as no more than a train of red dust along the grass. Others already half consumed by time, still yet preserve their shape. Then there are those that, fallen yesterday, still stretch their long branches on the ground, and hold the traveller up by an obstacle he had not expected. In the midst of all this debris the work of new creation goes ceaselessly forward. Offshoots, creepers and plants of every sort press across every obstacle to the light. They ramp along the trunks of fallen trees, they push their way into the rotten wood, and they lift and break the bark still covering them. Life and death meet here face to face as if they wished to mingle and confuse their labours.

We have often admired one of those calm and serene evenings on the ocean, when the sails flap quietly by the mast leaving the sailor doubtful whence the breeze will rise. This repose of all nature is no less impressive in the solitudes of the new World than on the immensity of the sea. At midday when the sun darts its beams on the forest, one often hears in its depths something like a long sigh, a plaintive cry lingering in the distance. It is the last stir of the dying wind. Then everything around you falls back into a silence so deep, a stillness so complete that the soul is invaded by a kind of religious terror. The traveller halts and looks round; pressed one against the other and with their branches interlaced, the forest trees seem to form but one whole, an immense and indestructible edifice under whose vaults eternal darkness reigns. On whatever side he looks, he sees nothing but a field of violence and destruction. Broken trees and torn trunks, everything testifies that the elements are here perpetually at war. But the struggle is interrupted. One would say that at the behest of a supernatural power, movement is suddenly halted. Half broken branches seem still held by secret ties to the trunks that no longer support them; uprooted trees have not yet had time to reach the ground, and stay suspended in the air. He listens and holds his breath in fear to better catch the least echo of life; no sound, no murmur reaches him.

More than once in Europe we have found ourselves lost deep in the woods; but always some sound of life came to reach our ears. Perhaps the distant tinkle of the nearest village bell, a traveller's footstep, the woodcutter's axe, a gunshot, the barking of a dog or just that confused sound that pervades a civilised country. Here not only is man lacking, but no sound can be heard from the animals either. The smallest of them have left these parts to come close to human habitations, and the largest have gone to get even further away. Those that remain stay hidden from the sun's rays. So all is still in the woods, all is silent under their leaves. One would say that for a moment the Creator had turned his face away and all the forces of nature are paralysed.

But that is not the only occasion on which we noticed the strange analogy between the sight of the ocean and that of a wild forest. In both the one and the other you are assailed by a sense of immensity. The continuity and monotony of like scenes both astonishes and overwhelms the imagination. Again in the solitudes of the New World we felt, perhaps more strongly and more poignantly, that sense of isolation and of abandonment that had weighed on us so heavily in the middle of the Atlantic. On the sea at least the traveller looks towards the vast horizon on which his eyes and hopes are set. But in this ocean of leaves who could point out the way? Whither turn one's looks? In vain to climb to the top of very high trees, for others still higher surround you. It is useless to climb the hills, for everywhere the forest seems to walk in front of you, and this same forest stretches before your feet right up to the Arctic Pole and the Pacific Ocean. You can travel on for thousands of leagues under its shade, and you go forward the whole time without appearing to change place.

But I must get back to the road to Saginaw. We had already been going forward for five hours in the most complete ignorance of where we were, when our Indians halted, and the elder, who was called Sagan Cuisco, drew a line in the sand. He pointed to one of the ends saying 'Miché-Couté-Ouinque' (that is the Indian name for *Flint River*), to the other pronouncing the name Saginaw, and, making a point in the middle of the line, he showed us that we had come half-way and ought to rest for a few moments. The sun was already high in the sky, and we would gladly have accepted the suggestion he made to us, if we had seen any water within reach. But seeing none anywhere near, we made a sign to the Indian that we wanted to eat and drink at the same time. He understood at once, and set off again as rapidly as before. An hour on from there he halted again, and pointed to a spot thirty paces away in the wood where his

gestures indicated that there was water. Without waiting for
our answer or helping us to dismount, he went there himself;
we hastened to follow him. A great tree had recently been blown
over by the wind on that spot. In the hole where its roots had
been there was a little rain water. That was the fountain to
which our guide had led us without appearing to think that one
could hesitate to make use of such a drink. We opened our knapsack; another blow! The heat had completely ruined our provisions, and we were reduced to a very small piece of bread, all
that we had been able to find at *Flint River*, for all our dinner.
Add to that a cloud of mosquitoes congregating near the water,
so that one had to fight them off with one hand while one put a
bite into one's mouth with the other, and you will have some idea
of a picnic in a virgin forest. While we were eating, our Indians
stayed sitting with arms crossed on the trunk of the fallen tree I
mentioned before. When they saw that we had finished, they
made a sign that they were hungry too. We showed our empty
knapsack. They shook their heads without saying a word. The
Indian has no conception of what regular hours for meals are.
He gorges himself on food when he gets the chance, and then
fasts until he gets another chance of satisfying his appetite.
Wolves behave the same in like circumstances. We soon thought
of mounting our horses, but saw with great alarm that our
mounts had disappeared. Stung by the mosquitoes and pricked
by hunger they had strayed from the path where we left them,
and it was only with difficulty that we succeeded in getting on
their tracks. If we had stayed for a quarter of an hour more
without paying attention, we should have woken up, like Sancho,
with the saddle between our knees. We heartily blessed the
mosquitoes that had made us think so soon of moving, and set
off again. Every moment our horses had to force their way
through thick bushes or jump over the trunks of huge trees that
barred our way. At the end of about two hours of very difficult
going, we came to a stream that was not very deep but had very
high banks. We crossed it by a ford and when we had climbed
up to the top of the opposite bank, we saw a field of corn and
two cabins very like log-houses. We realised as we came close
that we were in a little Indian settlement. The log-houses were
wigwams. Otherwise the deepest solitude prevailed there as in
the surrounding forest. When he came to the first of these

abandoned dwellings, Sagan Cuisco stopped; he paid close attention to all the objects around, and then putting his carbine down, he
came up to us. First he drew a line in the sand, showing us in the
same manner as before that we had not yet covered more than
two-thirds of the way; he then got up, pointed to the sun and
made signs to indicate that it was descending rapidly to the
horizon. He then looked at the wigwam and shut his eyes. This
language was very easy to understand; he wanted us to sleep
on that spot. I admit that the proposition surprised us a lot, and
did not please us at all. We had not eaten since the morning,
and were but moderately anxious to go to bed without supper.
The sombre and savage majesty of the sights we had seen since
the morning, the complete isolation in which we were, the
fierce countenances of our guides with whom it was impossible to
make any contact, in all that there was nothing to inspire us with
confidence. Moreover there was something strange in the
Indians' behaviour that was far from reassuring us. The way we
had gone for the last two hours seemed even less frequented
than that we had travelled on before. No one had ever told us
that we should have to pass an Indian village, and everyone had
on the contrary assured us that one could go in one day from
Flint River to Saginaw. So we could not conceive why our guides
wanted to keep us for the night in this wilderness. We insisted
on going on. The Indian made a sign that we should be surprised
by darkness in the forest. To force our guides to continue the
journey would have been a dangerous attempt. We decided
to tempt their cupidity. But the Indian is the most philosophic of
all men. He has few needs and so few desires. Civilisation has no
hold on him; he is unaware of, or scorns its charms. But I had
noticed that Sagan Cuisco had paid particular attention to a little
wicker-covered bottle that hung at my side. A bottle that does
not get broken. There was an object whose usefulness struck his
senses, and which had aroused his real admiration. My rifle and
my bottle were the only parts of my European gear that had
seemed able to rouse his envy. I made him a sign that I would
give him my bottle, if he would take us at once to Saginaw. The
Indian then seemed to be struggling violently with himself.
He looked at the sun again and then at the ground. Finally
making up his mind, he seized his carbine, and putting his hand
to his mouth raised a cry of 'Ouh! ouh!' and darted in front of

us into the bushes. We followed him at fast trot, and forcing a way through for ourselves, had soon lost sight of the Indian dwellings. Our guides ran like that for two hours faster than they had yet gone; but night gained on us, and the last rays of the sun were beginning to disappear behind the forest trees, when Sagan Cuisco was suddenly seized with a violent nose-bleed, Accustomed though this young man, like his brother, seemed to be to bodily exercise, it was clear that fatigue and want of food were beginning to drain his strength. We ourselves began to be afraid that they would give up the undertaking and want to sleep under a tree. So we took the decision to make them ride in turns on our horses. The Indians accepted our offer without surprise or difference. It was an odd sight to see these half-naked men solemnly seated on an English saddle, and carrying our game-bags and our slung rifles with bandoliers, while we laboured along on foot in front of them. At length night came on and a freezing damp began to spread under the foliage. Then darkness gave a new and terrible aspect to the forest. All around one could see nothing but gatherings of confused masses, without shape or symmetry, strange disproportionate forms, incoherent sights and fantastic images that seemed to come from the sick imagination of a fever bed. (The gigantic and the ridiculous rubbed shoulders there as close as in the literature of our day.) Never had our footsteps raised more echoes; never had the silence of the forest seemed more fearsome. One might say that the buzzing of the mosquitoes was the only breathing of this sleeping world. The further we went on, the darker did the shadows grow, and nothing but the occasional flight of a fire-fly through the woods traced a thread of light in their depths. Too late we realized how right the Indian's advice had been, but there was no question now of retreat. So we pressed on as quickly as our strength and the night would allow. After an hour we came out of the wood and into a vast prairie. Three times our guides yelled out a savage cry that echoed like the discordant notes of a tom-tom. An answer came from the distance. In five minutes we came to the edge of a river in such darkness that we could not see the opposite bank. The Indians made a halt at this spot; they wrapped themselves up in their blankets to escape the mosquitoes' stings, and, lying down on the grass, they soon formed no more than a scarcely perceptible heap of wool in which no one could have recognised the shape of a man. We, too, got to the ground, and patiently waited what was going to happen. A few minutes later a faint sound could be heard, and something approached the bank. It was an Indian canoe, about ten feet long, and shaped out of a single tree. The man who crouched in the bottom of this fragile bark, was dressed and looked completely like an Indian. He spoke to our guides who at his order hastened to take our saddles off and put them in the canoe. As I was getting ready to get into it myself, the supposed Indian came up to me, put two fingers in my shoulder, and said in a Norman accent that made me jump: 'Don't go too fast, sometimes people get drowned here.' If my horse had spoken to me, I do not think I should have been more surprised. I looked at the man who spoke to me and whose face lighted by the first rays of the moon shone like a ball of copper: 'Who are you then,' I said to him, 'French seems to be your language, and you look like an Indian?' He told me that he was a *bois-brulé*, that is to say the son of a French Canadian and an Indian woman. I shall have frequent occasion to speak of this race of half-castes that covers all the frontiers of Canada and part of those of the United States. For the moment I only thought of the pleasure of speaking my mother tongue. Obeying the advice of the savage, my compatriot, I sat down in the bottom of the canoe and kept balance as well as might be. The horse went into the water and began to swim, while the French Canadian propelled the little boat with an oar, singing under his breath the while an old French song of which I only caught the first two lines:

> 'Between Paris and Saint Denis
> There lived a girl.'

We reached the further bank without mishap. The canoe went back at once to fetch my companion. All my life I shall remember the moment when it came up to the bank for the second time. The moon which then was full, rose at that very moment above the prairie we had just crossed. Only half its orb showed above the horizon; one might have thought it a mysterious gate from which light flowed towards us from another sphere. Its rays reflected in the water glinted close around me. The Indian canoe slid forward right along the line of the pale moonbeams; one saw no oars; one heard no sound of rowing; it glided on quickly and effortlessly, long, narrow and black, like an alligator on the Mississippi that makes for the bank to seize its prey. As he crouched in the tip of the canoe with his head on his knees, one could only see the shining tresses of Sagan Cuisco's hair. At the other end the French Canadian rowed in silence, while behind him the horse's plunging chest sent the water of the Saginaw splashing. The whole scene had something of savage grandeur in it, which then made and has since left an enduring impression on our souls. Landing on the bank we hurried up to a house which we saw in the moonlight a hundred paces from the stream, where the French Canadian assured us we could find accommodation for the night. We did in fact get ourselves suitably fixed up, and probably sound sleep would have restored our strength, if we had been able to get rid of the myriads of mosquitoes in which the house abounded. But that is something we never achieved. What is called a 'mosquito' in English and 'maringouin' by the French Canadians, is a little insect like to its French *cousin* in everything except size. It is generally bigger, and its sting is so strong and sharp that only woollen stuffs can protect one from its attacks. These little gnats are the scourge of the solitudes of America. Their presence is enough to make a long stay unbearable. For my part I avow that I have never suffered torments like those they inflicted on me throughout the journey and particularly during our stay at Saginaw. By day they stopped us sketching, writing or staying one moment in the same place; by night they circled in their thousands round us; any bit of your body that you left uncovered at once became their rendezvous. Woken by the pain of their stings we covered our heads in the sheets, but their needles went through them; thus hunted and harried by them we got up and went to breathe the air outside until fatigue at last brought on troubled and interrupted sleep.

We got up very early in the morning, and the first sight that struck us as we left the house was that of our Indians rolled in their blankets near the door, asleep beside their dogs.

Then for the first time we saw in daylight the village of Saginaw which we had come so far to seek.

A small cultivated plain bounded on the south by a lovely,

tranquil stream, on the east, west and north by the forest, is up to now the whole territory of the city to be.

Near us was a house built in a style showing its owner's affluence. It was that in which we had just passed the night. There appeared another house of the same sort at the other end of the clearing. Between the two, along the edge of the wood, were two or three log-houses half lost among the leaves. On the opposite bank of the stream the prairie stretched like a boundless ocean on a calm day. At that time a column of smoke was coming up from it and rising peacefully into the sky. Tracing its line back down to the ground one could finally discern two or three wigwams whose conic form and pointed top lost themselves in the prairie grass.

A cart turned over, some oxen going back on their own to work, and some half-wild horses complete the picture.

Whichever way you looked, the eye would never find the spire of a Gothic belfry, a wooden cross marking the way, or the moss covered threshold of a presbytery. None of these venerable relics of old Christian civilisation have been transported into the wilderness; nothing there awakens thoughts of the past or of the future. One does not even find sanctuaries sacred to those who are no more. Death has not had time to claim its dominion nor to define the graveyard's limit.

Here man seems furtively to enter upon life. There is no meeting round his cradle of several generations to express hopes that are often vain and give rein to premature joys to which the future gives the lie. His name is not inscribed on the registers of the city. None of the touching solemnities of religion are mingled with the family's solicitude. A woman's prayers, a few drops of water sprinkled on a baby's head by his father's hand, are the quiet opening for him of the doors of heaven.

The village of Saginaw is the last point inhabited by Europeans to the northwest of the huge peninsula of Michigan. One may regard it as an advanced station, a sort of observation post, which the whites have established in the midst of the Indian tribes.

The revolutions of Europe and all the noisy bustle forever ringing in the well-policed part of the world, hardly reach here at long intervals, and ring like the echoes of a sound whose nature and origin the ear cannot identify.

A Fortnight in the Wilds

Perhaps an Indian incidentally recalls in the poetic manner natural to a man of the wilds some of the sad occurrences in the affairs of the world; a forgotten newspaper in a hunter's haversack; or just that vague rumour spread by unknown voices which hardly ever fails to let men know that something extraordinary is happening under the sun.

Once a year a ship going up the Saginaw comes to renew this broken link in the great European chain which already encircles the world. It brings the new settlement the varied products of industry and takes back in return the fruits of the soil.

Thirty people, men, women, old people and children were all that made up at the time of our visit that little society, a scarcely formed embryo, a growing seed entrusted to the wilds, which the wilds must fertilize.

Chance, interest or desire had brought together these thirty people in this narrow space. There was no other common link between them and they were profoundly different. One found French Canadians there, some Americans, some Indians and some half-castes.

Some philosophers have believed that human nature everywhere the same only varies according to the institutions and laws of different societies. That is one of the opinions to which the history of the world seems to give the lie on every page. In history all nations, like individuals, show their own peculiar physiognomy. Their characteristic traits reproduce themselves through all the transformations that they undergo. Laws, morals, religions alter; dominion and wealth change hands; external appearances vary; the dress is different; prejudices vanish or are replaced by others. Through all these diverse changes you always recognize the same people. Something inflexible shows through in spite of all man's adaptability.

The people inhabiting this little bit of cultivated plain belong to two races who for nearly a century have lived on American soil and obeyed the same laws. But there is nothing in common between them. They are English and French, just like those one finds on the banks of the Seine or the Thames.

Once inside that leafy hut you will find a man whose cordial welcome and open features at once indicate his taste for social pleasures and carefree attitude to life. At the first moment perhaps you will think him an Indian. Forced to live the life of a savage, he has freely adopted its habits, customs and almost its manners. He wears moccasins, otterskin cap and woollen cloak. He is an unwearying hunter, sleeps in the open, and lives on wild honey and bison flesh. Nonetheless this man has still remained a Frenchman, gay, enterprising, haughty, proud of his origin, passionate lover of military glory, vain rather than mercenary, a man of instinct following his first inclination rather than reason, preferring renown to money. To get to the wilds he seems to have broken all the ties that bind him to life; one does not find him with wife or children. This condition is unnatural to him, but he accepts it and everything else easily. Left to himself, his naturally stay-at-home temper would reassert itself; no one has a stronger taste than he for the domestic hearth; no one delights more in the sight of the ancestral clock-tower; but he has been snatched away in spite of himself from his tranquil habits, his imagination has been inflamed by new sights, and he has been transplanted under another sky; the man is the same but he has suddenly felt an insatiable desire for violent emotions, vicissitude and danger. The most civilised of Europeans has turned into a worshipper of the savage life. He prefers savannas to city streets and hunting to agriculture. He is taking chances with his life and lives without a care for the future.

The white men of France, say the Canadian Indians, are as good hunters as we. Like us they despise the comforts of life and brave the dangers of death. God made them to dwell in a savage's hut and live in the wilds.

A few steps away from this man lives another European who, having to face the same difficulties, has hardened himself against them.

This latter is cold, tenacious and relentless in argument; he attaches himself to the ground and snatches from savage life all that can be got out of it. He is in continual contest against it, and daily despoils it of some of its attributes. Bit by bit he carries into the wilds his laws, his habits and his customs, and if he could, he would introduce everything down to the smallest refinements of advanced civilisation. The emigrant from the United States is only interested in victory for its results; he holds glory but a vain clamour, and thinks that man has only come into the world to gain affluence and the comforts of life. He is brave nonetheless, but brave by calculation, brave because he has found out that there are several things harder to bear than death. An adventurer surrounded by his family, but one who sets little store by intellectual pleasures and the charms of social life.

On the other side of the river, down in the reeds by the Saginaw, the Indian occasionally casts a stoic glance on the dwellings of his European brethren. Do not go imagining that he admires their works or envies their lot. For nearly three centuries by now the American savage has been in contest with the civilisation that presses on him and surrounds him, but he still has not learnt to know or esteem his enemy. In vain does generation follow generation in both races. Like two parallel rivers they have been flowing for three centuries towards a common abyss; a narrow space separates them but their waters never mingle. It is not that the native of the New World is always lacking in natural aptitude, but his nature seems obstinately to repulse our ideas and our skills. Sleeping in his cloak in the smoke of his hut, the Indian looks with mistrust at the European's comfortable house; he for his part prides himself on his poverty, and his heart swells and rejoices at the thought of his barbarian independence. He smiles bitterly as he sees us plagueing our lives to get useless wealth. What we call industry, he calls shameful subjection. He compares the workman to an ox laboriously tracing out a furrow. What we call the comforts of life, he calls children's playthings or women's affectations. He envies us nothing but our weapons. When a man can find cover at night in a tent of leaves, when he can find enough to light a fire to keep off the mosquitoes in summer and cold in winter, when his dogs are good and the country full of game, what more can he ask from the Eternal Being?

On the other side of the Saginaw, near the European clearings and so to say on the border of the old and new world, one finds a rustic hut more comfortable than the savage's wigwam but ruder than the civilised man's house. That is the half-caste's dwelling. The first time that we presented ourselves at the door of such a half-civilised hut, we were surprised to hear a gentle voice singing the Psalms of penitence to an Indian air. We stopped a moment to listen. The modulations of the sound were slow and profoundly melancholy; it was easy to recognize the plaintive harmony of all the songs of men of the wilds. We came in. The master was away. Seated cross-legged on a mat in the middle of the room, a young woman was making some moccasins; with one foot she rocked an infant whose copper colour and whose features made its double origin clear. This woman was dressed like one of our peasants except that her feet were bare and her hair fell freely on her shoulders. When she saw us, she fell silent with a sort of respectful fear. We asked her if she was French. 'No,' she answered smiling.—'English.'—'Not that either.' she said; she lowered her eyes and added, 'I am only a savage.' Child of two races, brought up to use two languages, nourished in diverse beliefs and rocked in contrary prejudices, the half-caste forms an amalgam as inexplicable to others as to himself. What his rude mind takes in of the sights of this world, present themselves as something like an inextricable chaos from which his spirit knows no escape. Proud of his European origin he scorns the wilds, and yet he loves the freedom that prevails there. He admires civilisation but cannot completely submit to its dominion. His tastes are in contradiction with his ideas, and his views with his habits. Not knowing how to find his way by his uncertain lights, his soul is the painful battleground of all the arguments of universal doubt. He adopts contradictory customs; he prays at two altars; he believes in the Redeemer of the world and in the mountebank's amulets; and he reaches the end of his life without ever being able to sort out the difficult problem of his existence,

So in this corner of the earth unknown to the world God's hand had already sown the seeds of diverse nations; here there are already several different races, several distinct peoples facing one another.

Several exiled members of the great human family have met together in the immensity of the forests and their needs are all alike; they have to fight against the beasts of the forest, hunger and hard weather. There are scarcely thirty of them in the midst of the wilds where everything resists their efforts, but they cast only looks of hatred and suspicion on one another. Colour of skin, poverty or affluence, ignorance or enlightenment have already built up indestructible classifications between them; national prejudices, and prejudices of education and birth divide and isolate them.

A Fortnight in the Wilds

Where could one find a more complete picture of the wretchedness of our nature in a narrower frame? But there is yet one feature still unmentioned.

The deep lines that birth and opinion have ruled between these men by no means end with life but stretch out beyond the tomb. Six religions, or different sects, divide the faith of this nascent society.

Catholicism with its formidable immobility, its absolute dogmas, its terrible anathemas and immense rewards, the religious anarchy of the Reformation and ancient paganism are all represented. Already the one Eternal Being who made all men in his image is worshipped in six different ways. Disputes rage about the heaven that every one claims as his exclusive heritage. Beyond that even, in the midst of the wretchedness of solitude and the troubles of the present, human imagination wears itself out inventing inexpressible sorrows for the future. The Lutheran condemns the Calvinist to eternal fire, the Calvinist the Unitarian, and the Catholic embraces them all in a common condemnation.

The Indian, more tolerant in his rude faith, does not go beyond exiling his European brother from the happy hunting grounds he reserves for himself. For him, faithful to the confused traditions bequeathed by his fathers, there is an easy consolation for the ills of this life and he dies peacefully dreaming of the ever green forests which the pioneer's axe will never bring down, where deer and beaver will come to be shot through the numberless days of eternity.

After lunch we went to see the richest landowner in the village, Mr. Williams. We found him in his shop busy selling Indians a quantity of objects of little value such as knives, glass necklaces and ear-rings. It was a shame to see how these unfortunates were treated by their civilised European brethren. Moreover everyone we saw was loud in praise of the savages. They were good, inoffensive, a thousand times less inclined to theft than the white men. It was only a pity that they were beginning to learn about the value of things. And why that, if you please? Because the profits made by trading with them were daily becoming less considerable. Do you appreciate there the superiority of the civilised man? The Indian in his rude simplicity would have said that he was finding it daily more difficult to cheat his neighbour. But the white man discovers in the refinements of language a happy nuance that expresses the fact but hides the shame.

Coming back from Mr. Williams' it occurred to us to go some way up the Saginaw to shoot the wild duck on its banks. While we were so engaged, a canoe came out from the reeds in the river and some Indians came to meet us to look at my rifle which they had seen in the distance. I have always noticed that that weapon, which however has nothing unusual about it, wins me altogether special consideration from the savages. A rifle that could kill two men in one second and be fired in fog, was in their view a wonder beyond value, a priceless masterpiece. Those who came up to us as usual expressed great admiration. They asked where my rifle came from. Our young guide said that it had been made on the other side of the great water, in the land of the fathers of the French Canadians; a circumstance which, as you will believe, did not make it less precious in their eyes. But they pointed out that as the sights were not placed in the middle of each barrel, it was difficult to be sure of your shot, a criticism to which I admit I could not find an answer.

When evening came on we got into the canoe again, and trusting to the experience we had gained in the morning, we went out alone to go up a branch of the Saginaw of which we had only had a glimpse before.

The sky was cloudless and the air pure and still. The river waters flowed through an immense forest, but so slowly that it would have been almost impossible to say in which direction the current was running. We had always found that to get a true idea of the forests of the New World, one must follow up one of the streams that wander beneath their shade. The rivers are like main roads by means of which Providence has been at pains, since the beginning of the world, to open up the wilds and make them accessible to man. When one forces a way through the woods, one's view is generally very limited. Besides the very path on which you walk is the work of man. But the rivers are roads that keep no marks of tracks, and their banks freely show all the great and strange sights that vigorous vegetation left to itself can provide.

The wilds were there surely just the same as when our first fathers saw them six thousand years ago; a flowering solitude, delightful and scented; a magnificent dwelling, a living palace built for man, but to which its master had not yet reached. The canoe glided without effort and without sound; the serenity of universal calm reigned around us. We, too, soon felt the tender influence of such a sight. We talked less and less and soon found that we only put our thoughts into whispers. Finally we fell silent, and working the oars simultaneously, both of us fell into a tranquil reverie full of inexpressible charm.

Why is it that human language that finds words for every sorrow, meets an invincible obstacle in trying to make the most gentle and natural emotions of the human heart understood? Who will ever paint a true picture of those rare moments in life when physical well-being prepares the way for calm of soul, and the universe seems before your eyes to have reached a perfect equilibrium; then the soul half asleep hovers between the present and the future, between the real and the possible, while with natural beauty all around and the air tranquil and mild, at peace with himself in the midst of universal peace, man listens to the even beating of his arteries that seems to him to mark the passage of time flowing drop by drop through eternity. Many men perhaps have seen long years of existence pile up without once experiencing anything like what we have just described. They will not understand us. But there are some, we are sure, who will find in their memory and at the bottom of their heart something that gives colour to the picture that we paint, and, as they read, will feel the memory awakening of some fugitive hours which neither time nor the demanding cares of life have been able to efface.

We were woken from our reverie by a gun-shot that suddenly echoed through the woods. The sound at first seemed to roll crashing along both banks of the river; then it rumbled into the distance until it was entirely lost in the depths of the forest. It might have been the long, fearsome war cry of civilisation on the march.

One evening in Sicily we happened to get lost in a vast marsh that now occupies the place where once was the city of Himera; the sight of that once famous city turned back to savage wilds made a great and deep impression on us. Never have we seen beneath our feet more magnificent witness to the instability of human things and the wretchedness of our nature. Here too it

was indeed a solitude, but imagination instead of going back-
wards to try and get back into the past, went rushing on ahead
and got lost in an immense future. It struck us as a peculiar
privilege of fate that we who had been able to look on the ruins
of perished empires and to walk through wilds of human making,
that we, children of an ancient people, should be brought to
witness one of the scenes of the primitive world and to see the
still empty cradle of a great nation. Here it is not a question of
the more or less doubtful anticipations of the wise. The facts
are as certain as if they had already occurred. In but few years
these impenetrable forests will have fallen. The noise of civilisation and of industry will break the silence of the Saginaw.
Its echo will be silent. Embankments will imprison its sides,
and its waters which today flow unknown and quiet through
nameless wilds, will be thrown back in their flow by the prows
of ships. Fifty leagues still separate this solitude from the great
European settlements and we are perhaps the last travellers who
will have been allowed to see it in its primitive splendour, so
great is the force that drives the white race to the complete conquest of the New World.

It is this consciousness of destruction, this *arrière-pensée* of
quick and inevitable change that gives, we feel, so peculiar a
character and such a touching beauty to the solitudes of America.
One sees them with a melancholy pleasure; one is in some sort
of a hurry to admire them. Thoughts of the savage, natural
grandeur that is going to come to an end, become mingled with
splendid anticipations of the triumphant march of civilisation.
One feels proud to be a man, and yet at the same time one
experiences I cannot say what bitter regret at the power that
God has granted us over nature. One's soul is shaken by contradictory thoughts and feelings, but all the impressions it receives
are great and leave a deep mark.

We wanted to leave Saginaw on the next day, the 27th July;
but as one of our horses had been badly rubbed by its saddle we
decided to wait one day more. For want of any other way to
pass the time, we went shooting along the meadows that fringe
the Saginaw above the clearings. These meadows are not at all
marshy, as one might have supposed. They are more or less
large open spaces that the wood does not cover although the
soil is excellent. The grass there is tough and three or four feet

high. We found but little game and came back early. The heat was stifling as if before a storm, and the mosquitoes were even more troublesome than usual. We could not move without a cloud of these insects on whom we had to make perpetual war. Bad luck to any one who had to stop. That was to give oneself over defenceless to a pitiless foe. Once I remember having to keep moving while I was loading my rifle, so difficult was it to stay still for a moment.

As we were crossing the meadow on our return, we noticed that the French Canadian who acted as our guide, kept to a narrow trodden path and was very careful to look at the ground before putting his foot down. 'Why are you so careful?' I asked him. 'Are you afraid of getting wet?' 'No,' he answered. 'But I have got the habit when I am walking through the meadows, of looking where I put my feet so as not to tread on a rattlesnake.'—'What the devil,' I answered jumping onto the path. 'Are there rattlesnakes here?'—'Yes indeed,' our Norman American answered with imperturbable sang-froid. '*The place is full of them.*' I reproached him then for not having told us sooner. He made out that as we were wearing good boots and a rattlesnake never bites above the ankle, he had not felt that we were running great danger.

I asked him if a rattlesnake bite was mortal. He replied that one always died in less than twenty-four hours unless one turned to the Indians for help. They knew of a remedy which, if given in time, he said saved the victim.

However that may be for the rest of the way we imitated our guide and looked as he did to our feet.

The night that followed this burning day was one of the worst I have passed in my life. The mosquitoes had become so troublesome that, though worn out with fatigue, I could not shut my eyes. Towards midnight the long threatened storm finally broke. With no more hope of getting any sleep, I got up and opened our hut door so as at least to breathe the fresh night air. The rain had not started yet and the air seemed calm; but the forest shook already, and was filled with deep groans and lingering wails. Now and again a lightning flash illuminated the sky. The tranquil flow of the Saginaw, the little clearing that edges its banks, the roofs of five or six huts and the leafy fence that surrounded us appeared then for an instant like an evocation of the future. Then all was in the deepest darkness and the fearsome voice of the wilds was heard again.

While I stood, struck by this great spectacle, I heard a sigh at my side and in the flash of the lightning I saw an Indian leaning as I was doing against the wall of our dwelling. No doubt the storm had broken his sleep, for it was a a fixed and troubled gaze that he cast around the scene.

Was this man afraid of the thunder? Or did he see in the clash of the elements something beyond a passing convulsion of nature? Had the fugitive images of civilisation which rose unbidden in the midst of the tumult of the wilds a prophetic meaning for him? Did these groans of the forest that seemed to be fighting an unequal battle strike his ear as a secret warning of God, a solemn revelation of the final fate reserved for the savage races? I could not say. But his agitated lips seemed to be murmuring prayers and all his features were stamped by superstitious terror.

At five o'clock in the morning we thought about leaving. All the Indians in the neighbourhood of Saginaw had disappeared. They had gone to receive the presents that the English give them every year, and the Europeans were busy harvesting. So we had to make up our minds to get back through the forest without a guide. The undertaking was not as difficult as one might have supposed. Generally speaking, there is only one path in these vast solitudes and it is only a question of not losing track of it to reach the end of one's journey.

So then, at five o'clock in the morning, we crossed the Saginaw again; our hosts said good-bye to us and gave us their last words of advice. Then, turning our horses' heads, we found ourselves alone in the forest. I must admit that it was not without apprehension that we began to penetrate its humid depths. This same forest that surrounded us then stretched behind us to the Pole and to the Pacific Ocean. Only one inhabited point separated us from the endless wilds and we were going to leave that. But such thoughts only served to make us press our horses on and at the end of three hours we reached an abandoned wigwam and came to the solitary banks of the Cass River. A turf covered point projecting above the river in the shade of great trees served us as a table and we sat down to luncheon with a view of the river whose waters clear as crystal snaked through the wood.

A Fortnight in the Wilds

Going out of the wigwam on the Cass River we came upon several paths. We had been told which to take; but it is easy to forget some points or not to make oneself clearly understood in receiving such explanations. That is what we discovered on that day. They had told us about two ways; there were three. It is true that of these three ways there were two which joined up again further on, as we later found out, but we didn't know that then and great was our distress.

When we had well looked and well argued, we did what almost all great men do and acted more or less on chance. We got across the stream as best we could by a ford and forced our way quickly towards the South-West. More than once the path seemed ready to disappear amid the undergrowth; in other places the way seemed so little frequented that we could scarcely believe that it led to anything more than some abandoned wigwam. Our compass, it is true, showed us that we were always walking in the right direction. Nonetheless, we were not completely reassured until we found the place where we had had dinner three days before. A gigantic pine whose trunk, torn by the wind, we had admired made us recognize it. Nonetheless, we went on our way as quickly as before, for the sun was beginning to go down. Soon we came to a glade such as generally comes before the clearings and just as night was beginning to surprise us, we saw the Flint River. Half an hour later, we reached our host's door. This time, the bear greeted us as old friends and only got onto its hind legs to show its delight at our happy return.

Throughout the whole of that day we had not met a single human face. The animals too had disappeared; no doubt they had retreated under the foliage to escape the heat of the day. Only at long intervals did we notice, on the bare top of some dead tree, a sparrow hawk, motionless on one foot and sleeping peacefully in the rays of the sun, seemed sculptured out of the very wood on which it rested.

It was in the midst of that profound solitude that we suddenly thought of the Revolution of 1830 whose first anniversary had just arrived. I cannot describe the impact with which memories of the 29th July took possession of our minds. The cries and smoke of battle, the roar of guns, the rattle of rifles, the even more horrible ringing of the tocsin, that whole day with its delirious atmosphere seemed suddenly to rise out of the past and to stand before me like a living picture. This was only a sudden hallucination, a passing dream. When I raised my head and looked around me, the apparition had already vanished; but never had the silence of the forest seemed so icy, the shadows so sombre, the solitude so absolute.

Appendix[1]

24 hours in New Orleans,
describe the Mississippi when I shall have time

You know, Mon cher ami, that our intention was on leaving Philadelphia to go to New Orleans[2] and pass two weeks there, but shipwrecked at Wheeling, stopped by the ice at Louisville, held back ten days in Memphis, we were a hundred times on the point of giving up the trip that we had undertaken. We were going to turn back on our steps when the ———[3] December (note well the dates they are precious) a steamboat took us on board and offered to carry us down to Louisiana.

After all our calculations were made there remained of our two weeks not more than three days to pass in New Orleans. What was there to do however? We had to submit.

We set out then; but you see the implacability of fortune. In the night of the 26–27 of December, in the most beautiful moonlight that ever lit up the solitary banks of the Mississippi our boat suddenly touched bottom and after having tottered a while like a drunken man, she established herself tranquilly on the bar. To describe our despair at this affair would in truth be a difficult matter; we prayed to the heavens which said not a word, then to the captain who sent us to the pilot. As to the latter he received us like a potentate. After having blown a cloud of smoke in our faces, he observed peacefully that the sands of the Mississippi were like the French and could not stay a year in the same place. The comparison, you will admit, was insolent enough to be punished (*probablement insolente*)[4] but he was on his own ground and we on a ladder, we therefore pardoned him and came down

[1] Transcription of Yale Manuscript translated by Paul Lambert White; the present text has been established by K. P. Mayer. Cf. Pierson, op. cit., 619 ff. The French in this text is often faulty but we decided to reproduce exactly the Yale Manuscript.

[2] N.O. in photocopy.   [3] Blank in photocopy.   [4] French in photocopy.

to await the results of the efforts which the crew were going to make to get us out (*tirer*)[1] of the desperate position in which we found ourselves. We stayed there two days, At the end of that time they finally succeeded in tearing us loose from the sand and the first of January 1852, the sun rising in a shining (*étincelant*)[1] tropical sky revealed to us New Orleans across (*à travers*)[2] the masts of a thousand ships. We disembarked hastily, as you will readily conceive. (*nous débarquerons à la hâte vous le concevez sans peine.*)[3] There was no time to lose: to make the acquaintance of all those to whom we had been recommended, to enjoy the pleasures so celebrated of New Orleans,[4] to study the laws, learn the usages, to enter into the ways of life (*moeurs*),[5] to know the statistics and the history of the country. Only 24 hours remained to us: I (*je vous défie d'y ajouter une seule minute mais n'allez pas me juger avec trop de rigeur*)[6] defy you to add a single minute, but don't go and judge me too harshly; know that 24 hours usefully employed teach many things. I have this maxim from a young attaché of the French Embassy with whom I talked the other day. He appeared to speak very pertinently (?)[7] of England. An Englishman present pretended (*prétendait*)[8] that it was very impertinent but I, who saw that he was cutting into the quick at every stroke, and that he had a formed opinion (*une opinion faite*)[8] upon everything pertaining to that country; I began to be seized with admiration and I asked him that minute (*momentamment*)[9], how long a time he had passed among our neighbours. One week he replied. "*Monsieur a sans doute habité longtemps chez nos voisins? il me t——*[10] *et répondit: huit jours. . . .*"[11] I appeared surprised, I had not then my present experience. Seeing my astonishment he added (*reprit*)[12] with that air at the same time mysterious and engaging, deep and light—with a *diplomatic* "*qui distinguent tous les hommes d'une grande capacité et tous les diplomats*"[13] air in a word: one week, when one knows how to observe, is sufficient for many things. That is my excuse. *Voila mon excuse.*[14]

---

[1] French in photocopy.   [2] French deleted in Photocopy.
[3] French in photocopy.   [4] N.O. in photocopy.   [5] French in photocopy.
[6] French in photocopy; inserted and deleted. [7] Question mark in photocopy.
[8] French in photocopy.   [9] French inserted and deleted in photocopy.
[10] Blank in photocopy.   [11] French in margin in photocopy.
[12] French in photocopy.   [13] French in margin in photocopy.
[14] French deleted in photocopy.

Appendix

If one week is sufficient indeed for a superior man to have an opinion upon the British Empire and all her colonies, it is clear that a man of an inferior capacity can still hope to learn something of New Orleans in 24 hours.

Besides we had no choice. After we had laid out our best clothes, (therefore, *après donc nous être mis dans la tenue la plus soignée*)[1] we tried to introduce into our dress as much as possible a happy mixture of the Philosopher and the man of the world. We were under the necessity, without being able to return to our quarters during the whole course of a long day, of being alternately very deep and very amiable. We put on a black tie for the members of the legislature, a white vest (*gilet*)[2] for the women, we carried in our hand a little swagger stick (*badine*)[2] to raise (*relever jusqu'à*)[2] us into intimacy with the fashionable world, and, very contented with ourselves, we descended the stairs. There the difficulty of putting order into our activities presented itself for the first time to our mind: we established ourselves on a curbstone as a deliberating assembly and after a discussion which lasted an hour we adopted the following plan. We made an infinite number of classifications. We created principles of observation, then we made deductions from our principles, then deductions from our deductions; we discussed, classified, unclassified for an hour and noon was smiling upon us when we finally adopted the following plan: you see that I possess indeed the style of the *procès-verbal*:[2] we resolved to consecrate two hours to an examination of the city, to knowing its external appearance, to seeing the character of its population, to studying the most apparent aspects of its morals and its customs (*ce qu'il y a de plus apparent dans les moeurs et dans les usages.*)[3]

A short visit to our counsel would bring us to three o'clock. There would then remain for us four hours of daylight during which we would visit all the celebrated men, legislators, publicists, lawyers, poets and orators of New Orleans. Between these calls we would insert visits to the most beautiful women solely for the purpose of resting ourselves, I swear. (*Je vous jure.*)[2]

At 7 o'clock we would go to the play. After the play would

[1] French inserted and deleted in photocopy.   [2] French in photocopy.
[3] French deleted in photocopy.

come the *bal*. At midnight we would go back to our lodgings to collect (*rédiger*)[1] our notes. Has this plan your approbation? It received ours and we set out.

Coup d'oeil[1] of New Orleans

Marginal notes:

> *duc de Bourbons garde nationale pourquoi les mulatus coup d'oeil de la Nouvelle Orléans visite au consul M. Mazureau. un spectacle promenade bal des quad*[2]

> *Jeudi jeune—jour populaire jour de l'an.*

But do you not count upon making these *noirs blancs* some-day your equals? Never. Then I much fear (*je crains bien*) that they will one day make themselves your ministers. (*qu'il ne se fasse un jour vos ministres*).

> —[3] *à côté de marché à esclaves.*

> *ces êtres dégradés peuvent-elles cependant depraves?*[4] *jamais devenir vos femmes? non la loi le defend au terms expres—ajoute-t-elle alors quelle seront vos maîtresses? non—que je sache—en effet, il n'en était pas besoin.*

The course of our observations had led us to the door of our consul whose name by chance I am able to say (*dont par hasard, je puis dire le nom*):[5] M. Guillemain. We knocked. The negro who opened the door seemed completely surprised that we should wish to visit his master but of[6] what importance is it what goes on in a negro's head? We went in. M. Guillemain appeared in his turn surprised to see us enter his office but he got possession of himself (*il se réunit*)[5] immediately and received us in the most polite manner. He wished first to speak with us about France, about our friends, our relatives. . . . It was in truth a question of that (*c'etait bien de cela en verité qu'il s'agissait*):[1] he believed that we had come to make a visit and that informal questions (*il s'agissait d'une interrogation informal*)[5] were in order. We, therefore, turned the conversation as decently as we

[1] French in photocopy. [2] Probably quadroons.
[3] Incomprehensible. [4] Question mark in photocopy.
[5] French deleted in photocopy. [6] Deleted in photocopy.

could and by an adroit and well managed circuit we led him back to New Orleans.[1] Finally he began to speak of it and to speak very directly. He made us feel how important it was to France for French morals (*moeurs*)[2], customs, and habits to continue their sway in Louisiana. This has happened (*c'est jusqu'à présent ce qui arrive*)[3] up to the present, he added, to such an extent that the other day the people, learning what had happened in the Church of St. Germain L'auxerrois in Paris, remembered that a curé of the city had refused to bury a man who had committed suicide and ran to break his windows (*courut entrer ses vitres*).[3] The consul then spoke to us of the prosperous state in which Louisiana found herself. In the 15 years I have been here, he said, the prosperity of this country has (*centuplé*)[3] increased a hundredfold, I have seen suburbs (*quartiers*)[2] rear themselves in the midst of infested swamps, palaces replace cabins, the city increase in population (*se peupler*)[2] in spite of the yellow fever. The same impulse is imprinted upon all the districts of the state. All are prospering, all are growing visibly, the future of Louisiana is admirable (*les destinées de la Louisiane sont admirables*).[2] Ten states in which will soon be found the force and the populations of the union have as their only outlet the Mississippi and we hold the key to it. New Orleans is the natural *entrepot*.[2]

Thus spoke M. Guillemain and we kept very quiet the reason being that we were occupied in registering in our mind every one of his words. M. Guillemain (*Plus que (?)*[4] *cela des autres qui se complaisait à la vue de leurs oeuvres pour de pareils hommes un bavard est un ennemi naturel et qui se tait a toujours un égotisme du mérite*)[5] had one of those egotistical intelligences (minds) which speaks but does not converse and which finds pleasure in the sight of their own thought.

Meanwhile the hour was passing, the time of the inquest was about over. I thought that we should in leaving, leave one of these outstanding and deep thoughts which remain in the mind of the listener and show him that every man who keeps quiet is not necessarily a fool.

I slid in then cleverly between two of his ideas and I said: the extreme prosperity of this country of which you have been

---

[1] N.O. in photocopy. [2] French in photocopy. [3] French deleted in photocopy.
[4] Question mark in photocopy. [5] Margin, opposite this remark.

the witness, (*ne dit plus*)[1] more than any one, Monsieur, commenced with the union of Louisiana with the United States. Such a union (parallelism?) (*rapprochement*)[1] tells more than (*en dit plus*)[1] all the theories in favour of republican institutions. Imagine my surprise when (*qui fut surpris je vous le demande lorsque*)[1] M. Guillemain, interrupting me, cried: ah, Monsieur, one must live 15 years as I have done in the heart of a small democratic republic such as this one to lose such ideas. Do you wish to have an idea of the public administration. Examine the streets of the city, what holes (?)[2], what lack of order and alignment: the city however has more than a million of revenue. But into what hands it passes, God only knows. Do you want to have a clear cut opinion about the wisdom of the deliberating bodies? Read the names of those who compose them, obscure people, lawyers of the third order, village intriguers. One would (be tempted to) say that the law prevents the choice of people of merit and talent. Nothing simpler. It is the lower classes of people who have the majority in the electoral colleges. They choose from their own kind (*il choisit à sa portée . . .?*[3] *qui par nature ou par efforts sont descendus à sa portée*). Open the (*compte-rendus*) acts of the sessions. It is a veritable statute of Penelope (*Toile de Pénélope*).[4] To make, unmake, remake is the work of our legislators. The spirit not of (a)[5] party but of (a)[5] coterie absolutely directs the state. They suppress a position to ruin a man or create another to give a living to an honest friend persecuted by fortune. These, gentlemen, are the republican institutions which have made and still make everyday the prosperity of Louisiana. But I am mistaken, this government has one merit that one must not deny it. Without force as it is without skill (*habilité*)[1], without plans as it is without energy, incapable of harm as it is incapable of good, powerless and passive (*impuissant et passif*)[6] it lets society go its way (*marcher toute seule*)[7] without trying to direct it. Well, in the present state of affairs America in order to prosper does not need either able leadership (*une conduite habilé*)[7] or deep laid plans or great efforts, but liberty and still more liberty. The reason for that is

---

[1] French deleted in photocopy. [2] Question mark in photocopy.
[3] Illegible in photocopy. [4] Underlined in photocopy.
[5] Parentheses in photocopy. [6] French in photocopy.
[7] French underlined in photocopy.

that no one has yet any interest to abuse that liberty (*personne n'a encore intérêt à en abuser*).[1]

I pray you to believe, my dear friend, that this tirade against republics had not in the least downed me (*ne m'avait point abattu*)[1] and I was going to reply vigourously; but at the moment that I opened my mouth the clock struck four.

We hastened to take our hat and we set out congratulating ourselves that France had not yet lost the right (*n'eut point encore prescrit*)[1] to be represented abroad by people worthy of her (*des gens indignes d'elle*)[1]

Dossier I

Suite ʽa la Nouvelle Orléans[2]

We had if I am not mistaken 71 (21?) letters for New Orleans It was a difficult task only to put in order this formidable correspondence and classify each letter according to the merit of the person to whom it was addressed. But we are as you know of the number of those who think that, no matter how hurried one is, one can not sacrifice too much time in favour of logic. Order finally established, we directed ourselves towards the house of a M. Mazureau who had been pointed out to us as the eagle of the New Orleans bar; furthermore as speaking French, an advantage which we had learned to appreciate in our travels. We had much trouble and lost much precious time in finding his house. The houses of New Orleans have no numbers or the numbers do not run in sequence at all. Number 2 precedes 1 and 30 follows 70. It is an arithmetic peculiar to (*a l'usage de*)[3] the corporation of New Orleans with which we were not yet acquainted. This, *du reste*,[4] ended in giving us a real consideration for our consul. How indeed can one imagine a good government in a city where a stranger cannot find his way!

We arrived at last: the negro who opened the door for us and from whom we asked to see M. Mazureau at first regarded us fixedly without having the air of understanding us. He said to us finally: Now, Massa, today?—and yes without doubt Butor why not? . . .

---

[1] French deleted in photocopy. [2] Cf. above, pp. 101, 164, 171.
[3] French underlined in photocopy. [4] French in photocopy.

Appendix

There was some energy in our reply but of argument not a word. The slave, however (*toute pris*)[1] had the air of recognizing himself vanquished and, lowering his head with a submissive air, he opened the door of the salon.

The eagle of New Orleans, wrapped in the folds of a flowered dressing gown (*à ramage*)[1] and seated tranquilly in the corner of what is called a French fireplace in Louisiana and an antique fireplace in France was receiving at that very moment the homage of his assembled posterity.

We saw there children, grandchildren, nephews, great nephews, first cousins, distant cousins, bonbons, sweets and toys[2] the family picture was complete. Joy seemed to shine on all the faces. Union reigned in all hearts. One is such good friends the day of New Year's gifts. (*On est si bons amis le jour des étrennes.*)[1] I do not want to add a thing to this painting for fear of moving you too much. Know at least that at this sight there is not an 18th century philosopher who would not have wept with sensibility and tenderness.

As for us we remained as though struck with stupor at this spectacle: a ray of light finally managed to penetrate our intelligence (*saurait enfin de percer jusqu'à nous*).[1] We understood (*nous nous expliquons*)[1] now the embarrassment of the consul, the astonishment of the negroes, of the good negroes we had treated as Butors. To set out with a letter of introduction on New Year's day. What a monstrous incongruity! Alas! Where is the happy time when I would rather have forgotten my name than the arrival of the first of January. At the sight of the two unwelcome visitors M. Mazureau rose brusquely and advanced towards the door enveloping in the folds of his dressing gown two small children who, lost in the midst of this obscure labyrinth, let out sharp cries. We on our part were hastening to go towards him but our precipitation was fatal to several playthings[2] which were crushed pitilessly in our course. We at last met out host in the middle of the salon and there we reciprocally assured ourselves of all the pleasure we had in seeing each other.

---

[1] French deleted in photocopy.
[2] 'Bonbons . . . toys' in margin in photocopy with reference.

Index[1]

[1] I wish to thank Mrs. N. H. Feeny who kindly compiled this Index.

Index

Characteristics, national, 161–2, 163, 365
  American characteristics, 182–183
    American is the Englishman left to himself, 177
    Association, discussion and meeting, habit of, 51, 55, 57, 212–15, 239, 252–3; conventions, 60, 213–15; colony of Economy, 219
    Casualness, 274
    Coarseness, 193
    Coldness, 181, 193
    Enlightenment, 86–7, 92, 120, 179, 206, 211, 235, 258, 271
    Enterprise, spirit of, 75, 245
    Equality, spirit of: see Social relations
    Interest as only bond of different nationalities, 211
    Locality, spirit of, 59
    Morals: see Morals
    North and South compared, 72, 75, 109, 115, 160, 177, 269
    Pride, 274
    Rationalism, 181
    Religion: see Religion
    Social relations: see Social relations
    Tipping, opposition to, 217
    Tolerance, 31, 135, 227, 256
    Virtue, lack of, 180, 211, 245, 258
    Vulgarity, 274
  English characteristics: see England and English people
Children, illegitimacy and law concerning, 223–4, 231–2; paternal authority, 231, 256
Cincinnati: see Ohio
Civilisation producing few outstanding men, 17, 86–7, 160
Commentaries III (Blackstone), 281 n.

Commentaries on American Law (Kent): see Kent, James
Communications:
  Canals, 133 and n., 159, 265, 270, 271, 272, 334
  Post, 268, 270
  Prosperity and, 270–3
  Railways, 272
  Roads, 117–8, 129, 178, 270–1, 272–3
Confederations: see Government, forms of
Congress, 18, 28–9, 55, 66, 149, 228
  Choice of candidates, 67–8, 165–6, 254
  Constituents' rights, 233, 255
  Doctor members. 79
  Ecclesiastics elected, 79, 206, 208
  Electioneering, 83, 95, 254
  Franchise: see Elections
  Landowner members, few, 119
  Laws, Congress subject to, 252
  Lawyer members, 119
  Majority not essential for President, 59, 88–9, 178
  President's right to order militia to take command of Senate, 228
  Record of proceedings difficult to obtain, 120
  Roman Catholic priest elected by Protestants, 206, 208
Connecticut, criminal investigation organisation, 151–2; counties, 151, 152; education, 220, 231, 256; no State Attorney, 311
Constitution: see Union
Contracts, law concerning, 281–2
Conventions: see Characteristics, national; American characteristics; Association
Copyright, 251
Corporations, 232–3, 253

Index

Index

New England—*contd.*
tion, 220; laws, 292; juries,
291–2; judges, 307
New Orleans, 71–2, 101–4, 117,
164–5, 178, 236, 378–83
New Year celebrations, 172, 384
New York and New York State,
legislature, 28, 216; Court of
Chancery, 53, 54 and n.; laws,
53, 54 and n., 58, 230, 256–7;
juries, 153; society; differences
from Massachusetts, 202–3;
Roman Catholics, 206; slavery,
232, 254
Nullificators: *see* Political parties

Oaths, 173–4, 226
Ohio, 90, 92, 93, 261–5; irreligion
in newspaper, 80; movement
and mixture of population, 89,
90–1, 97–8, 161, 162, 261;
judicial institutions, 89–90, 93,
94, 306–8; morals, 90; land
fertility and prosperity, 90,
161, 261–2; education, 91;
local government, 91, 92–3;
universal suffrage, 92; elections, 93, 94–5, 98; banks, 94,
264; governors, 94; religion,
97; Negroes, 97, 98, 265;
compared with Kentucky, 97–
98, 99, 263–4; laws, 98, 261,
307–8
*On the Administration of Criminal
Justice in England and the
Spirit of the English Government* (Cottu), 318 n.

Patent rights, 250–1
Paternal authority, 231, 255–6
Penitentiary system: *see* Law and
crime
Pennsylvania, legislature, 28,
216; governor, 59; Negroes,
77, 225; counties, 280; law,
280–87, 308
Philadelphia, bankrupts, 181,

245; Negroes, 225; laws, 287–
289, 312; Quakers: *see* Religion; Protestantism
Pierson, George William, 14
Political parties, 74, 88, 163,
170–1, 238 and n.–239, 273;
nullificators, 96n., 114–15, 177;
coteries; no party of integrity,
239
Politics, no great men in, 17, 20,
160; religion and, 114, 150,
206, 207, 208, 226; public
enlightenment: *see* Character-
istics, national; American characteristics
Poor and poor law, 31–2, 223
Post: *see* Communications
Presbyterians: *see* Religion; Protestantism
Presidents:
Adams, John Quincy, 60 and
n.–62, 80
Congress, relations with:
majority not essential for
President, 59, 88–9, 178;
President's right to order
militia to take command of
Senate, 228
Election, 118
Jackson, Andrew, 50, 59, 83,
88, 96–7, 156, 158, 161, 194,
195
Jefferson, Thomas, 80
Public indifference, 178
Re-entry into public affairs, 63
Washington, George, 80, 116,
227 and n.
Press, 58, 203, 239, 266, 268,
270; powers, 30; freedom, 30;
233; irreligion in, 80, 97; jour-
nalists in public posts, 97
Pride, national: *see* Characteris-
tics, national; American char-
acteristics
Prisons: *see* Law and crime: Peni-
tentiary system
Prosecutor, public: *see* Law

392

Index

THE YALE PAPERBOUNDS